Queer Science

The Use and Abuse of Research into Homosexuality

Simon LeVay

The MIT Press
Cambridge, Massachusetts
London, England

This book was set in Bembo by The MIT Press.

Printed and bound in the United States of America.

Library of Congress Cataloging-in-Publication Data

LeVay, Simon.
    Queer science: the use and abuse of research into homosexuality / Simon
LeVay.
        p.   cm.
    Includes bibliographical references and index.
    ISBN 978-0-262-62119-9
    1. Homosexuality—Research—Social aspects.   2. Sexual orientation—
Research—Social aspects.   I. Title.
HQ76.25L497   1996
306.76'0723—dc20   96-12906
                                                                     CIP

Queer Science

As kingfishers catch fire, dragonflies draw flame;
  As tumbled over rim in roundy wells
  Stones ring; like each tucked string tells, each hung bell's
Bow swung finds tongue to fling out broad its name;
Each mortal thing does one thing and the same:
  Deals out that being indoors each one dwells;
  Selves—goes itself; *myself* it speaks and spells,
Crying *What I do is me: for that I came.*

Gerard Manley Hopkins

Contents

Acknowledgments

In 1991, while on the faculty of the Salk Institute in San Diego, I published a report in the journal *Science* on differences in brain structure between heterosexual and homosexual men. Although I had conducted that piece of research fairly "innocently"—that is, without a great deal of knowledge of or interest in its potential social implications—these implications were brought home to me by the ensuing media attention and by many strongly expressed individual responses, some full of praise and others critical in the extreme. In addition, I had the opportunity a few months later to act as presenter on a documentary film, *Born That Way?*, produced by the British director Jeremy Taylor for Windfall Films of London. This gave me the chance to focus on some of the social issues raised by research in the field of sexual orientation, and I have to thank Jeremy for helping germinate the thought processes that led to this book.

Over the last four years I have had the opportunity to meet with an extraordinarily diverse collection of people and to hear their views on this field of research and what it does or does not mean for society. Far too numerous to mention individually, these people have included sexologists, neurobiologists, psychologists, historians, lawyers, doctors, ministers, queer theorists, pro- and antigay activists, and many regular citizens both gay and nongay. I owe them collectively an enormous debt.

I do need to thank specifically a number of individuals who took the time to read a part or the whole of the first draft of this book, and whose comments helped improve the book enormously. They include Michael Bailey, David Bianco, Vern Bullough, Ralf Dose, George Ebers, Dean Hamer, Richard Isay, Laurie Saunders, Ritch Savin-Williams, and Kenneth Zucker, as well as Fiona Stevens (who was until recently my editor at The MIT Press), and several readers whose comments were provided to me anonymously. Because many of these individuals read only a portion of the book, and because I did not always incorporate their suggestions, it should not be assumed that any particular statement or opinion reflects their views.

Introduction

What causes a person to be gay, straight, or bisexual? And who cares? These are the twin themes of this book.

The first question is one that has intrigued people since antiquity. In Plato's *Symposium*, the playwright Aristophanes offered a whimsical answer: all human beings, he said, are descendants of original "double" creatures who were cut in two by an angry god. Sexual desire, he said, is the desire to be reunited with one's other ancestral half. Some of the original beings were hermaphrodite (half female, half male): their descendants are heterosexual, because their missing halves are of the opposite sex to their own. Others of the original creatures were all male or all female: their descendants are homosexual, because their missing halves have the same sex as themselves. Today Aristophanes (as Plato represented him) would be considered an "essentialist": his account implies that a person's sexual orientation is an objective, inborn characteristic.[1]

A few hundred years later Saint Paul made a radically different claim: he asserted (in Romans 1:26–27) that homosexual behavior is undertaken in conscious opposition to one's true nature, which is heterosexual.

Although the passage has been subject to a variety of interpretations, it is probable that Paul was denying the existence of any intrinsic differences between people who experienced same-sex attraction and those who did not.[2]

The second question—who cares?—is essentially modern. The idea that research on sexual orientation might significantly affect people's lives, by influencing medicine, law, or religious teachings, or by changing social attitudes toward homosexuality, arose first in the nineteenth century. Since then, this field of research has been closely linked with the struggle by gays and lesbians for social acceptance and legal rights, as well as with the countervailing effort to continue their exclusion and oppression.

Of course, this linkage is not entirely justified either in a moral or a legal sense. Gay rights should not depend entirely on finding out what makes people gay—in particular, on proving that gays and lesbians are "born that way." Nor should the idea that homosexuality is a "chosen lifestyle" be a justification for discrimination and prejudice. There are other grounds for believing that gays and lesbians should be respected and protected from oppression: their right to privacy and freedom of action and expression; the "victimless" nature of homosexual relations; and the many valuable contributions that gays and lesbians make to society.

Nevertheless, the linkage exists. Attitudes toward gays and lesbians are inextricably tied up with beliefs about what causes them to be homosexual. Let us look at a recent survey. A New York Times/CBS News poll taken in early 1992[3] found that the U.S. population is about equally split into those who believe homosexuality is "something people choose to be" and those who believe it is "something they cannot change." When these two groups of respondents were asked about their attitudes toward gay people, the answers were radically different. Asked, for example, whether they would object to having a homosexual as a child's elementary school teacher, 71 percent of the "choice" brigade said they would object, while only 39 percent of the "no-choicers" objected. The logic of the connection here is clear enough: if you don't want your child to be gay, and you think that teachers can influence children toward homosexuality, then it's understandable that you might not want your child to have a gay teacher. If homosexuality is not "catching," on the other hand, then having a gay teacher poses no risk. But the interviewees also differed in their answers to the question, "Would you object to having an airline pilot who is homosexual?" Of those who thought homosexuality was a choice, 18 percent said yes to this question, while only 4 percent of those who thought it was not a choice did so. The logic of this connection is less clear: pilots, whether gay or straight, have little opportunity to influence their passengers' sexual orientation. Therefore, objecting to flying with a gay pilot must reflect a negative belief about gay people—perhaps that they are unreliable in an emergency or that they have difficulty finding their way from one airport to another—or a dislike of gay people that is expressed in a wish for them to be denied employment opportunities. Evidently, such attitudes are more common among those who think homosexuality is a choice than among those who do not. Finally, many more of the "no-choicers" than the "choicers" believed that homosexual relations should be legal (62 percent versus 32 percent)—clear evidence of a connection between beliefs about causation and attitudes toward gay rights.

The connection exemplified in this survey has also been documented in psychological studies,[4] and it exists across different cultures.[5] Indeed, Aristophanes and Saint Paul themselves typify the relationship: the essentialist Aristophanes poked fun at gay sex in a couple of his plays (particularly at the idea of a grown man taking the receptive role in anal intercourse), but he was evidently at ease with those of his friends who praised and engaged in same-sex relationships. Saint Paul, on the other hand, unequivocally branded homosexual behavior as sinful, and his words have been the justification for centuries of Christian persecution of gays and lesbians.

Given that this connection exists, is it causal? Does the belief that homosexuality is a matter of choice lead to negative attitudes toward gays and lesbians, and conversely, does the belief that it is not a matter of choice lead to favorable attitudes? Two psychologists—Julie Piskur and Douglas Degelman—set out to answer this question in a very direct manner.[6] They took 105 college students and divided them at random into three groups. One group was asked to read a research summary that emphasized a biological basis for sexual orientation. Another group read a summary that did not support such a basis, and the third group read nothing. Afterwards, all the students completed a questionnaire that tested their attitudes toward gays and lesbians. It turned out that the students who had read the "biological" material expressed significantly more favorable attitudes toward gay people than students in either of the other two groups. The experiment suggests that there is indeed a causal connection, at least within the short timeframe of Piskur and Degelman's experiment.

One can gain more insight into the same phenomenon by listening to people who have changed their attitudes toward gays and lesbians. While participating in the making of a documentary film on homosexuality,[7] I interviewed such a person, William Cheshire, who is the editorial page editor of a conservative newspaper, the *Arizona Republic*. Reflecting Cheshire's own views, the newspaper had previously published numerous editorials arguing against extending any rights to gays and lesbians. "My moral perspective came out of a religious background," he told me, "a perception in this instance that homosexuality was a sin." In late 1991 he met with a group of gay and lesbian activists, who provided him with some scientific papers on the topic of homosexuality. "I became persuaded that it was not. . .something voluntary," he said, "not something that you embraced, it was the way you were born. If it's the way you were born then it ceases to be a sin, and then one's whole theological and moral perspective shifts, and then you begin to view the problem entirely differently, and that's what happened to me." As a result of this experience, Cheshire published an editorial retracting his earlier views and arguing *in favor* of gay rights —an editorial that may have contributed to the passage of a gay-rights ordinance by the city of Phoenix in 1992.

Obviously, there are many issues to be debated here. Theologians, for example, might want to distinguish between the moral status of homosexual *acts* and that of homosexual *orientation*; most gay people would dispute the immorality of homosexuality even as a totally voluntary state; psychologists might criticize the "choice/no choice" dichotomy as a hopeless oversimplification of the actual range of possibilities. For the moment, though, I just wish to make the point that beliefs about the causation of homosexuality clearly *do* influence attitudes toward gay people. Therefore, research that attempts to find the cause of homosexuality is inherently a social and political enterprise as well as a scientific one. Not that scientists who work in the field are necessarily committed to any particular social or political agenda, but whether they are or not, their findings will inevitably be used by others in ongoing public debate about homosexuality and gay rights.

The political content of this area of research leads to a bias that might not otherwise be present. Even with the best will in the world, it is hard not to think about the "cause of homosexuality" without implying that heterosexuality is the "normal" state that requires no explanation. Of course, the entire spectrum of sexual orientation is in need of explanation. But homosexuality is the stigmatized condition, the one that all the fuss is about. And it is a condition that seems to flout one obvious function of sexuality, which is to produce offspring. So it is inevitable that attention be focused on its cause at the expense of the cause of heterosexuality or even bisexuality.

What should be emphasized, though, is that seeking the cause of homosexuality is really the same thing as seeking the cause of heterosexuality. When people ask what makes people gay, they are not asking about the total sequence of events responsible for the creation of a homosexual human being. That would require the study of earwax, philosophy, the distance from the earth to the sun, and myriad other topics. Rather, they are simply asking: What happens differently in the development of a homosexual person from the development of a heterosexual person that causes that person to be gay? It is just the differences that are at issue. But whatever makes a gay person different from a straight person is the same thing that makes a straight person different from a gay person. If "gay genes" make a person gay, then "straight genes" make a person straight. If a hostile father makes his son gay, then a loving father makes his son straight. And so on. When we study homosexuality we are inevitably studying heterosexuality also, even if we do not always express it that way.[8]

Most gay men and lesbian women have their own opinions about why they are homosexual. Although there are exceptions, gay men in the United States today generally tend to claim that they were "born gay." Ninety percent of gay men surveyed by the *Advocate* in 1994 claimed to have been born gay, and only four percent believed that choice came into the equation at all.[9] Lesbians surveyed by the *Advocate* gave somewhat more diverse reasons: about half of them believed they were born gay, 28 percent thought that environmental circumstances (generally early childhood experiences) had played some role, and 15 percent said that choice had something to do with their sexual orientation.[10] Although there are significant differences between the attitudes of lesbians and gay men, it is clear that both groups are far more inclined to consider their sexual orientation a biological "given" than is the general population.

Should one take these assertions seriously? Not entirely, of course. No one even remembers being born, let alone being born gay or straight. When a gay man, for example, says he was born gay, he generally means that he felt different from other boys at the earliest age he can remember. Sometimes the difference involved sexual feelings, but more commonly it involved some kind of gender-nonconformist or "sex-atypical" traits—disliking rough-and-tumble play, for example—that were not explicitly sexual. These differences, which have been verified in a number of ways (see chapter 4), suggest that sexual orientation is influenced by factors operating very early in life, but these factors could still consist of environmental forces such as parental treatment in the early postnatal period.

Conversely, when lesbians or gay men assert that they chose to be gay, one has to ask whether they are really talking about choosing their sexual orientation, or whether what they chose was simply to come to terms with a preexisting orientation, and to express it in sexual relationships and community identity. As an example, the late Darrell Yates Rist, an author and gay activist who claimed to have chosen his homosexuality, wrote: "It seems to me to be cowardly to abnegate our individual responsibility for the construction of sexual desires. Rather, refusing the expedient lie and insisting instead on the right to fulfill ourselves affectionally—in what ever directions our needs compel us, however contrary to the social norm they may be—is both honest and courageous, an act of utter freedom."[11] But what is the "compelling need" Rist is referring to, if not his own homosexual orientation? As I see it, he exercised his choice in responding to that need, not in creating it.

In spite of these caveats, I do claim that gay people have a certain privileged insight into their own natures. If homosexuality is a conscious choice made at puberty or later (and this is still the belief of a large part of the U.S. population), then gays and lesbians should remember making that choice. If homosexuality results from intrafamily conflict, the residue of that conflict should still cloud the gay person's view of him- or herself. If, on the other hand, homosexuality is an innate attribute like handedness, gays and lesbians should feel as comfortable with their homosexuality (in the absence of negative forces from outside themselves) as straight people feel with their heterosexuality. As society's acceptance of homosexuality increases, we are indeed seeing the emergence of a new generation of lesbians and gay men who are far more at ease with their homosexuality than their predecessors could ever have been.[12]

Because this book attempts to portray research into homosexuality in its social context, I have included a considerable amount of historical review. Nevertheless, the overall organization of the book is not chronological, but thematic. I begin, in chapter 1, with the life story of one particular sex researcher, the German physician and gay-rights pioneer Magnus Hirschfeld (1868–1935). Hirschfeld was only one of several influential sexologists of his period who paid special attention to the nature and causes of homosexuality. But Hirschfeld is particularly interesting because he took a more uncompromisingly biological view of homosexuality than other, perhaps better-known researchers such as his predecessor Richard Krafft-Ebing or his English contemporary Havelock Ellis. Furthermore, this biological view, encapsulated in his notion of a "third sex," was the explicit basis for the gay-rights movement that Hirschfeld founded and led for thirty years. Thus, by looking at Hirschfeld's life and work, which predated most of the important scientific findings in the field, we can gain an outline view of the issues that occupy the remainder of the book.

In the following eight chapters I look at a variety of different approaches that have been taken toward understanding the basis of sexual orientation. Chapter 2 asks whether sexual orientation is in fact a meaningful basis for categorizing human beings, and if so, what fraction of the population is homosexual, bisexual, or heterosexual. Chapters 3 and 4 survey two non-biological approaches to the subject: psychoanalysis and learning theory. Chapter 5 deals with attempts to understand sexual orientation in terms of hormonal mechanisms, and chapter 6 looks at possible brain mechanisms that may be involved. As will become clear, the hormonal and brain theories are closely interrelated. Chapter 7 surveys research on mental traits that may be associated with sexual orientation: the evidence, in other words, that homosexuality and heterosexuality are not isolated phenomena but occur as part of a "package" of sex-atypical or sex-typical traits. In chapter 8 I review one very specific theory of causation that attributes male homosexuality to stress experienced during fetal life. Concluding this section, chapter 9 is devoted to the evidence for a genetic influence on sexual orientation. Although this section of the book is focused on the science itself, I also describe how, in the past, the research findings (or purported findings) were used. In great part, this means recounting how efforts were made to convert gay people to heterosexuality—whether through psychoanalysis, behavioral "therapy," hormone treatment, or even brain surgery. This dismal saga, which hopefully is now coming to a close, illustrates the extent to which research into homosexuality was embedded in the general mind-set of its time, specifically in the belief that, whatever the determinants of sexual orientation, heterosexuality was a far preferable state to homosexuality.

The final five chapters of the book focus more explicitly on the social aspects of research into homosexuality. Chapter 10 is somewhat transitional in this respect: it deals with same-sex behavior in nonhuman animals. This is a topic that has been the subject of objective ethological research, but it is also commonly taken up in the context of moral questions about homosexuality—specifically, whether homosexual behavior is "unnatural." In chapter 11 I review the long-running debate over whether homosexuality should be considered a disease, a debate that (in the United States) climaxed in 1973, when the American Psychiatric Association (APA) voted to remove homosexuality from its *Diagnostic and Statistical Manual of Mental Disorders (DSM)*. Specifically, I ask whether the APA's decision was based on the findings of scientific research or on sociopolitical factors such as gay activism. Chapter 12 takes a look at how research findings have been used in attempts to influence the law toward a more positive, or alternatively a more hostile, attitude toward lesbians and gay men. In chapter 13 I look into the crystal ball and consider whether some of the fears that have been expressed about the future of biological research are justified: will we develop the technology to engineer homosexuality out of the human race, for example, and if so, should we be taking steps to prevent this from happening? In the concluding chapter I attempt to make the case that research into homosexuality is worth pursuing, not merely because of the intrinsic interest in understanding the basis of human diversity, but because this research may indeed, as Hirschfeld believed, help the larger society recognize what gays and lesbians have generally believed about themselves: that their sexual orientation is a central, defining aspect of their identity.

Scientists are supposed to live in ivory towers. Their darkrooms and their vibration-proof benches are supposed to isolate their activities from the disturbances of common life. What they tell us is supposed to be for the ages, not for the next election. But the reality may be otherwise.

1

Hirschfeld and the Third Sex

America was not the birthplace of the gay-rights movement. The first substantial effort to organize gay men and lesbians in this country was the founding of the two "homophile" organizations, the Mattachine Society and the Daughters of Bilitis, in the early 1950s. But in Europe the history of the movement goes back much further. In Germany, in fact, an active gay-rights movement existed already at the beginning of the century. Of particular relevance to the themes of this book is the close connection between the political efforts of the early German activists and the development of ideas about the nature and causes of homosexuality. This connection was especially obvious in the life and work of the movement's leader, the Jewish physician and sexologist Magnus Hirschfeld.

Hirschfeld's Predecessor—Ulrichs

In his thinking about homosexuality, as well as in his political engagement, Hirschfeld owed a major debt to a gay man of an earlier

generation, the German jurist Karl Heinrich Ulrichs (1825–1895).[1]
If, as some people assert, the word "gay" should be reserved for people who are self-conscious, open members of the homosexual community, then Ulrichs was the first gay man of modern times. Certainly he was the first gay activist. Driven by a stubborn streak that was the leading feature of his personality, Ulrichs argued tirelessly for the rights of homosexuals. In 1867 he made a speech before the Congress of German Jurists in Munich, in which he appealed for the abolition of the sodomy statute. He also corresponded widely with gay men, and published numerous pamphlets and monographs on homosexuality.

Ulrichs had a sense of himself as being considerably more feminine than the average man. He recalled that as a young child he wore girls' clothes, preferred playing with girls, and in fact expressed a desire to be a girl. As an adult, he was sexually attracted to virile young men, especially to soldiers in uniform. As far as we know, however, he did not cross-dress as an adult; in fact, he was perceived by his contemporaries as a rather conventionally gendered man.

Ulrichs put forward two important ideas about homosexuality. First, he declared that homosexuals were a distinct class of individuals, innately different from heterosexual people. At that time there was no word to describe this class of people, aside from the pejorative, behavior-based term "sodomite." (The word "homosexual" was introduced later by the Hungarian Karl Maria Kertbeny.) Ulrichs therefore coined the word "urning," meaning follower or descendant of Uranus. The name is a reference to a passage in Plato's *Symposium*, in which Pausanias calls same-sex love the offspring of the "heavenly Aphrodite," daughter of Uranus. Ulrichs later added the feminine form "urningin" to define women we now refer to as lesbians. Heterosexuals, in Ulrichs's parlance, became "dionings"—descendants of the "common Aphrodite," daughter of Zeus by the mortal woman Dione.

Second, Ulrichs put forward a theory to account for the development of sexual orientation. In his earliest conception of this theory, propounded in 1864,[2] the human embryo was viewed as having the potential for bodily and mental development in either the female or the male direction. In most people the sexual development of the body and the mind was concordant: either both were male or both were female. In fetuses destined to become *urnings*, however, the sex of bodily development was male, while the sex of mental development was female. These individuals, being neither totally male nor totally female, constituted a "third sex." He later put forward a similar explanation for the origin of *urningins*: in them, the sex of bodily development was female, while that of mental development was male.

Although Ulrichs's theory was biological and framed in terms of fetal development, it did not offer an ultimate explanation for why particular individuals were gay or straight, because it did not explain why the development of mind and body was sexually concordant in some people and discordant in others. Ulrichs does not seem to have been especially interested in this question. As long as homosexuality was inborn, Ulrichs felt he could justly claim that homosexual behavior was natural for homosexual people, and therefore should not be criminalized or viewed as sinful. In essence, Ulrichs was saying that Saint Paul made a mistake in calling same-sex behavior "against nature"—it would only be against nature for some-one who was innately heterosexual.

Ulrichs soon understood that his theory was not fully adequate to account for the diversity of human sexual orientation. For one thing, he realized that sexual orientation is not an either-or phenomenon but a continuum: there are people who to one degree or another are sexually attracted to both men and women. These people, who we now call bisexuals, Ulrichs referred to as "urano-dionings."[3] But he did not consider that the existence of intermediate degress of sexual orientation conflicted in any way with his theory. After all, as he pointed out, there are also intermediate stages of physical sex, as evidenced by the existence of hermaphrodites or intersexes. The urano-dionings were simply people in whom mental development had proceeded partially along male lines and partially along female lines.

A more serious problem with Ulrichs's original theory had to do with the urnings' sexual partners. Those virile young men who were the preferred sexual partners of Ulrichs and his kind—if they responded to the urnings' advances, did that make them urnings themselves? And if not, what then was their biological nature, and what was their moral status?

Ulrichs said that these men were not urnings—they were young heterosexual men who would eventually become sexually active only with women. Their sexual activity with urnings, whatever its motivation, was justified simply because it was justified for urnings. After all, urnings could not be expected to have sex with each other, because they were insufficiently masculine to form suitable objects for urning love. Another likely factor behind Ulrichs's neglect of the urnings' sex partners was social snobbery: the partners were mostly working-class youths or young men, whose own motivations were not of great significance to a cultured professional like Ulrichs.

As he came to know a large number of gay men, Ulrichs had to acknowledge that they were not as uniformly feminine as he perceived himself to be. In fact, he corresponded with some men who seemed to be masculine in every way, aside from the direction of their sexual desire. In some cases, to be sure, these men had been somewhat cross-gendered in childhood and had become more conventionally masculine after puberty. That might be, as Ulrichs pointed out, because of social pressures that forced them to conceal the feminine side of their nature. But there were also men who were sexually attracted to men who lacked even a childhood history of femininity.

Ulrichs therefore revised his theory by proposing that there was a spectrum of urning natures. At one end was the *weibling* or "female-type." Such an individual was very feminine in personality and even in physical appearance, and was typically attracted to masculine young men. At the other end was the *mannling* or "male-type," who was conventionally masculine in every way except for his sexual orientation. The mannling was typically attracted to somewhat androgynous youths or young men. Between these two extremes were any number of intermediate stages.

In addition, Ulrichs acknowledged that urnings varied in terms of their preferences for particular sexual acts. Some were "active": like heterosexual men, they took the insertive role in sexual intercourse. Others were "passive": like heterosexual women, they took the receptive role. Still others could derive pleasure from either role.

In making these revisions Ulrichs had moved a considerable distance from his original conception of the urning as a person with the mind of a woman and the body of a man. That conception corresponds more to what we nowadays refer to as a male-to-female transsexual. The revised conception was far more in accord with our current ideas about the variety of gay men and their sexual relationships. The only major missing element was the possibility of relationships between pairs of mannlings—the type of companionate relationships between conventionally masculine gay men that are at the center of the self-image projected by the gay male community today.

If Ulrichs's revised model was descriptively superior, was it superior in explanatory power? Ulrichs had been forced into positing the existence of not one but at least three psychic entities that developed in a sexually differentiated fashion. One of these entities was sexual orientation (urning, urano-dioning, or dioning), another was preferred sexual behavior (passive, no preference, or active), and a third was a broader collection of gender characteristics (weibling, intermediate, or mannling). The direction of sexual differentiation of these three entities was not necessarily the same: Ulrichs himself, for example, was feminine in two (he was an urning and a weibling) but masculine in the third (he was active in his preferred sexual behavior). Did this multiplication of entities, and the possibility of discordance among them, undermine the very basis of Ulrichs's argument, reducing it to the mere tautological statement that homosexuals are the way they are because their minds exhibit same-sex attraction?

Rather than attempting to answer the question at this point, let us see how Ulrichs's ideas were further developed. Ulrichs himself, in a pamphlet published in 1879,[4] tried to simplify the whole question of male sexual diversity by presenting it as a unidimensional continuum. At one extreme was the *weibling*, feminine in everything but his genital anatomy; at the other was the virile heterosexual man. Along the continuum were found an infinite number of intermediate stages (*Zwischenstufen*), including the *mannling* as well as less-than-masculine heterosexual men. How complex discordances could be represented in such a continuum (say an effeminate male-to-female transsexual who is nevertheless sexually attracted to women) was left unclear. More significant than Ulrichs's later writings, however, was the development of his ideas by Hirschfeld.

Fin-de-Siècle Berlin

Forty years younger than Ulrichs, Hirschfeld came of age in a society very different from the one Ulrichs knew. By 1896, when Hirschfeld took up residence in Berlin, that city was already the home of a diverse and self-aware gay and lesbian community. This community and this self-awareness did not come into being as a consequence of the "naming" of homosexual people by nineteenth-century sexologists. Rather, the prime cause was the explosive growth of Berlin during the years after 1871, when it became the German capital. By the time Hirschfeld moved there only London, another gay mecca, was larger. Gay people were attracted to large cities, as Hirschfeld himself observed, "like gnats to a bog" (*wie Mücken zum Sumpf*), for only in large cities were they able to find sexual outlet, acceptance, and anonymity.

We can gain some idea of the gay and lesbian scene at that time from an engaging book entitled *Berlins Drittes Geschlecht* ("Berlin's Third Sex"),[5] published by Hirschfeld in 1904. At its simplest, gay male culture might consist of anonymous meetings between strangers in a secluded corner of the *Tiergarten*, or the picking up of a hustler on "the Strip" (*der Strich*) or in one of the city's many gay bars. At its most elaborate, gay culture involved public drag balls (attended by both men and women) and exclusive private parties for gay aristocrats. Hirschfeld described one of these parties:

> We sat at small tables and dined most opulently, while chatting about the most recent performances of Wagner's operas—a topic in which nearly all educated urnings are interested. The conversation moved on to travel and literature, but kept clear of politics. Gradually it turned to court gossip. People dwelt in great detail on the recent court ball. The appearance of the young duke of X. had set many an urning's heart aflutter: everyone was ecstatic about his blue uniform and his charming personality, and people related how they had contrived to be introduced to His Royal Highness. . .

At the heart of lesbian and gay culture, then as now, were countless stable lesbian and gay male relationships—relationships that were far less visible than we are accustomed to today, yet that often gained a measure of acceptance, even outside of homosexual circles. It was not uncommon, for example, for a young lesbian or gay man to bring her or his lover to live in the parental household, and for the parents to consciously accept their new "daughter-in-law" or "son-in-law" as one of the family. Many of these relationships, in Hirschfeld's description at least, were "transgenderal," involving for example the pairing of a conventionally masculine man with a markedly feminine man.

But there was a dark side to Berlin's gay culture. Paragraph 175 of the German penal code, inherited from the earlier Prussian code, made sex between men a felony punishable by imprisonment for up to six months. Unlike the sodomy statutes that still exist in many American states today, paragraph 175 was no dead letter. It was actively enforced by police surveillance, by entrapment, and by the use of informers. About 500 men were imprisoned under paragraph 175 each year. In a much larger number of cases, prosecution was dropped after preliminary inquiries, but even this was enough to cost a man his job and his position in society. In addition, blackmail was a constant threat. A book about male prostitution in Berlin, published in 1906, makes it clear that for many hustlers blackmail was the whole point and purpose of the trade.[6] Countless men were driven to suicide by blackmail, by the actual disclosure of their homosexuality, or simply by the prospect of having to live under such oppressive conditions. Hirschfeld recounts one case:

> On Christmas Day of last year, very early in the morning, I was called to the room of a homosexual student in the western part of Berlin. The word was that he had suffered an attack of delirium during the night.
>
> When I arrived, I was met by a frightful scene. The entire room was strewn with broken dishes, pieces of furniture, torn fabric, books and papers, all stained with blood, ink and paraffin oil. By the bed there was a large pool of blood, and on the bed lay a young man with a waxen-pale face and deep-set, blazing eyes. Locks of black hair framed his finely sculpted, regular features. His forehead and his arms were covered with blood-soaked rags.
>
> He had had an argument with his father, a respected citizen of Berlin, concerning his homosexuality. Neither had been able to attempt a reconciliation,

and now, on Christmas Eve—the first since he had moved out of his parents' home—he had been wandering alone through the deserted streets of the metropolis. Concealing himself in a passageway, across the street from his parents' house, he had watched the bright lights within, and heard the laughter of his younger brothers and sisters. For a moment he caught a glimpse of the outline of his mother as, lost in thought, she leant her brow against the windowpane.

After the lights went out, he went to the nearest bar, took a seat in a hidden-away corner, and emptied one glass of *schnapps* after another. He went on to a second and third bar and did the same. In empty cafes he gave the last of his money for black coffee and *kirsch*.

After he had made his way home through the cold winter's night, and had staggered up the four flights of stairs to his room, he had been seized by a wild frenzy. He reduced everything within reach to splinters, and he smashed the burning lamp, in the expectation that he would open his arteries and bleed to death. One of the landlord's family called a doctor, who merely looked through the doorway and speedily wrote out an order committing the student to the psychiatric section of the Charité Hospital.

One of the student's friends called me to him. I washed and bandaged one wound after another on that Christmas morning. He did not wince or speak a single word, but his blazing eyes and his pale lips and his gaping wounds spoke of his intense pain, and of the sacred task of those who work for the urnings' liberation.

The story was doubtless a true one, but the way it is told also illustrates something of Hirschfeld's mind-set: his messianic fervor, his inclination to romanticize, and his almost mechanical approach to psychology, an approach in which feelings are not so much communicated as acted out. Compared with Freud, who undertook long voyages within his patients' unconscious, Hirschfeld was most comfortable in the outer world of action.

"Sappho and Socrates"

In the same year that Hirschfeld moved to Berlin, he published his first work on homosexuality, a pamphlet entitled *Sappho and Socrates*.[7] Although Hirschfeld mentioned Ulrichs only rather briefly in this pamphlet, the debt to his predecessor was obvious. Like Ulrichs, Hirschfeld accounted for diversity in sexual orientation in terms of the bisexual nature of the developing fetus, but, in keeping with his training as a physician, he spoke of the "brain" where Ulrichs had spoken of the "mind." Hirschfeld posited the existence, in the embryos of both sexes, of rudimentary neural centers for attraction to both males and females. In most male fetuses, the center for attraction to women developed, while the center for attraction to males regressed, and vice versa for female fetuses. In fetuses destined to become homosexual, on the other hand, the opposite developmental sequence took place.[8] While admitting that the location of these centers was still unknown, Hirschfeld predicted that when they were identified, it would be found that adults of each sex carried the vestigial remnants of the centers typical for the other sex. Although he did not spell this out, there was also the implicit prediction that differences would be found between the brains of heterosexual and homosexual individuals: in gay men, for example, the centers for attraction to women would be vestigial, while those for attraction to men would be relatively large.

Unlike Ulrichs, Hirschfeld concerned himself with the question of why the neural centers for sexual attraction developed atypically in fetuses destined to become homosexual. In keeping with the then current ideas about "degeneracy" (*Entartung*), he suggested that the cause might lie with a weakening of the parents' seed on account of alcoholism, syphilis, and so forth. Perhaps recalling that his own parents had led exemplary lives, he added rather lamely that homosexuals could also crop up in apparently healthy families. In his later writings Hirschfeld played down the notion of a connection between homosexuality and degeneracy, but never seemed to abandon it completely. He suggested more than once, for example, that homosexuality might be a device invented by Nature to prevent people from having degenerate offspring, and he used this idea as an argument against gay people marrying.

The notion of an early bisexual stage of development is somewhat confusing. It is one thing to say that at an early stage of development the brain is sexually undifferentiated, that it may subsequently follow one of two developmental pathways depending on external factors, and that a person's ultimate sexual orientation depends on which pathway was followed. It is quite another to say that at some early stage the individual is actually experiencing sexual attraction to both men and women. Hirschfeld seems not to have recognized this distinction at all clearly. At one point he wrote that the human fetus, up to the end of the third month, was "completely without a sex (or more accurately, is both male and female)." Later in the pamphlet he wrote that it was ". . .beyond scientific doubt that the original state of the individual is hermaphroditic, and the mental drive is originally directed with equal strength toward both men and women. . ." Hirschfeld seems to have conceptually telescoped the individual's sex life backwards into the fetal period. Other writers of the period who discussed bisexuality, most notably Wilhelm Fliess and Sigmund Freud, also tended to project active sexuality backwards into the postulated bisexual (or "polymorphous") period; the validity of their approach is discussed later.

Like Ulrichs, Hirschfeld argued that the prenatal origin of homosexual attraction removed homosexuality from the categories of sin or crime. Of course, he recognized that the law punished behavior, not feelings. But Hirschfeld also "biologized" the connection between feeling and action by positing an innate sexual drive, whose strength varied between individuals, and which determined whether homosexual feelings were inevitably translated into action, or were capable of repression. In most bisexual people, Hirschfeld believed, the strength of same-sex desire was relatively low, and therefore its development could and should be restrained. He recommended that young people in general be allowed the company of the opposite sex and not be kept in single-sex environments which might nurture the germ of homosexuality. In this way, he believed, same-sex feelings would develop only in exclusively homosexual individuals, in whom the strength of the same-sex drive lay beyond what could be modified by experience.

In fact, *Sappho and Socrates* contains numerous passages that reveal Hirschfeld's ambivalent attitude toward homosexuality at that time. He was emphatic that same-sex behavior should be decriminalized, and he cited the homosexuality of notable historical figures to bolster his assertion that urnings and urningins could be healthy and valuable members of society. Yet, at the same time, he repeatedly drew an analogy between homosexuality and congenital deformities such as hare lip. The main difference was that hare lip was correctible, whereas homosexuality, in the full urning, was not.

Although this attitude may seem surprisingly negative, it was probably inevitable, given the social conditions then existing. Hirschfeld failed to spell out emphatically that the "problem" lay with the homophobic attitudes of society, not with homosexuality itself. He had, as we would say nowadays, "internalized" some of that homophobia. But exactly the same phenomenon was apparent in the early days of the gay-rights movement in the United States fifty years later. The manifesto of the first gay-rights organization, Harry Hay's Mattachine Society, conceded that gay people suffered from "physiological handicaps"—a rephrasing of Hirschfeld's "curse of Nature"—and the first lesbian organization, the Daughters of Bilitis, invited speakers to discuss possible cures. Only Ulrichs had been immune to self-loathing: extraordinary man that he was, he simply hurled back with redoubled force every rock that society cast his way.

Notably absent from *Sappho and Socrates* was any attempt to link homosexuality with a broader gender nonconformity in the way that Ulrichs had tried to do. It is possible that the reason for this lay in Hirschfeld's own nature. Hirschfeld seems to have been more of a *mannling* than a *weibling*, to use Ulrichs' terminology. He had a conventional childhood and was on the best of terms with his father; in adulthood, he was apparently drawn to fairly unmasculine men, not to the soldiers and *Burschen* (strapping lads) that Ulrichs found so irresistible. Unfortunately, in all his voluminous writings Hirschfeld was remarkably silent about his own sex life. In fact, he never formally came out of the closet, although his homosexuality eventually became known to a very wide circle of colleagues and acquaintances. At any event, it seems likely that Hirschfeld, like Ulrichs, based his earliest ideas about homosexuality primarily on his own experience and modified these ideas later when he came to know larger numbers of homosexual men and women.

A final point worth emphasizing about *Sappho and Socrates* is how much Hirschfeld attempted to turn sexual feelings into concrete phenomena. This is evident, not merely in the way he equated sexuality with the development of (still hypothetical) brain centers, but also in his attempts to quantify sexual feelings. He represented the strength of sexual desire on a 10-point scale, and the direction of desire by the letters A (heterosexual), B (homosexual), or A + B (bisexual). Thus a particular individual's sexuality might be expressed by a figure such as A3,B9: such a person would be rather weakly attracted to the other sex and very strongly to the same sex. An individual might be completely asexual (A0,B0), violently drawn to both sexes (A10,B10), and so forth. This scheme actually goes beyond the Kinsey scale, developed fifty years later (see chapter 2), because that scale is unidimensional: it suggests (although Kinsey did not actually believe this) that every person has the same fixed endowment of sexual energy, which he or she then divides up between same-sex and opposite-sex attraction in a ratio indicative of his or her own sexual orientation.

This concrete, reifying approach to sexuality reflected the cast of Hirschfeld's mind. A stranger to any kind of religion or spirituality, and out of sympathy with abstract systems such as that constructed by Freud, Hirschfeld believed in the evidence of things seen. To him, a scientific theory was in essence a prediction that something presently unseen would be made visible in the future.

The Petition to the Reichstag

The publication of *Sappho and Socrates* initiated Hirschfeld's lifelong involvement in the gay-rights struggle. In the following year (1897), he and three associates founded the *Wissenschaftlich-humanitäres Komitee* (*WhK* or "Scientific-humanitarian Committee"), the world's first gay-rights organization.

The *WhK* grew rapidly. Already in 1897 it submitted a petition to the two legislative bodies (the Bundesrat and the Reichstag), signed by about two hundred jurists, professors of medicine, and others. The text of the petition, first of several that were submitted to the legislature over the ensuing thirty years, was as follows:[9]

To the Legislative Bodies of the German Reich

Considering that already in 1869 the leading public health officials in both Austria and Germany, including men such as Langenbeck and Virchow, lent their collective voice to the demand that sexual intercourse between individuals of the same sex be decriminalized, basing their argument on the fact that the behaviors under consideration are in no way different from behaviors that have never been subject to criminal sanction, such as those performed on the person's own body, between two women, or between men and women;

Observing that the lifting of similar penalties in France, Italy, Holland and numerous other countries has not led to any decline in public morals or to any other unfavorable consequences;

Recognizing that scientific research, especially that carried out over the last twenty years in German-, English- and French-speaking countries, has thoroughly investigated the question of homosexuality (sensual love towards people of the same sex), and has without exception confirmed the view of the earlier authorities who studied the topic, namely that this phenomenon, which has been so uniformly encountered in all countries and at different periods of history, must represent the expression of a deep constitutional predisposition;

Emphasizing that it is now virtually proven that this phenomenon, which at first sight is so mysterious, actually results from developmental conditions linked to the early bisexual (hermaphroditic) state of the human fetus, and as a consequence no moral blame should be laid on a person for possessing the capacity for such feelings;

Considering that this capacity for same-sex attraction generally seeks physical expression with the same strength as does the normal sex drive, and often even more strongly;

Recognizing that, according to the statements of all experts on the matter, *coitus analis* and *oralis* [anal and oral penetration] take place relatively seldom in same-sex intercourse, and certainly no more commonly than in normal sexual intercourse;

Taking note of the fact that, among those subject to feelings of this kind, not just in classical antiquity but up to and including our own time, have been counted men and women of the highest intellectual achievement;

Noting that the existing law has not freed a single homosexual from his sexual drive, but condemns very many upright, valuable individuals, who already suffer enough at the hands of nature, to disgrace, despair, insanity or death, even when they are sentenced to a single day's imprisonment—the least penalty permissible under the laws of the German Reich—and in fact even when the case does not proceed beyond a preliminary inquiry;

Considering that these regulations have greatly contributed to the wide prevalence of blackmail, as well as to the highly reprehensible practice of male prostitution;

The signatories listed below, whose reputation attests to the seriousness and purity of their motives, inspired by the quest for truth, justice and humanity, declare the present version of paragraph 175 of the Penal Code of the German Reich to be inconsistent with the current status of scientific knowledge, and therefore call upon the Legislature promptly to alter this paragraph so that, as in the countries mentioned above, sexual acts between persons of the same sex (homosexual), like those between persons of the opposite sex (heterosexual), shall only be punishable when involving duress, when one of the participants is under 16 years of age, or when they take place in such a way as to offend public decency (i.e., in violation of paragraph 183 of the Penal Code).

The petition was in large part a précis of *Sappho and Socrates*. In describing as "virtually proven" Hirschfeld's speculations about the origin of homosexuality in a bisexual embryo, the petition was of course milking the science for a lot more than it was worth. But few of the other arguments were likely to carry much weight either. That France, Germany's recently defeated enemy, or Italy or Holland had abolished their sodomy statutes was of little consequence, when England, Austria, and the American states were still actively upholding theirs (Oscar Wilde had completed his prison sentence a few months earlier). The assertion that anal and oral intercourse were not common features of sex between men could reasonably be doubted. And the fact that numerous prominent historical figures may have been homosexual carried little weight, not only because their identities were unknown to most Germans, but because, in the progress-oriented mentality of the time, history was when bad things happened. To a modern American ear, the petition's most notable shortcoming is its failure to frame its demands in terms of fundamental human rights. To contemporary Germans, however, it was most probably the failure to address the traditional Christian injunctions against homosexuality that was the petition's major weakness. In fact, some church leaders made considerable use of the biblical prohibitions in their denunciations of the petition, and the *WhK* later added clauses specifically responding to the religious objections.

Probably more important than the actual arguments used in the petition was the fact of its existence and the impressive list of signatories attached to it. As the petition was presented again and again, the numbers of signatories climbed, so that a total of well over three thousand people signed it at one time or another. These included such notables as the eminent sexologist Richard Krafft-Ebing, Albert Einstein, Thomas and Heinrich Mann, Rainer Maria Rilke, Gerhart Hauptmann, Käthe Kollwitz, and Stefan Zweig. But because many of the signatories, like Hirschfeld himself, were Jewish, their voices carried little weight in a country that was increasingly giving way to anti-Semitism.

Research and Education

Athough there was evidently broad support for the repeal of paragraph 175 among the intelligentsia, it became obvious, after the petition was rebuffed by the legislature, that the *WhK* would need to generate much wider public support if it were ever to succeed in its aim. Hirschfeld and his supporters therefore began a program of broadly based research and education, the aim of which was to present a true picture of homosexuality and of the gay and lesbian community to public view. In this way Hirschfeld hoped to get away from the concept of homosexuality as a psychopathological rarity—a concept derived from clinical studies such as those of the influential nineteenth-century sexologist, Richard Krafft-Ebing—and to emphasize the participation of gays and lesbians in every aspect of German society.

On the research side, Hirschfeld used several approaches. One was to obtain detailed information about a large number of gays and lesbians through "psychobiological questionnaires," which sought information about the respondent's childhood traits, parental relationships, sexual development, adult sexuality, health, personality, and interests. The information from these questionnaires was summarized in several books. Another approach was to carry out surveys of the prevalence of male homosexuality and bisexuality in nonclinical populations. This was done by mailed inquiries, which in 1903 were sent to three thousand male college students in Berlin. The following year they were sent to five thousand male metalworkers. About half the inquiries were answered, and the figures obtained were quite similar to those that have been obtained in recent surveys in the United States: about 4 percent of the respondents stated that they were sexually attracted to both men and women, and 1 to 2 percent were only attracted to men. As with the more recent studies, the figures must be considered as minimum estimates. This piece of sociological research cost Hirschfeld dearly: six of the polytechnic students brought an action against him for disseminating obscene documents, and he had to pay a substantial fine.

Yet another research method used by Hirschfeld was the exploration of Berlin's gay subculture. The results of this research, in the course of which Hirschfeld evidently mixed business and pleasure, were presented in the book mentioned earlier, *Berlins Drittes Geschlecht*.

Hirschfeld did not abandon the traditional method of sexological research, the individual consultation. As his reputation as a gay-positive clinician grew, Hirschfeld attracted increasing numbers of gay men to his consulting room. In a radical departure from earlier medical practice, Hirschfeld developed a psychotherapeutic procedure that emphasized the client's ability to accept his own homosexuality, rather than to change it. The therapeutic task, as Hirschfeld saw it, was to help the client develop mental skills for surviving as a gay man in a still hostile world. Typically, the therapeutic sessions would involve talking through the client's childhood and adult life in an attempt to link the client's symptomatology to the negative influence of homophobia. He encouraged his clients to meet other gay people, and in fact arranged group meetings for this purpose.

This is not to say that Hirschfeld in a single leap made the transition to the gay-positive style of psychotherapy as we know it today. He still maintained that gay men had the right to attempt to change their sexual orientation if they so wished, and recommended them to practitioners who claimed the ability to accomplish this task. Because of Hirschfeld's biological orientation, he was especially disposed to imagine that this transformation might be achieved by purely medical means. This belief had serious consequences for some of his clients, as we shall see later.

On the educational side, Hirschfeld and the *WhK* used pamphlets, books, lectures, conferences, and eventually films to spread the word. Hirschfeld himself must have given thousands of public lectures in his career: a populist by instinct, he was never so happy as when addressing large groups of students or workers. He traveled extensively: toward the end of his career he made an eighteen-month trip around the world, which included numerous lecture engagements in the United States as well as in many countries of Asia. He left his long-term companion, Karl Giese, at home to manage his affairs. While in China, however, Hirschfeld acquired a personal disciple in the form of a medical student named Li Shiu Tong (Hirschfeld referred to him as Tao Li or "beloved disciple"), who accompanied him on his travels across Asia and back to Europe. Thereafter Hirschfeld, Giese, and Tao Li formed an uneasy threesome.

The film *Anders als die Anderen* ("Different from the Others"), which Hirschfeld helped make in 1919, is of particular interest because portions of the film are still extant. Directed by Richard Oswald, the film starred the leading German actor Conrad Veidt, who is best known to American moviegoers in his role as the German commandant in *Casablanca*. Veidt, who was himself gay, played a gay violinist who was driven to suicide by blackmail and legal persecution. The film ends with an impassioned speech by Hirschfeld, in which he sees a vision of a future in which paragraph 175 has been swept away. The film was a major box-office success, but in the following year it was banned after a bevy of prominent psychiatrists testified that it portrayed homosexual life in too rosy terms![10]

Hirschfeld founded and edited a journal, the *Jahrbuch für sexuelle Zwischenstufen* ("Yearbook of Sexual Intermediaries"), which was published annually from 1899 to 1923. Like Hirschfeld, the *Jahrbuch* was devoted both to the scientific explication of homosexuality and to the political struggle for gay rights. It published writings by a great diversity of authors, some of whom totally disagreed with Hirschfeld's ideas.

In 1919 Hirschfeld founded the world's first institute for sex research, the *Institut für Sexualwissenschaft*. It was located in an elegant neoclassical mansion that had once belonged to the great violinist Joseph Joachim. It housed consulting rooms, an auditorium for public lectures, an ever-growing library, and the offices of the *WhK*. It also served as Hirschfeld and Giese's residence.

The Harden Trials

As an expert on homosexuality, Hirschfeld testified in numerous court cases and was able to help many men who had been indicted under Paragraph 175 escape imprisonment. One legal affair, however, ended up as a public-relations disaster for him. This was a sequence of suits and countersuits concerned with the purported homosexuality of two close associates of the kaiser: the general Count Kuno von Moltke and the diplomat Prince Philipp von Eulenburg. In 1907 Moltke brought a libel suit against a journalist, Maximilian Harden, who had written an article that, according to Moltke's complaint, implied that he and Eulenburg were homosexual. Rather than trying to deny that this was the meaning of his article, Harden took the offensive and called Moltke's ex-wife as a witness, who testified that the two men had in fact engaged in an amorous relationship. Hirschfeld also testified for the defense, asserting that on the basis of the evidence, as well as his own scientific analysis of Moltke's demeanor in court, the plaintiff was indeed "psychically homosexual."

Harden was acquitted, but undercover machinations led to a new trial later in the year. This time Moltke's ex-wife withdrew her former testimony, and Harden himself said he had never meant to imply that Moltke was homosexual. Thus sandbagged, Hirschfeld had to beat a hasty retreat: he testified that Moltke had merely cultivated the old German virtue of male friendship, something that had nothing to do with sodomy or homosexuality. Harden was convicted of libel, and Hirschfeld was publicly reviled. Among the press comments dug up by Charlotte Wolff are the following: "We are of the opinion that the scientific method of Dr. Magnus Hirschfeld is more madness than method" (the right-wing *National-Zeitung*), and "Dr. Hirschfeld makes public propaganda under the cover of science which does nothing else but poison our people" (the liberal *Münchener Neueste Nachrichten*).[11]

Although Hirschfeld certainly had blurred the line between science and politics, the fact is that Moltke and Eulenburg were indeed homosexual both in disposition and in practice. This came out in later trials in which Hirschfeld was not involved. The full byzantine story has been recounted by James Steakley, who has emphasized the coupling of anti-Semitism and homophobia in the public response to the case.[12]

Hirschfeld and Women

Hirschfeld's original interest was primarily in male homosexuality, and the political movement focused on men because sex between women was not illegal. But over time Hirschfeld became increasingly interested in lesbianism, in female sexuality in general, and in women's rights. He joined the *Bund für Mutterschutz* (League for the Protection of Mothers), the feminist organization founded by the writer Helene Stöcker in 1904, and he campaigned for the decriminalization of abortion, as well for the abolition of rules that imposed celibacy and nonmaternity on female teachers and civil servants. A number of women, including the heterosexual Stöcker, joined the *WhK*, especially in 1910 and 1911, when there was talk of extending paragraph 175 to apply to women as well as men. For all these positive interactions, Hirschfeld remained a creature of his time, believing (as did many feminists themselves) that women were intellectually inferior to men.

Development of Hirschfeld's Views

In 1903 Hirschfeld published *Der Urnische Mensch* ("The Homosexual"—the phrase is sex-neutral). This book represents his mature views on homosexuality, and his later writings, although far broader in scope, did not break radically new ground.[13] In *Der Urnische Mensch* Hirschfeld asserted that homosexuals are indeed sexual *Zwischenstufen* (intermediate stages), although not quite in the same sense that Ulrichs had used the word. Hirschfeld did not think that there was a single male-female continuum, along which any individual could be assigned a unique position. Rather, he held that there are a number of sex-related traits, including gonadal anatomy, genital anatomy, anatomy of other parts of the body, personality, and sexual orientation, any one of which could be used to describe an individual as being more male-like or more female-like. Thus sex was multidimensional, and "male" and "female" were abstractions. Homosexual women and men were *Zwischenstufen* because they possessed a mixture of traits, some of which were male-like, some female-like, and some intermediate.

Hirschfeld now believed that same-sex orientation was sometimes accompanied by physical characteristics of the opposite sex: the hips of some gay men were broader than average, for example, while those of some lesbians were sometimes narrower. Similarly, facial appearance might be typical of the other sex, making it relatively easy for the individual to pass as the other sex if he or she so desired. Later in his career, Hirschfeld even speculated that some gays and lesbians were intersexed in terms of their reproductive physiology: he suggested that it would be worthwhile to examine the vaginal secretions of lesbians for the presence of spermatozoa, and the urine of gay men for menstrual blood.[14] In part, such groundless speculations were the result of Hirschfeld's failure to clearly distinguish among homosexuals, transsexuals, genital intersexes, and gonadal hermaphrodites. But another factor was Hirschfeld's need for visual proof of his theories: he could not rest his case, it seemed, until "lesbian sperm" were laid out for the world to behold.

Hirschfeld also believed that, in terms of personality traits, gays and lesbians were often partially shifted toward the other sex: gay men, for example, were often less aggressive, more caring, and more esthetically inclined that heterosexual men, whereas for lesbians it was often the reverse: they were often more adventurous and forceful than heterosexual women.

On the basis of thousands of interviews, questionnaires, and written reports that he had collected over the previous seven years, Hirschfeld maintained that lesbians and gay men were most gender-nonconformist during their childhood, and that one could fairly speak of a "homosexual child," even though such children did not necessarily feel or express same-sex attraction. The homosexual girls looked and dressed like boys, preferred boys' company and boys' activities, whereas for the homosexual boys it was the reverse. These gender-nonconformist traits did not result from parental treatment (from the parents' wish for a child of the other sex, for example), but from an inborn sexual variance that manifested itself already in childhood.

Thus, in certain respects, Hirschfeld had returned to a close approximation of the views of Ulrichs, in that he firmly linked homosexuality with a broader constellation of sexually variant traits, the entirety of which he attributed to an atypical sexual differentiation of the brain and body during fetal life.

Steinach

In considering how this atypical development might come about, Hirschfeld was influenced by the current developments in endocrinology, most especially by the research of the Viennese endocrinogist Eugen Steinach (1861–1944). During the first decade of the twentieth century, Steinach performed transplantations of testes and ovaries in rats and guinea pigs. His research showed that these glands secrete hormones into the bloodstream that influence not only the animals' physical development but also their sexual behavior. These secretions, he argued, were responsible for the "sexualization" of the brain as male or female.[15] He suggested that this sexualization occurs early in life, because the most dramatic effects were seen when the transplantations were performed shortly after birth.

Steinach developed the notion, partly under the influence of Hirschfeld's biological theories, that the testicular secretions in homosexual men were abnormal and that they drove brain development in a female rather than a male direction. He even claimed to see microscopic differences in the structure of the testis between homosexual and heterosexual men; these differences were not in the sperm-forming cells but in the "interstitial" cells, the cells that he had shown to be responsible for the secretion of testicular hormones.

True to his training as an experimentalist, Steinach tested his hypothesis by conducting transplants in humans. In 1917 he published a sensational report in the *Jahrbuch* that described the results of transplanting a testicle from a heterosexual man into an "effeminate, passive homosexual man." According to the report, the man was totally "cured"—he was said to have lost all attraction to men and to have developed normal heterosexual feelings.[16]

Steinach's experiment seemed to provide dramatic support for a biological explanation of homosexuality. "The decisive factor in contrary sexual feeling," Hirschfeld wrote in 1920, "is not, as Ulrichs believed, in the mind or soul (*anima inclusa*), but in the glands (*glandula inclusa*)."[17] Whatever reservations Hirschfeld may have felt about the desirability of changing a person's sexual orientation were laid aside in favor of promoting Steinach's research. He sought and found volunteers for the procedure—gay men who were desperate to become heterosexual—and directed them to Steinach. Some further successes were reported, but eventually the procedure was exposed as ineffective. If only one of the volunteer's own testicles was removed, there was no permanent effect on his sex drive or sexual orientation. In cases where both of the volunteer's own testicles were removed, however, the consequences were more serious. Hirschfeld published one man's account of his experience.

> After my wife gave her consent, I underwent a bilateral castration. The operation was performed by a well-known surgeon, with the understanding that it would be followed later by the implantation of a testicle from a heterosexual man. As I was already over forty, the initial operation didn't have any dramatic effects. My voice and facial hair weren't affected. My sex drive declined in strength but didn't change its direction. I did lose my body hair, though. A year later the testicle of a heterosexual man was implanted in my abdominal cavity. My body hair began to regrow, but six months later it disappeared again. My sex drive gradually declined until it finally disappeared, but it never changed its direction. My desire to drink and use drugs did go away—I've been clean and sober for years now. So I achieved what I wanted. But I've been destroyed as a man: my drive and will-power are gone. I don't blame anyone—I asked for the procedure myself. But maybe I could have given up drinking if only my feelings of inferiority had been alleviated, by social or moral means. Steinach's transplants were much overrated in those days, even by doctors. I've researched the literature—there isn't one reported case of lasting improvement after a transplant.[18]

Steinach's experiments were doomed to failure because of the immunological rejection of the transplanted glands. But as we shall see later, the underlying scientific hypothesis that so excited Hirschfeld was also incorrect: according to the present scientific consensus, the testicular secretions of gay men differ neither in quality nor in quantity from those of heterosexuals. The gay men who were unmanned by

Steinach, far from making history, earned only a macabre footnote in the annals of medical homophobia.

Freud

If Steinach pulled Hirschfeld in one direction, another Viennese physician—Sigmund Freud—pulled in quite another. Freud in his early career was quite interested in the brain basis of mental life, and was open to the notion that "constitutional factors" played an important role both normal and abnormal psychic development. In 1905, however, Freud published his *Three Essays on the Theory of Sexuality*, in which he declared that "perversions" and neuroses were merely alternative ways of dealing with unresolved Oedipal conflicts: by arrest of development in the one case, or by redirection of the sexual drive in the other. In a letter to Carl Jung written four years later, Freud spelled out the fateful circumstances that lead male children to homosexuality. "In their earliest childhood, later forgotten," they had "an intense erotic attachment to a female person, as a rule their mother, provoked and fostered by the excessive tenderness of the mother herself, further buttressed by the recessiveness of the father in the child's life." At a later stage "the boy represses his love for his mother by putting himself in her place, identifies himself with her, and takes his own person as a model in whose likeness he chooses his new love objects. Thus he has become homosexual; in fact he had slid back into autoeroticism, since the boys whom the growing youngster now loves are, after all, only substitute persons and renewals of his own childish person, boys whom he loves as his mother had loved him as a child."[19]

Through the first decade of the century, Hirschfeld and Freud were on good terms and had a lively interest in each other's ideas. Hirschfeld helped found the Berlin Psychoanalytical Society in 1907, and Freud for his part used some of Hirschfeld's insights in his *Three Essays*. But the two men's views increasingly diverged. In 1911 Hirschfeld left the Psychoanalytical Society, an act that triggered an outburst of the invective which Freud reserved for errant disciples. Magnus Hirschfeld was "no great loss, a flabby, unappetizing fellow, absolutely incapable of learning anything."[20] Hirschfeld did not return the salvo, but he increasingly distanced himself from psychoanalytic theory. The divergence between the two men epitomized the subsequent history of twentieth-century psychology, with its deep division between psychodynamic and biological theories of the mind. (Freud's ideas about homosexuality are considered further in chapter 3.)

Adolf Brand and the Gemeinschaft der Eigenen

Although Hirschfeld and the *WhK* were by far the most influential gay-rights activists of the time, there were other homosexual groups, some of which were opposed to Hirschfeld's approach. The most interesting of these groups was the *Gemeinschaft der Eigenen* (loosely translated: "Community of Free Spirits"), led by the anarchist Adolf Brand. Brand was a proponent of "outing" closeted homosexuals in high places, a strategy aptly referred to as the "path over corpses" (*Weg über Leichen*). In fact, at least one of the men who were outed in that period, the industrialist Friedrich Alfred Krupp, died shortly after his exposure, probably by suicide. Brand himself was jailed several times for his activities. Unlike Hirschfeld, he was unafraid to refer to himself as homosexual, even in court.

Brand and several of his followers joined the *WhK* in its early years. But there were serious conceptual and political disagreements. Brand and his group adamantly rejected Hirschfeld's notion that homosexual men were feminine. To them, love between men was a sign of manliness, a product of the finest German traditions of brotherly love and a sentiment that any man was capable of. In thus blurring the boundary between homosexual attraction and same-sex friendship, the *Gemeinschaft* anticipated the stance taken by lesbian feminists in America in the 1970s. But Brand's followers were no feminists; in fact they tended toward outright misogyny. They were also intellectual and racial elitists who often framed their ideals of male good looks in terms of Germanic racial purity.

The writings of Brand and his followers are preserved in the pages of *Der Eigene*, the magazine published by Brand from 1896 to 1931.

(Selections from the magazine have been republished in English translation.[21]) Besides their objection to the "feminization" of male homosexuality, the members of the *Gemeinschaft* objected to the very fact that the *WhK* was led by a physician, and a sexologist to boot. In their view, this inevitably perpetuated the image of homosexuality as a mental disease, whatever Hirschfeld's actual views on the subject. Even more seriously, Hirschfeld's approach focused the public debate on homosexual practices, which they felt demeaned the homosexual movement by distracting attention from the nobler attributes of love between men.

The *Gemeinschaft* was never a prominent political organization in the manner of the *WhK*, but to the extent that it had its own political platform it was based on human rights, especially on a perceived right to privacy. (No such explicit legal right existed, even in the Weimar constitution of 1919.) This point of view is exemplified in a 1907 article by the *Gemeinschaft's* cofounder Benedict Friedländer. The article explains why Brand, Friedländer, and others resigned from the *WhK* in the wake of the Harden debacle.

> . . .Let it be sharply emphasized here that we lay far less weight on a scientific theory than Herr Hirschfeld and see the question much more from the standpoint of natural rights as one of personal freedom. . .
>
> In truth the medical writers [i.e., Hirschfeld and others] presented to the public, partly in thick volumes, partly in tract format, everything that the Hannoverian *Amtsassessor* [Ulrichs] had brought into the world, supplied with the stamp of medical authority almost without any criticism, partly translated into the jargon of medical quackery, and decorated with so-called "case histories."
>
> . . .Certainly there are "sexual intermediates". Earlier they were called hermaphrodites. They are the rare malformations, which may be estimated to make up—at most—a small fraction per thousand. Of those who are aware of their same-sex feelings, however, there are whole percents. . .[he goes on to cite Hirschfeld's own survey data, albeit without ackowledging their source]
>
> As long as the love for a male being is presented as a specific and exclusively feminine characteristic. . .it will not help to deny sickness: there remains an unavoidable image of a partial hermaphrodite, that is, a kind of psychic malformation. . .
>
> As for the worst in our question, that is, paragraph 175 itself, we shall fight it from purely juridical and moral viewpoints. For whereas the medical theory

is controversial and in part really quite vacuous, the juridical and moral consideration is clear, simple and convincing:

Two responsible people, freely consenting and without harm to a third or even merely to themselves, produce for each other a pleasant feeling. Then comes the state—if by exception it once learns of it—and locks up the culprits, as if they had done something wrong!. . .

Since we renounce in principle making propaganda for homosexual activity, viewing sexual matters rather as a private affair, and fight against paragraph 175 purely on juridical grounds, and since that which we positively advocate is nothing other than male friendships and men's unions—our propaganda will be strictly legal and much safer from police intervention than that of Hirschfeld, which on the basis of its medical theory is forced to go into all kinds of sexual details openly in public. (translation by Hubert Kennedy[22])

The Fate of the Movement

Hirschfeld's movement persevered for years in its single-minded struggle. Sometimes success seemed near. In 1911 a measure to repeal paragraph 175 came to a floor vote in the Reichstag but was defeated. With the new liberal spirit of the Weimar Republic, optimism reigned again, and Brand's *Gemeinschaft* and other gay groups joined with the *WhK* to form an action committee which was to guide policy. In 1925 several other groups, including the *Bund für Mutterschütz*, joined with the *WhK* to form the "Cartel for Reform of the Law against Sexual Offenses". In 1929 a commission of the Reichstag recommended that sex between men over twenty-one be legalized, albeit with various restrictions that would have greatly diminished the impact of the proposed change.[23] The proposal never came to a vote.

The 1920s did indeed see an enormous flowering of gay and lesbian culture in Berlin, a culture far more open and visible than the scene described by Hirschfeld in 1904. It attracted gays and lesbians not just from other parts of Germany but from many other countries. Perhaps the best known of these visitors was Christopher Isherwood, who lived in Berlin from 1929 to 1933 and came to know Hirschfeld and Giese.[24] Gender nonconformity was the heart and soul of this culture, and many of the men and women who created it found the "third sex" an appropriate enough designation for people of their kind. It seemed that Hirschfeld's ideas about homosexuality were being borne out by a new and freer generation of lesbians and gay men.

There were probably several factors at play here. First, Hirschfeld's ideas may have been at least partly correct. Second, his efforts over two decades may have helped to create a culture in the image of his own theories. Lastly, the gender nonconformity of 1920s Berlin was probably in part a reaction to a series of blows inflicted on the German ideals of the virile man and the feminine women, most notably by the military debacles of the Great War and the increasing role of women in the workplace and public life.

If the 1920s were a time of optimism, they were also a time of increasingly dire warnings. In October 1920, Hirschfeld was assaulted and severely injured by a group of Nazi thugs. Shortly thereafter Hitler singled him out as a "Jewish swine" who was being protected by the government: he urged the *Volk* to work its own justice on him.[25] Hirschfeld's public appearances were increasingly disrupted by heckling, stinkbombs, and so on. He withstood the attacks for years, but the increasing political disorders in 1931 and 1932, during which time Hirschfeld was on his world tour, made it impossible for him to return to Germany. In May 1933, sitting in a Paris cinema, he watched newsreels that showed the looting of his Institute for Sexual Science in Berlin and the burning of its books and files. For a while, Hirschfeld planned to found a new institute in France, aided by his ever-present companions, Giese and Tao Li. But deteriorating international conditions made the enterprise impossible. Hirschfeld moved to Nice, where in May 1935 he died of a stroke.

The gay-rights movement in Germany was utterly destroyed by the Nazis. Between 1933 and 1945, about fifty thousand people were convicted of homosexuality by Nazi judges. Of these, about five thousand—virtually all men—were sent to concentration camps, where most of them died.[26] The gay organizations, including the *WhK* and the *Gemeinschaft der Eigenen*, were banned. Adolf Brand had given up gay activism in the early 1930s; he married a woman and settled down in retirement. The aging anarchist might have survived the Nazi period unscathed, had he not been killed in an Allied air raid.

Hirschfeld in Retrospect

History has not dealt kindly with Hirschfeld. After the Second World War and through the 1970s, the fields of psychology and psychiatry were dominated by psychodynamic concepts that paid little attention to possible biological origins of mental diversity. In Germany especially, where memories of Nazi "eugenics" hung heaviest, the notion developed that Hirschfeld's theories had actually paved the way for the extermination of homosexuals. Manfred Herzer cites a passage written by two West German sexologists in the mid-1970s.

> ...[Hirschfeld's] decisive argument was that what is natural cannot be condemned by moral criteria. Fascism taught homosexuals how little this argument was worth—how easily, in fact, it could be turned into its very opposite. For if homosexuality is conceived of as natural and innate, then under the ruling social conditions that could—and still can—lead only to an image of homosexuality as an anomaly, even a deformation. If normal, non-deformed nature is to remain "healthy", then—in the framework of a racist and nationalistic ideology—the sick and the degenerate must be rooted out.[27]

In fact, however, the Nazis did not generally consider homosexuality to be innate or a sign of degeneracy. Rather, they considered homosexuality to be the moral equivalent of an infectious disease that, by means of seduction, could spread all too easily through the ranks of Germany's finest youth. That Hitler himself espoused this theory is made clear in a memorandum issued by his headquarters on August 19, 1941, which read in part:

> Yesterday evening the Führer spoke for a long time about the plague of homosexuality. He said that we must prosecute it with ruthless severity, because there was a time in youth when boys' sexual feelings could easily be influenced in the wrong direction; it was precisely at that age that boys were corrupted by homosexuals. More often than not, a homosexual seduces a huge number of boys, so that homosexuality is actually as infectious and as dangerous as the plague.[28]

Thus what the Nazis "turned into its very opposite" was not Hirschfeld's philosophy but that of Brand and the *Gemeinschaft*.

A conception of Hirschfeld as fundamentally antigay has percolated into the consciousness of the contemporary American gay community. Paul Russell, for example, a professor of English at Vassar College, has published a brief account of Hirschfeld's life in which he claims that Hirschfeld attempted to blackmail the gay men who entrusted information about themselves to him.[29] A gay librarian told me that Hirschfeld regularly handed lists of gay men over to the Berlin police for prosecution. Neither of these allegations appear to be true.

Hirschfeld's memory has also suffered through the failure to acknowledge the influence of the German gay-rights movement on the early gay-rights movement in America. Yet this influence was significant. The very earliest gay-rights organization in the United States was the short-lived Society for Human Rights, based in Chicago. The society was founded in 1924 by Henry Gerber, after he had returned from a three-year stay in Germany, during which time he made contact with gay groups there. The influence of Hirschfeld's thinking on Gerber has been documented.[30]

Another way that Hirschfeld's ideas contributed to the American gay movement was through the person of Rudi Gernreich, an Austrian emigré who was a cofounder of the Mattachine Society in 1950. According to Stuart Timmons's biography of Harry Hay, which is based largely on interviews with Hay, the immediate inspiration for the founding of the Mattachine Society was the meeting of Hay and Gernreich in July 1950, at which Gernreich told Hay about Hirschfeld and his movement.[31] Yet Hay has not been forthright in acknowledging this connection. In an interview for the 1986 documentary film *Before Stonewall*,[32] for example, Hay said: "We didn't know at that point, none of us knew, that there had ever been a gay organization of any sort anywhere in the world before; we had absolutely no knowledge of that at all." Thus the myth has developed that the Mattachine Society had no antecedents.[33]

Hirschfeld's use of science in the cause of gay rights has, for many, made the science itself suspect. In his biography of Freud, Peter Gay described Hirschfeld as a "far from disinterested partisan of homosexual rights," and "interested only in sexual liberation," and he felt compelled to emphasize that Freud "did not share [Hirschfeld's] sexual tastes."[34] Even Hirschfeld's own biographers have placed little stock in Hirschfeld's ideas about homosexuality. Charlotte Wolff presents a sympathetic portrayal of the man, and Manfred Herzer offers an insightful analysis of his social, political, and sexological work, but they are in agreement that his faith in biology as the key to sexual orientation was misplaced.

There is no doubt that some of Hirschfeld's views—especially with regard to bodily differences between homosexual and heterosexual people—were extreme and uncritical. Other aspects of his theory, however, have held up better. In later chapters I will discuss some of the more recent work that may lead us to revisit the notion of the "third sex." For now, it may be appropriate simply to express my own feeling toward Hirschfeld: a profound admiration for the man, his ideas, and his cause.

2

The Nature and Prevalence of Homosexuality

The previous chapter introduced a number of divergent points of view about homosexuality, as they were expressed in Europe early in the twentieth century. Sometimes it seems as if nothing has changed since then. Hirschfeld, Brand, Freud, and Steinach are long dead, but their intellectual heirs are still with us and still going at it hammer and tongs. It is common to read passages in scientific papers, or hear speeches by pro- or antigay activists, that could have been lifted bodily from the records of that long-vanished epoch.

Yet there have also been significant changes. For one thing, important scientific discoveries have been made in the areas of sex and sexual orientation; speculation has, to a degree, been replaced by knowledge. Second, the social climate for gays and lesbians has improved immeasurably, both in Europe and America. Because of this, scientific findings that seemed to have a certain social consequence then might be seen as having a very different consequence now. And lastly, women have added their perspective to a debate that, in Hirschfeld's time, was dominated by men. We will see, in this and the following chapters, how the various themes introduced by Hirschfeld and the others have been reworked over the ensuing decades.

In this chapter I discuss questions relating to the very concept of homosexuality. Can one truly speak of homosexual and heterosexual people, and if so, how common are they? What are the criteria for defining sexual orientation? Are these criteria universal, or are they relevant only to contemporary Western cultures?

The Question of Categories

There has been much debate about the validity of categorizing people according to their sexual orientation. This debate has scientific, ethical, legal, and philosophical aspects. Because the question of categories recurs so often in this book, I begin with a brief discussion of what categorization is.

Categorization involves an interaction between the mind and the things and events that fill the universe—"phenomena." While there is a school of thought that questions the existence of objective phenomonena, I will stay within the commonsense tradition that recognizes a world "out there"—a world that exists independently of our contemplation of it, but to which we have access through our senses. That world includes not just non-human Nature but also humans and everything concerning them, such as human sexuality.

Because the process of categorization involves the activity of the mind, skepticism has arisen about the reality of the "categories" that result from this process. To take an example, pretty much at random, of how this skepticism shows itself, here is a quotation from a 1982 court ruling in which a judge was discussing the question of classifying people by race: "The notion of race," he wrote, "is a taxonomic device and, as with all such constructs, it exists in the human mind, not as a division in the objective universe."[1]

What the judge seemed to suspect about race, namely that people make a "black and white" issue of something that in reality is far more blurred and subjective, is probably right on target. But was he right in suggesting, as he seemed to be doing, that all attempts at categorization or taxonomy construct divisions that do not exist in the objective universe? To me it seems fairer to say that some classifications are not based on objective divisions at all, some are based on incomplete divisions, and some on sharp divisions.

A good example of a classification that does not reflect an objective division is classification by color—not racial color, but colors in general. All that is out there in the world is an infinitely graded continuum of wavelengths of light, but we call certain ranges of wavelength "red," "green," and so on. This grouping of wavelengths into color categories is a perceptual contruction, but it is a construction that is remarkably constant across cultures. Our tendency to form color categories is, to a considerable extent, biologically fated: it depends on the particular spectral sensitivities of the photoreceptor cells in our eyes and on the computations performed by the retina and brain on the inputs from the photoreceptors. Because of this innate perceptual apparatus, we see and name color categories, but we also know, on the basis of information from measuring instruments, that the rainbow is in truth a smooth continuum of wavelengths.

Many classifications, though, *do* reflect objective divisions, divisions that may be sharp or less sharp. When we classify different parts of the earth's surface as "land" or "sea," for example, we are recognizing a division whose reality can be measured, tested, and confirmed. There are of course parts of the earth's surface that are intermediate between the two categories (intertidal zones, coastal marshes, and so on), as well as parts that do not fit comfortably into either category, such as rivers and lakes. But we could apply a test (say for the presence of salt water) to every small patch of the earth's surface, and we could repeat this testing many times during the course of, say, a year, and then plot in histogram form the number of observed patches that are covered in salt water 100 percent of the time, 90 percent of the time, and so on. If we did this, we would end up with a histogram with one very large peak at 100 percent (the ocean), a somewhat smaller peak at zero percent (dry land), and much lower values between these two (intertidal zones). In a word, the histogram will be "bimodal," and it is this bimodality, whose degree can be accurately measured, that is the objective basis of the classification that our minds make when we inspect the world.

Observation and measurement alone cannot tell us whether the "sea/land" classification is the most appropriate way to divide up the world's surface, for that depends on the purpose to which we wish to use the information. Furthermore, as a result of choosing to make our measurements over the course of a year, we obtain a histogram whose degree of bimodality is different than it would be if the measurements were made over the course of a minute (when tides would not have the chance to ebb or flow) or over ten million years (when the continents themselves would have time to move). Again, the period chosen depends on the purpose for which we want to use the information. And lastly, the exact criteria used for measurement will affect the results—if the presence of salt water is used, then lakes will be counted with the land, but if the presence of a hard surface is used, then lakes will be counted with the sea, except when they are frozen over. Yet again, it is the purpose that sets the appropriate criteria: are we concerned with protecting whales, planning an airport, or looking for drinking water? In other words, human affairs affect how we define categories, but, if these definitions are made sufficiently explicit, we can objectively assess whether and to what degree these categories are based on an objective segregation of the phenomena being considered.

Sexual Orientation: The Criteria

Although a great variety of criteria have been used to assess the distribution of sexual orientation in the population, we can group them into four general classes. In the first class are criteria that depend on people's physiological responses to potentially erotic stimuli. For example, one can measure whether a man develops an erection when viewing pictures of naked men, or naked women, or both. Similarly, one can measure whether a woman's vagina becomes engorged with blood in response to the same stimuli. Physiological measurements of this kind have the advantage that they seem to tap into very basic mechanisms of erotic arousal over which individuals have little conscious control. Certainly, if one is looking for a biological basis for sexual orientation, this approach seems very appropriate. On the other hand, it is not feasible to perform such measurements on large, randomly selected groups of people. In addition, the results will not necessarily be predictive of the direction of people's affections, their self-identity, and so on. Yet another problem lies with the very specificity of these kinds of tests. Are visual cues as erotically significant to women as to men? Are olfactory cues more "basic" than visual ones? And so forth.

Another set of criteria involves asking people about their sexual attraction toward men and women, their use of male and female imagery in sexual fantasy, and the like. Such "feelings-based" criteria probably most closely address what we commonly mean by sexual orientation, and have therefore been used very frequently. A drawback to these criteria is that they depend both on the respondents' honesty and on a shared understanding of the meanings of terms like "sexual" and "attraction."

A third set of criteria is based on people's actual sexual behavior. This approach avoids some of the vagueness of the attraction-based criteria: one can frame fairly precise questions such as "With how many men have you had genital contact to orgasm over the past five years?" Behavior-based criteria are particularly appropriate when the purpose of the inquiry is to develop strategies for the prevention of AIDS or other diseases; for that reason many of the recent large-scale surveys have focused on behavior. From the point of view of studying sexual orientation, one has to bear in mind that people's actual sexual behavior may be influenced by factors only loosely connected to their sexuality: their moral beliefs, their opportunities, even their desire to make money. Therefore, behavior-based criteria could be considered less "primary" than those based on feelings. Still, it is important to know how well the "feelings-based" and "behavior-based" criteria correlate with each other, particularly when considering some of the social implications of research in this field. If they correlate very closely, for example, then one could argue that laws penalizing same-sex behavior discriminate against a class of people defined by their underlying sexuality. If they correlate poorly, the argument is not so convincing.

Lastly, one can ask people about their own sense of what categories they belong to. Do they consider themselves to be "homosexual," "lesbian," "gay," "bisexual," and so forth? This "self-labeling" approach does not contribute much to the question of whether homosexuality, bisexuality, and heterosexuality are objective categories of human beings. Nevertheless, people's responses to these questions have a lot to do with the social and political aspects of homosexuality. By correlating the results of this approach with the other tests, one could hope to find out how much people's engagement in the gay community and in gay activism actually reflects their underlying sexuality. Given phenomena like the "political lesbianism" of the 1970s—the adoption of a lesbian identity as an expression of solidarity with the community of women—this issue is by no means a trivial one.

Continuum or Categories?

One of the concerns about classification by sexual orientation that has frequently been expressed is this: perhaps sexual orientation is a broad continuum in the direction of sexual desire, like wavelength, and there is no actual clustering of individuals at the two ends of the spectrum (or at three points in the spectrum, if we include bisexuals as a category). If so, sexual orientation categories are entirely constructs—either perceptual constructs like color categories, or more likely social constructs. There might still be intrinsic differences between individuals, with some experiencing only same-sex attraction and some only opposite-sex attraction, but the "classes" of homosexuals, heterosexuals, and bisexuals would not correspond to any objective groupings in the population.

Hirschfeld stated explicitly that there were intermediate stages between homosexuality and heterosexuality, and his early surveys (described in chapter 1) indicated that bisexuals were in fact more numerous than homosexuals. But, over the course of his career, Hirschfeld seemed to become more confident that gays and lesbians were a discrete category of people who could be identified without any great concern about overlap or dividing lines. He carried out larger surveys, relying on secondhand reports from gay people in various professions, in which he assessed the numbers of "homosexuals" in the population and generally disregarded the existence of bisexuality. Certainly Hirschfeld's work as a whole was taken as strengthening the notion of homosexuals as forming something like a "species"—a point of view that he not only believed in but also considered beneficial to the advancement of gay people.

One person who attempted to demolish this point of view was the American sexologist Alfred Kinsey, lead author of the "Kinsey Reports" that were published in 1948 and 1953.[2] Kinsey and his colleagues interviewed several thousand men and women about their sexual feelings and behavior and came to the conclusion that sexual orientation was a continuum. In the first volume, Kinsey wrote:

> Males do not represent two discrete populations, heterosexual and homosexual. The world is not divided into sheep and goats. Not all things are black nor all things white. It is a fundamental of taxonomy that nature rarely deals with discrete categories. Only the human mind invents categories and tries to force facts into separated pigeon-holes. The living world is a continuum in each and every one of its aspects. The sooner we learn this concerning human behavior the sooner we shall reach a sound understanding of the realities of sex. (p. 639)

Although this sounds very like the judge's statement about race, cited earlier, it is in fact less extreme. The judge seemed to believe that his conclusion was derived from logical first principles and had universal validity. Kinsey was only saying that people who studied living things generally failed to find discrete categories, and deduced from this that biological categories are usually man-made.

If we look at Kinsey's actual data we find that, in the case of men, they do not support his conclusion very strongly. The subjects' sexual orientation was expressed in terms of the famous seven-group Kinsey scale, in which "zero" indicates complete heterosexuality, and "six" complete homosexuality. Kinsey never published histograms of the percentages of subjects in each group, but I have constructed one from the tabulated data (figure 2.1, panel A). The distribution is of course

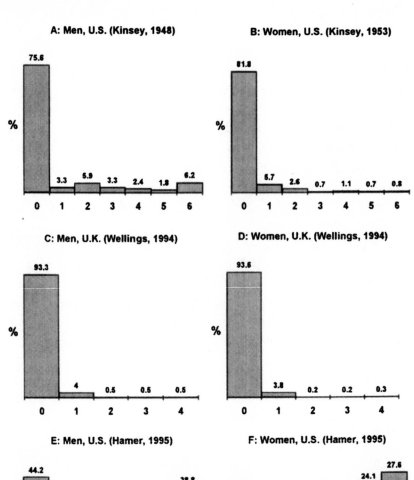

Figure 2.1

Distribution of sexual orientation in men and women, as shown by seven- or five-point "Kinsey scale" histograms. Column 0 in each case contains individuals who are completely heterosexual, column 6 (or 4 in the histograms of panels C and D) contains individuals who are completely homosexual, while the remaining columns are for varying degrees of bisexuality. Panels A–D are population studies; panels E and F are from samples deliberately chosen to contain large numbers of homosexual individuals. The criteria used to assign individuals to particular Kinsey scores vary considerably from one study to the next. (See note on following page.)

Note: A: male U.S. population aged 16–55, age corrected; each individual is placed in the highest Kinsey group to which he belonged for a period of at least three years after he turned 16, based on both feelings and experience (N = 4,275). Derived from bottom line of Table 150 of Kinsey et al., *Sexual Behavior in the Human Male*, p. 654. B: Women aged 30 or above, reporting their "psychological responses and overt experience" at age 30 (N = 2,061). Derived proportionately from lines 6, 12, and 19 of Table 142 of Kinsey et al., *Sexual Behavior in the Human Female*, p. 499. C: Men aged 16–59, lifetime heterosexual/homosexual attraction (N = 8,384). Based on column 1 of Table 5.1 of Wellings et al., *Sexual Behaviour in Britain*, p. 183. D: Women aged 16–59, lifetime heterosexual/homosexual attraction (N = 10,492). Based on column 2 of Table 5.1 of Wellings et al., p. 183. E: Unpublished data of Dean Hamer and Angela Pattatucci. The sample consists of gay men recruited for a study of handedness, along with some of their relatives (N = 522). F: Women, as for D (N = 892).

---

skewed toward heterosexuality, but it certainly looks bimodal, given that the two end-groups are the two largest, and together account for over 80 percent of the population. There might even be a third, "bisexual" mode. In the case of women, however, Kinsey's data do suggest a gradual tapering off of the numbers in the direction of homosexuality: there is no distinct "homosexual" mode (figure 2.1, panel B).

Whatever his data actually showed, Kinsey clearly felt that they disproved Hirschfeld's theories. "From all this," he wrote, "it should be evident that one is not warranted in recognizing merely two types of individuals, heterosexual and homosexual, and that the characterization of the homosexual as a third sex fails to describe any actuality."[3] Kinsey urged that the words "homosexual" and "heterosexual" not be used to define people, although he departed from his own precept long enough to make some prejudicial statements about "homosexual males."[4] Kinsey himself was a heterosexual male.

Curiously, while Ulrichs and Hirschfeld had argued that homosexual acts should be decriminalized because they were the natural behavior of a special class of people, Kinsey also argued for decriminalization, but for exactly the opposite reason, namely that there was *nothing* special about people who engaged in these acts, and that there was no such thing as "a homosexual." Thirty-seven percent of the male population, he reported, had had some same-sex contact to orgasm between adolescence and old age. Therefore "[t]he judge who is considering the case of the male who has been arrested for homosexual activity, should keep in mind that nearly 40 percent of all the other males in the town could be arrested at some time in their lives for similar activity, and that 20 to 30 percent of the unmarried males in that town could have been arrested for homosexual activity that had taken place within that same year. The court might also keep in mind that the penal or mental institution to which he may send the male had something between 30 and 85 percent of its inmates engaging in the sort of homosexual activity which may be involved in the individual case before him."[5]

Although the Kinsey Reports were based on interviews with very large numbers of people, the methods used to recruit people were rather haphazard. As a result, there has been considerable debate about the reliability of the Kinsey data. Rather than review this debate, let us move on to recent surveys that have employed modern sampling techniques. One such survey was carried out in Britain in the early 1990s.[6] Nearly 19,000 men and women, age sixteen to fifty-nine, were interviewed in depth about their sexual feelings and behavior. In figure 2.1 (panels C and D) I have plotted Kinsey histograms (simplified to five-point scales) based on life-time sexual attraction. The histograms are not bimodal either in men or in women: people who have been attracted exclusively to the same sex are no more common than people with varying degrees of attraction to both sexes. The histograms derived from behavior-based questions are very similar (not shown). These results lend support to Kinsey's claim that sexual orientation is a continuum. It should be borne in mind, however, that the histograms collapse the interviewees' complete life experience into a single scale; thus they may blur distinctions that would be clearer if they were based on questions about recent life history. This would be true, for example, if substantial numbers of people who experienced some opposite-sex attraction and behavior at adolescence or in early adulthood moved to a more exclusively homosexual orientation at maturity (see below). A comparable U.S. study, published in 1994, obtained roughly similar results.[7]

One difficulty with attempting to answer the question about the discreteness of the categories "homosexual" and "heterosexual" has to do with the skewness of the distribution. Homosexuality is far less common than heterosexuality; therefore the details of the distribution at the homosexual end of the spectrum tend to get lost in the noise, even with large samples. Recently, some researchers have looked at the question of discreteness by using samples that have been "enriched" in gay people. A good example is the work of Dean Hamer and his colleagues, who have published Kinsey scale histograms for the subjects involved in their genetic studies of sexual orientation and related traits (see chapter 9). Figure 2.1 (panels E and F) shows two of these histograms; the subjects comprise the original "gay" volunteers as well as some of their relatives, who were selected without regard to their sexual orientation. The histograms are highly bimodal: in the male histogram especially, almost no one falls into the three central groups (2, 3, and 4). Hamer commented: "This is what would be expected for a discrete, or bimodally, distributed phenotype [observed characteristic]. If sexual orientation were a quantitative, or continuously, distributed phenotype, we would have found more of a bell-shaped curve."[8]

Histograms like Hamer's may exaggerate the apparent bimodality of sexual orientation. After all, the alternative to bimodality is not really a "bell-shaped curve" but one half of such a curve, with its peak right at the "heterosexual" end of the histogram and a tail dropping away to the "gay" end. By adding gay men selectively to this tail, Hamer may have produced the appearance of a trough in the middle of the distribution where none really existed. Some studies avoid this problem by only reporting the Kinsey scores of the relatives of the gay people who volunteer, not the volunteers themselves. For example, Michael Bailey (of Northwestern University) and Richard Pillard (of Boston University) have reported that the monozygotic ("identical") co-twins of gay men fall clearly into two groups, heterosexual and homosexual (see also chapter 9).[9] But the relevance of this unusual population to the distribution of sexual orientation in general is uncertain, and indeed Bailey and Pillard made no claims in this regard.

One thing that Hamer and many other researchers seem to agree on is that the distribution of Kinsey scores is less strongly bimodal in women than in men. In fact, even women who identify as "lesbian" nevertheless often state that they are aware of some opposite-sex attraction.[10]

On the whole, the results of the various sex surveys suggest that there is a good correlation between people's sexual orientation as assessed by their feelings, their behavior, and their declared identity. The survey results do not support the notion that, in contemporary Western cultures, large numbers of men and women are sexually attracted to the same sex but fail to act on that attraction. The great majority of men and women have sex only with members of the other sex, and they do so for a simple reason: they don't find members of the same sex sexually attractive.

Physiological Tests of Sexual Orientation

As mentioned earlier, physiological tests offer a means to study sexual arousal rather directly. The pioneer in this field was the Czech-born psychologist Kurt Freund, who in the 1960s invented a gadget named the penile plethysmograph.[11] This device measures changes in penile volume or pressure that occur in response to erotic stimuli. It is sensitive to small changes occurring before the subject attains a recognizable erection. A comparable device has been developed for measuring the engorgement of the vaginal walls during arousal—it is a light-sensitive device that responds to color changes as the vaginal walls become engorged with blood.[12]

According to Freund, the great majority of men show plethysmographic responses to pictures of naked adult women, or to pictures of naked adult men, but not to both. In fact, Freund identified few if any men who were bisexual by plethysmographic criteria.[13] Freund's observations therefore supported the notion that there are objective categories of sexual orientation in men, at least at this basic level of erotic arousal. There is reason to be cautious in generalizing from Freund's results, however, because they were not derived from broad, randomly selected samples of the population.

Very recently, a comparable study has been done on women by Ellen
Laan and her colleagues at the University of Amsterdam.[14] They tested
the vaginal responses of lesbian and heterosexual women to film clips
showing either a man or a woman performing oral sex on a woman ("heterosexual" and "lesbian" clips). In sharp contrast to Freund's data for men,
both groups of women responded about equally to the heterosexual and
the lesbian clips, both in terms of the measured vaginal responses and their
subjective sense of arousal. The interpretation of Laan's findings are complicated by the presence of two actors in the clips, with resulting uncertainty as to who the subjects were focusing on or identifying with.
Further research may clarify these points. The results so far, however, suggest that the kind of stimuli found to be sexually arousing may not be a
good indicator of whether a woman prefers to have sex with women or
with men. If so, sexual orientation as usually defined would seem to be
a more "high-level" aspect of personality in women than in men.

Stability of Sexual Orientation

Whether homosexuality and heterosexuality are objective categories
(as may be the case in men), or arbitrary divisions of a spectrum of
sexual orientation (as seems to be true in women), the question still
remains of how stable sexual orientation is over the life span. At one
extreme, one could imagine that sexual orientation is sufficiently fixed
that it contributes a data point to a person's unique and permanent
identification—like a particular digit of a person's social security number. At the other extreme, a person's sexual orientation might be essentially fluid, congealing at "homosexual" or "heterosexual" only for
the duration of particular relationships.

As we have seen, Hirschfeld believed that sexual orientation was a
life-long attribute. He asserted that it was determined by prenatal developmental events, that it was discernible in childhood on the basis of
gender-related traits, and that it generally remained stable after emergence at sexual maturity, even in the face of attempts to change it.

Several of these claims have received at least partial support from
research conducted since Hirschfeld's time—research that will be

reviewed in the following chapters. But the question of lifetime stability is still rather uncertain. The ideal way to answer the question would be by means of a study that followed a group of individuals as they grew up, matured, and aged. Yet there have been few studies of this kind, and these have been limited to the childhood-to-adulthood transition (see chapter 4). Most studies that have addressed the question of stability have actually been concerned with the success or failure of efforts to convert gay people to heterosexuality. Thus they have not provided information about whether sexual orientation can change naturally over a course of many years.

In one recent study, by Angela Pattatucci and Dean Hamer, the sexual orientation of several hundred women was assessed (using feelings-, behavior-, and identity-based tests), and the tests were then repeated after an interval of twelve to eighteen months.[15] The results obtained at the two time points were very similar: in only about 20 percent of the women was there a measurable change in sexual orientation, and nearly all these changes were small (one Kinsey group) and within the central bisexual range; the Kinsey group 0's and 6's hardly changed at all. Thus in the short term women's sexual orientation, whether heterosexual, bisexual or homosexual, seems to be quite stable.

On the basis of another study, however, in which several hundred women who identified as lesbian were asked how they identified in the past, it appears that significant number of women change from a bisexual to a lesbian identity. In the majority of such cases, the bisexual identity is a transitional phase on the way to a homosexual identity, but some women fluctuate between the two identities. What *is* uncommon is for a woman, once she has adopted a bisexual or lesbian identity, to subsequently adopt a heterosexual identity.[16]

A comparable survey of gay-identified men also indicated that many of them (about 40 percent of the total) had previously identified as bisexual. In the majority of cases the period of bisexual identification was at a young age (between sixteen and twenty-five) and was transitional to the adoption of a homosexual identity.[17]

Thus it appears that sexual orientation as measured by *identity* can change—usually in the direction heterosexual→bisexual→homosexual. No doubt this represents in considerable part the "coming-out process," that is, a process of increasing honesty (to oneself and others) about a same-sex attraction that one has been experiencing all along. But this does not seem to be the whole story, especially for women. In my own informal discussions with men and women who have come out as gay or lesbian later in life, the men have usually asserted that they "knew they were gay" all along. The women, however, have been quite diverse in their recollections: some have told me that they "knew they were lesbian" all along, but others said they never experienced any kind of same-sex attraction until quite late in life. Thus, unless one chooses to drag in the awkward concept of "latent homosexuality," one has to conclude that some women truly change their sexual orientation from heterosexual to homosexual.

The existence of bisexuality, as well as the fact that sexual orientation sometimes changes, have frequently been used in arguments against biological theories of sexual orientation—particularly against genetic theories. Such arguments hold little water. First, genes do not necessarily have either/or effects: genes produce not just black cats and white cats but also grey cats. Second, the effects of genes may not become apparent until late in life: male-pattern baldness, for example, is influenced very strongly by genes, but most bald men once had a full head of hair. And as we shall see in chapter 9, the scientists who currently espouse genetic theories claim only that genes *influence* sexual orientation, not that they *determine* it. The remaining, non-genetic influences, whatever they are, doubtless add to the diversity and malleability of human sexuality.

Essentialism versus Social Constructivism

Because Hirschfeld believed that sexual orientation was a fixed, objective aspect of human nature, he was what nowadays would be called an "essentialist." But there has also been another tradition which has claimed that the categories of "homosexual" and "heterosexual" have emerged from the social, political, and scientific debate about sexuality that has taken place over the past century or so, and that these categories have then been applied as labels to unsuspecting citizens, in effect *making* them homosexual or heterosexual. This is "social constructivism," a school of thought in which concepts like "representation," "signification," "discourse," and "power" are more important than the details of individual development. Probably the leading figure in this school was the French philosopher Michel Foucault, who died in 1984,[18] but American exponents of these ideas include writers like David Halperin, a professor of literature at MIT. Halperin's essay *One Hundred Years of Homosexuality* encapsulates, in its very title, the notion that homosexuality was brought into existence by the invention, in the late nineteenth century, of the word used to define it.[19]

It seems to me quite artificial to make the existence of homosexuality dependent on the coinage of a term to describe it. The philosopher Richard Mohr has argued persuasively that, even without the word, people could and did formulate the equivalent concept.[20] But Mohr does not go far enough, for even the ability to formulate the concept is irrelevant to the existence or nonexistence of homosexuality. Sexual attraction is an aspect of consciousness; it is directly experienced, like hunger, thirst, seeing the color red, taking fright, loving one's mother, and countless other aspects of our mental life. Just as people experience hunger (and indeed cravings for particular classes of food) without having to say to themselves "I'm hungry," or even "I have that same feeling I had last Monday when I didn't eat all day," so a woman can repeatedly and consistently be sexually aroused by women and not by men, without ever having to say to herself "I'm lesbian," "I'm different from the others," or anything else. Social constructivists, particularly of the "strong" variety represented by Halperin, seem to want to replace consciousness with self-consciousness, and a highly linguistic self-consciousness at that.[21]

According to "strong" social constructivists, scientific researchers like myself, who have searched for the determinants of sexual orientation in the processes of individual development, are the victims of a crass literalmindedness; we are like those biblical scholars of bygone days, whose idea of understanding Genesis was to figure out where the Garden of Eden was historically located. There is in fact so little common ground between the "strong" social-constructivist approach and that of biological science that little interaction between the two is possible.

There is, however, a "weaker" form of social constructivism, according to which individuals do have an intrinsic sexual orientation (possibly biologically caused), but this intrinsic orientation is far less relevant to human affairs that the "extrinsic" orientation that people are assigned. A representative exponent of this form of constructivism is Janet Halley, a legal scholar at Stanford University. In her essay "The Construction of Heterosexuality,"[22] Halley writes: "The...class of heterosexuals is a default class, home to those who have not fallen out of it. It openly expels but covertly incorporates the homosexual other, an undertaking that renders it profoundly heterogeneous, unstable, and provisional." Thus closeted homosexuals are indeed homosexual, but because society reads them as heterosexual their homosexuality is of little importance.

Weak social constructivism does not challenge the intellectual validity of research into sexual orientation so much as it challenges the relevance of such research to practical issues like gay rights. There is a lot to be said for this point of view. In many contexts, what matters is not the inner feelings that people experience or the private behavior that they may engage in, but the form in which they present themselves to the world or are identified by the world. This presentation and identification can be quite remote from the psychological structures that genes, hormones, and brain development help set up.

Yet even if one accepts the message of weak social constructivism, one can still make a case for the relevance of biology. First, one's own inner life is important, as much as or more than one's social status. Even the most closeted gay person undergoes the central experience of homosexuality: his or her life course is indelibly affected by it. Homosexuality, in a very real sense, is inescapable. And second, as our society becomes increasingly permissive and even accepting with regard to sexual diversity, people's "intrinsic" and "extrinsic" orientations are becoming more and more congruent. As the surveys discussed earlier have shown, sexual behavior and self-identification nowadays correspond fairly closely to the direction of sexual attraction that an individual experiences, and the closet is a thing of the past for increasing numbers of gays and lesbians. Thus the study of what factors set up the direction of a person's sexual feelings is becoming, to an increasing extent, the study of a person's behavior and social status too. Biology and "weak" social constructivism may therefore be on converging paths.

Cross-Cultural Studies

Homosexual relationships fall into a number of different patterns. Among these patterns, three seem to recur widely in different cultures: I will refer to them as *transgenderal*, *age-disparate*, and *companionate* relationships. Transgenderal homosexual relationships are those in which one of the two individuals is markedly cross-gendered, while the other is more or less conventional for his or her own sex. In many traditional Native American cultures, for example, there were individuals, known to anthropologists as *berdaches* (male) or *amazons* (female), who cross-dressed and took on some of the social roles and attributes of the other sex. (They are sometimes referred to as "two-spirit people.") Berdaches and amazons often married more conventional individuals of the same sex as themselves. These transgenderal relationships aroused little comment, perhaps because they so closely mimicked—except in the minor detail of one partner's anatomy—the socially prescribed pattern for heterosexual relationships. Age-disparate homosexual relationships, which are more common between men than between women, are those in which a difference in age between the two partners is a key aspect of the relationship. The celebrated male homosexual cultures of Classical Greece and pre-Western Japan mostly involved relationships of this kind. Companionate homosexual relationships are those between two individuals who are not markedly different from each other in age, gender-related characteristics or, other traits. Not especially common in the historical or anthropological record, such relationships have nevertheless become highly visible in our own society.[23]

The existence of these various patterns forces us to consider carefully what we mean by "homosexual" and "heterosexual." Today, a person is usually described as homosexual if he or she is sexually attracted predominantly to people of the same anatomical sex as him- or herself. Thus both partners in a transgenderal relationship may be considered equally homosexual. In Ulrichs's and Hirschfeld's writings, however, there was always the sense that the transgendered partner is "more" homosexual than the conventionally gendered partner. Their concept of homosexuality was colored by the concept of "inversion," the idea that homosexuality is related to a broader sex-atypicality involving preferred sex acts (penetrating or being penetrated), mental traits, and social roles.

I adhere to the contemporary definition of homosexuality, because I think it is useful to distinguish between sexual object choice and other aspects of sexuality. But cross-cultural studies suggest that homosexuality tends to be a more fixed and permanent trait in transgendered than in more conventionally gendered individuals. In native American cultures, for example, the men who married berdaches, and the women who married amazons, might also (before or after the homosexual relationship) couple with persons of the other sex. The amazons and berdaches themselves, on the other hand, tended to avoid heterosexual relationships for most or all of their lives.[24]

The time course of age-disparate homosexual relationships seems to have varied in different cultures. As Aristophanes paints it in Plato's *Symposium*, the man-loving youth becomes, as he matures, a youth-loving man; there is a smooth continuity of homosexual identity. Perhaps this was something of an idealization: one might guess that some youths entered into liaisons with adult men on account of the advantages to be gained from such liaisons and the difficulty of finding an outlet for heterosexual desires, rather than from a homosexual orientation in the sense we use the word. If so, they might not have formed relationships with youths when they matured, or only until they could find a wife.

In another form of age-disparate male homosexuality, described by Gilbert Herdt among the Sambia of New Guinea, the entire phenomenon is compressed into the late-childhood and teenage years: starting at seven to ten years of age, boys perform ritualized fellatio on older

teenagers, switching roles around puberty.[25] After the older partners leave
the all-male cult houses, most of them marry women and cease engaging in sex with males, although a few continue to do so. Rather than
say that the male Sambia "change" sexual orientation after leaving the
cult houses, it seems more appropriate to say that homosexual behavior has been institutionalized for the entire teenage male population,
heterosexual, bisexual and homosexual. In a comparable way, *heterosexual* behavior has traditionally been institutionalized for both heterosexual and homosexual teenagers in American society—by means of
high-school proms and a myriad other explicit or subtle pressures.[26]

In taking a scientific approach to the study of sexual orientation,
one is making the assumption that a certain sameness underlies the
diversity observed in different cultures. Sociologist Fred Whitam has
provided some evidence for consistency across cultures, particularly
with respect to childhood traits that are to some extent predictive of
adult sexual orientation.[27] But in large part, this assumption is one that
remains to be tested. Not only has much of the research been restricted
to the United States and Europe, it has also often focused on narrow
groups within the population. Psychoanalytic studies have generally
involved "patients," brain studies have focused on people who have
died of AIDS, cognitive studies have concentrated on college under-
graduates, surveys have often reported selectively on "out" gays and
lesbians, and genetic studies have recruited through clinics, gay organizations, and friendship networks. Even within these narrow groups,
the results have often been inconsistent, as the following chapters will
document. It will be an important but daunting task to determine
which findings can be generalized to the entire human race.

Prevalence

Given all the foregoing, it will be obvious that any attempt to estimate
the prevalence of homosexuality is fraught with hazards. At the very
least, it is necessary to spell out the criteria used to assess sexual orientation, the cutoff point used to define "homosexuals," and the time
span over which sexual orientation is considered.

Hirschfeld assessed the prevalence of homosexuality at about 1 percent to two percent, and of bisexuality at about 4 percent (see chapter 1). Kinsey, in contrast, refused to come up with global estimates of this kind; instead he produced long charts showing the prevalence of different ratios of same- and opposite-sex attraction and behavior over different periods of life. Admirable though this cautious approach may have been, it did him little good. His data were rapidly distilled and transformed in the public imagination, reemerging as a simple statistic: one in ten Americans is "gay." Kinsey was re-invented in a Hirschfeldian mold, in fact as a "super-Hirschfeld," because he had found gay people to be five times commoner that Hirschfeld's estimate.

Self-identified gay people were largely responsible for this transformation. Already in 1950 the 10 percent figure was trumpeted in Harry Hay's manifesto for the Mattachine Society.[28] Since then, it has been elevated to a central tenet of gay culture, appearing in articles, on posters, in the titles of organizations and publications, and even in scholarly texts.[29] Conversely, studies that have come up with lower figures have been widely dismissed as biased or technically flawed. Evidently, the prevalence of homosexuality is a research topic that speaks very directly to gay people's self-esteem, as well as to their perceived (and therefore their actual) political leverage.

Most people know that the 10 percent figure derives from the Kinsey Reports, but few people know that it applies only to men, and only refers to the percentage of men who are predominantly homosexual (group 5 or 6) for at least three years of their adult life. Given that adult lives extend for several decades, the figure is compatible with a much lower prevalence of homosexuality in the male population at any given moment of time. In fact, Kinsey estimated that only about 4 percent of men were exclusively homosexual throughout their adult lives, and the figures for women were even lower: between 1 percent and 3 percent of never-married or previously married women and less than 0.3 percent of married women.

The recent surveys have consistently produced figures lower than 10 percent. In the British study cited earlier, 1 percent of the men and only 0.5 percent of the women said that they were sexually attracted

"mostly" or "only" to people of their own sex, and the same percentages stated that they had had "genital contact" with a person of their
own sex within the previous five years. Higher percentages of men
and women (3.6 percent and 1.7 percent respectively) said that they
had had a least one same-sex experience with genital contact. Quite
similar results have been obtained in surveys carried out in France (men
only)[30] and Norway,[31] although the Norwegian study differed in that
it found no sex difference in the percentages of men and women with
recent homosexual experience (0.9 percent of both sexes).

Recent surveys in the United States have also come up with prevalence figures well below 10 percent. Most studies agree that about 2
percent of the population have had at least one homosexual experience in the previous few years.[32] In a large survey conducted by the
National Opinion Research Center in 1992, 2.8 percent of men and
1.4 percent of women identified as "homosexual" or "bisexual." Another 3.2 percent of men and 4.1 percent of women identified as "heterosexual" but acknowledged some degree of same-sex attraction.
The highest percentages reported in recent random-sample studies
come from a market-research firm, Yankelovich Partners, Inc., who
stated that 5.7 percent of their respondents identified as "gay/homo-
sexual/lesbian."[33] This survey did not offer any "bisexual" option,
however; it is likely that a significant fraction of those choosing the
"homosexual" option would have switched to "bisexual" if it had
been available. Another recently published study, from the Harvard
School of Public Health, found relatively high rates of homosexual behavior and attraction (for example, it concludes that 6.2 percent of U.S.
males and 3.6 percent of U.S. females have had sexual contact with
someone of the same sex in the previous five years), but the study is
rendered problematic by poorly-phrased questions.[34]

Homosexuality is a stigmatized condition, and one has to be concerned that some of the surveys' respondents were less than frank about
their homosexual feelings or behavior. Although most of the surveys
used techniques designed to reduce this problem (for example, by not
requiring the respondents to make direct statements to the interviewers about their sexuality), most of them also emphasize that, be-

cause of this potential problem, their figures should be considered as minimum estimates. There have also been technical criticisms of some of the studies.[35] Thus gay people or others who wish to cling to a 10 percent figure still have a possible line of argumentation.

Yet these same surveys also reveal what may be the reason why gays and lesbians have such a hard time accepting low estimates of prevalence. This is the fact that so many gay people live in places where the prevalence of homosexuality is far above the norm. In the British survey, for example, fully 43 percent of men who were gay by a behavior-based criterion (at least one same-sex "partner" in the previous five years) lived in London, most of them having moved there from other parts of Britain. By contrast, only 13 percent of the nongay men lived in London. As a consequence, gay men formed nearly 5 percent of London's male population, but only 0.5 percent of the population of Wales or Scotland. The phenomenon was not so marked for lesbians, but still, twice as many lesbians as nonlesbians had moved to London. In the United States the aggregation of gay people, especially of men, may be even more extreme. In one "gay ghetto"—the city of West Hollywood, California—self-identified gays and lesbians form about 30 percent of the population,[36] while rural and small-town America is over 99 percent "gay-free."[37] Thus gay people, especially men, are liable to develop a wholly inflated notion of the prevalence of homosexuality, based on their immediate environment.

Prevalence data for countries outside of Europe and the United States are very sketchy. Reports of cultures where everyone is homosexual, or where no one is homosexual, are doubtless fictitious.[38] So is the belief, widespread around the world, that one's own culture was free of homosexuality until foreigners imported it.[39] Sociologist Fred Whitam has made the case, based partly on his own studies of diverse cultures, that the prevalence of male homosexuality is similar in all countries: aside from special cases such as San Francisco, he has estimated that about 5 percent of the male population of large cities is homosexual.[40]

As with the topics of bisexuality and the stability of sexual orientation, so the question of prevalence across cultures has been used in the debate about a biological or genetic basis for sexual orientation. One frequently hears statements to the effect that, because homosexuality is much more common in one country or ethnic group than another, it cannot be genetically based. In fact, of course, the prevalence of many genes varies between different countries and ethnic groups (that is a part of the reason why ethnic groups exist). Thus, even if it could be shown that homosexuality were significantly more common in one part of the world than another, such a finding would not by itself speak to the question of what determines people's sexual orientation. The only kind of prevalence data that could undermine a purely genetic theory would be the demonstration that homosexuality had rapidly become more common or less common within a single culture. Longitudinal data of this kind are very limited, but comparison of Hirschfeld's data with the recent surveys suggests that the prevalence of same-sex attraction in Western culture has remained fairly stable over the last century. What *has* changed dramatically is the fraction of the homosexual population that is out of the closet—a finding that leads to an unsurprising conclusion, namely, that gay people's willingness to come out is strongly influenced by the culture in which they find themselves.

Overview

All in all, the question of whether people can be assigned to objective categories of sexual orientation on the basis of their Kinsey scores remains somewhat unclear. It seems likely that the distribution in men is bimodal, although there are clearly individuals at all positions on the scale. Thus it is reasonable, at least on a provisional basis, to speak of homosexuals and heterosexuals as classes into which most men can be objectively categorized. With women, there is no strong evidence at this point for objective categories; therefore, when I use "homosexual," "lesbian," or "gay" with respect to women, it should be borne in mind that the group of women I am referring to may well be an arbitrary sector of a continuum of sexual orientation. "Bisexual" does not seem to be an objective category in either sex, although bisexual men and women can of course be defined as forming an arbitrary sector of the Kinsey scale or on the basis of their self-identification as bisexual.

Even more problematic is the question of the consistency of patterns of sexual orientation across cultures and in different historical periods. Nothing in the historical or anthropological record contradicts the notion that the general pattern we see in our own culture—a majority of individuals attracted predominantly to the other sex and a minority attracted predominantly to the same sex—has been true of all cultures. But the record is so incomplete, and so distorted by changing attitudes and beliefs, that we cannot be sure that this pattern is universal. It seems appropriate to proceed on the assumption of universality, but with a willingness to be corrected if new evidence warrants it.

Finally, we do not know whether different forms of homosexuality (e.g., age-disparate, transgenderal, and companionate) have developmental mechanisms in common, or whether they are better thought of as completely distinct entities arising from completely different programs of development. It is important that (where possible) researchers obtain detailed information about their subjects' sexuality, so that diverse pathways of homosexual development, if they exist, will eventually become apparent. On the other hand, excessive splitting of entities can be counterproductive. Science proceeds most easily when assumptions are kept simple. An enormous amount has been learned about sex on the assumption that there is only one relevant way to class people—as men and women. Now we know that is not the whole story, and that sexual orientation must also be considered. A lot is being learned on the assumption that sexual orientation is the only important classification beyond sex, but eventually, the inadequacy of that classification will become apparent too. To try to take all this potential diversity into account right at the beginning would be a recipe for paralysis.

3

The Talking Cure

Freud

"Psycho-analytic research," wrote Sigmund Freud in 1915, "is most decidedly opposed to any attempt at separating off homosexuals from the rest of mankind as a group of a special character."[1] With this statement Freud distanced himself once and for all from the ideas of Ulrichs and Hirschfeld (or the "spokesmen of the inverts" as he liked to call them), for it was precisely this attempt to which Ulrichs and Hirschfeld had dedicated their lives.

Why did Freud make this statement? He was of course aware that one can separate the human population into two groups on the basis of their answers to questions like "Do you experience same-sex attraction?" or "Do you have sex with people of the same sex as yourself?" But he believed that the categories so defined would be trivial—that they would not tell us much of significance about human nature or the psychology of the individuals involved. This was because, in Freud's eyes, the significant workings of the mind were hidden from view. In the passage cited above he continued as follows:

By studying sexual excitations other than those that are manifestly displayed, it has been found that all human beings are capable of making a homosexual object-choice and have in fact made one in their unconscious. Indeed, libidinal attachments to persons of the same sex play no less a part as factors in normal mental life, and a greater part as a motive force for illness, than do similar attachments to the opposite sex. On the contrary, psycho-analysis considers that a choice of an object independent of its sex—freedom to range equally over male and female objects—as it is found in childhood, in primitive states of society and early periods of history, is the original basis from which, as a result of restriction in one direction or another, both the normal and the inverted types develop.

At first glance this does not sound so very different from Hirschfeld's developmental theory outlined in chapter 1: an early bisexual phase is followed, through selective elimination of same-sex or opposite-sex attraction, by heterosexuality or homosexuality. But the two theories are in reality quite different. The early bisexual phase, in Hirschfeld's model, involves the simultaneous existence of two different neural centers, one for attraction to males and one for attraction to females. Furthermore, the question of whether these two centers actually *function* at this early stage, although apparently answered by Hirschfeld in the positive, is not at all crucial to his model. In Freud's view, on the other hand, there are no such separate centers. What exists in infancy is a sexual drive, a *libido*, that is not yet attached irreversibly to a specific class of objects. What is crucial is that the libido *does* function in early infancy: it is this very functioning that drives development.

As Freud defined it in his *Three Essays on the Theory of Sexuality*, the libido is the sexual instinct: the equivalent in the sexual realm of hunger in the realm of nutrition. Thus it is not a general motivating force but a specifically sexual one. Nevertheless its specificity with regard to its object is much less fixed, according to Freud, than we commonly believe. Even in the sphere of the conscious sexual feelings experienced by adults, sexual desire to some extent can be separated from its object or objects. The word "horniness" captures, at least for men, the sense of nonspecific sexual arousal that might eventually find release in any of a number of ways. But in the unconscious mind, according to Freud, the libido ranges even more freely. Not only may it be directed to classes of objects that are not consciously recognized as sexually attractive (for example, toward persons of the same sex in "heterosexual" individuals), it may also, through sublimation and other processes, gain expression in artistic creativity, intellectual work, or charitable endeavors, as well as in personality traits such as thriftiness, ambition, even religious faith. The operation of the libido, in Freud's view, is the cause not only of "perversions" (which are explicitly sexual) but also of the neuroses, whose sexual origins have been repressed from consciousness. Even diseases such as anorexia nervosa, bulimia, and obesity, which might be viewed simply as disorders of the instinct of hunger, are supposedly the result of the unconscious, repressed operations of the libido. In short, Freud believed that the libido shapes and motivates a very large part of human nature.

The problem with this broad conceptualization of the libido is that it becomes all but impossible to verify or refute its relevance in any particular instance. Most especially is this true for infants and young children. Faced with this problem, Freud took a particular behavior—thumb sucking—as a paradigm of infantile sexuality. He asserted that thumb sucking was sexual because it was the infant's attempt to repeat a remembered sexual pleasure, namely the pleasure experienced when suckling at its mother's breast.

There are two problems with this interpretation. First, the invention of ultrasonographic imaging has led to the discovery that, like young babies, fetuses also often place and keep a thumb in their mouths. Whether or not they actively suck, the placement of the thumb in the mouth evidently offers some gratification prior to any experience of the mother's breast.

More crucially, what is the reason for considering even sucking at the nipple to be driven by the libido rather than (or as well as) by hunger or thirst? According to Freud, simple observation gives the answer: "No one who has seen a baby sinking back satiated from the breast and falling asleep with flushed cheeks and a blissful smile can escape the reflection that this picture persists as a prototype of the expression of sexual satisfaction in later life."[2] Yet might one not equally well assert that the infant's behavior after breast-feeding resembles that shown by adults after a hearty meal or a few beers? It is not obvious that it specifically resembles postcoital behavior.

One could of course ask whether the suckling infant has a penile erection or vaginal engorgement or contractions, whether it shows the signs of orgasm, or (in a thought experiment at least) whether the brain circuits involved in coitus or in sexual object-choice are activated during suckling. But even if none of these things happen, it could always be argued that the pathways that mediate the physical expression of sexual arousal or orgasm are not functional in infants, or that the libido has not yet developed to the genital stage, or that the libido is not represented by the activity of any particular set of brain neurons. Freud's theory is not exactly unfalsifiable in the Popperian sense, but it is certainly slippery enough (on account of the uncertain definition of the word "sexual") to make it difficult either to prove or disprove.

At any event, Freud considered that the mouth, by virtue of its engagement in breast-feeding and thumb sucking, was an "erogenous zone," and the infant was in the "oral phase" of its psychosexual development. But other zones could become erogenous also. "A child who is indulging in sensual sucking," he wrote, "searches about his body and chooses some part of it to suck—a part which is afterwards preferred by him from force of habit; if he happens to hit upon one of the predestined regions (such as the nipples or genitals) no doubt it retains the preference."[3]

This passage contains an assumption that is not merely falsifiable but manifestly false, namely, that infants are capable of sucking their own nipples or genitalia. But even if an occasional baby were capable of such gymnastics, why would sucking the nipples or the genitalia confer erotogenicity on those parts? Freud never claimed, after all, that the *thumb* became an erogenous zone as a result of being sucked. Freud did not want to be forced into the "biological" interpretation, that is, that there are specific neural pathways leading from the genitalia and nipples (but not from the thumb) to the brain circuits that mediate sexual arousal. He therefore finessed the whole problem, in a later edition of the book, by saying that "After further reflection...I have been led to ascribe the quality of erotogenicity to all parts of the body and to all the internal organs." Unfortunately, this conclusion left unanswered the original question, which was why the genitalia and nipples, but not the thumb or, say, the back of the head, are generally experienced as erogenous zones.

Of particular relevance in the context of male homosexuality is the erotic role of the anus. According to Freud, young children derive sexual pleasure from defecation. Later, he claimed, this pleasure is forbidden and the child must repress the libido associated with it. In neurotic adults, the repressed libido reemerges in a transformed shape, involving constipation, secret scatological practices, or the like. If this aspect of the libido is not repressed, it will persist into adulthood and will be manifested as a perversion, namely as the desire for receptive anal intercourse. Presumably, although Freud was not explicit about this, the failure of repression could occur either in boys or girls and would not necessarily be associated with same-sex attraction. Nevertheless, a failure to progress beyond the anal phase was seen by Freud as a feature of the sexual development of some homosexual men. Furthermore, this kind of adult sexuality was *narcissistic*, because it arose from a period of development when the libido was focussed on a part of the individual's own body.

After the (normal) repression of anal eroticism, the child's libido focusses on the penis. This is the so-called phallic phase. The only problem is, girls do not have a penis to focus on, but "only" a clitoris; therefore they become envious of boys and believe that they have been castrated. Boys, on the other hand, fear that they may be castrated in the future, most probably by their fathers. ("Castration" in psychoanalytic parlance means removal of the penis, or of the entire male genitalia, not just of the testicles.)

So far, the child's sexuality has been autoerotic: it has been focused on his or her own body. In the case of boys, the next developmental stage is the direction of the libido toward other individuals who, like themselves, possess the admired male genitalia. This is a homosexual phase (although occurring in a period of childhood that is not consciously recalled later). Some individuals simply remain in this phase. "Persons who are manifest homosexuals in late life," Freud wrote in 1911, "have, it may be presumed, never emancipated themselves from the binding condition that the object of their choice must possess genitals like their own. . ."[4]

That there truly is a "homosexual" phase (as opposed to an auto-erotic or bisexual phase) in early childhood is questionable. There is certainly no observational evidence to support the idea: Freud's evidence is solely based on the uncovering, by means of psychoanalysis, of supposedly repressed memories of a homosexual period. Furthermore, the idea that gay men have never freed themselves from the requirement that their sex-objects have male genitalia conflicts with Freud's more famous explanation for male homosexuality, cited in the previous chapter, whereby the gay man's central problem is not being able to break off a sexual attraction to his own mother—a person who lacks male genitalia. Apparently, Freud believed that there were two separate routes to male homosexuality—a "pre-Oedipal" and an "Oedipal" route.

The heterosexual, mother-directed libido appears in boys at about four years of age and persists, albeit in a more-or-less latent form, until puberty. At that time the libido is normally redirected to other females and becomes much stronger and more explicit. It is the failure of this redirection (or resolution of the Oedipal complex) that is the basis, in Freud's better-known theory, of male homosexuality. Seeking to reenact the sexual bond between his mother and himself, the growing boy identifies himself with his mother and chooses as sex objects individuals who represent himself during the Oedipal phase, that is, males. Castration anxiety, aroused earlier in childhood by a father's hostility or a mother's excessive intimacy, is thought to be an important factor in driving a boy along this route to homosexuality.

The awkwardness of this theory is most apparent when one considers how much more readily it would account for *hetero*sexuality than homosexuality: a straight man, after all, could easily be viewed as reenacting the Oedipal relationship every time he falls in love with a woman. For a gay man, on the other hand, a switch of identities is required (from his own to that of his mother) in order that the preferred sex object be male. There is no compelling evidence that such a switch takes place. Evidence of femininity in gay men, for example, is equally compatible with an inborn gender nonconformity à la Hirschfeld as with an Oedipal switch à la Freud. Nor does there seem to be anything about the objects of a gay man's attraction that suggests that they represent himself in his relationship with his mother. One would expect, for example, such sex objects to be prepubescent, or pubescent at the oldest. In fact, however, gay men are generally attracted to adult men: according to one study, the preferred partners of gay men are actually significantly older than the preferred partners of heterosexual men.[5]

Freud put forward an even more convoluted explanation for male homosexuality in a 1922 monograph.[6] In this account, the originating factor, an excessively intense mother fixation, is the same as in his earlier writings. But in cases where the boy has an older brother, this fixation sets up a bitter rivalry with the brother for the mother's love. Because the rivalry cannot be expressed in the actual killing of the older brother, the rivalrous impulse is repressed and transformed, reemerging as sexual attraction. Thus the gay man's attraction to men is not an attraction to himself, as in the earlier scenario, but to a brother. Freud believed that this mechanism explained nonexclusive homosexuality.

Freud's writings on the subject of female homosexuality are quite limited. His one extended treatment of the topic is contained in his 1920 work, *The Psychogenesis of a Case of Homosexuality in a Woman*.[7] The key causal event in this woman's life, according to Freud, was the birth of a younger brother when she was sixteen.

> She became keenly conscious of the wish to have a child, and a male one; that what she desired was her *father's* child and an image of *him*, her consciousness was not allowed to know. And what happened next? It was not *she* who bore the child, but her unconsciously hated rival, her mother. Furiously resentful and embittered, she turned away from her father and from men altogether. After this first great reverse she foreswore her womanhood and sought another goal for her libido.

Sensing perhaps that the birth of a younger brother was not by itself sufficiently traumatic to drive a woman to lesbianism, Freud looked for other contributing factors operating earlier in her life. In her childhood, Freud learned, she had been "a spirited girl, always ready for romping and fighting," a sign of a "strongly marked 'masculinity complex.'" After seeing her older brother's genitalia she became consumed by penis envy. "She was in fact a feminist; she felt it to be unjust that girls should not enjoy the same freedom as boys, and rebelled against the lot of women in general. At the time of the analysis the idea of pregnancy and child-birth was disagreeable to her, partly, I surmise, on account of the bodily disfigurement connected with them." Thus Freud was invoking childhood gender-nonconformist traits as important antecedents of this woman's homosexuality—traits whose origin he did not attempt to explain, although they would fit well with Hirschfeld's notion of a broad gender-atypical development. By the end of the essay Freud made a complete about-face, declaring that this was in fact a case of congenital homosexuality, which the events of her teen years had merely served to fix and make manifest.

Luckily, the young woman in question seems to have been impervious to all of this. "Once," Freud wrote, "when I expounded to her a specially important part of the theory, one affecting her intimately, she replied in an inimitable tone, "How very interesting," as though she were a *grand dame* being taken over a museum and glancing through her lorgnon at objects to which she was completely indifferent."[8] Eventually the analysis was broken off.

The ambivalence that Freud seemed to be experiencing as he wrote this essay extended to the causes of male homosexuality as well as those of lesbianism. At the end of the essay he attacked the "tendentious literature" (i.e., Ulrichs and Hirschfeld again) that took notice only of a person's overt sexual orientation, not their unconscious sexual feelings, and that tied sexual orientation to biological factors. Once one realizes that homosexual men have experienced an unusually strong mother fixation, Freud wrote, "the supposition that nature in a freakish mood created a 'third sex' falls to the ground." Yet in the following paragraph he changed direction again and gave a positive assessment of Steinach's efforts to change men's sexual orientation through testicle grafts, and he acknowledges a link between homosexuality and "physical hermaphroditism" in some cases.

Freud agreed with Hirschfeld that homosexual people could not easily be converted to heterosexuality. "In a certain number of cases," he wrote in his famous 1935 letter to the American mother of a gay man, "we succeed in developing the blighted germs of heterosexual tendencies which are present in every homosexual, in the majority of cases it is no more possible."[9] The theoretical explanation for this failure was that homosexual was not a neurosis, which involved the repression and rechanneling of sexual energy, but a perversion, which was a failure or inhibition of sexual development. Psychoanalysis could expose repressed libido but could not cause the normal development of libido that had been "blighted" many years previously.[10] Thus, although Freud seems to have had a certain personal antipathy toward homosexuality and gay people, he did not consciously begin the "therapeutic" attack on homosexuals through psychoanalysis. His personal influence was, if anything, rather favorable toward them, because he rejected the notion of homosexuality as a disease and explicitly acknowledged that gays and lesbians were capable of leading normal, useful lives.

American Analysts

The real psychoanalytic attack on homosexuality was initiated by Freud's followers, particularly by those working in the United States. The attack was directed primarily against male homosexuality rather than lesbianism. Three names—Lionel Ovesey (who died in 1995), Irving Bieber (who died in 1991), and Charles Socarides—are especially prominent in this field. Socarides is still practicing in New York, and he still claims success in converting gay men to heterosexuality.

The theoretical justification for the attempt to "cure" homosexuality was a change in the psychoanalytic status of homosexuality from a perversion to a neurosis. According to Ovesey, a gay man is often fearful of female genitalia because they remind him of the danger of castration. Therefore he represses his attraction to women, and the libido associated with that attraction finds another channel for expression, namely in attraction to men. Thus, for many "homosexual" men, homosexuality is not their authentic orientation but merely a displaced route for sexual release. It follows that homosexuality can be cured like any neurosis, that is, by exposing the cause of the repression to view and allowing the patient to work through his unconscious anxieties.[11]

Ovesey's ideas are actually part of a larger revision of Freud's theory of sexuality, a revision that also cast doubt on the notion of the libido and of infantile bisexuality. But aside from the theoretical underpinnings, there were practical issues that may have contributed to the change of views. In America of the 1940s and 1950s, homosexuality had reached a nadir of acceptability. It was a condition that gay men, their families, and society in general very much wanted to be rid of. Thus there were powerful incentives for psychoanalysts to attempt to change gay men's sexual orientation. From this perspective, technical argumentation about the nature of homosexuality may have been little more than window dressing—the post hoc justification for a clinical intervention whose true motivation was more pragmatic.

We are accustomed to thinking of the role of the psychoanalyst as one of sympathetic detachment. We have the notion that he or she is supposed to be a good listener, able to guide the patient's thought processes toward the uncovering of unconscious conflicts, but not judgmental or directive. Yet the American analysts who tackled homosexuality were the very opposite of detached. One gay analysand, Martin Duberman, has told of his own experiences with a succession of East Coast analysts in the 1950s and 1960s.[12] The first of them insisted that Duberman break off his relationship with his boyfriend as a condition for the continuation of the analysis. The second urged Duberman to begin a sexual relationship with a woman, from whom he was to conceal his homosexuality. ("After all, homosexuality may soon be a thing of the past for you, and to bring it up would be to sabotage any prospect for a different kind of future.") The third analyst, after two years of fruitless sessions, forbade Duberman to even mention his homosexuality unless he made us his mind to give it up. Yet another therapist (not an analyst) organized group sessions with heterosexual activities ("If you *seriously* want to find out whether you're as sexually uninterested in women as you claim, then I suggest you and Joan go into the adjoining room and you let Joan try to turn you on").

In considering the appropriateness or otherwise of these therapists' approaches, one has to bear in mind that Duberman was an all-too-willing coconspirator in the torment to which he was subjected. Unlike Freud's lesbian patient, who never wished to become heterosexual and who only agreed to undergo analysis to please her parents, Duberman wanted desperately to be "cured" of his homosexuality. Like many gay men at that time, he did not believe in the possibility of a stable homosexual relationship. Fortunately, Duberman is now an eloquent gay historian and educator.

There are indications that some of these analysts were motivated by more than a simple desire to help unhappy homosexuals achieve their desired heterosexual adjustment. Several of them seem to have had a very low opinion of homosexuality and gay people, regardless of whether these people were happy or unhappy with their orientation. Thus Irving Bieber and Charles Socarides campaigned vigorously against the removal of homosexuality from the American Psychiatric Association's *Diagnostic and Statistical Manual of Psychiatric Disorders* (see chapter 11). Socarides argued that homosexuals had incapacitating pathology that rendered them unsuitable for responsible employment.[13] In his 1978 book, *Homosexuality*, Socarides put forward no fewer than fifteen characteristics of pre-Oedipal male homosexuality that attest to its pathological nature. These were:

1) femininity
2) fear of engulfment by women
3) primitive nature of mental processes
4) fear of bodily disintegration
5) fear of engulfment as evidenced by dreams of encasement in caves, and so forth
6) sexual acts carried out only with a person of the same sex. (Apparently this was not viewed as a natural consequence of being gay.)
7) damaging aggressive impulses: "the affects of love and affection are usually found to be surface rationalizations covering severe aggression."
8) sex acts are performed to lessen anxiety
9) addictive nature of homosexual acts
10) attraction to men really represents a search for love from the father and a wish to wreak vengeance on him
11) a deep sense of inferiority and guilt, caused not by social attitudes but by a realization that homosexual sex is anatomically inappropriate
12) psychic masochism
13) pre-Oedipal and Oedipal anxiety
14) severe anxiety engendered by any attempt to cease homosexual activities

15) homosexuality is commonly accompanied by fetishism, transvestism, or exhibitionism.[14]

When I asked Socarides, in a 1992 interview, what had caused his own son Richard to become homosexual,[15] he became incensed and said, among other things, "How would you like it if *I* asked *you* about your HIV status?" Apparently he considered homosexuality, whether it was accepted or not, as the equivalent of a potentially fatal infection.[16]

Another Freudian-oriented therapist who is still actively engaged in the attempt to convert homosexuals to heterosexuality is Joseph Nicolosi, who operates out of the Thomas Aquinas Clinic in Encino, California. (Saint Thomas Aquinas laid down the Christian doctrine that sex is sinful except when performed for the purpose of reproduction.) Nicolosi claims to focus on changing the sexual orientation of "non-gay homosexuals," that is, individuals who experience same-sex attraction but do not want to be part of the gay community. However, Nicolosi evidently considers homosexuality pathological regardless of whether one wants to be gay, as the following passage from his book, *Reparative Therapy of Male Homosexuality*, illustrates:

> Two men can never take in each other, in the full and open way. Not only is there a natural anatomical unsuitability, but an inherent psychological unsuitability as well. Both partners are coming together with the same deficit. Each is symbolically and sexually attempting to find fulfillment of gender in the other person. But the other person is not whole in that way either, so the relationship ends in disillusionment.
>
> The inherent unsuitability of same-sex relationships is seen in the form of fault-finding, irritability, feeling smothered; power struggles, possessiveness, and dominance; boredom, disillusionment, emotional withdrawal, and unfaithfulness. Although he desires men, the homosexual is afraid of them. As a result of this binding ambivalence, his same-sex relationships lack authentic intimacy.[17]

Bieber, Socarides, and other analysts have been vocal in their claims to be able to "cure" homosexuality, at least in a sizeable fraction of cases. Bieber orchestrated a survey of the experiences of psychoanalysts treating gay men in the late 1950s. According to his collected data, 19 percent of the men who had initially been completely homosexual converted to complete heterosexuality as a result of treatment, and another 19 percent became bisexual. Of the men who had initially been bisexual, 50 percent became completely heterosexual. Bieber emphasized certain features of gay patients that made for a high likelihood of conversion; these included an expressed desire to become heterosexual, a good relationship between the patient and his father, a history of having attempted heterosexual sex, and a history of dreams with heterosexual content. Younger patients were also more likely to become heterosexual than older ones. Conversion was unlikely when the patient was markedly gender-nonconformist in childhood, or when the patient's mother preferred her child to her husband.[18] A similar but much smaller survey of lesbians in analysis produced rather similar results: eight out of nineteen lesbians were reported as having become completely heterosexual after treatment.[19]

It is nearly impossible to assess the validity of these data. There have been no independent attempts to verify the reality or durability of the "cures," and the identity of the individuals concerned is of course cloaked by medical confidentiality. Within the psychoanalytic profession, there still appears to be a widespread belief that some homosexual individuals can be converted to heterosexuality through psychoanalysis.[20] Among nonanalytic psychiatrists, however, such a belief is probably uncommon. There are no counterparts to Martin Duberman's autobiography by gay men who succeeded in becoming heterosexual through psychoanalysis. It may be that individuals who are to some degree bisexual can be helped to invest their sexual energy in the heterosexual side of their nature, if they are very desirous of doing so. Whether this would be merely a behavioral adjustment, or a real change in a person's underlying orientation, is hard to say.

Psychoanalysis is of course an expensive and time-consuming process, generally available only to to a small sector of the population. But the attitudes of the analysts diffused out of their consulting rooms and influenced general attitudes toward homosexuality. An example is the 1968 book, *Growing Up Straight*, which is a popularization of Bieber's ideas.[21] Perhaps the most remarkable part of the book is the glowing preface written by the then director of the National Institute of Mental Health, Stanley Yolles, that concludes: "With broadened parental understanding and more scientific research, hopefully, the chances that anyone's child will become a victim of homosexuality will eventually decrease." This was written only five years before homosexuality was removed from the American Psychiatric Association's official list of mental disorders (see chapter 11).

Yolles's remark highlights something about the psychoanalytic approach to homosexuality that is insufficiently appreciated, which is how much it affected the *parents* of gays and lesbians. Bieber and his colleagues claimed that almost all these parents, but most especially the fathers of gay men, exhibited a florid psychopathology that included hostility, detachment, and rejection of the son. Not one of the fathers of the gay men in the study, according to Bieber, could be regarded as a "reasonably normal parent." During the 1960s and 1970s defective parenting was generally viewed as the cause of homosexuality, just as it was viewed as the cause of schizophrenia and many other mental problems. Thus it was not just gays and lesbians who were pathologized by the analysts but their parents too. Eventually some of these parents were goaded into rebellion. During the 1970s support groups for parents began to spring up, and in the early 1980s some of these groups coalesced to form Parents and Friends of Lesbians and Gays (PFLAG), a nationwide organization that stands up for the mental health of gay people *and* their families.

Gay-Positive Psychoanalysts

Although psychoanalysis has generally been the most conservative and antigay branch of the mental-health industry in America, gay-positive voices are beginning to be heard in the profession. One analytically oriented psychiatrist, Judd Marmor of USC and UCLA, began to speak out on behalf of gay people in the late 1960s, partly as a consequence of the fact that, unlike most psychiatrists, he had gay people among his circle of personal friends. Marmor was somewhat more open to biological views of sexuality than many of his colleagues, although he has never fully abandoned Freudian theories of causation. In the early 1970s, he became a significant figure in the campaign to declassify homosexuality as a mental disorder (see chapter 11), and since that time he has also offered progay testimony in court cases concerned with gay rights (see chapter 12). Although Marmor has written extensively on the topic of homosexuality,[22] my impression is that his contribution has been less in developing new theories and more in injecting a certain humanity and skepticism into the debate. In an interview with Eric Marcus a few years ago, he reminisced that:

> In those days we still assumed all explanations lay within the family dynamics. The fear of competing with the father. The incest barrier. Castration anxiety. God, we used to work that myth of castration anxiety! Not that people don't have castration anxiety, but I understand it in very different terms now. It's a symbol, not a fact. In those days we used to believe that it had a literal meaning—almost.[23]

Another analyst, Richard C. Friedman of Columbia University, has stressed the importance of a neutral view of homosexuality and its causes. Friedman, who is heterosexual, visualizes sexual orientation as a dimension of character that is orthogonal to (and therefore independent of) the dimensions of psychostructural level (sickness–wellness) and personality subtype (hysteric, obsessive, masochistic, etc.). Unlike most analysts, Friedman takes a lively interest in biological theories of sexual orientation and has been engaged in some biological research on the topic himself.

Friedman has been less than neutral with respect to gender nonconformity in childhood, a trait that, as Hirschfeld recognized, is a common precursor to homosexuality (see also chapter 4). In his 1988 book, *Male Homosexuality*, Friedman wrote:

> In addition to family pathology, effeminate [boys] often manifest diffuse psychopathology, indicating that the effeminacy syndrome is part of a global psychiatric disorder.[24] Projective psychological tests are frequently abnormal in characteristic ways, indicating that the syndrome involves not only cross-gender social behavior but also the internal self-object world of the child. Empirical studies of effeminate children have uncovered in many individual patients and their families the very symptoms that were once hypothesized by influential psychoanalysts to occur in the backgrounds of most homosexual adults. One wonders whether these psychoanalysts' database contained disproportionate numbers of children who in early life experienced full or partial effeminacy.[25]

It seems that Friedman wishes to separate off the class of gay men who had a childhood history of marked gender nonconformity and label them as the "sick" ones, or at least as the ones whose homosexuality has pathological origins. To my mind, this ignores an obvious fact about gender-nonconformist boys, which is that, unlike more conventional prehomosexual boys, they are exposed to virulent stigmatization and as well as traumatic "corrective" measures from a very early age (see chapter 4). To show that gender nonconformity in childhood is associated with generalized psychopathology, one would have to demonstrate that such pathology manifests itself even in families and societies where feminine boys are tolerated or accepted. There is some evidence that it does not.[26]

Friedman's supposed neutrality concerning homosexuality is in fact somewhat suspect. As Eve Kosovsky Sedgwick, a professor of English at Duke University, has pointed out, Friedman attributes full mental health only to those men (whether gay or straight) who have embraced a fairly stereotypical masculinity. Unfortunately, gay men and gay therapists have frequently followed Friedman's lead in this matter: they have often attempted to conceal or downplay the positive importance of gender nonconformity in gay development. "[T]he eclipse of the effeminate boy from adult gay discourse," writes Sedgwick, "would represent more than a damaging theoretical gap; it would represent a node of annihilating homophobic, gynephobic, and pedophobic hatred internalized and made central to gay-affirmative analysis."[27]

Kenneth Lewes, author of an important survey of psychoanalytic views on male homosexuality, has concluded that sexism (or "gynecophobia") has historically been the basis for the field's antigay bias. According to Lewes, psychoanalysts have thought poorly of gay men because their real or perceived feminine traits brand them as "deficient males."[28] If so, Friedman has failed to make the crucial break with sexism that would allow him (and many others) to view gay men dispassionately.

Richard Isay of Cornell of Medical College is that rare specimen, an openly gay psychoanalyst. In fact, he was instrumental in persuading the American Psychoanalytic Association to admit gays and lesbians as training analysts. Isay has seen many gay men in his practice, including some who had been severely traumatized by earlier efforts at conversion to heterosexuality. In 1989 Isay summarized his beliefs about male homosexuality in a very readable book, *Being Homosexual.*[29]

Isay has discarded many of the details of Freudian theory, conserving what he considers to be its core: the importance of unconscious conflicts in childhood as precursors to psychological problems in adult life and the usefulness of uncovering these conflicts as a means to resolve them. For gay men, Isay argues, this therapeutic regime can only be carried out successfully in an atmosphere that accepts homosexuality as a "given" and that recognizes the unique developmental processes that gay men undergo.

As Isay sees it, the development of homosexual boys diverges from that of heterosexual boys at the onset of the Oedipal phase (i.e., at about three to six years of age). Instead of developing sexual feelings toward his mother, the homosexual boy directs these feelings toward his father. Because he perceives his father to be heterosexual (or at least partnered with his mother), the boy takes on feminine attributes to make himself an attractive sex object. Thus gender nonconformity, in Isay's model, results from the boy's attempt to displace his mother in his father's affections, just as gender conformity, in heterosexual boys, results from their efforts to displace their father in their mother's affections.

Unfortunately, it is common for fathers to react negatively to their sons' seductive efforts, in part because of problems with unconscious homosexual feelings of their own. They may become detached or hostile or favor the company of other siblings. Thus Isay takes the well-known "hostile father, gay son" relationship and stands it on its head. Instead of the father's hostility *causing* the son's homosexuality, Isay suggests that it is a *reaction* to the son's homosexuality. This paternal rejection may in turn lead to poor self-esteem on the part of the growing boy.

Isay also believes that the hostile relationship with the father, recollected by so many gay men, is at least in part a distortion of memory. The purpose of this distortion is to conceal from consciousness the history of incestuous childhood desire. Isay finds it ironic that psychoanalysts, who are generally so averse to taking anything their patients tell them literally, have swallowed this particular fabrication whole and made it into the centerpiece of the traditional analytic theory of homosexuality.

Since writing *Being Homosexual*, Isay's views have moved toward a more globally "biological" view of homosexual development. As described in a forthcoming book, *Becoming Gay*,[30] Isay now places more weight on the idea that both homosexuality and childhood femininity are part of a package of gender-variant traits that have some common basis in prenatal development. He suggests that a father who reacts negatively to a gay son may be rejecting this inborn femininity as a quality inappropriate in a son, more than he is rejecting any seductive efforts on his son's part.

Very recently, there has been renewed interest in psychoanalytic theories of lesbian sexual development.[31] In part, this new lesbian-positive work has mirrored arguments made by Isay and others about gay male development. For example, Leslie Deutsch (among others) has suggested that lesbian girls go through an Oedipal phase that is the opposite of that experienced by gay boys: they fall in love with their mothers and are often rejected by their mothers as a consequence of their seductive efforts.[32] Another common theme is the importance of an accepting attitude toward a homosexual orientation in the therapeutic environment. However, lesbian-positive analytic thought also has its own unique threads. Among these are a greater emphasis on bisexuality in the childhood development of lesbians,[33] an unlinking of gender identity, sexual object choice, and lesbian self-identification,[34] and a generally lower estimation of the value of categories and of detailed theories of causation.[35]

Overview

As a direct therapeutic procedure, psychoanalysis has never served more than a niche market, but the influence of analysts, whether for good or bad, has always been much greater than their patient base might suggest. Analysts have been seen as the deep thinkers who have mapped the main channels of psychological development and have offered a strategy for the durable healing of psychic trauma. Yet over the last two decades, the intellectual authority of psychoanalysis has been eroded as biologists, armed with new techniques in molecular genetics, neuropharmacology, brain imaging, and the like, have scored remarkable successes with their more reductionist view of mental life.

Ultimately, though, as Freud himself foresaw, it will be necessary to reintegrate the different levels of investigation: the level of genes, synapses, and neurotransmitters, and the level of conscious and unconscious mental processes. It may be that psychoanalysts, who alone have the opportunity to observe—intimately, and over a long period—the workings of a naked, unaccommodated mind, may be uniquely positioned to approach this difficult synthesis. That some analysts, such as Friedman, have themselves become involved with biological research, makes this even more likely. What such a synthesis will ultimately have to say about sexual orientation is difficult to predict. But one thing does seem likely—that this new departure will also mark the end of the antigay tradition in psychoanalysis.

4

Learning and Unlearning Homosexuality

While Freud and his followers were using psychoanalytical techniques to explore the inner passageways of the mind, another school of psychologists took a radically different approach. These psychologists—the behaviorists—attempted to reduce the mind to a set of input-output functions. They proposed that the perceptual and behavioral systems of the mind are initially connected by innate reflex pathways that mediate a few basic responses. These pathways are later modified under the influence of experience, thanks to a set of mechanisms for forming associations and learning new responses. The behaviorists' philosophical antecedents lay with the seventeenth-century thinkers Thomas Hobbes and John Locke, who believed that the mind was built up of the sensations that impinged on it. But the impetus to apply this concept to the scientific study of the mind came from the Russian physiologists I. P. Pavlov (1849–1936) and V. M. Bekhterev (1857–1927), who demonstrated the modification of behavior through conditioning.

The two most well-known American behaviorists—J. B. Watson (1878–1958) and B. F. Skinner (1904–1990)—did not pay much attention to the question of sexual orientation and its origins. Nevertheless, their work challenged the Freudian approach in a number of ways: by emphasizing measurement, experiment, and testable hypotheses, by asserting the direct relevance of animal behavior to human behavior, and by taking a parsimonious rather than an expansive view of the mind. Behaviorism in the form that Watson and Skinner developed it is now long out of fashion: it is widely agreed that one must study the complex inner workings of the brain to get a handle on how any specific mental task is accomplished. Yet the rigorous standards set by the behaviorists have permeated the entire field of psychobiology. As a consequence, brain and cognitive scientists tend to be among the severest critics of psychoanalytic theory.

In classical conditioning, learning of new responses occurs when two stimuli occur simultaneously: one that already elicits a response, and another that does not. In Pavlov's famous experiment, the dog initially salivates to food but not to the sound of a bell; if the food and the bell are repeatedly presented together, the dog begins to salivate to the sound of the bell alone. In operant conditioning, which was largely Skinner's contribution, behavior is modified by means of judiciously timed "reinforcements" (rewards or punishments).

Behaviorism offered the possibility of a far simpler explanation of sexual orientation than did psychoanalysis. Whether a person sought sex with male or female partners, or with both, could be envisaged as the consequence of the particular schedule of reinforcements to which he or she had been exposed. The most obvious positive reinforcement was of course the pleasure associated with the sexual act itself, especially with orgasm. Thus, in the very simplest of behaviorist models, a person's sexual orientation depended on the sex of the first person with whom he or she first had sexual contact to orgasm. If that person was of the opposite sex, then heterosexuality was reinforced; if of the same sex, then homosexuality was reinforced. Conversely, an early sexual contact that was painful or frightening would act as a negative reinforcement, decreasing the attractiveness of one class of sex partners. A woman whose first sexual experience was being molested or raped by a man, according to this scheme, would likely end up as a lesbian. (Of course, the theory requires that the *sex* of one's initial sexual partner, not his or her occupation, dress, etc., be his or her most salient characteristic, otherwise one might end up always dating taxi drivers or never having sex with people in jeans.)

This theory, which was put forward in the 1960s by Wainwright Churchill[1] and others, is superficially quite plausible. It corresponds to our everyday experience: activities that give us pleasure tend to become habits, whereas we dislike doing things that have caused us pain. Even today, there are some people who believe that this is an important determinant of sexual orientation. Most outspoken among them is Paul Cameron, a psychologist who was expelled from the American Psychological Association in 1983 for the misrepresentation of scientific data. Many gay men, according to Cameron, had their first sexual experience with another male (often a brother), and it was this event that triggered a lifetime of homosexuality.[2] Cameron has used this argument in legal testimony aimed against gay rights (see chapter 12), as well as in the antigay documentary film, *The Gay Agenda*.

If one accepts this theory, and if one also shares the majority view that homosexuality is wrong, the door is opened to all kinds of preventive measures: discouraging single-sex education and single-sex youth organizations; encouraging early heterosexual experimentation and discouraging any kind of homosexual experimentation; keeping homosexuals away from children and teenagers, and so on.

There are, however, a number of problems with the theory. For one thing, many people end up with a sexual orientation different from that predicted by the nature of their first sexual encounter. For example, many gays and lesbians engage in heterosexual sex prior to any homosexual experience. This may be because of the pressure of social expectations or because they do not become fully aware of same-sex attraction until some years after puberty. It is also quite common for gays and lesbians to know that they are homosexual prior to any same-sex encounter or even prior to sexual experiences of any kind. And conversely, there are many heterosexual women and men whose first sexual contacts (and pleasurable ones at that) have been with the same sex. Perhaps the most striking evidence for this comes from the sex practices of the Sambia of New Guinea, mentioned in chapter 2. All teenage Sambia boys engage in culturally enforced homosexual behavior, but later they enter a predominantly heterosexual adult culture. Similarly, extensive same-sex behavior occurs among boys and girls at traditional British private boarding schools, which are sex segregated. Yet attendance at such schools does not increase the likelihood of a homosexual orientation in adulthood.[3]

Even if we concede that the initial sexual contacts of gays and lesbians tend to be with persons of the same sex, and those of heterosexual people tend to be with the other sex (and reliable statistics in this matter are hard to come by), this correlation would be equally consistent with many other theories of sexual orientation. If, for example, one believes that sexual orientation is entirely determined by genetic mechanisms, then one would naturally expect people to choose their first sex partners in accordance with their inborn sexual orientation. Cases where the initial encounter is nonconsensual are not informative, because the theorist can interpret such an encounter as providing either positive or negative reinforcement and thus make it fit any hypothesis.

Yet a further difficulty with the theory is that, in most operant conditioning paradigms, positive reinforcement of a single act is not enough to fix subsequent behavior. Biologically, one can see why this should be so: there is so much random noise in the universe of sensory experience that it would be disadvantageous to base a lifetime of behavior on one pleasurable episode. (Single-shot learning makes more sense with negative reinforcement, where life-threatening events may be involved.) To deal with this problem, R. J. McGuire, J. M. Carlisle, and B. G. Young[4] came up with the following ingenious hypothesis: although the initial encounter itself may not fix sexual orientation, the association is reinforced during subsequent solitary masturbation, because the individual is likely to use the recollection of the initial event as an aid to sexual arousal. Here is a "case history".

> An exclusively homosexual man of 32 recalled how, at the age of 15, he had been seduced by an elderly man in a train and how frightened he had been at the time. A few months later he masturbated for the first time in his life using fantasies of the incident. Later, in the Navy, he began to practise overt sexual activities. (p. 189)

This account is an example of how, just as with psychoanalytic theory, behaviorist theory can be manipulated to accommodate almost any case history. An unpleasant heterosexual experience (e.g., molestation of a girl by a man) causes a person to become homosexual, but an unpleasant homosexual experience (the one described here) does not turn the youth into a heterosexual man, because he provides his own positive reinforcement for the event later.

At any event, this reinforcement-through-masturbation theory led McGuire and colleagues to propose a simple technique for the prevention or cure of homosexuality: the patient should be advised to avoid homosexual fantasy during masturbation and to substitute heterosexual fantasy. Of course, if the patient is gay then homosexual fantasy may be necessary for masturbation to be successful. But as McGuire and colleagues knew, timing is everything in the world of operant conditioning: only behaviors that take place immediately prior to the reward (the orgasm in this case) are reinforced. Thus they suggest that the patient begin masturbating with homosexual fantasies and switch to a heterosexual fantasy five seconds prior to orgasm— by which time one could assume that the climax is too close to be derailed by the sudden change of imagery.

McGuire and colleagues do not recount whether they found a patient sufficiently in control of his or her fantasies to test their new cure. Nor apparently did they attempt to make themselves gay by this same technique, an experiment that (if successful) would have provided dramatic support for their theory. It seems that the behaviorist psychiatrists, in spite of their theories, always imagined homosexuality to be less securely fixed than heterosexuality, in that it could be disrupted by some rather trivial program of positive or negative reinforcement, a program that no-one imagined would be capable of converting a straight man or woman to homosexuality.

"Trivial" is perhaps not the right word to describe the major weapon in the behaviorists' arsenal: aversion therapy. In this approach the subject was brought into the laboratory and exposed to a set of potentially erotic stimuli, for example, photographic slides of nude men (most of the patients were gay men, not lesbians). In combination with this viewing, the psychologist did something unpleasant to the subject. By associating the erotic arousal with the unpleasant experience, the subject's homosexual drive was supposed to be reduced.

In one kind of aversion therapy the unpleasant stimulus was an injection of the drug apomorphine, which induces nausea or vomiting. One study by Kurt Freund, published in 1960, claimed some success, but the results were short-lived: by five years after treatment all of the patients were experiencing homosexual feelings again, and 87 percent of them were engaged in homosexual behavior.[5]

In 1962 a psychiatrist in Bristol, England, described a "complete cure" of a gay man who had failed to respond to other kinds of treatment, including psychotherapy and hormone treatments. During the period of apomorphine-induced nausea he was not only exposed to photographs of naked men but also made to listen to repeated playings of an audiotape: the tape explained his homosexuality as being a learned pattern of behavior, the learning having resulted from father deprivation and from his initial homosexual experiences. (Apparently the psychiatrist was not worried that the patient might develop an aversion to learning theories!) After a mere four days of this treatment the patient became "in all respects a sexually normal person."[6] But the follow-up was for only five months.

Interestingly, this study seems to have had a political motivation, at least in part. A few years previously, a British government commission had published a report (the Wolfenden Report) that had recommended that homosexual behavior be decriminalized. One of the reasons put forward by the commission was that homosexuals could not be converted to heterosexuality. In claiming to have demonstrated a rapid, simple, and effective "cure," the psychiatrist was explicitly refuting the report and thus undermining the validity of the commission's proposals. In 1967, however, the British parliament did legalize homosexual behavior between persons over twenty-one.

Reports of successful treatment continued to be published in the 1970s but were greeted with increasing skepticism and moral outrage. An Australian psychiatrist, Nathaniel McConaghy, who published several papers on apomorphine-induced aversion "therapy" for homosexuality,[7] was himself subjected to a kind of aversion treatment: one of his papers was accompanied by a sharp editorial critique by the Johns Hopkins sexologist John Money, who accused McConaghy of charlatanism,[8] and a lecture by McConaghy at the 1970 American Psychiatric Association convention in San Francisco was shouted down by gay activists.[9] The treatment worked: in 1976 McConaghy published a highly critical article about aversion treatment,[10] and since then he has worked on innocuous subjects such as the prevalence of homosexual feelings in different age groups.[11]

Another aversive stimulus used to treat homosexuals was electric shock. In some versions of this treatment, the subject was simply subjected to electric shocks while viewing photographs of naked men. This (like the apomorphine treatment described above) was an example of classical conditioning. But electric shock, because it is so short-lived, lends itself well to operant-conditioning procedures. In these forms of treatment the subject could turn off the shock by pressing a button, which also caused the photograph of the naked man to disappear and be replaced by a naked woman or by some neutral picture. In some forms of treatment, the subject could avoid being shocked altogether if he pressed the button quickly enough. Typically, a session lasted thirty minutes and a complete course of treatment might include twenty or so sessions over a period of a few months.

During the 1960s aversion therapy was widely practiced both in the United States and other countries. The results were mixed at best. One study, published by M. P. Feldman and M. J. MacCulloch in 1971[12], described the treatment of seventy-three homosexuals (including two women), some of whom were compelled to participate by court order. They reported that the "success" or "failure" of the procedure depended on the subjects' prior sexual history. Many of the subjects who had had some previous heterosexual experience or fantasy were apparently "improved" by the treatment: they reported a cessation of homosexual desires and activities that lasted at least a year after the end of the treatment. Subjects who had never experienced heterosexual feelings or activity were not changed by the treatment. Feldman and MacCulloch argued that the former group were "secondary" homosexuals who had acquired their homosexuality by some kind of learning: they were therefore susceptible to unlearning it. The other group, the "primary homosexuals," had been born gay, perhaps as a consequence of an "abnormal" hormonal environment *in utero.*

The Feldman and MacCulloch study was followed by others. Some asserted that even their rather moderate claims of success were inflated, and that in fact men who seemed to be cured by aversion therapy reverted to homosexuality within a few months.[13] Others claimed that Feldman and MacCulloch had not used the best techniques. In some treatment centers, the subjects' physiologocal responses were monitored with the aid of the plethysmograph, and they were shocked whenever an erection began to develop. This did prevent the subjects from getting an erection in the treatment environment, but the "learning" did not usually extend to real life. In one study, only one subject failed to get an erection during homosexual encounters after treatment, and even this subject was able to circumvent the problem through an ingenious technique: he simply told his male partner to "recite accounts of heterosexual orgies" while they were having sex.[14] Another study, from the Center for Behavior Change in Atlanta, claimed that better results could be obtained by simply increasing the intensity of the shocks.[15]

One institution that applied aversion therapy with particular enthusiasm was Brigham Young University (BYU), the Mormon school in Provo, Utah. The Mormon church had been relatively unconcerned about homosexuality until the McCarthy era, when church leaders began to denounce it and develop programs to root it out. At BYU, for example, a program was instituted for spying on the off-campus activities of BYU students, with the aim of identifying and expelling those who gave evidence of a gay lifestyle. Counseling was instituted for students who stated that they experienced same-sex feelings, and later this was expanded to include aversion therapy. The protocol employed at BYU's psychology clinic in the 1970s was described by M. F. McBride[16].

One Mormon student who underwent aversion therapy at BYU, Don D. Harryman, has provided an account of his experiences.[17]

Harryman, then a devout Mormon, was made aware of the church's teaching on homosexuality in 1970, at the end of his freshman year when he was preparing to go on a mission to Japan. "Homosexuality, we were warned, was consummate evil, and any unrepentant person was doomed to a mission filled with spiritual darkness and failure. I was certain they were right, and with my heart pounding, I requested to speak to the Mission Home president. Upon hearing my confession, he assured me that I was involved in the darkest of sins." Nevertheless, because he had not put his feelings into practice, Harryman was allowed to go on his mission. After returning to BYU he became even more certain that he was homosexual and even more determined to change. He sought counseling at the psychology clinic and was inducted into the aversion therapy program, where he underwent about eighty-five sessions of electric shock treatment over the course of a year. This took place in 1974 and 1975, that is, after the American Psychiatric Association had removed homosexuality from the *DSM*. In addition, he was treated with hypnosis: while under hypnosis he was told that he would become uncontrollably nauseated whenever he thought about men in an erotic way.

The treatments caused both physical injury (burns) and emotional trauma, but Harryman persisted. "The countless talks I had heard about knocking on the door until your hands were bloody rang in my ears, and in my desperation I began to feel that my suffering and hence my being a martyr was additional proof that what I was doing was right." After a year he was pronounced cured, but a few months later he fell in love with his male roommate, an event that led to an increasing involvement with gay and gay-friendly people. In his last year at BYU Harryman sought an interview with the stake president (bishop). "My frustration began to grow as did my anger when he confessed that as a professional—he had a Ph.D. in educational psychology—he knew that homosexuality was not a curable or changeable state. But in his position as a church leader, he felt compelled to support the official church position. Besides, he said, the brethren did not really mean that one could be cured, just that a homosexual should not act on his or her feelings. I was outraged. . .Finally, I knew that I had to get my own answers." Eventually Harryman accepted his homosexuality and became an active member of the gay community.

Yet another form of conditioning used to treat gay men involved what was termed "covert sensitization." Like the procedures already described, this technique involved pairing a sexually arousing stimulus with an aversive stimulus. The difference was that both stimuli took place entirely within the subject's imagination: the subject had to visualize participating in a same-sex encounter that had unpleasant consequences.[18] Here is a description of the technique in a 1973 study.

> For example, a man might be asked to imagine going to the apartment of a homosexual contact, approaching the man's bedroom, initiating sexual activity, feeling increasingly nauseous, and finally vomiting on the contact, on the sheets, and all over himself. A variation of this scene might involve the patient finding the homosexual contact rotting with syphilitic sores, or finding that the contact had diarrhea during the sexual encounter.[19]

The authors of this study claimed that covert sensitization was a more effective treatment than regular aversion therapy with electric shocks; but because the subjects were given both forms of treatment, it is not possible to say which treatment was responsible for long-term changes in behavior, if indeed any such changes occurred.

An account of attempts to "unlearn" homosexuality would not be complete without mention of another technique that was intended to achieve the same result through a brute-force approach. This involved the induction of *grand mal* epileptic seizures, either by delivering electric shocks to the head or by administering of a drug, metrazol. Convulsive therapy was believed to exert its effect by disrupting "engrams"—the traces laid down in the brain by repetitive thoughts or habits. Today, this kind of therapy is used almost exclusively for the relief of severe depression, and it is often very effective in this application. In the past, however, it was been used for all kinds of conditions in which it conferred little if any benefit.

In 1940 a psychiatrist in Atlanta reported remarkable successes in the treatment of both male and female homosexuality by convulsive therapy with metrazol.[20] Here is a case history.

> A white male of 19 years had been arrested and sentenced to prison because of moral turpitude (homosexuality). He was paroled for treatment and

promised a pardon if his perversion was corrected. The family history was not enlightening. Homosexual experiences began during his fourteenth year and continued thereafter. Feminine mannerisms were evident. Metrazol was administered until fifteen shocks [*grand mal* seizures] were produced. All homosexual desires had disappeared after the ninth shock, but treatment was continued until all feminine mannerisms had been removed. Normal sex relations were established and eighteen months later there had been no return of homosexual tendencies. He was granted a pardon. (p. 65)

One does not have to be especially cynical to imagine that the young man simply lied about becoming heterosexual, with the motivation of avoiding incarceration. In fact a subsequent study, carried out on prisoners at a state hospital in California, found that not a single one of the treated men became heterosexual. One man, however, was apparently converted from homosexuality to kleptomania![21]

In spite of this negative result, the use of electroconvulsive therapy (ECT) on gay men continued. The historian Jonathan Ned Katz has published an interview with a gay man who underwent seventeen ECT sessions in 1964. The case is particularly disturbing because the treatments took place during his involuntary commitment to a mental hospital: the commitment was instigated by his parents who disapproved of his homosexuality. The man himself had no desire to change his sexual orientation, and in fact it did not change as a result of the treatment. He was finally released from the hospital when a new doctor arrived and told him "There's nothing wrong with being gay." He suffered memory impairment and depression for several years after his release.[22]

Childhood Learning

Hirschfeld's assertion that homosexual men and women tend to be gender-nonconformist during their childhood (see chapter 1) has been substantiated by numerous studies. Some of these studies have been retrospective surveys that ask adult lesbians and gay men (and comparison groups of heterosexual men and women) about their childhood. Recently Michael Bailey (of Northwestern University) and Kenneth Zucker (of the Clarke Institute of Psychiatry in Toronto) reviewed the data from forty-one such studies.[23] They found that gays and lesbians were significantly more nonconformist than heterosexuals in the following gender-differentiated traits: (1) participation in rough-and-tumble play, competitive athletics, or aggression, (2) toy and activity preference, (3) imagined roles and careers (significant difference for men only), (4) cross-dressing, (5) preference for same- or opposite-sex playmates, (6) social reputation as "sissy" or "tomboy," and (7) gender identity.

Other studies (which so far have been done only in males) have taken the reverse approach: identifying gender-nonconformist children and then following them through to adulthood to see what sexual orientation they develop.[24] The most extensive and detailed of these prospective studies was carried out by Richard Green, a psychiatrist at UCLA. In his study, about four-fifths of the markedly effeminate boys became rather conventional homosexual or bisexual men, one boy became a transsexual man, and the remainder became heterosexual men. (Actually, many of these were still under eighteen at their most recent interview, raising the possibility that they might become homosexual, or come out as homosexual, at some later time.) Of the comparison group of boys who were selected without regard to gender characteristics, none became homosexual and only one became bisexual. The other studies reported similar findings.

Thus the association between childhood gender nonconformity and adult homosexuality is well established, especially in men. This is not to say that any individual's ultimate sexual orientation can be predicted with certainty from his or her gender-related behavior childhood, because there is overlap between the characteristics of prehomosexual and preheterosexual children. Nevertheless, the association is one of the most striking and consistent findings in developmental psychology.

The demonstration that sexual orientation has antecedents in childhood gender characteristics tends to weaken the theories that ascribe homosexuality to sexual experiences at puberty or later, or to other learning processes in adulthood. Thus, for those who believe that sexual orientation (or homosexuality at least) is learned, attention becomes focused on whether this learning might actually take place during the development of gender-related traits in childhood.

The name most closely associated with the idea that gender is learned is that of John Money, a long-time sexologist at Johns Hopkins University. In 1957 Money and his colleagues suggested that gender was established by a process of imprinting.[25] Citing Konrad Lorenz's famous experiment, in which the naturalist fooled ducklings into following him as if he was their mother, Money and colleagues thought that young humans might adopt whatever gender role that they were exposed to. They reached this conclusion from a study of children who were intersexes: that is, children who had ambiguous genitalia as a result of hormonal abnormalities during fetal life. According to Money, these children adopted the gender of whatever sex they were treated as during the first two years of life, but afterwards this gender became fixed and was no longer susceptible to modification.

The imprinting model is not really a good analogy for what Money proposed. Imprinting does not require reinforcement but merely exposure. Yet most children under two see far more of their mothers than of their fathers. Why then, if gender is imprinted, do not most boys become feminine? In actuality, operant conditioning seems to be a better description of what Money had in mind: the idea that parents shaped the child's identity and behavior by countless subtle rewards and punishments.

Richard Green, who trained with Money, searched for factors that might predispose to gender nonconformity in children. In his 1974 book, *Sexual Identity Conflict in Children and Adults*,[26] Green explored these factors by means of extensive interviews with gender-nonconformist boys and their parents. Although he was cautious in attributing causality, Green named several factors that he believed were associated with femininity in boys: the failure of parents to discourage feminine behaviors, their active encouragement of feminine behaviors, their active discouragement of boyish behaviors, maternal overprotection, and so on. He explained to parents that they might have unwittingly caused or promoted their son's femininity, and that they stood the best chance of correcting the problem if they started to actively discourage it and encourage masculinity instead. In particular, the fathers should take a more active role in the boy's life. "You've got to get these mothers out of the way," Green told the parents of one seven-year-old. "Feminine kids don't need their mothers around."

Green's 1974 book was written at a time when the connection between childhood gender nonconformity and adult homosexuality was less well established than it is now. If anything, Green expected that the markedly feminine boys he studied would become transsexual adults, something that actually happened with only one of them. Nevertheless, it is apparent that the specter of homosexuality loomed in the minds of some of the boys' parents, and it was the hope of steering their sons away from this fate that caused them to bring them to a psychiatrist. One such case history is particularly well documented: it concerns a child referred to variously as "Kraig" or "Kyle," who became the behaviorists' poster boy, and later their nemesis.

Kyle's femininity became apparent to his parents when he was about two years old. He had a strong interest in doll-play, and by four or five was saying that he wanted to be a girl and become a mother when he grew up. When Kyle was five his parents saw a television program that featured Green talking about childhood gender nonconformity and that also featured an adult gay man who described how he had played with dolls when he was a child. Out of concern that Kyle would become homosexual or transvestite, they brought him to Green, who in turn referred him to an operant-conditioning program run by a psychology graduate student at UCLA by the name of George Rekers.

Kyle's treatment with Rekers lasted ten months. He and his parents came periodically to the laboratory and underwent training, in which the parents learned to positively reinforce masculine behaviors and negatively reinforce feminine behaviors. They also carried out a similar program in the home: Kyle was given blue tokens for masculine behavior and red tokens for feminine behavior—the blue tokens entitled Kyle to ice cream and other rewards, whereas the red tokens earned loss of blue tokens, confinement, or spanking. Later, Kyle's schoolteacher also took part in the program.

Apparently Kyle modified his behavior greatly under this regime. According to accounts published by Rekers and his colleagues, by age eight Kyle's femininity had completely disappeared.[27] At fifteen he was "indistinguishable from any other normal teenage boy. . .developing normal masculine roles, [with] a normal male identity [and] normal aspirations for growing up to be married and have a family."[28] When Kyle was seventeen, his mother visited Green again. "I am indeed still thankful the day I saw you on TV and you took me in," she told him, "because I knew that there was going to be a problem if something wasn't done. . .If he had not become homosexual, I'm sure he would have become very, very fetish" (her word for "enjoying wearing women's underwear and stuff like that").

But when Green interviewed Kyle himself at age eighteen, a very different picture emerged. He complained that he was unable to make friends because of an overwhelming fear of appearing feminine. Under lengthy questioning, Kyle conceded that he was predominantly homosexual but was deeply conflicted about it. In his first and only homosexual experience, he fellated a stranger in a toilet, apparently through a "glory-hole." Thus he was not required to reveal himself as gay even to his sex partner. Soon after this experience he attempted suicide. He believed homosexuality was sinful and attributed his own homosexuality mainly to a lack of affection from his father. "Because when you are a child," he said, "I think you copy what you see. And I didn't have any strong male influence." He expressed gratitude that Rekers's treatment had at least saved him from becoming 100 percent homosexual. A less charitable interpretation would be that the treatment did nothing but instill Kyle with an incapacitating fear of revealing his femininity, a fear that remained with him through adolescence and also affected his emerging homosexuality. In fact, according to Green's figures, nine out of twelve gender-nonconformist boys who were subjected to behavior modification treatment became gay or bisexual adults—no different from what was seen in the boys who were not subjected to the treatment.[29]

With the removal of homosexuality from the *DSM* in 1973 and the rise of gay activism and gay-affirmative psychology, the ethical basis of trying to head off homosexuality by subjecting gender-nonconformist children to operant conditioning came into question. Two gay activists from San Francisco, Stephen Morin and Stephen Schultz, wrote a seminal paper in 1978 that asserted the rights of prehomosexual children to follow their own developmental pathway, free of efforts to mold them to a conventional sexuality. Rekers's program, they claimed, was "pernicious and ill-conceived," and "[t]he most insidious attempt to stamp out the development of gay identity in young children."[30] Rekers and his colleagues defended themselves vigorously, claiming that marked gender nonconformity in childhood leads to dire consequences in adult life: transsexuality, transvestism, and effeminate homosexuality, with accompanying risks of suicide and self-castration. "Given the strong evidence that the gender-disturbed boy would have a poor prognostic outlook in the absence of treatment...it would be unethical for the psychologist not to assist the parents...in providing intervention techniques currently held to have the greatest therapeutic potential..."[31] Later Rekers began to reveal a virulent antipathy towards homosexuality. In his 1982 book, *Shaping Your Child's Sexual Identity*, Rekers described homosexuality as a "promiscuous and perverted sexual behavior," and he bemoaned the fact that "homosexuality has been sold to the unwary public as a right between consenting adults."[32]

It should be stressed that there are contemporary psychologists and psychiatrists who treat "gender identity disorder" in children from a nonhomophobic perspective. Kenneth Zucker and Susan Bradley (of the Clarke Institute of Psychiatry and the Hospital for Sick Children in Toronto) have argued that some gender-nonconformist children can and should be treated, without making the likelihood of adult homosexuality a reason for undertaking such treatment.[33]

Green has kept to a middle-of-the-road position. He still believes that patterns of parental reinforcement are a major influence on children's sex-typed behaviors, and that the lack of a warm father or brother or male playmate (a condition he calls "male-affect starvation") predisposes to homosexuality in adulthood. But he has also come to acknowledge that constitutional factors may play a significant role. Interestingly, Green's wife, Melissa Hines, is a developmental psychologist whose work has lent considerable support to biological theories of gender and sexual orientation (see chapters 5 and 6). Between them the couple seems to have evolved to a "centrist" position. Certainly Green's attitude toward homosexuality, as expressed in the transcripts of interviews with his emerging gay teenagers, has been consistently positive and reassuring. If in hindsight we can question his attempts to discourage their childhood femininity, he can only be praised for choosing not to make a battlefield of their adult sexuality.

If "Kyle" was the behaviorists' poster boy, their poster-*girl* was a truly unfortunate individual, variously named "Joan" or "John," whose entire life became a battleground for gender theorists. The child was born as a normal male, one of two identical twins. At the age of seven months his penis was accidentally destroyed during circumcision. Because there seemed no hope of reconstructing the penis, the parents elected to have the child surgically transformed into a girl. The first stage of the surgery—removal of the scrotum and testicles—was performed when the child was seventeen months old, and the child was given a girl's name. John Money gave the parents advice on how to socialize her into a girl's role, and he assured them that she would develop a female gender identity.

For the first few years, all seemed to go well. John Money and Anke Ehrhardt, in their 1972 book, *Man & Woman, Boy & Girl*, described how by age seven Joan had become appropriately feminine.[34] "She likes for me to wipe her face," said her mother. "She doesn't like to be dirty, and yet my son is quite different. I can't wash his face for anything." Joan loved to have her hair set, liked frilly dresses, wanted dolls for Christmas, and enjoyed helping her mother do housework, unlike her brother, who "could not care less about it." Joan was however very tomboyish and was often the dominant one in a girl's group. "Of course, I've tried to teach her not to be rough. . .she doesn't seem to be as rough as him. . .of course, I discouraged that. I teach her more to be polite and quiet, I always wanted those virtues. I never did manage, but I'm going to try to manage them to—my daughter—to be more quiet and ladylike."

In spite of this one masculine trait, the effort to turn the child into a girl was adjudged a success, and the case was taken as a major boost to the theory that gender is determined by socialization, not by bio-logical mechanisms. As recently as 1985, the leading textbook of neu-robiology, Kandel and Schwartz's *Principles of Neural Science*, claimed that the case illustrated "the overriding role of life experiences in molding human sexuality."[35]

Yet even on the basis of the childhood data, the case was a poor one from the behaviorist standpoint. Not only was at least one trait clearly masculine (her enjoyment of rough-and-tumble play), but the case his-tory depended, not on close study of the girl herself, but on the as-sertions of the mother, who after all had every motivation to believe that the conversion had been successful. More important, the case did not dissociate learning from hormonal effects, given that the child had been turned anatomically and endocrinologically into a girl. Only pre-natally and in the first seventeen months of postnatal life was she en-docrinologically a male.

Puberty was induced by administration of estrogens at age twelve. At this point Money and Ehrhardt claimed to have lost contact with the girl. But in 1980, when the twins were adolescents, a BBC tele-vision documentary reported that, according to psychiatrists familiar with the case, the girl had a very masculine gait, looked quite mascu-line, and was being teased and called "cave-woman."[36] According to detective work by Milton Diamond of the University of Hawaii, Joan began dressing and living as a male shortly after puberty, using the name "John." At fourteen, she requested and received a mastectomy. At fif-teen and sixteen years of age she underwent operations to reconstruct a penis and scrotum, thus becoming one of the few people to have changed sex twice in the course of a single lifetime.[37] John was al-ways sexually attracted to girls and not to boys, and from eighteen years of age he had sex with girls with the aid of a prosthesis. John is now living with a woman and has adopted children. In the end this extra-ordinary case, far from being a triumph for socialization theory, actu-ally suggested the very opposite: that prenatal events specify gender and sexual orientation rigidly enough to prevail even when anatomy, postnatal hormones, and socialization all conspire to produce a dif-ferent result.

Money and Green's theory is one example of a "social-learning" theory of gender development. Many such theories have been put forward, each with its own unique wrinkle and its own message to parents. In one class of theories, boys imitate the parent who exerts more power or is more loving. Thus a boy might become feminine (and, by extension, homosexual) if the mother dominates the father.[38] Obviously these theories shade into Freud's ideas about close-binding mothers and absent or hostile fathers as factors predisposing to homosexuality.

In opposition to social-learning theories, another school of thought has proposed that the young child first identifies itself as male or female by some intrinsic mechanism.[39] Having made this identification, the child imitates behavior by individuals of that sex. In partial support of this "cognitive developmental" theory are studies showing that children as young as one year already act as if they know which sex they are.[40] There are also theories that combine aspects of social-learning and cognitive developmental thinking: in these so-called social interactionist models the child's sense of its own sex is "given," but it requires validation by appropriate responses from parents, siblings, and so on.[41]

Overview

There is surely no period of one's life that seems so long and so crowded with momentous happenings and powerful characters as childhood. Yet what exactly childhood is good for still perplexes us. We learn something, certainly. But is that something merely the means to adapt to the particular environment we happen to find ourselves in, rather in the manner we might learn to deal with life in a foreign country, picking up the language and the local customs, forming acquaintances, and so on, but preserving our original identity intact within ourselves? Or are our very own selves the product of the circumstances we are exposed to during those "formative" years?

In this and the previous chapter I have sampled only a fraction of the theories that have been put forward to explain gender and sexual orientation in terms of the life experiences a person undergoes. No doubt the reader can think up others of his or her own. Because gender and sexual orientation are such bedrock aspects of a person's identity, these theories can be considered part of a broader point of view about human nature: one that minimizes the significance of "constitutional factors" in the development of the self.

The problem with most of these theories is that they have not been tested—they are mere surmises concerning what might have happened to bring about a certain result. But it is all too easy to look back in a person's life and to "explain" how a person got to be a certain way in terms of childhood events, family relationships, sexual experiences, and so on. As Freud himself wrote in a moment of unusual frankness, "the chain of causation can always be recognized with certainty if we follow the line of [retrospective] analysis, whereas to predict it along the line of synthesis is impossible."[42] Yet unless there is prediction, there is no explanation.

The work of Green and Rekers comes closer than most to a scientifically valid treatment of the topic. They had a fairly explicit learning theory of the development of gender identity, involving positive role modeling and affection from the same-sex parent. According to the theory, boys who lacked such modeling became feminine, and this femininity later led into adult transsexuality or effeminate homosexuality. They tested the predictions of the theory in two ways, first by observing the outcome of untreated childhood gender nonconformity (Green), and secondly by examining the effects of reversing the learning process in feminine boys before the development of adult sexuality (Rekers). The results were counter to prediction. First, most of the boys became more or less conventional gay men, not transsexuals or highly effeminate gay men. Second, behavioral treatment, even though it did remove the boys' feminine traits (or their visible manifestations), did not prevent the emergence of homosexuality in adulthood. Thus, in the simplest interpretation, adult homosexuality is indeed often preceded by childhood gender nonconformity, but it is not a causal chain in the way their theory had envisaged. Rather, childhood gender nonconformity and adult homosexuality may independently develop from some common prior cause.

Of course there are any number of reservations and complications. Very likely, the boys who were treated by Rekers maintained an "inner" femininity despite the treatment. Perhaps it is this inner femininity, rather than any social expression of femininity, that is the necessary prelude to adult homosexuality. Also, the mere fact that the boys apparently "unlearned" their femininity does not prove that it was learned in the first place, any more that the failure of behavioral therapy in the treatment of adult homosexuality proves that sexual orientation is inborn. But the point is, here was a theory and a prediction, and the prediction was not fulfilled. For the great majority of theories that have been put forward, there have been no predictions, let alone any experiments to tests them. Therefore the whole field tends to suffer from unfruitful speculation.

It is hard to make and check predictions that span decades, and there are ethical problems with experimenting on humans, especially children. (The experiments conducted by Rekers under the guise of therapy should never have been undertaken, in my judgment.) This is where the biological approach, discussed in the ensuing five chapters, has an enormous advantage. By starting with the realization that humans are animals, it becomes possible to fill many of the gaps in the human story with evidence acquired in rats and monkeys. This is not to deny any role for human culture in the development of sexual orientation but merely to acknowledge that, in our present situation, a biological approach seems to offer the best prospect for advances in our understanding.

5

Hormones

In chapter 1 I recounted how one of the early endocrinologists, Eugen Steinach, attempted to convert gay men to heterosexuality by replacing their testes with testes taken from heterosexual men. Steinach's early reports caused a flurry of enthusiasm. One German surgeon even claimed to have "cured" a man of homosexuality without his knowledge, by slipping a piece of testicle into his body during a hernia operation. Within a few weeks, the surgeon reported, the man developed "normal" sexual desires and even desired to marry.[1] But by the mid-1920s the failure of these experiments had become evident, and for a while the idea of a connection between hormones and sexual orientation lost favor.

The issue came up again a few years later when the sex hormones themselves were isolated. The first of these to be purified was estrone, a member of the *estrogen* family of ovarian hormones. Estrone was isolated in pure form from human urine in 1929. Progesterone, a member of the *progestin* family of ovarian hormones, was purified in 1934, likewise from urine. In the following year testosterone, the principal hormone of the *androgen* family, was purified from bulls' testicles. The

hormones were found to be *steroids*—compounds built up of four in-
terlocking rings of carbon atoms.

For a while the use of sex steroids in medicine and research was
limited by their availability: to produce a few milligrams of testosterone,
for example, the early researchers had to start with a ton or so of bulls'
testicles. Methods of production gradually improved, however. In 1935
Russell Marker, an organic chemist at Pennsylvania State College,
began looking for new sources for the hormones. Improbably enough,
he found a substance that could easily be converted into sex hormones
in the roots of a wild yam growing in the mountains near Veracruz,
Mexico. This discovery led to the founding of the Mexican pharmaceutical company Syntex and to the ready availability of the various
classes of sex steroids.[2]

In 1935 a Los Angeles psychiatrist, Clifford Wright, reported that the
hormone levels in the urine of gay men differed from those seen in
heterosexual men: the urine contained a lower concentration of androgens and a higher concentration of estrogens.[3] In a word, the gay
men's urine was feminized, suggesting that the hormones in their blood
were feminized too. Wright's finding was soon replicated,[4] and the stage
was set for a campaign to convert gay men to heterosexuality by pharmacological means—a procedure that was termed "organotherapy."

The first attempt in this direction involved giving gay men testosterone and/or extracts of pituitary gland. (The latter substance contained hormones that were believed to cause the testis to increase its
own secretion of testosterone—see chapter 6.) The logic of the experiment was clear: if the men were deficient in male hormones then
making up the deficit might offer a cure. Wright tried this treatment
on fourteen gay men who were "under custodial care" (i.e., in prison
or a hospital for the criminally insane) and reported numerous cures,[5]
but tests on nonprisoner populations failed to replicate Wright's results. S. J. Glass and R. H. Johnson, for example, who had worked with
Wright on the urine studies, reported that most of their subjects complained of an actual *intensification* of their homosexual drive while they
were taking testosterone.[6] Glass and Johnson commented that a patient in custody "has a strong impulse either to deceive the physician

or at least to show a bias in his statement"—a perception that many workers in the field could profitably have taken to heart. Other studies confirmed that testosterone increases the strength of the libido without changing its direction.[7] According to testimony by Alfred Kinsey, a U.S. Army unit attempted to treat three hundred homosexual men during the Second World War by injecting them with testosterone. As a result of this treatment "they had the worst homosexual problem on their hands that they had ever had, because they increased the intensity of the drive of these men, you see. It did not modify the direction of their behavior at all."[8]

Among the darkest episodes in the history of research on homosexuality was the set of experiments carried out by the Danish endocrinologist Carl Vaernet at Buchenwald concentration camp in 1944.[9] Vaernet had developed an "artificial male sex gland," a slow-release capsule that, once implanted under the skin, was supposed to deliver testosterone into the circulation for a prolonged period. He suggested to the Nazi medical authorities that the artificial gland could be used to convert gay men to heterosexuality. With the encouragement of SS-chief Heinrich Himmler and the assistance of the camp doctor Gerhard Schiedlausky, Vaernet implanted the capsules in at least ten male homosexual prisoners. At least one of the prisoners died during the experiment, but Vaernet reported success with some of the others. In a letter to the Nazi authorities Vaernet described the first five cases as follows:

> Subject: Report on the implantation of the "artificial male sex gland" at Weimar-Buchenwald. Report No. 6, up to 30.10.44.
>
> The operations at Weimar-Buchenwald were carried out on 5 homosexual persons on 13.9.44. Of these
>
> 2 had been castrated
> 1 sterilized
> 2 not operated on.
>
> *The purpose of the operations*
>
> 1. To investigate whether implantation of the "artificial male sex gland" can normalize the sexual orientation of homosexual persons.
> 2. To establish the support dose.
> 3. Control standardization of the "artificial male sex gland."

The "artificial male sex gland" is implanted in varying amounts, so that the absorbed quantities of hormone can be expressed as 1a, 2a and 3a.

The investigations are far from complete. But:

I. The provisional results show that the 3a dose *transforms homosexuality into a normal sex drive.*
The 2a dose reawakens the sex drive in a person castrated seven years earlier. *The reawakened sex drive* is without any homosexual elements.
The 1a dose produces a reappearance of erection among castrated persons, but no sex drive.
II. The absorbtion doses—1a, 2a and 3a—supplied by the "artificial sex gland" transform severe depression and tension into optimism, calm and self-confidence. All three absorbtion doses brought about an excellent sense of physical and psychological well-being. . .

The apparent changes in sexual orientation were presumably feigned in an attempt to receive a discharge from the camp. Early in 1945 Vaernet left Buchenwald. At the close of the war he was arrested, but he escaped to Argentina, where he took employment in the Buenos Aires health service. Schiedlausky was executed for other crimes committed at Buchenwald.

When it became apparent that androgens were not having the desired effect, some psychiatrists turned to estrogens. There was little scientific basis for the expectation that giving estrogens would make gay men straight, because the reports were that estrogen levels were too *high* in gay men, not too low. It may be that the aim was to desexualize gay men entirely rather than to convert them to heterosexuality; or possibly doctors simply took a blunderbuss approach, trying every drug in the book with the hope that something would work. This was certainly the case with one unfortunate man, an inmate of Worcester State Hospital, Massachusetts, who was treated sequentially with three different estrogen preparations, as well as with testosterone, gonadotropins, thyroid powder, and pituitary extract, over a period of six months in 1939 and 1940. His homosexuality remained unaffected, as did his other traits, which included "the mannerisms of a clinging-vine type of female."[10]

Nevertheless, there were several reports that estrogens did have an effect. In 1940 an American psychiatrist, C. W. Dunn, stated that he had been able to extinguish completely the libido of a heterosexual sex offender by estrogen treatment.[11] In 1949 psychiatrists in Britain issued a similar report: they had been able to abolish the sex drive of thirteen men, of unspecified sexual orientation, by means of large doses of estrogens.[12] These results led to the use of estrogen treatment in a legal setting, where there was more concern with stopping homosexual behavior than converting people to heterosexuality. The most celebrated victim of this treatment was the British mathematician Alan Turing, who was convicted of gross indecency in 1952. (His crime was engaging in consensual sex with a nineteen-year-old man.) He was sentenced to a year's estrogen treatment as an alternative to imprisonment. Although he grew miniature breasts as a result of the treatment, he apparently did not lose his sex drive or his potency. A year after the completion of the treatment, however, he committed suicide.[13]

Another medical strategy used for the elimination of homosexual behavior was castration. This operation results in a marked lowering of testosterone levels in the blood, although variable amounts of testosterone and other androgens are still secreted by the adrenal glands. As far back as 1779 the state of Pennsylvania mandated castration as the punishment for sodomy and other sexual crimes.[14] As late as 1950, eleven states permitted courts to order castration, and fifty thousand cases of court-ordered or legally sanctioned castration are recorded according to Arno Karlen.[15] Probably only a very small fraction of these castrations were for homosexual offenses.

In Germany during the Nazi period, castration of gay men *was* commonly performed. At first, it was "voluntary," but later forced castrations were performed in prisons and concentration camps. It was generally justified with the claim that castration caused the decline or cessation of homosexual drive and behavior. Castration does indeed lead to a reduction or elimination of the sex drive in many cases (regardless of sexual orientation), although the full effects may take years to become apparent. The Nazis believed that castration of gay men would decrease the incidence of homosexuality in the next generation, but not because of the elimination of "gay genes." Rather they expected that it would decrease the frequency with which young men were "infected" with homosexuality through seduction by older gay men.[16]

The scientific studies that had given birth to organotherapy—the reports of anomalous hormone levels in gay men—were actually beset with methodological problems, chief among them being the insensitivity of the measuring techniques then available. During the postwar years much more refined analytical procedures were developed, such as the radio-immunoassay and mass spectrometry. In addition, medical scientists became much more aware of the importance of proper controls (comparison groups), "blind" measurements, and appropriate statistical procedures. Between 1968 and 1984, no less than twenty-five studies on the blood levels of testosterone in gay men were published, and the results were remarkable: twenty of the studies reported no differences between gay and heterosexual men (or between gay and bisexual men); two studies reported that testosterone levels were actually *higher* in gay men than in heterosexuals, and only three supported the original claims that testosterone levels were lower. Furthermore, these three studies had methodological problems that might have confounded the results. It is reasonable to conclude that there are no consistent differences in testosterone levels between gay and straight men. There seem to be no differences in estrogen levels either: two studies reported slightly higher estrogen levels in gay men, but four studies reported failing to find any differences.[17] In other words, the efforts to "cure" gay men through organotherapy had been based on an incorrect hypothesis about the relationship between sex hormone levels and sexual orientation.

The studies that have been done in women are much less extensive. By and large, they suggest that sex hormone levels are about the same in lesbian and heterosexual women. One study reported that about one-third of the lesbians had testosterone levels above the range encountered in heterosexual women, although still below the levels seen in men. The significance, if any, of this finding remains to be explored.[18]

The investigation of hormone levels in adults thus seems to have been a blind alley, although it did lead to unfortunate, sometimes tragic consequences in terms of attempted "therapy" of gay men. But this still left open the question of hormone levels earlier in life, most especially during the fetal period. The reasons for focusing on early development derived to a large extent from animal experiments, so I need to describe some of these experiments before returning to the human work.

As mentioned in chapter 1, Steinach carried out transplantation experiments in rats and guinea pigs prior to the human experimentation. In the animal work Steinach noticed that the effects on sex behavior were greater the earlier in life the operations were performed. This finding in itself should have made him think twice about attempting to change people's sexual orientation by testicle transplants in adult life.

More recent work has reinforced Steinach's finding. The manipulation of sex hormone levels during an early developmental period can change the kind of sexual behavior displayed by an animal during adult life. Doing the same thing during adult life, on the other hand, can change the *amount* of sexual behavior that an animal displays but not the *kind* of behavior. The first type of hormone effect is described as an *organizational* effect, because it seems to organize the brain in such a way as to predispose to certain kinds of behavior later in life. The second kind of effect is called *activational*, because it activates (or conversely prevents the appearance of) a behavior pattern that had been laid down earlier.

The laboratory that made the most important discoveries in this field was that of William Young at the University of Kansas. In a 1959 study, Young's group showed that treating female guinea pigs with testosterone while they were fetuses prevented them from showing the typical female sex behavior during adulthood, in particular the behavior called *lordosis*—the raising of the rump which permits the male to mount her. Furthermore, if these females were treated again with testosterone in adulthood, they would mount other females, a typically male behavior. In other words the testosterone exposure during fetal life had apparently *defeminized* the developing brain and also *masculinized* it, at least with respect to these particular sex-linked behaviors.[19]

The converse experiment—removing testosterone from male fetuses by castration—is technically hard to do, because it requires surgery on the fetuses while they are still in their mother's uterus. Young's group, however, got around this problem by switching from guinea pigs to rats, who are born at a very early stage of development (fetal life lasts only twenty-two days in rats, as compared with sixty-eight days in guinea pigs). Thus castrating a newborn rat is equivalent to castrating a fetus of other species. When these castrated male rats were allowed to grow up they failed to show the normal pattern of male sex behavior, even if they were supplemented with testosterone by injection. If on the other hand they were treated with female hormones in adulthood, they were unusually willing to display female-typical sex behaviors such as lordosis. The researchers concluded that the lack of testosterone during early life *demasculinized* and *feminized* the male pup's developing brains.[20] Subsequently, similar results were obtained in rats by administering androgen-blocking drugs such as flutamide to pregnant females. The male rats deriving from these pregnancies were likewise demasculinized and feminized in their sexual behavior.[21] Thus it appears that the major factor driving the brain to differentiate in a male or female direction is the presence or absence of high levels of testosterone in the animal's blood during a certain *critical period* of development. The ovarian hormones, on the other hand, do not play a significant role in early development. In fact the ovaries do not secrete sufficient estrogens or progestins to influence sexual characteristics until puberty.

These pioneering studies opened the door to a whole field of endocrinological research. One line of study, conducted mostly but not entirely in rats, investigated the kinds of behaviors that were influenced by early hormone levels. It was found that a whole range of behaviors were affected: not just behaviors concerned directly with mating but a variety of other behaviors that typically differed between males and females. These included juvenile play, exploratory and marking behavior, maze-solving abilities, parental behavior, aggressive behavior, and so on.[22] It was if a whole constellation of traits, which in humans we might lump together under the catch-all designator "gender," differentiated under the influence of prenatal or perinatal androgen levels.

Another question was: Do the findings in rodents apply to primates too? To answer this question, Robert Goy and his colleagues at the University of Wisconsin, Madison, began a multi-year study of female macaque monkeys who had been exposed to testosterone while they were fetuses. These monkeys began to act differently from other females while they were still juveniles. They engaged in more play fighting, and they also took the male role in "play-sex," something that juvenile females never do.[23] When they became sexually mature, they showed a higher frequency of male-typical sexual behavior and a lower frequency of female-typical behavior than untreated females.[24] Thus there appears to be a critical period for the organization of sex-typed behavior in primates also, and in rhesus monkeys this period is before birth. Because of the long duration of fetal life in monkeys, the Madison group was able to show that different aspects of psychosexual differentiation were influenced by hormone levels at different times. In other words, there is not just one critical period but several, which partially overlap each other.[25]

One complication concerning the organizing effects of testosterone has to do with what happens to the testosterone once it enters the brain. In the simplest model, the hormone binds to target molecules in the nuclei of brain cells—the *androgen receptors*— and this binding triggers the developmental events responsible for the "organization" of male-typical development. The brain, however, contains an enzyme, whose name is *aromatase*, that is capable of converting testosterone into *estradiol*, the principal estrogenic hormone (see figure 5.1). It turns out that, for some of the organizing effects of testosterone to take place, the hormone must first undergo this conversion. The resulting estradiol then binds to its own receptor molecules, the *estrogen receptors*, that in turn trigger the organizing effects. The main evidence supporting this scheme comes from experiments with another androgen called *5-alpha-dihydrotestosterone* or DHT. DHT can bind to the androgen receptor, but it cannot be converted into estradiol by aromatase. When DHT is administered to developing animals, it does not have all the organizing effects of testosterone. Those effects that fail to occur are presumed to be mediated by estradiol, formed by the aromatase conversion.

There seem to be considerable differences among species in how important the aromatase conversion is. But, to the extent that it is important, one immediately comes up against a puzzle, which is this: The blood of pregnant females contains high levels of estradiol, and this estradiol can cross the placentas and enter the blood circulation of the fetuses. Why then are not the brains of all fetuses masculinized by the maternal estradiol? The reason, it turns out, is that fetuses have specific mechanisms to prevent this from happening. The mechanisms include special proteins and enzymes that prevent the maternal estradiol from ever reaching the fetal brain. Therefore, only the estradiol formed locally from testosterone within the brain itself can have an organizing effect.

Is all this animal work relevant to the question of human sexual orientation? For many years one scientist, the German endocrinologist Günter Dörner, was the loudest voice saying "yes." During the late 1960s and 1970s, Dörner and his colleagues replicated and extended the work on rats begun by the Madison group. Dörner claimed that the male rat castrated at birth was a model for human male homosexuality, and the female rat treated with androgens at birth was a model for lesbianism.[26] Dörner has called homosexuality a case of "central nervous pseudohermaphroditism"—a restatement in technical jargon of Ulrichs's original concept of a female mind in a male body (or vice versa). Unfortunately Dörner, who traces his academic heritage back to Steinach,[27] also believed for many years that homosexuality was something to be cured or prevented. In this vein he labeled homosexuality an example of "functional teratology"—in plain English, a psychological monstrosity. In the 1970s he promoted the idea of a public-health program for the elimination of homosexuality, that was to involve the measurement of sex hormone levels in the amniotic fluid of pregnant women and the correction of these levels in those cases where homosexuality seemed a likely outcome. The following passage is from his 1976 book *Hormones and Brain Differentiation*:

> ...[A]n important preventive therapy of sexual differentiation disturbances might become possible in the future by administration of androgens in...male foetuses with androgen deficiency during the critical differentiation periods of genital organs and, in particular, of the brain...On the other hand, in...fe-

male foetuses with unphysiologically high androgen levels, a prenatal treatment with antiandrogens could be taken into consideration.

Finally, it may be discussed whether a possible preventive therapy of inborn sexual deviations should be inaugurated at all. The more so as numerous prominent personalities of universal history were homosexuals. . .On the other hand, about 3% of homosexuals were reported to commit suicide...Even about 25% of homosexuals are said to attempt suicide. In view of these data a great deal of males and females with inborn sexual deviations are suffering from psychosexual pressure.

Dörner went on to state that he had received letters from unhappy homosexuals and transsexuals asking for help, and that he believed the medical profession had an obligation to ease the existence of such people.[28] Of course, the amniotic testing program would do nothing for adults who were already homosexual, but as we shall see in the next chapter, Dörner had something in mind for them too.

Others reacted vigorously to Dörner's claims. In 1982 the German Society for Sex Research issued an official statement that criticized Dörner's work on both technical and moral grounds.[29] In an American review article written in 1984, the author (H. H. Feder) stressed the ethical dangers of Dörner's ideas and laid out two arguments to counter the idea that the animal models were useful for understanding human sexuality.[30] First, Feder argued that human behavior has been liberated from the "mechanical" developmental processes that occur in nonhuman animals. Traits that in animals might be brought about by hormones were in humans more likely to be the results of learning, culture, or free will. Second, Feder argued that the behavioral traits studied in animals—mounting, lordosis, and so on, really had nothing to do with sexual orientation. To confuse the two, Feder argued, was to confuse the question "Who is a person sexually attracted to?" with the the question "What role does a person take when he or she has sex?"

This second argument had considerable merit. Being gay does not necessarily mean that one always prefers to take the receptive role in anal intercourse, even if there is a subset of gay men who do have this preference. Similarly, being lesbian does not mean that one desires always to take a "male" role in sex, even if some lesbians do have this desire. Conversely, the fact that a female rat readily mounts other rats does not necessarily mean that she prefers females as sex partners, nor does the fact that a male rat submits to being mounted necessarily mean that he prefers males as sex partners. In fact, Dörner has published photographs of a hormonally manipulated female rat mounting a hormonally manipulated male: in this case both animals are engaged in sex-atypical behavior, but the sexual encounter is unquestionably heterosexual!

Thus, by the early 1980s, endocrinological theories of sexual orientation seemed to have reached a low point of credibility, and those who still espoused them were labeled the "bad guys," who were on a mission to eliminate homosexuality by a technical fix. In Dörner's case the label was well deserved. But Fortune's wheel continued to turn, and new findings brought hormone theories to the surface again.

For one thing, new experiments on hormonally manipulated animals suggested that they really did have an atypical sexual orientation.[31] These experiments, which have now been done in rats,[32] hamsters,[33] ferrets[34], pigs,[35] and even zebra finches,[36] involved giving the animal a choice of sex partner. For example, a test animal might be put in one arm of a three-armed maze, the other two arms of which contained a tethered male and a tethered female respectively. The experimenter would observe which arm the test animal entered, how long it spent with the male or the female, and whether it engaged in sex with either of them. Experiments of this kind revealed that females treated with androgens during the critical period were shifted in their partner preference toward females, while conversely, males that had been castrated, or treated with androgen blockers or aromatase inhibitors were shifted in their partner preference toward males. Collectively, these experiments have greatly strengthened the case that the hormonal manipulation of animals offers a valid model for the study of sexual orientation in humans.

Researchers really hit pay dirt, however, when they studied *humans* who had been hormonally manipulated before birth. Of course, no one actually injected pregnant women with testosterone or testosterone blockers to see if their children became lesbian or gay. But experiments that would be grossly unethical if conducted deliberately sometimes happen by natural circumstances or through human misadventure. In the case of hormones and sexual development, two types of circumstances provided the necessary data. One was a natural genetic disorder called *congenital adrenal hyperplasia* (CAH), and the other was a pharmaceutical nightmare involving a drug called *diethylstilbestrol* (DES).

In fetuses afflicted with CAH, a genetic error disrupts the synthesis of hormones in the cortex (outer rim) of the adrenal gland. Instead of secreting its usual hormones, which are corticosteroids and mineralocorticoids, the gland secretes large amounts of androgens (see figure 5.1). Because the adrenal glands develop later than the gonads, the initial sexual differentiation of the fetus proceeds normally. But in female fetuses with the CAH syndrome, androgen levels rise to levels that are much higher than usual, although still below the levels usually seen in male fetuses. These androgens often have a virilizing effect on the external genitalia: sometimes surgery is required to convert them to the normal female appearance. After the child is born the syndrome is quickly recognized and treated with drugs that replace the missing adrenal hormones and suppress the adrenal secretion of androgens. Thus, in most cases, the period of abnormal androgen exposure is limited to fetal life and a few days of postnatal life.

Studies of girls with CAH have shown several significant differences from other girls (such as their unaffected sisters). During childhood, these girls have an unusual interest in playing with toys such as trucks that boys typically play with. Conversely, they are less interested in traditional girls' toys such as dolls and kitchen implements. These differences are not merely anecdotal but have been established in rigorously controlled observations of the children's behavior. They also score better than their sisters on tests of spatial ability in which boys typically outperform girls. CAH girls also typically express less interest in becoming mothers than unaffected girls.[37]

When CAH girls grow up, they are more likely than other women to experience sexual attraction to women, or to both women and men. This has been documented in a number of studies using different subject populations and methods of analysis.[38] Although there has been

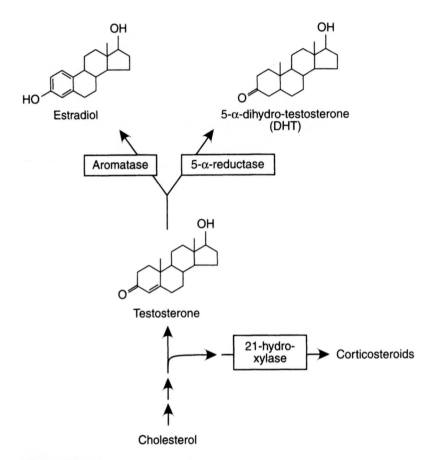

Figure 5.1
Pathways for synthesis of sex steroids. Cholesterol can be used for synthesis either of
testosterone (in testis and ovary) or corticosteroids (in adrenal gland). If the enzyme
21-hydroxylase is defective (the condition of *congenital adrenal hyperplasia* or *CAH*),
the adrenal glands secrete testosterone or similar androgens instead of corticosteroids.
In the skin, testosterone is converted to 5-alpha–dihydrotestosterone (DHT), the androgen that is responsible for the development of the male genitalia. In the brain,
testosterone is converted (by the enzyme *aromatase*) to estradiol. Both testosterone
and estradiol influence the prenatal differentiation of the brain in a male direction:
they activate androgen and estrogen receptors respectively. In the ovary, most testosterone is converted immediately to estradiol before secretion into the blood. The four-
ring core structure of the sex steroids consists of seventeen carbon atoms linked by
single or double bonds (the latter are shown by double lines).

some disagreement about the mechanism for this effect, the most likely explanation is that the high androgens during prenatal life influenced organization of brain circuits for sexual orientation in the male-typical direction. It should be emphasized that not all CAH girls become lesbian women; in fact the majority do not. This could be for a variety of reasons: the androgen levels may not have been high enough, the timing of the increased androgen levels may not have coincided with the critical period for partner preference, the women might not have been followed long enough to allow their homosexual feelings to become apparent, or (and this is surely at least part of the explanation) prenatal hormones may not be the sole determinants of adult sexual orientation. But the results strongly support the belief that hormones do play a significant role.

DES is a synthetic estrogen that between 1940 and 1971 was widely prescribed to pregnant women who were at risk of miscarriage. It has been estimated that a total of between four hundred thousand and 2.8 million pregnancies were treated with the drug, meaning that approximately this number of people now living (between twenty-five and fifty-five years old), were exposed to DES during fetal life.[39] The use of DES in pregnancy was banned in 1971 because it was found to cause serious side-effects in some cases. In particular, it caused a rare form of cancer of the cervix and vagina in some of the female offspring of these pregnancies. It is also doubtful that it actually had any of the beneficial effects for which it was prescribed.

DES is not a steroid, and therefore it escapes inactivation by the mechanisms that fetuses use to prevent maternal estrogen from reaching the brain. It does bind to the estrogen receptor and activate it, however. It does not bind to or activate the androgen receptor, and it does not cause virilization of the external genitalia. To all appearances, girls exposed to DES are indistinguishable from girls who were not exposed.

Thus the study of DES-exposed girls or women allows one to ask the question: Is the organizing action of prenatal testosterone, which has been observed in CAH patients, a result of the direct action of testosterone on the brain's androgen receptors, or must the testosterone first be converted to estradiol by the aromatase pathway? If the former, then one would not expect DES to have a similar effect, because DES cannot bind to androgen receptors. If the latter, however, one *would* expect DES to have an effect—it would simply short-circuit the aromatase step and home in directly on the real target, the estrogen receptors.

Heino Meyer-Bahlburg, Anke Ehrhardt and their colleagues at Columbia University have shown that DES-exposed women are indeed significantly more likely to experience same-sex attraction than their unexposed sisters or other comparison groups.[40] For example, in one of the comparisons eight out of twenty (40 percent) of the DES women reported that they had experienced a significant degree of sexual attraction to women throughout their adult lives (in addition to some degree of attraction to men), while only one out of the twenty non-DES sisters had experienced such an attraction. The results suggest that the estrogen pathway is indeed involved in the organization of brain circuits responsible for sexual orientation. The effects of DES exposure, however, did not seem to be as great as was seen in the CAH women. In particular, the effects of DES on other gender-related traits, such as childhood sex-typed behavior, seem to be weak. Thus it is very possible that the estrogen pathway and the direct androgen pathway both play a role in the development of these traits: because androgens activate both pathways, CAH causes bigger effects than DES exposure.[41]

Taken together, the CAH and DES studies lead very persuasively to the conclusion that prenatal hormone levels can influence a person's ultimate sexual orientation. But beyond that, they leave many uncertainties. How strong is that influence? When exactly is the critical period? Do environmental factors interact in an important way with the hormonal events? It is hard to answer these questions because the human studies are by necessity "sloppy": no one knows exactly what hormone levels any individual was exposed to as a fetus, or when; nor are their subsequent life experiences known in any detail. Just because hormones played a role in causing these women to experience same-sex attraction, we cannot conclude that every lesbian or bisexual woman was exposed to atypical hormone levels as a fetus. Indeed, the fact that gays and lesbians are generally so similar to heterosexual men and women (and certainly do not usually have intersexed genitalia) should make us skeptical of the notion that atypical hormone levels are the simple and sole cause of homosexuality.

But another issue is this: if differences in prenatal hormone levels do play some role in the determination of sexual orientation, how do these differences arise? One could imagine a variety of possible mechanisms, some of which, if they were proven to play a role, might have a significant effect on public attitudes toward homosexuality.

One possibility would be that they arise from genetic differences among individuals. That is actually the case for CAH, which is a genetically caused disease, but I am thinking of something much more subtle: slight differences in the genetic regulatory mechanisms that would increase or decrease the production of androgens at a certain time of fetal development, rather in the same way as genetic mechanisms influence the timing and degree of the growth spurt at puberty. We simply do not know whether such genes exist, but there is nothing implausible about the notion. If this mechanism were found to play an important role, this would of course support the "born that way" school of thought, with consequences that are discussed elsewhere in this book.

It is equally possible, however, that differences in prenatal hormone levels might come about as a result of some environmental process, such the kind and amount of food consumed by the pregnant mother, the amount of daylight she is exposed to, or any number of other factors. One environmental theory of this type has attracted particular attention. This is the idea, put forward by Dörner in 1980, that stress on pregnant women predisposes the male offspring of these pregnancies to homosexuality. This theory will be discussed in chapter 8.

There are also "prenatal hormone" theories of sexual orientation that do not require that hormone levels themselves be different in fetuses that become homosexual and those that become heterosexual. For example, one could hypothesize that the *receptors* for sex hormones might differ between the two, either in their number or in their characteristics. Such differences could affect the sexual differentiation of the brain as profoundly as differences in the levels of the hormones themselves.

One well-known syndrome depends on exactly this kind of effect. This is a condition called the *androgen insensitivity syndrome* or AIS. In AIS, a mutation of the gene that codes for the androgen receptor causes the receptor to be totally nonfunctional: androgens no longer bind to it or, if they do, they no longer trigger the usual developmental events that follow binding. Thus the affected fetus, even if it is swimming in testosterone, develops as if testosterone were completely absent. These fetuses, even if they are genetically male, develop with the external genitalia of females; in other words, they are females according to the usual definition. When these girls grow up they are sexually attracted to men. This finding is consistent with the prenatal hormone theory, in that a nonfunctional androgen system leads to sexual attraction to males, but it is not really informative, because these individuals have the bodies of women (on the outside, at least) and not just the brains of women.

But there might be more subtle mutations of the androgen receptor that affect its function only in certain parts of the body. One example is known, in fact. There is a rare disorder called Kennedy's disease that is marked by degeneration of parts of the spinal cord and brain stem. The disorder is caused by a mutation of the androgen receptor gene that apparently affects its function only in those parts of the nervous system, not in the rest of the brain or in the body as a whole. What then if there were mutations of the androgen receptor gene that affected its function selectively in those parts of the brain that are concerned with sexual function?

As will be described further in chapter 9, experiments to test this idea have come up negative. Even so, there are plenty of other genes concerned with sex-hormone signaling that remain to be examined: the gene for the estrogen receptor, for the aromatase enzyme, and probably many others. There is no special reason to quit prospecting just because the first well was dry.

So far, then, there has been evidence that prenatal hormones do play a role in the establishment of sexual orientation, but the exact nature and strength of this role remains to be established. Furthermore, we have seen that prenatal hormonal theories are actually a mixed bag, some being essentially genetic, others environmental. It is possible that prenatal hormones could be the "final common path" for a wide variety of factors that influence sexual orientation. The only thing they would all have in common is that they operate prior to birth, and therefore are very distinct from the processes envisaged by psychoanalytic or social-learning theories.

In this chapter I have spoken of the hormone-brain connection as if it were a one-way street. After we have discussed some of the brain circuits that are involved in sexuality, we shall see that the brain and the gonads are in fact engaged in a delicate two-way communication. The discovery of these reciprocal interactions has led to further theories about the origins of homosexuality, which I will discuss later.

6

The Brain

In previous chapters I have referred to a number of conflicting ideas about the brain and its involvement in sex and sexual orientation. According to one school of thought, the brain is a general-purpose learning machine. At birth, this theory goes, the brains of different individuals do not differ from one another in important respects, but they become different as life progresses. As a result of different life experiences they store different memories. As a result of different rewards and punishments they lay down different patterns of response. Eventually, these differences become so ingrained that aspects of personality and behavior—sexual orientation among them—seem like innate characteristics.

According to another school of thought, the brain is a collection of special-purpose modules, each one designed to function in a certain way. Major differences among individuals, according to this theory, exist because different modules developed when the brain was first assembling itself. One person might have a better memory than another because more nerve cells, or more connections between nerve cells, developed in the part of the brain concerned with memory. Similarly, one person might be sexually attracted to men, and another not, because different numbers of cells, or connections between cells, developed in the brain system that is concerned with sexual attraction to men.

These two models are not really as diametrically opposed to each other as one might think. For example, brain development continues after birth—not in terms of new brain cells being generated but in terms of new synaptic connections being laid down. Therefore there is the opportunity for learning and other interactions with the environment to influence brain development. Indeed, all learning probably involves a kind of drawn-out development—a fine tuning of the synaptic connections whose main outlines were laid down during fetal life. And furthermore, we will see in chapter 8 how an environmental factor (stress) can influence development even before birth, at least in rats.

For these reasons it is not very useful to take refuge in generalities about the brain, if we want the answers to questions like "What makes people gay or straight?" We need to know the particulars. What parts of the brain are involved in the regulation of sexuality and sexual orientation? What structural or functional differences underlie the preference for male or female sex partners, and how and when do these differences develop?

Sex Centers

In chapter 1, I described how Hirschfeld proposed the existence of two neural centers in the brain, one for sexual attraction to men, the other to women. He suggested that rudiments of both these centers existed in every fetus, but generally only one underwent extensive development, while the other atrophied. As for what decided which center developed, a good candidate soon emerged: the level or nature of the gonadal hormones reaching the developing brain.

It took much longer to identify locations in the brain that might correspond to Hirschfeld's hypothesized centers. During the 1930s Steinach's student Walter Hohlweg began to gather evidence pointing to a general region of the brain known as the *hypothalamus* as playing an important role in sexual life. The hypothalamus, which is shown in figure 6.1, is a tiny region at the base of the brain. It actually consists

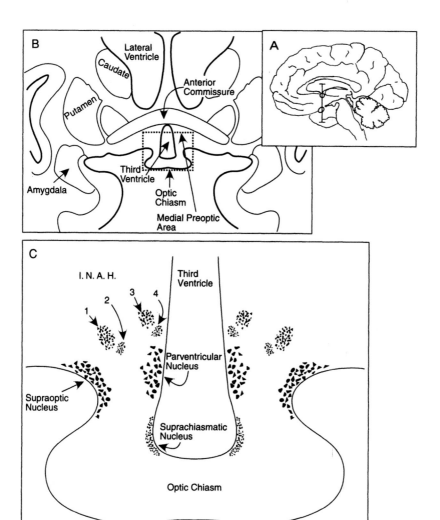

Figure 6.1

Location of the Interstitial Nuclei of the Anterior Hypothalamus (INAH). A: Midline of a human brain (front is to the left), showing where transverse slice illustrated in B was taken. B: Transverse slice at the level of the anterior hypothalamus. The boxed region at the center is shown at higher magnification in C. C: The medial preoptic area of the hypothalamus, showing the location of the four Interstitial Nuclei on each side. They are labeled 1 to 4 from lateral to medial. The drawing is semidiagrammatic: all four nuclei are not usually seen in the same transverse slice. The size of INAH3 varies both with sex and with sexual orientation. (Other structures: the optic chiasm is the crossing of the left and right optic nerves, the third ventricle is a fluid-filled space at the midline of the brain, the supraoptic and paraventricular nuclei are groups of large hormone-secreting cells, and the suprachiasmatic nucleus is a group of small cells involved in the regulation of circadian rhythms.

of symmetrical left and right halves that flank the *third ventricle*, a fluid-filled cavity in the midline of the brain. In spite of its small size the hypothalamus is involved in a number of vital functions in addition to sex: eating and drinking, temperature regulation, hormonal regulation, and so on. In evolutionary terms it is an ancient structure, being found in all vertebrates, even in those, like fish, which lack a cerebral cortex.

During the 1950s detailed investigations in animals revealed that different regions within the hypothalamus play a role in the generation of "male-typical" and "female-typical" sexual behavior. The region that helps produce male-typical behavior is towards the front end of the hypothalamus, in a zone called the *medial preoptic area*, whereas the region contributing to female-typical behavior is a little further back, in a zone called the *ventromedial nucleus*. (A *nucleus*, in neuroanatomy, is a cluster of nerve cells that can be reliably identified on the basis of its size and position and the appearance of the nerve cells forming it.)

The evidence for these conclusions came from several different kinds of experiments. In one kind of experiment, adult male or female rats were gonadectomized (i.e., the testes or ovaries were surgically removed). With their brains deprived of sex hormones, the animals' sex behavior soon ceased. Now the experimenters tried the effect of implanting pellets containing minute amounts of sex hormones at various locations within the rats' brains. They found that the sex behavior of male rats could most easily be restored if pellets containing testosterone were implanted in the medial preoptic area. The sexual behavior of females was most easily restored by implanting pellets containing estrogens and progestins in the ventromedial nucleus. Thus these two sites seemed to be key sites of action of the hormones.[1]

In another kind of experiment, the effects of destroying various parts of the hypothalamus were observed. It was found that destruction of the medial preoptic area impaired or did away with the ability of male rats to mount females, whereas damage to the ventromedial nucleus prevented females from showing lordosis behavior when paired with a stud male.[2]

In a third kind of experiment, electrodes were implanted in the hypothalamus, and the medial preoptic area or the ventromedial nucleus were stimulated electrically. It was found that stimulation of the medial preoptic area made male animals more likely to approach and mount females, whereas stimulation of the ventromedial nucleus made females more likely to show lordosis.[3]

Finally, recordings of the electrical activity in these regions revealed that the activity of some cells was correlated with the animal's sexual behavior. For example, the activity of some cells in the medial preoptic area of male animals increases as the male approaches and copulates with a female, and ceases after the animal has ejaculated.[4]

Several cautionary statements need to be made at this point to avoid creating an overly simplistic view of how the brain generates sexual behavior. First, behaviors like lordosis and mounting, although typically shown by female and male rats respectively, can be shown on occasion by rats of the "wrong" sex, even if these rats have not been subjected to any hormonal manipulation during fetal life. Thus the neural circuitry for lordosis must exist, even if in some simplified or attenuated form, in the brains of male animals, and conversely the circuitry for mounting must exist in the brains of female animals. In fact, lesion and stimulation studies have shown that the medial preoptic area serves mounting behavior in females as well as males, and the ventromedial nucleus serves lordosis in males as well as females.[5] Thus, even before we actually look inside the brain, we know that females are not going to be completely lacking a medial preoptic area, nor are males going to be completely lacking a ventromedial nucleus.

More important, it needs to be emphasized that the hypothalamus is just one element, albeit an important one, in the brain systems concerned with sexuality. The medial preoptic area and the ventromedial nucleus are connected with other regions outside the hypothalamus, regions with names that are daunting to the nonspecialist: the *amygdala*, the *septal area*, the *bed nucleus of the stria terminalis*, the *periaqueductal grey*, and quite a few others. Some of these areas have been shown by experiments like those just described also to play a role in sex behavior. One can even trace neural pathways from the cerebral cortex to the hypothalamus, as well as in the reverse direction.

Because the hypothalamus is only one element in the system, there is much uncertainty and debate about what precisely the hypothalamus does for a rat's sex life, or for our sex lives. Some researchers believe that the hypothalamus plays a very "low-level" role. According to this school of thought, it is responsible primarily for regulating the behavioral patterns of copulation, such as mounting and lordosis, but not for "higher-level" functions such as choice of partner and the preliminaries of sex such as approaching and signaling to the chosen partner. According to other researchers, the hypothalamus plays a key role in the initial sex drive and its direction, as well as the execution of the sex act itself. Data obtained in different species have led to conflicting conclusions. In rats, for example, lesions in the medial preoptic area interfere with mounting but leave the male rat with some interest in estrous females. They behave as if they still want to do something with the female but have forgotten what it is. In primates, on the other hand, even quite small lesions within the medial preoptic area can cause males to lose all interest in estrous females; they still have a sex drive (as evidenced by their continuing to masturbate), but they seem to lose any notion that females offer a means to satisfy it.[6]

In view of these uncertainties, we should be very cautious about equating the medial preoptic area and the ventromedial nucleus with the neural centers proposed by Hirschfeld. It is probably safer to suggest that what Hirschfeld proposed as "centers" are actually extended networks, in which the medial preoptic area and the ventromedial nucleus may be elements.

Hypothalamic Surgery

Given what has been recounted in previous chapters, it will come as no surprise to learn that the findings of brain science have been used in attempts to "cure" homosexuality. During the 1960s and 1970s, Günter Dörner and his colleagues studied the effects of brain surgery on his "homosexual" rats. In one kind of experiment, they used male rats who had been castrated early in life. As described in the previous chapter, when such rats are treated with androgens in adulthood they do display sexual behavior, but this behavior is more likely to take the form of the female-typical behavior, lodorsis, and less likely to take the form of the male-typical behavior, mounting, than is seen in normal male rats. Dörner destroyed the ventromedial nucleus in these animals. He reported that after the operation the animals not only ceased to display lordosis but actually mounted females more frequently than before.[7] Dörner's original research papers are somewhat vague about the size and reliability of this effect, but in his public pronouncements he was more outspoken. In a documentary film that Dörner made to illustrate the effects of the neurosurgery, the narrator said boldly "By stereotaxic hypothalamic operation the homosexual male rat was thus transformed into a heterosexual animal."[8] In his 1976 book Dörner explicitly put the operation forward as a possible therapy for human homosexuality.[9]

The first destruction of the ventromedial nucleus in a human being was carried out in 1962 by Fritz Roeder, a neurosurgeon at the University of Göttingen (in what was then West Germany). This operation predated Dörner's research: according to Roeder, he selected his target at the recommendation of H. Orthner, a neurobiologist who had helped define the ventromedial nucleus as playing a role in sexual behavior by means of lesion experiments in rats. The patient was a fifty-two-year-old man who was in prison for having sex with several twelve to fourteen-year-old boys. He volunteered for the operation as an alternative to castration. After the operation, which destroyed the nucleus on one side of the brain only, he experienced a decrease or loss of his homosexual feelings, but did not develop significant attraction to women. He was released from prison and apparently led an uneventful life thereafter.[10]

After this "cure," a number of other men—about forty altogether—were subjected to the same operation. Some of these were operated by Roeder, others by another West German group, led by Gert Dieckmann of the University of the Saarland and R. Hassler of the Max Planck Institute of Brain Research in Frankfurt.[11] The latter group specifically acknowledged the importance of Dörner's work as providing the scientific background for the surgery. All the men who were operated were in prison or in a hospital for the criminally insane. Some were heterosexual rapists, others were described as "pedophile homosexuals." Most of the "pedophiles," however, committed their offenses with post-pubertal youths, not prepubertal boys, suggesting that they did not have the medically defined condition of pedophilia.[12] Their activities (leaving aside the question of consent) would in some cultures be considered to fall within the range of normal sexuality.

For the most part, the operated men experienced a diminution or even extinction of their sex drive. Dieckmann's group wrote: "Concerning the question of sexual reorientation from homosexual to heterosexual interests, it can be stated in general, that in our pedophilic patients the homosexual interests were not eliminated but fewer pedophilic acts occurred and they were able to control their behavior better. In these cases a marriage occurred for reasons of family care and some reported heterosexual intercourse." The most common side-effect of the operation was obesity: this effect, which was also seen in the operated rats, resulted from damage to nearby cell groups in the hypothalamus that play a role in regulating the appetite.

Roeder's results were similar to Dieckmann's, but in his public utterances he was more positive about the procedure. In 1970, for example, he told a reporter for *Medical World News* that he had actually changed his patients' sexual orientation from pedophilic to heterosexual.[13] In the same article John Money of Johns Hopkins Medical School, then one of America's leading sexologists, expressed qualified enthusiasm for Roeder's work and stated that the operation could be performed at Hopkins. As far as I am aware, however, no such operations were ever performed in the United States.

Dörner cited the human experiments as supporting his theories. After the operation, he maintained, the medial preoptic area is liberated from an inhibitory influence exerted by the ventromedial nucleus, and thus does its normal thing, which is to produce male-typical sex behavior. In reality, however, very little male-typical behavior emerges after the operation, either in homosexual men or in "homosexual" rats.

One potential explanation for this result would be that in gay men the medial preoptic area is not merely inhibited but—in accordance with Hirschfeld's theory—has actually developed to a lesser degree than in heterosexual men. In this conception, destroying the ventromedial nucleus does not convert gay men to heterosexuality because there simply is not enough hardware in gay men's medial preoptic area to sustain male-typical behavior, regardless of whether the ventromedial nucleus is present or absent.

The LH Response—A Marker for Homosexuality?

In 1975 Dörner and his colleagues reported that a simple hormonal test distinguished, with a moderate degree of accuracy, homosexual from heterosexual men.[14] The test involved injecting the men with one hormone—estrogen—and measuring their blood levels of another hormone, luteinizing hormone (LH), over the following few days. In most of the gay men, but very few of the straight men, the estrogen injection was followed, three days later, by a marked increase in the concentration of luteinizing hormone in the blood. A "diagnostic test" for homosexuality, it seemed, was coming close to a reality.

To understand the rationale for this piece of research, we need to delve briefly into an aspect of brain function that has not been touched on so far in this book. The hypothalamus is not just influenced in a passive way by sex hormones coming from the gonads; it also secretes hormones of its own that travel back to the gonads and influence *their* function. There is a loop, in other words, whereby brain and gonads influence each other.

The brain-to-gonad influence works via what seems like an unduly complex pathway. There is a set of specialized neurons in the hypothalamus that synthesize and secrete a hormone known as *gonadotropin releasing hormone* or GnRH.[15] GnRH does not enter the general blood circulation but is transported in special blood vessels to the pituitary gland, which sits immediately beneath the hypothalamus, on the floor of the skull. Here it causes a set of glandular cells to release a second hormone, luteinizing hormone. LH in turn travels in the bloodstream to the testes (in men) or the ovaries (in women). In the testes, LH promotes the synthesis and secretion of androgens—mainly testosterone. In the ovaries, LH also promotes the synthesis of androgens, but most of these androgens are immediately converted into estrogens. In both sexes, the gonadal steroids have a feedback influence on the hypo-thalamus. Among other things, they inhibit the release of GnRH from the hypothalamus and hence decrease the secretion of LH from the pituitary gland. Thus, the brain → gonad → brain loop is controlled by *negative feedback*, which tends to keep androgen or estrogen concentrations at stable levels. There is a second mechanism, however, whereby at very high estrogen levels the secretion of LH is *stimulated* rather than being inhibited. This introduces an instability into the control loop and allows LH to rise to very high levels for a brief period. This is one of the key elements of the menstrual cycle; in particular it is involved in triggering ovulation.[16]

In rats, there is a clear difference between the sexes in the way estrogen controls LH release. After a small injection of estrogen, both males and females show a depression of LH release (negative feedback). After large estrogen injections, however, female rats secrete LH in a surgelike fashion (positive feedback), whereas male rats do not.[17] The origin of this difference lies in the early development of the hypothalamus: if testosterone levels are low during the critical perinatal period, as in females, the hypothalamus develops the capacity to respond to estrogen with an LH surge, but if testosterone levels are high, this capacity does not develop.[18]

Thus, when Dörner and his colleagues reported that gay men exhibit an LH surge after an estrogen injection, he was suggesting that the hypothalamus of gay men had developed in such a way as to allow it to participate in the menstrual cycle, and that it must therefore have been exposed to unusually low levels of androgens during prenatal development.

Subsequent research has not lent much support to Dörner's claim. In a study by the Dutch endocrinologist Louis Gooren, no significant differences in the LH responses of gay and straight men were found.[19] In fact, Gooren did not even find any significant differences between the LH responses of men and women.[20] One U.S. study did obtain data supportive of Dörner's results,[21] but a more recent study that attempted to replicate Dörner's methods exactly, found no differences at all between the gay and the straight men.[22] In addition, animal experiments have suggested that a sex difference in the LH response to estrogen may not exist in primates at all, contrary to the picture in rats.[23] In one particularly convincing experiment, two endocrinogists at Texas Tech University transplanted ovaries into male macaque monkeys. These monkeys then proceeded to undergo ovarian cycles like females, suggesting that both male and female monkeys have the same brain mechanisms to sustain the cycle.[24] Thus Dörner, in neglecting to test for the basic sex difference in humans, may have been relying on unwarranted assumptions about the equivalence of hormonal mechanisms in humans and rodents.

Sexual Dimorphism

There are structural differences between male and female brains in humans as in other species. These differences, which are called *sexual dimorphisms*, offer an inviting target for those interested in sexual orientation from a biological perspective. If homosexuality, as Hirschfeld proposed, reflects a sex-atypical process of brain development, then one might expect to find signs of this most readily in the sexually dimorphic structures.

One sexual dimorphism relates to the size of the entire brain. After allowing for differences in body size, men's brains are about one hundred grams (or 7 percent to 8 percent) heavier than women's.[25] It is a matter of debate whether the larger size of men's brains is related to a slightly higher average general intelligence in men, as has been reported in some studies,[26] or to the fact that mental abilities in which men excel (see chapter 7) are unusually expensive in terms of neural hardware.[27] The size difference may even have no functional significance at all. But in any case, at least three studies have reported that the brain size of gay men is the same as that of straight men.[28] Thus, in men at least, homosexuality is not associated with a sex-atypical brain size.

Much more interesting than overall brain size is the question of sexual dimorphism in the hypothalamus. The key discovery in this area was made in 1977 by Roger Gorski and his colleagues at UCLA. They examined stained tissue slices from the hypothalamus of male and female rats and found that a portion of the medial preoptic area, recognizable on account of its darkly staining, closely packed cells, was about eight times larger in males than in females. This region has since been named the *sexually dimorphic nucleus* of the preoptic area, meaning a cell group that is structurally different in the two sexes.[29]

Gorski's discovery was made at a time when the question of innate differences between the sexes was a matter of broad public debate. Many feminists at that time denied the existence of "biological" differences between men and women, outside of the obvious facts of reproductive anatomy and physiology. Thus Germaine Greer, in *The Female Eunuch*, stated categorically that there were no differences between the brains of men and women.[30] Another group of feminists took the very opposite view, promoting the notion that men and women were all but separate species.[31] Caught in the crossfire, Gorski and his colleagues kept a fairly low profile. For one thing, they made no attempt, for over a decade after Gorski's original discovery, to extend their research to the human brain. Rather they concentrated on understanding how the sexual dimorphism in rats comes about.

In brief, the difference in the size of the sexually dimorphic nucleus arises because of differences in the levels of androgens circulating in the blood of male and female rats during the critical period, that straddles the time of birth. If testosterone is administered to female rats for a few days before and after birth, the size of the nucleus in adulthood will be within the male range. (This treatment will also masculinize the rat's sexual behavior, as described in the previous chapter.) It is believed that the hormonal effect requires the conversion of testosterone to estradiol via the aromatase pathway, for males rats who are treated with an estrogen receptor blocker during the critical period fail to develop a nucleus of the usual size. Hormonal treatments in adult rats, on the other hand, fail to alter the size of the sexually dimorphic nucleus.[32]

Since the discovery of the sexually dimorphic nucleus in the preoptic area of rats, comparable nuclei have been recognized in several other species, including guinea pigs, gerbils, ferrets, and possibly also in macaque monkeys.[33] The developmental mechanisms seem to be similar in the different species. One report, however, claims that the size of the gerbil's sexually dimorphic nucleus is affected by sex hormone levels in adulthood, not just during the critical developmental period.

Another line of research, conducted mostly in rats, has focused on the fine details of the sexually dimorphic nucleus: its internal structure, the distribution of neurotransmitters and other substances within it, and its connections. These detailed reports confirm that the medial preoptic area is organized very differently in male and female animals. They also offer potential means to establish whether structures seen in the preoptic area of different species are really homologous or not.[34]

Although the sexual dimorphic nucleus of the preoptic area is the most dramatic example of a sex difference in the rat's brain, there are other structures that show more modest differences. These other structures (the *medial nucleus of the amygdala* and a portion of the *bed nucleus of the stria terminalis*) are about twice as large in males as in females. These structures are interconnected with the sexually dimorphic nucleus of the preoptic area, forming what may be a chain of structures involved in the generation of male-typical sexual behavior. It is believed that these other structures become dimorphic via a hormonal mechanism too, but the details remain to be worked out.[35]

One might expect, on the basis of the findings I have described so far, that there would be a sexual dimorphism of the opposite kind in the ventromedial nucleus of the hypothalamus, that is, that this nucleus, or some part of it, would be larger in females than in males. To date, however, no such difference has been reported. Of course, this could be simply for lack of sufficiently careful observation. But it may also be that the infrequency with which male rats display female-typical behavior (especially lordosis) is not a result of their having a relatively small brain region to generate this behavior. Perhaps there are subtler differences, such as in the neutransmitters or the synaptic connections of this region, that underlie the behavioral differences between the sexes. Another possibility is that the ventromedial nucleus is under some kind of inhibitory or suppressive control from the medial preoptic area. If this were the case, one would expect damage to the medial preoptic area not merely to impair male-typical behavior but also to facilitate female-typical behavior (because the inhibitory input to the ventromedial nucleus would have been removed). Such an effect has not been described in rats, but it does happen to some degree in ferrets.[36]

There is one cell group in the rat's hypothalamus that *is* larger in females than in males. This is a nucleus at the very front of the hypothalamus named the *anteroventral periventricular nucleus* or AVPVN. This nucleus seems to be involved not in the generation of sexual behavior but in the regulation of the ovarian cycle. Again, the size difference results from differences in androgen exposure during development. It is interesting that, in the case of AVPVN, high androgen levels cause the structure to be small, the converse of what happens in the sexually dimorphic nucleus.[37]

In the late 1980s Gorski's group (in particular his graduate student Laura Allen) began looking for sex differences in the human brain. This they did by examining the hypothalamus from brains obtained at autopsy. In 1989 they reported that two nuclei in the medial preoptic area, which they code-named INAH2 and INAH3, were significantly larger in men than in women (see figure 6.1).[38] "INAH" stands for *interstitial nucleus of the anterior hypothalamus*—the nuclei are interstitial in the sense that they lie among fiber tracts. The sex difference for INAH2 was somewhat equivocal in Allen's data, but the difference for INAH3 was robust: on average, INAH3 was between two and three times larger in men than in women, and the difference seemed to exist at all ages. INAH3 is located at a site within the medial preoptic area that corresponds to the location of the sexually dimorphic nucleus in rats; however, it would take more detailed studies of the connections and other characteristics of these cell groups before one could state confidently that the rat and human nuclei are homologous.

Subsequently, Allen and her colleagues extended their work to other parts of the brain. Specifically, they showed that, just as in rats, the bed nucleus of the stria terminalis and the amygdala contained groups of cells that were sexually dimorphic.[39] As with the medial preoptic area, the dimorphism favored men. They also found a structure, however, that was larger in women than in men: this was the *anterior commissure*, a band of fibers that runs between the left and right sides of the brain, interconnecting the two halves of the cerebral cortex. The difference was not very great, and there was considerable overlap in the data from the two sexes; but in a statistical sense the finding appeared to be robust.[40] Yet another connection between the two hemispheres, the *corpus callosum*, also differs between the sexes: the posterior part of the callosum is larger, relative to overall brain size, in women than in men.[41]

Brain Structure and Sexual Orientation

In 1991, while at the Salk Institute in San Diego, I set out to test the idea that the size of structures such as INAH3 might vary with sexual orientation as well as with sex. My specific hypothesis was that the size of INAH3 (and/or INAH2) would be correlated with a sexual drive directed toward females; that is, it would be large in heterosexual men and lesbian women and small in heterosexual women and gay men. I was in fact able to confirm the part of the hypothesis that related to men: INAH3 was between two and three times larger, on average, in the heterosexual men than in the gay men whose brains I examined (see figure 6.2). I also confirmed Allen's report that INAH3 was generally small in women. I was not able to determine whether there were differences related to sexual orientation in women, however, for the simple reason that the medical records of the women whose brains I studied contained no information about their sexual orientation. Given that the women were deceased, it was not a practical possibility to obtain this information.[42]

The findings on INAH3 fit very well with the model put forward by Hirschfeld nearly a century ago, and in my view they greatly strengthen the notion that the development of sexual orientation, at least in men, is closely tied in with the prenatal sexual differentiation of the brain. But it is important to stress several limitations of the study. First, the observations were made on adults who had already been sexually active for a number of years. To make a really compelling case,

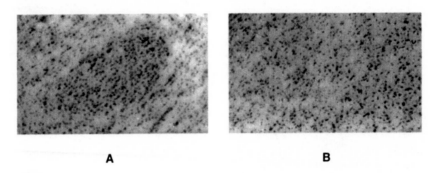

Figure 6.2
Photomicrographs of the region of INAH3 in a heterosexual (A) and a homosexual (B) man. Each small dot is a single nerve cell. In A, INAH3 is clearly recognizable as an oval cluster of cells occupying most of the center of the field. In B, nerve cells are present, but they are not of the same kind as in A and are not clustered into any recognizable nucleus. The difference between A and B is more marked than typically seen: on average, INAH3 is between two and three times larger in heterosexual than in homosexual men.

one would have to show that these neuroanatomical differences existed early in life—preferably at birth. Without such data, there is always at least the theoretical possibility that the structural differences are actually the *result* of differences in sexual behavior—perhaps on the "use it or lose it" principle. Furthermore, even if the differences in the hypothalamus arise before birth, they might still come about from a variety of causes, including genetic differences, differences in stress exposure, and many others. It is possible that the development of INAH3 (and perhaps other brain regions) represents a "final common path" in the determination of sexual orientation, a path to which innumerable prior factors may contribute.

Another limitation arises because most of the gay men whose brains I studied died of complications of AIDS. Although I am confident that the small size of INAH3 in these men was not an effect of the disease,[43] there is always the possibility that gay men who die of AIDS are not representative of the entire population of gay men. For example, they might have a stronger preference for receptive anal intercourse, the major risk factor for acquiring HIV infection. Thus, if one wished, one could make the argument that structural differences in INAH3 relate more to actual behavioral patterns of copulation than to sexual orientation as such. It will not be possible to settle this issue definitively until some method becomes available to measure the size of INAH3 in living people who can be interviewed in detail about their sexuality.

I should emphasize that INAH3 is not the only sexually dimorphic cell group in the human brain. As mentioned earlier, Allen and her colleagues have located at least two others, located within brain regions called the amygdala and the bed nucleus of the stria terminalis. Whether these cell groups also vary with sexual orientation remains to be determined. For that reason alone it would be presumptuous to lay the entire "cause" of a person's sexual orientation at the feet of just one of these cell groups simply because that one was the first to be identified. When future research has delineated the entirety of the sexually dimorphic circuitry within the human brain and has established which parts of this circuitry are sex-atypical in homosexual individuals and which are not, it will be possible to form a more educated hypothesis about the brain basis of sexual orientation.

Since I published my findings on INAH3, Laura Allen and her colleagues have reported on a second difference between the brains of gay and heterosexual men. This difference is in the size of the anterior commissure. As mentioned earlier, the anterior commissure is generally somewhat larger in women than in men. When Allen and her associates compared the size of the structure in gay and straight men, however, they found that it was larger in the gay men. In fact, after standardizing their data by taking differences in overall brain size into account, the anterior commissure was about the same size in gay men as in women. Here again then we have a brain structure that is sexually dimorphic, but whose size is sex-atypical in gay men. The significance of this finding is uncertain. The anterior commissure is not a group of brain cells but a bundle of nerve fibers interconnecting the two cerebral hemispheres. It is not likely to be directly involved in the regulation of sexual behavior. It is possible that differences in the size of the commissure are related to differences in the lateralization of brain functions (see chapter 7).[44]

Because my findings on INAH3 and sexual orientation attracted a great deal of media attention and public interest when they were published in 1991, they have also faced intense scrutiny and criticism. One person who has been especially critical is William Byne, a psychiatrist and neurobiologist, now at Mount Sinai Medical Center in New York. Byne has in the past conducted neuroanatomical research on sex differences in the hypothalamus of guinea pigs;[45] he is therefore well qualified to point out the problems with this kind of work, and he has done so in a number of publications.[46] He has at one time or another suggested that: (1) INAH3 may not exist at all, (2) if it does, it may not be sexually dimorphic, (3) if it is, it may not differ between gay and straight men, and (4) if it does, that does not prove that the size of INAH3 is the cause of a man's sexual orientation. Byne has based his case on a variety of arguments: he has, for example, pointed out that there is a long history of conflicting reports concerning sexual dimorphism in the brain, and he has suggested that the small size of INAH3 in gay men who died of AIDS might be caused by certain drugs used in the treatment of that disease. Byne's publications have been used (probably much against his desire) by anti-gay activists and lawyers, for example, in the litigation concerning Amendment 2, the antigay rights measure in Colorado (see chapters 12 and 14).

Rather than merely voice criticisms, however, Byne has set out to determine the facts of the matter for himself by collecting and examining his own sample of human hypothalami. On the basis of his results so far, Byne has concluded that INAH *does* exist, that it *is* sexually dimorphic, that it may well be homologous to the sexually dimorphic nucleus of the rat's hypothalamus, and that its size is not affected by AIDS.[47] At this point, neither Byne nor anyone else has replicated (or refuted) the key finding, namely, the difference between INAH3 in gay and straight men. Furthermore, even if he or other researchers do replicate that finding, his last point (which I also have been at pains to stress) will remain valid.

It seems likely that the finding of morphological differences between the brains of gay and straight men will be followed by findings of other differences—in neurotransmitter distribution, for example—just as happened in the rat research. It is also possible that differences may be found in the patterns of functional activity—patterns that can be visualized in the brains of living people through imaging techniques such as positron emission tomography or PET.

The recent findings on the brain basis of sexual orientation have succeeded, as few previous studies on the topic have, in arousing the attention both of the gay community and of the general public. Although earlier biological reports on sexual orientation were generally received with suspicion or hostility by gay people, and were often put to use in ways that were harmful to them, the more recent findings have generally been welcomed. Among the reasons for this may be the improving climate for gays and lesbians in this country, a climate that makes the abuse of biological knowledge to oppress gay people far less likely than it was ten or twenty years ago. In addition, the fact that the current wave of scientists working in the area are either themselves gay, or are well disposed to gay people, tends to diminish anxiety that the research is intended to harm the gay community. Nevertheless, some gays and lesbians still express the fear that science is likely to harm them, whatever the sympathies of the scientists themselves. I will explore these issues further after I have completed the survey of the science itself.

7

Mental Traits

Do gays and lesbians differ from heterosexual men and women in psychological traits other than their sexual orientation? If so, do these differences result from the experience of being gay or lesbian in a generally homophobic culture, or are they evidence that homosexuality is one item in a broader package of inborn traits? And if homosexuality does come as part of a package, is there any generalization one can make about it—for example, that it represents a global shift in gender? The answers to these questions are of obvious relevance in any attempt to understand the nature and origins of sexual orientation. In addition, however, they are relevant to the question of whether gay people are distinct enough from heterosexuals that they should be thought of like an ethnic or other minority, with all the social and legal implications that such minority status carries with it.

Sex Differences

Because the "gender-shift" theory is the conceptual framework for so many of the psychological studies on sexual orientation, it makes sense to begin with a review of what is known about cognitive and other psychological differences between men and women. Historically, of course, the field has been contaminated by sexism: women were intellectually and emotionally weaker than men, or they had talents that suited them only for certain roles in life—in the kitchen, the nursery, or the home generally. Much of feminist thought over the last thirty years has been devoted to overthrowing such stereotypes, and thus has tended to minimize any inborn psychological differences between men and women. There has always been another current within feminism, however, which has portrayed women as markedly different from men—almost as a separate (although enslaved) species. In this vein some feminist writers have emphasized the existence of innate psychological differences between the sexes, albeit with a more positive assessment of women's qualities than tradition had accorded them. In the face of these strong and conflicting pressures, psychologists have tried to remain objective by concentrating on traits that can be measured with simple, replicable tests.[1]

One area of mental skill that has rather consistently yielded sizable sex differences is that of spatial ability. Men generally outperform women in a variety of spatial tasks.[2] One such task is mental rotation: a subject is shown a two-dimensional view of an object and asked to match it with other views—the task requires forming a three-dimensional mental image of the object and rotating it.[3] Another spatial task in which men excel is targeting: in a typical experiment, the subject is asked to throw a ball or a dart as accurately as possible to a point that is several feet away.[4] Men also learn mazes faster than women, especially when global cues are available, but women do as well or better than men when the maze-learning task requires the memorization of local landmarks.[5] Women do outperform men in some spatial tasks that require speedy and accurate manipulation of objects close to the body, for example putting pegs rapidly into a pegboard.[6]

Men also do better than women (on average) on tests of mathematical reasoning and geometry, but women tend to be faster and more accurate calculators.[7] This higher ability at calculation may be linked to a general female superiority at tasks requiring rapid processing of information: thus women also tend to be faster than men at certain verbal tasks, such as naming as many words as possible that fall in a particular category, finding a match for a particular object among a set of objects, or determining which object in one set of objects is missing from another set.[8] Sometimes these abilities are referred to collectively as "perceptual speed," although it may be more than simply the perceptual processes that are faster in women.

There is considerable evidence that the sex differences in some of these traits result in significant part from biological processes, and in particular that they are connected with the sexual differentiation of the brain under the influence of circulating sex hormones, a process that in humans probably takes place before birth. Among the lines of evidence pointing to this conclusion are the following. Some of the sex differences are present very early in life and do not seem to depend on environmental differences. Taking targeting skills as an example, differences in this task are evident already in preschool-age children, before the sports experience of boys and girls begins to diverge.[9] The difference seen in adults persists after allowing for differences in sports experience, or after minimizing the effects of sports experience (for example, by making the subjects use their nonpreferred hand or throw in an unusual manner).[10] Women with congenital adrenal hyperplasia (CAH), who were exposed to unusually high levels of androgenic (testosterone-like) hormones during fetal life, score better on several tests of spatial ability, including mental rotation, than their unaffected female relatives,[11] whereas individuals with the androgen insensitivity syndrome (AIS—see chapter 5) do worse than their unaffected male or female relatives.[12] Somewhat comparable sex differences in spatial ability have been measured in laboratory animals, and manipulation of sex hormone levels during development alters the animals' spatial abilities in adult life.[13] There is even evidence that in adult humans changes in circulating hormone levels associated with the menstrual cycle or with the seasons of the year can influence cognitive abilities.[14]

Finally, some of the differences make evolutionary sense. In early human societies, men were probably responsible for exploration, hunting, and warfare, tasks that place a premium on skills involving extrapersonal space. Women, on the other hand, probably spent much of their time in gathering and in tasks centered on the home site. Such tasks may have emphasized skills in intrapersonal (within-reach) space. It would make sense if this division of labor, perpetuated over countless generations, led to selective pressure for genetic changes that caused women's and men's brains to develop somewhat differently. There have been eloquent critics of these kinds of evolutionary hypotheses, however,[15] and one has to admit that they are not easy to test in any meaningful way.

Differences also exist between women and men in the distribution of cognitive functions between the two sides of the brain. It is generally true of both sexes that language skills are more dependent on the left than the right hemisphere of the cerebral cortex, whereas spatial skills are more dependent on the right hemisphere. This is known from studies of the effects of injuries to the left or right hemisphere, as well as from the use of imaging techniques such as positron emission tomography that allow the patterns of brain activity to be visualized in living subjects during verbal or other tasks.[16] But there are differences between the sexes in this pattern of functional lateralization: for example, in women the two hemispheres tend to collaborate more in the execution of language and spatial tasks.[17] Damage to the left hemisphere tends to cause more severe and long-lasting language impairment (aphasia) in men than in women, perhaps because women have a greater residual capacity for language in the right hemisphere. (Doreen Kimura and Elizabeth Hampson have some evidence for an alternative explanation: they suggest that in women language functions are located further forward in the left hemisphere, away from the regions most commonly affected by strokes.[18]) If women do use their two hemispheres more collaboratively than do men, this might be related to the larger size of the anterior commissure and of part of the corpus callosum in women (see chapter 6); in other words, more connections between the two hemispheres may be required if they are working jointly on tasks than if they are parceling out tasks between them.

Handedness is another characteristic that seems to differ between the sexes. The majority of both men and women are right-handed—a bias that is displayed already before birth[19]—but, according to a number of studies, a slightly larger fraction of men than of women are left-handed or mixed-handed (performing some tasks with their left hand and some tasks with their right hand).[20] Actually, complete left-handedness is uncommon: many people who write with their left hand do preferentially use their right hand for some tasks.

Handedness is related to cerebral lateralization. Right-handedness reflects the predominant role of the left cerebral hemisphere in the planning and execution of body movements, a function known as *praxis*. The reason for this is that the neural connections between the brain and the body are crossed, so that the cerebral praxis system has more direct access to the right hand and foot than to the left. In left-handers and mixed-handers there is an increased likelihood of finding right-hemisphere or bilateral representation of the praxis and language systems; however, left-hemisphere representation is the most common arrangement for all groups, even for exclusive left-handers. Thus, the brain basis of left-handedness is not fully understood. There are reports of brain structural differences related to handedness, especially involving the corpus callosum and the language area of the cerebral cortex.[21]

Men are generally are more competitive, more aggressive, and more criminally violent than women.[22] This difference is already apparent in childhood in that boys participate more in play fighting and rough-and-tumble play. As with spatial skills, observations of CAH girls[23] and hormonal manipulations in animals[24] suggest that hormone differences during fetal life contribute to sex differences in aggressive behavior. Doubtless these biologically programmed differences are modified or bolstered by differences in the way boys and girls are treated in our or other societies.

There are also psychological differences between man and women in the sphere of sexuality itself.[25] Men desire to have a greater number of different sex partners than do women.[26] Women reject the sexual advances of men more frequently than men reject the sexual advances of females.[27] In addition, men have a greater interest than women in visual sexual stimuli,[28] put more emphasis on their partners' youthfulness[29] and physical beauty,[30] and are less concerned with their partners' social status.[31] Men are more upset by their partners' sexual infidelity than are women, but women are more upset by their partners' emotional infidelity.[32] Many of these sex differences are seen in animals as well as humans and fit well with evolutionary theory.[33] For example, the fact that females are less open to casual sex than males reflects the greater investment they make in reproduction and the limited number of offspring they can have. When it comes to mating strategy, females do best to emphasize quality over quantity.

Women spend more time looking after infants than do men. Certainly anatomical differences (the fact that women have breasts) as well as cultural constraints are important here. But there is good reason to think that inborn mental differences also play a role. Young girls spend more time than boys on activities that could be construed as rehearsal for motherhood, especially on doll play,[34] whereas CAH girls spend less time on such activities and express less interest in becoming mothers than do their unaffected sisters.[35] Animal experiments as well as observations of human parenting suggest that maternal behavior develops out of a complex interaction between innate programs of brain development, hormonal influences on the brain during pregnancy, and sensory interactions with infants.[36]

It should be emphasized that both the existence and the causes of cognitive differences between the sexes are still disputed. Even among biologically trained researchers, there are those who take a very "antibiological" view of the subject.[37]

Cognitive Differences with Sexual Orientation

Among studies comparing the cognitive traits of homosexual and heterosexual people, one finding has been rather consistent: gay men do worse that straight men in tests of spatial ability. In some studies, lesbians outperform heterosexual women in such tests. One such study was carried out in 1993 by Jeff Hall, a student in the laboratory of

Doreen Kimura.[38] Hall and Kimura tested the accuracy of heterosexual men and women in throwing a ball to a target. They confirmed the basic sex difference in this task (the heterosexual men were significantly more accurate than the heterosexual women), but they also found that the gay men were significantly less accurate than the straight men; in fact, they were about as bad as the heterosexual women. Conversely, the lesbians did *better* than heterosexual women, although the difference did not quite reach statistical significance. The gay men in the sample had less sports experience than the heterosexual men, and the lesbians had more sports experience than the heterosexual women, so one might be tempted to think that it was this difference in sports experience, rather than any innate differences in targeting ability, that was responsible for Hall and Kimura's results. But statistical analysis of the data suggested that this was not the case: after allowing for this difference in experience, the difference between the homosexual and heterosexual groups persisted. Common sense suggests that native talent and sports experience go together: if a lesbian throws well, for example, she will be more likely to enjoy softball and thus to hone her throwing skills further.

This particular result was of course consistent with the "gendershift" model. But in another part of the study Hall and Kimura examined their subjects' skill and speed at a pegboard task and got different results. They confirmed the basic sex difference in favor of females,[39] but the performance of gay men and lesbians was not transposed: rather, gay men performed like straight men, and lesbians performed like straight women.

Other studies have reported that gay men do worse than straight men on mental rotation and other visuo-spatial tasks, although the results are not all consistent.[40] Three studies that compared spatial abilities in lesbian and heterosexual women, on the other hand, failed to detect any differences.[41] Thus the difference observed in women by Hall and Kimura may simply have been due to chance, or possibly it reflected the use of a performance task rather than the pencil-and-paper tasks that most researchers employ.

There is little evidence that gays and lesbians differ from heterosexuals in general perceptual speed or in verbal fluency. Although

there is one study reporting that gay men outperform both heterosexual men and women on tests of "verbal IQ,"[42] other studies have
failed to detect any differences,[43] or have reported slight differences
that did not reach statistical significance.[44] In the context of the gender-shift model, it is perhaps not surprising that it has been difficult
to show differences in verbal skills related to sexual orientation, given
that the basic sex difference is a weak one.

Brain Lateralization and Handedness

So far, few studies have directly examined brain lateralization in lesbians or gay men. One study reported that gay men are less strongly
lateralized in visual function than straight men.[45] Another study found
no difference in cerebral lateralization between homosexual and heterosexual men and women in a language perception test.[46]

There are quite a number of studies of handedness and homosexuality. Such studies are of course much easier to carry out than direct
studies of brain lateralization: all one needs to do is to find a sample
of gay people and some heterosexual controls and ask them which
hand they use for various tasks. Yet the results are very conflicting. According to Hirschfeld's data (gathered in Germany before 1920), gay
men were almost twice as likely to be left-handed as were heterosexual men.[47] Two reports have claimed that both lesbians and gay men
are left-shifted compared with heterosexual women and men (i.e., they
are less consistently right-handed).[48] There are also reports limited to
men that agree with Hirschfeld that gay and bisexual men are left-
shifted.[49] Yet several other studies, some based on large samples, have
failed to see any relationship between handedness and sexual orientation.[50] And according to a preliminary report, Dean Hamer and his
colleagues replicated the finding that lesbians are left-shifted but found
that gay men are *right*-shifted.[51] Hamer's finding is what one would
predict on the basis of the gender-shift hypothesis, but until the researchers can reach some consensus on the facts of the case, it seems
unwise to draw any conclusions from handedness studies. Why the
different studies are so conflicting is unclear: it may have to do with dif-

ferences in the definitions of sexual orientation and handedness used in the particular studies, the small size or atypical nature of some of the samples, or changes in handedness that may have occurred in the population over the years.

Fingerprints

Recently, Jeff Hall and Doreen Kimura extended the search for a connection between lateralization and sexual orientation by studying physical asymmetries of the body. Such asymmetries are common and to some extent are related to sex. In women, for example, there is a statistically significant tendency for the left breast to be larger than the right, and in men, the right testicle tends to be larger than the left.[52] Interestingly, there is a connection between this asymmetry and cognitive function. Kimura has shown than, even within each sex considered separately, individuals whose right breast or testicle is larger perform statistically better on cognitive tests at which men typically excel, such as tests of spatial ability or mathematical reasoning. Conversely, individuals whose left breast or testicle is larger do better on tests at which women typically excel, such as tests of perceptual speed.[53]

The asymmetry that Hall and Kimura studied was in the pattern of ridges in the fingerprints. In the majority of people, both women and men, there are more ridges on the fingers of the right hand than on the fingers of the left hand, but more women than men have the minority, leftward asymmetry. When Hall and Kimura compared the fingerprint patterns in gay and straight men, they found that more gay than straight men have the leftward pattern of asymmetry.[54] In other words, the distribution of fingerprint patterns is sex-atypical in gay men. They have yet not reported on fingerprint patterns in lesbians.

Hall and Kimura have also studied the connection between fingerprint asymmetry and cognitive function in gay men. They used a listening task[55] that provides information about the lateralization of language functions in the brain. They found that gay men with a rightward fingerprint asymmetry usually have language represented in the left cerebral hemisphere, whereas gay men with a leftward fingerprint asymmetry have a more bilateral representation of language.[56] Gay men with the leftward fingerprint asymmetry are also more likely to be left-handed or ambidextrous than gay men with the rightward asymmetry or with symmetrical patterns.

Fingerprint patterns are established by about the sixteenth week of fetal life.[57] Hall and Kimura's findings (which have not yet been replicated) therefore support the notion that sexual orientation is connected with prenatal processes of sexual differentiation.

Hall and Kimura's findings are a faint echo of the notion, propounded by Hirschfeld and many other sexologists of the nineteenth and early twentieth centuries, that one can recognize homosexual people on the basis of sex-atypical bodily characteristics such as hip width, body fat distribution, hairiness, facial appearance, and so on. But no one, least of all Hall and Kimura, is attempting to resurrect those ideas. There may be a few special cases, such as that of congenital adrenal hyperplasia, where homosexuality and an intersexed anatomy are linked. Generally, however, the bodies of gay male are unambiguously male, and the bodies of lesbians are unambiguously female. Any biological theory that attempts to explain homosexuality in terms of atypical sexual differentiation must also explain why there is a discordance between the sexual differentiation of the body and that of the brain circuits that mediate sexual attraction.[58]

Aggressiveness

As discussed already in chapter 4, there is strong evidence that children who later become homosexual exhibit a constellation of gender-nonconformist traits that include differences in participation in play fighting, team sports, and so on. In particular, the lower aggressiveness of boys who later become gay, compared with boys who later become straight, has been documented both by retrospective[59] and prospective[60] studies.

Although these childhood gender-nonconformist traits seem to become less marked and less consistent after puberty,[61] there is still evidence for some connection between aggressiveness and sexual orientation in adulthood. In a survey conducted by Lee Ellis and his colleagues at Minot State University, for example, gay men reported having engaged in significantly less criminal or violent behavior than did straight men, whereas for bisexual or lesbian women it was the reverse: they reported more criminal or violent acts than heterosexual women.[62] Another study, by Brian Gladue and Michael Bailey, broke aggressiveness down into three components: physical aggressiveness, verbal aggressiveness, and competitiveness. They found that gay men showed significantly less physical aggressiveness that heterosexual men but were similar in verbal aggressiveness and competitiveness. They found no differences in aggressiveness between lesbian and straight women.[63] Thus the evidence, limited as it is, suggests that gay men at least are gender-atypical in aggressiveness, and that this difference may be limited to physical acts of aggression.

Sexuality

Promiscuity (by which I mean a tendency to have many different sex partners) is one sexually differentiated trait that seems not to be "transposed" in gay people. Surveys of the actual sex behavior of lesbians and gay men have indicated that gay men have far more sex partners than do lesbians. Sometimes the reported differences have been extreme. In a study conducted in the San Francisco Bay area in the 1970s, for example, almost one-half of the white gay men and one-third of the black gay men claimed to have had at least five hundred different male sex partners, whereas most of the lesbians had had less than ten female sex partners.[64]

Far from being sex transposed in this trait, it seems likely that gay men in contemporary western cultures have more different sex partners than even heterosexual men—a kind of hypermasculinity, if you will.[65] But the reason for this may not be that gay men *desire* more sex partners than straight men but simply that they come closer to *fulfilling* their desire, because they are not constrained by the unwillingness of women to have sex with them.[66] This interpretation was supported by the results of a recent study by Michael Bailey and his colleagues.[67] They asked gay men, lesbians, and straight men and women a series of questions about their actual sexual behavior as well as their interest in uncommitted sex. They found that, in terms of interest, gay men scored like straight men and lesbians scored like straight women. But in terms of actual behavior, the gay men scored higher—they achieved more uncommitted sex—than the straight men.

Bailey's group looked at a number of other traits connected with sexuality. They found some cases where the scores for gay men or lesbians were shifted toward those of the other sex. Gay men placed less emphasis than straight men on their partners' youthfulness and also placed less emphasis on sexual fidelity (as opposed to emotional fidelity). Lesbians were more interested than heterosexual women in visual sexual stimuli and were less interested in their partners' status. But in other cases, gays and lesbians scored like heterosexuals. For example, gay men were as interested as straight men in visual sexual stimuli and in their partners' physical attractiveness, whereas lesbians, like heterosexual women, emphasized emotional over sexual fidelity, had little interest in uncommitted sex, and rated their partners' physical attractiveness as relatively unimportant. Although Bailey's group found that lesbians were "sex-typical" in terms of not emphasizing youthfulness as a criterion for sexual attractiveness, another study did find a difference between lesbians and heterosexual women in this regard—the lesbians did not prefer older partners as the heterosexual women did.[68]

Overview

It is only in the last five years or so that substantial, objective research has been done on the normal mental characteristics of gays and lesbians. Given the brief history of this field it is perhaps not surprising that there are so many conflicting findings. It will require several more years at least before any kind of consensus is reached, particularly with regard to topics like verbal skills and handedness, where the differences, if they exist at all, are probably very small.

Clearly the available data offer some support for the idea that homosexuality is part of a package of sex-transposed traits, and in that sense they back up the ideas of Ulrichs and Hirschfeld with some cold statistics. It could well be that there are other sex-atypical traits awaiting scientific investigation—empathy in gay men, leadership qualities in lesbians, and so on, and that together these traits powerfully influence the career choices, public image, and self-image of lesbians and gay men. Equally, though, it seems that some sex-linked traits are not shifted in homosexual men and women. It may be this combination of sex-typical and sex-atypical characteristics that give gays and lesbians some claim to be a third sex, or better, a "third gender."

There are three major caveats to this line of thought. First, no amount of psychological investigation of adult lesbians and gay men can establish conclusively which aspects of their minds developed as part of some prenatal program of brain differentiation, which in response to socialization, and which from some subtle interaction between the two. Even the parallels with animal development are less than fully persuasive: it is a clear possibility that nature achieves similar results in different species through different means—through prenatal hormonal control in rats, say, and through social interactions in humans.

Second, many of the findings need to be replicated in cross-cultural studies to see whether they have universal validity or whether perhaps they result from peculiarities of the way gay and lesbians are reared and treated in the United States or westernized countries generally.

The third limitation of the research that has been done so far is that is has generally treated gays and lesbians as uniform groups, with little concern for differences within each group. This kind of simplification is inevitable and necessary in a new field of study. But there are obvious gender distinctions *within* the populations of lesbians and gay men— the butch and femme lesbians, the straight-acting and "queeny" gay men, and probably many variations on these. Until cognitive psychology has told us something about this kind of diversity, it will not have explained homosexuality or even have drawn a persuasive likeness of it.

Stress

In 1980 Günter Dörner suggested that stress might be a major cause of homosexuality in men.[1] Not stress during childhood or adult life—although gay men are certainly exposed to enough of that—but stress before birth, during the critical period for the sexual differentiation of the brain. His idea was that stress experienced by a pregnant woman somehow communicates itself to the male fetus and prevents it from undergoing the normal process of brain masculinization. Thus the fetus is predisposed to homosexuality in adulthood.

Dörner's theory is an interesting one in that the proposed mechanism operates at the interface of "nature" and "nurture"—the ultimate cause of homosexuality, according to the theory, is environmental, but it operates before birth through biological processes of brain differentiation. Thus, from the point of view of the newborn child, his predisposition to become gay is an inborn characteristic—as natural to him as if it were laid down in his genes.

The stress theory is also a troubling one. For while stress in some form or another is part and parcel of human existence, what Dörner had in mind was overwhelming, catastrophic stress—the kind of tragic life events that we would do anything to avoid. To anyone who thinks well of gay people, who believes that they are a valuable facet of the kaleidoscope of human diversity, the notion that gay men acquire their defining characteristic as a result of such events is threatening, even repellant. For if the cause of homosexuality (in men at least) is so undesirable, then must not homosexuality itself be undesirable—if not with the force of logic, then at least through "guilt by association"? It seems fitting that Dörner, who in the past at least was an advocate of measures to prevent or eliminate homosexuality, should come up with a theory of this kind, a theory that seems to lend justification, even urgency, to preventive measures.

To give Dörner his due, his theory does have one thing going for it: it is based on a solid body of research conducted on animals. Much more questionable, as we shall see later, is the applicability of this animal research to the issue of sexual orientation in humans.

The Animal Model

Before getting to the crucial animal experiments, it is necessary to describe briefly the body's response to stress, which involves a complex cascade of events originating in the hypothalamus. The sequence is analogous to the GnRH→LH→gonadal steroid cascade described in chapter 6, but it involves the adrenal glands rather than the gonads. During stress, a group of hypothalamic neurons secrete a hormone known as corticotropin releasing factor or CRF. The CRF travels through special blood vessels to the pituitary gland, where it causes the release of a second hormone, adrenocorticotropic hormone or ACTH. ACTH travels through the general bloodstream to the cortex (outer rim) of the adrenal glands, where it causes the synthesis and release of a class of "stress hormones" known as *glucocorticoids*. (The most important glucocorticoid in humans is hydrocortisone, whereas in rats it is a slightly different compound named corticosterone.) A second component of the stress system, involving the release of adrenalin and similar compounds from the adrenal glands, is less important to the present story.[2]

Activation of the stress system mobilizes the body's emergency energy supplies and also suppresses nonessential body systems such as the digestive, immune, and reproductive systems. It is this last effect that is important to us here. The stress system depresses the reproductive system in several ways. First, stress blocks the secretion of GnRH by the hypothalamus. This blockage involves the action of another set of chemical messengers, the brain's "endogenous opiates" or *endorphins*. Second, CRF not only promotes the release of ACTH but also *depresses* the release of luteinizing hormone (LH). A third interaction between the stress and reproductive systems occurs at the level of the gonads: glucocorticoids reduce the sensitivity of the testes and ovaries to LH. The net effect is that, in males, stress causes a drop in the levels of testosterone in the blood, and can inhibit sperm formation. In females, stress lowers estrogen levels and can prevent ovulation.

Dörner's idea that prenatal stress might have something to do with homosexuality has its origins in experiments on rats carried out during the 1970s. These experiments were carried out primarily by Ingeborg Ward and her colleagues at Villanova University.[3] In a typical experiment, Ward stressed pregnant rats by confining them in narrow plastic tubes for forty-five minutes, during which time they were exposed to bright lights. This experience was repeated three times a day during the third week of pregnancy (days fourteen to twenty-one of the twenty-two-day pregnancy). Later, when the male offspring of these pregnancies were tested for sexual behavior with estrous females, they generally failed to perform. If they were then castrated and given estrogen and progesterone (a treatment that mimics the hormonal status of an estrous female rat) they would display lordosis and allow themselves to be mounted by stud males. Ward hypothesized that prenatal stress of the mother stresses the fetuses too, and that this fetal stress alters androgen levels in the blood of the fetuses during the critical period for the organization of sexual behavior. Later it was verified that there are such changes: the stress systems of the fetuses are indeed activated during the periods of maternal stress,[4] and testosterone levels are altered in the fetal circulation: on the seventeenth day of gestation testosterone levels are higher than in unstressed fetuses, whereas on the following two days, which probably constitute a more important period for the sexual differentiation of the brain, testosterone levels are markedly *lower* than in the unstressed fetuses.[5] In addition, the levels of aromatase (the enzyme that converts testosterone to estrogen) in the brains of the stressed animals was lower than in unstressed animals on days eighteen, nineteen, and twenty.[6] Thus it is likely that less estrogen was produced in the brains of the stressed fetuses.

Probably as a result of these hormonal changes, prenatal stress affects the structure and function of brain regions involved in generating sexual behavior. This is most obvious in the medial preoptic area of the rat's hypothalamus. The sexually dimorphic nucleus (SDN) in the prenatally stressed male rats is smaller than that of unstressed male rats (although it is remains larger than the SDN of female rats).[7] In addition, the neurons of the medial preoptic area of prenatally stressed rats are less strongly activated by the presence of sexually receptive females than are the same neurons in unstressed rats.[8] Structural effects of prenatal stress have also been observed in other sexually dimorphic regions of the nervous system: in the cerebral cortex,[9] the anterior commissure,[10] and in a region of the spinal cord that controls the musculature of the penis.[11]

Ward's "prenatal stress syndrome" has been replicated in other laboratories and extended in various ways: it has been shown that the same syndrome can be produced in mice,[12] that other kinds of stress, such as crowding[13] or malnutrition,[14] have a similar effect, and that the males exposed to prenatal stress are atypical not only in their sexual behavior but in other sex-differentiated traits—they are less aggressive,[15] and they more readily display parental behavior toward pups.[16]

It has become apparent more recently that other treatments besides environmental stress can produce very similar effects. In particular, treatment of pregnant rats with alcohol or with opiate-like drugs leads to a similar syndrome in the male offspring.[17] Furthermore, the effects of prenatal stress are prevented if, simultaneously with the stress, the pregnant rats are given an opiate-blocking drug such as naltrexone. Thus it may be that the effects of maternal stress on the fetuses are mediated at least in part by the endorphin system of the brain. This makes sense because, as was noted above, endorphins are involved in the suppression of GnRH secretion by stress.

Research on Humans

Dörner seized on Ward's observations to develop a stress theory of homosexuality in humans, specifically in men. He argued that stress on pregnant women might predispose their male offspring to engage in same-sex behavior. As a first attempt to test the hypothesis, he attempted to determine how many gay men were born during wartime compared with peacetime: this he did by checking the birth dates of several hundred gay men who were registered by venereologists in various parts of East Germany. In his 1980 paper, he reported that there was an excess of men who were born during the Second World War or the two years following the war (when conditions were still very stressful in Germany).

In a second study, Dörner asked sixty gay men and one hundred heterosexual men about stressful events affecting their mothers during pregnancy. The results were remarkable: according to the men's reports, 35 percent of the mothers of gay men had suffered severe stress during pregnancy (events such as the death of the husband at war, the home being bombed, rape, or the pregnancy being unwanted), and another 33.3 percent had suffered moderate stress. Among the mothers of the heterosexual men, on the other hand, not a single one had suffered severe stress, and only 6 percent had suffered moderate stress.[18]

It is rare to find such large differences between groups in any kind of psychological study. If one took these data at face value, one would have to admit that Dörner had hit on the major cause of homosexuality. As if to ram home the social implications of his hypothesis, Dörner ended his paper with the following sentence: "These findings indicate that prevention of war and undesired pregnancies may render possible a partial prevention of the development of sexual deviations."

Efforts to replicate Dörner's findings have largely failed. Two German psychologists who made a close study of the sexual behavior of men born during the Second World War found no evidence for an increased incidence of homosexuality. That they considered their research a rebuke to Dörner's sociopolitical stance was made evident by their concluding comment: "Homosexual men can go on loving peace and getting involved in the peace movement."[19] In another German study, from the University of Kiel, three researchers located detailed medical records of a cohort of women who were pregnant during the early 1960s. The records included information on stressful events, diseases, and so on. The researchers tracked down fifty of the men who were born of these pregnancies and found no correlation between their sexual orientation and the occurrence of stressful events during their mothers' pregnancies.[20]

In 1988 Lee Ellis and his colleagues at Minot State University published a report in which women who had had gay, lesbian, bisexual or heterosexual children were asked about stressful events during and before their pregnancies.[21] In contrast to Dörner's findings, the number and severity of stressful events during "homosexual" and "heterosexual" pregnancies were not significantly different. When Ellis and his colleagues broke the data down into three-month periods, they did find a marginally significant trend for there to be more severe stress during the second trimester in pregnancies that gave rise to gay males. This might have been the result of random variations in the data, however, given that they found a similar difference for a three-month period a year *before* the women became pregnant. Thus, at most, Ellis's data provide very weak support for Dörner's hypothesis.

Probably the most careful study of the issue was done by Michael Bailey and his colleagues (then at the University of Texas, Austin).[22] They recruited a large number of mothers, some of whose sons were gay and some heterosexual, and gave them questionnaires about potentially stressful events during their pregnancies. The mothers of homosexual children were also asked about other pregnancies that had given rise to heterosexual children. There was absolutely no tendency for the mothers to report more (or more severe) stressful events during pregnancies that gave rise to gay men than during pregnancies that gave rise to heterosexual men.

Bailey's data were therefore in radical disagreement with Dörner's. One obvious reason for the discrepancy is that Dörner had relied on the recollections of the gay men concerning what they had been told about their mothers' pregnancies, rather than asking the mothers directly. The gay men might have reported more stressful events for any number of reasons, for example, because their mothers had been more confiding with them. It is also very possible that the interviewers unconsciously pressured the gay men to report more stressful events: there is no indication that the interviews were conducted "blind" to the men's sexual orientation. Probably the most favorable comment one could make on Dörner's hypothesis at this point is that it might conceivably be part of the explanation in a minority of cases, but the great majority of gay men seem to be homosexual for some other reason entirely.

Before we breathe too deep a sigh of relief, though, I should mention that Bailey's group did make one unexpected finding. When they carried out a similar survey of the mothers of *lesbians*, they did find an effect: the mothers reported more stressful events during the pregnancies that gave rise to lesbian daughters than during pregnancies that gave rise to heterosexual daughters. The difference was not very great, but it was statistically significant. Because there was no theoretical reason to expect this result, its meaning is unclear. It may simply reflect a tendency for mothers to remember more stressful events during the "lesbian" pregnancies because, ever since they found out that their daughters were lesbian, they had been racking their brains to figure out what "went wrong." But the finding means that the stress theory of homosexuality may not yet have been finally put to rest.

Given that the prenatal stress syndrome is so well documented in animals, one might well ask why prenatal stress does not seem to cause homosexuality in men, as Dörner had postulated. First, one could point out that the published reports on prenatally stressed rats do not actually include tests of sexual orientation—that is, the animals were not tested in a T-maze where they could choose to go and have sex with a male or a female. Rather, they were tested for copulatory performance separately with stud males and estrous females. However, all we know about the syndrome suggests that the animals would perform in a sex-atypical fashion in a T-maze situation, just as hormonally manipulated animals do.

Another possibility is that the endocrinological reponse to stress is different in rats and humans. In fact, it has been reported that the secretion of stress hormones by the adrenal glands in reponse to stress is much less marked in humans than in rats.[23] Furthermore, the human reproductive system seems to be more resistant to stress than that of rats or even of other primates.[24] Thus, the apparent failure of prenatal stress to predispose boys to homosexuality does not undermine the general hypothesis that endocrinological events before birth can influence sexual orientation in adulthood.

Given that the stress theory of homosexuality is so loaded with social and political implications, one might think that researchers who study the prenatal stress syndrome would be quite engaged in public discussion of the issue. Far from it. The two major groups working on the syndrome in rats (Ingeborg and Byron Ward at Villenova University, and Reuben Rhees and his colleagues at Brigham Young University) rarely mention the human relevance of their work and, on occasions when I have asked them about this directly, seemed not especially interested in the topic. Dörner, meanwhile, has gone on to other theories.

9

Genes

Of the various biological approaches to the study of sexual orientation, none arouses more ambivalence among gay people than the
search for genes that might influence people to become homosexual.
On the one hand, this search, if successful, seems to promise the most
direct support for a liberating "born that way" argument. On the
other hand, it raises what is invariably described as the "specter of Nazi
eugenics"—the possibility that attempts will be made to eliminate homosexuality through genetic "therapy," through the selective destruction of fetuses that carry "gay genes," or through the sterilization of
gay adults.

In reality, the genetic approach has so far been the least harmful of
the various disciplines that have been brought to bear on the topic. As
mentioned earlier, the Nazi persecution of gay men was not based on
the belief that homosexuality was inherited, but that it was a learned
behavior, spread by seduction. There have been few if any attempts to
prevent gay people from reproducing.[1] On the contrary, there has been
uniform and relentless pressure on them to marry and have children,
and the general consensus has always been that gay people who do

marry and have children are no longer homosexual, or that their ho-mosexuality is no longer a problem.

Of course, the relatively benign history of genetic research on ho-mosexuality does not preclude the possibility of future harm. The dra-matic advances in molecular genetic techniques over the last decade, the introduction of gene therapy into the medical arsenal, and the rapid progress of the human genome project raise the possibility that, if sex-ual orientation is indeed influenced by genes, these genes could be manipulated in such a way as to eventually eliminate lesbians and gay men from the population. Such concerns about the future will be con-sidered further in a later chapter. For now, I will review the history of research on the genetics of sexual orientation and assess the current status of the field.

Early sexologists such as Krafft-Ebing and Hirschfeld believed that homosexuality, especially in men, was at least partially inherited. As mentioned in chapter 1, Hirschfeld originally bought into the con-cept of "degeneracy": that is, he proposed that homosexuality might arise as a result of the weakening of the genetic stock through disease, alcoholism, and the like. He later rejected this point of view, but he still believed that genetic factors played a role. In support of this be-lief he asserted that male homosexuality clustered in families: the brothers of gay men, he claimed, were far more likely to be gay them-selves than were men without gay brothers. Furthermore, he reported a few cases of identical male twins, both of whom were homosexual. Although Hirschfeld's data certainly suggested that male homosexu-ality clustered in families, they did not distinguish clearly between ge-netic factors and other possible causes for the clustering, such as a tendency for certain parents to treat all their children in a fashion that predisposed them to become gay.

During the 1930s a German geneticist, Theo Lang, published a se-ries of studies concerning the siblings of gay men.[2] These studies were concerned, not with the incidence of homosexuality among these sib-lings, but with the ratio of males to females. Basing his analysis on data in German police files, Lang reported that for every 100 sisters of gay men there were 121 brothers, a sex ratio significantly more biased to-

ward males than is the general population ratio, which is about
106:100. Lang suggested that the "missing" females were the gay men
themselves: in other words, that gay men are chromosomal females
who in the course of fetal life develop a male anatomy, but preserve
at least one female trait, namely, a sexual attraction to men.

Lang's theory is certainly incorrect. Subsequent cytological studies
have demonstrated that gays and lesbians have the chromosomal
makeup appropriate to their sex.[3] Furthermore, if gay men were chro-
mosomally female, that is, lacking a Y chromosome, then they would
be unable to father sons and most likely would be completely infer-
tile. Neither of these predictions are true. Still, some subsequent studies have replicated Lang's basic observation, although generally with
less skewed ratios.[4] The reason for the skewed sex ratio is unclear.

Family and Twin Studies

In 1952 a New York psychiatrist and geneticist, Franz Kallmann, presented what seemed to be dramatic evidence for the genetic determination of sexual orientation in men.[5] Kallmann investigated the
distribution of sexual orientation (using the Kinsey scale) among the
monozygotic and dizygotic co-twins of gay and bisexual men.
(Monozygotic or "identical" twins share all the same genes,[6] while
dizygotic or "fraternal" twins, like ordinary siblings, share about half
their genes.) If we focus on the twins of exclusively or nearly exclusively gay men (Kinsey groups 6 and 5) his results are particularly remarkable: among the thirty *monozygotic* co-twins of such men,
twenty-five also fell in groups 6 or 5, three fell in groups 4 or 3, and
none fell in groups 2, 1, or 0. In contrast, among thirty *dizygotic* co-
twins of such men, fifteen fell in groups 0 or 1, two fell in groups 2–4,
and none fell in groups 5 or 6. (The remainder were female or un-
available for study.) On the face of it, Kallmann's data suggested that
genes are more or less decisive in the development of sexual orientation in men.

A German twin study published in 1962 presented data very similar to Kallmann's,[7] but around the same time case studies began to

appear that described pairs of monozygotic twins who were discordant for sexual orientation.[8] In addition, Kallmann's research methodology came under severe criticism.[9] During the 1970s the whole issue of a genetic influence on sexual orientation took a back seat to social-learning theories of various kinds.

The 1980s saw a revival of interest in genetic factors in the development of sexual orientation. One of the key players in this new wave of research has been Richard Pillard, a psychiatrist at Boston University Medical Center. Pillard is gay himself—he was one of the first openly gay psychiatrists in the United States and was actively involved in the efforts to remove homosexuality from the American Psychiatric Association's *Diagnostic and Statistical Manual* (see chapter 11). He also has several close relatives who are or were gay, lesbian, or bisexual. Thus he had good reason from his own experience to reopen a line of inquiry that seemed to have been discredited.

Pillard first wanted to determine whether it was generally true that homosexuality clusters in certain families. Specifically, he tested the hypothesis that the siblings of gay men or lesbians are themselves more likely to be gay or lesbian than the siblings of heterosexual men and women. With the collaboration of James Weinrich he first recruited a sample of gay men and a comparison sample of heterosexual men, and investigated the sexual orientation of the men's brothers and sisters. Among the brothers of the heterosexual men, about 4 percent were homosexual or bisexual (Kinsey groups 2–6), a figure that, not suprisingly, is about the same as the general incidence of these groups in the population. Among the brothers of the gay men, on the other hand, about 22 percent were gay or bisexual. Thus, finding one gay man in a sibship substantially increases the likelihood of finding others. The sisters of the gay men, on the other hand, were no more likely to be lesbian than the sisters of the heterosexual men.[10]

Four studies have described comparable investigations of the siblings of lesbians.[11] Again, a much higher fraction (5 percent to 25 percent) of the sisters of lesbians than of the comparison groups of women (0 percent to 11 percent) were themselves lesbian. (The exact figures depended considerably on the precise definitions used, but in all comparisons the percentages were much higher for the sisters of the lesbians.) The brothers of the lesbians were also, in some of the studies, more likely to be gay than were comparison groups of men, although the rates were not as high as for the sisters. It seems therefore that both male and female homosexuality cluster in families and that there is some tendency, although a relatively weak one, for lesbians and gay men to crop up in the same families.

The observation that homosexuality is familial is not in itself proof of a genetic influence on sexual orientation, for many environmental mechanisms can have the same effect. If parents treated one child in such a way as to make him or her homosexual, for example, they might well treat other children in the same way. But if homosexuality did *not* cluster in families, it would be difficult to sustain a genetic theory.

Pillard, Bailey, and others have gone on to perform twin studies of the same kind as Kallmann's, but with more attention to appropriate methods of sampling and data analysis. These studies have come up with concordance rates for homosexuality in monozygotic twins that are much higher than in dizygotic twins, but that do not come close to the near-100 percent concordance reported by Kallmann. In a study of male twins by Bailey and Pillard,[12] 52 percent of the monozygotic co-twins of gay men were themselves gay, while only 22 percent of the dizygotic male co-twins were gay. In a study led by Frederick Whitam of Arizona State University, the concordance rates were somewhat higher: 65 percent for the monozygotic and 29 percent for the dizygotic twins.[13] In a study of female twins by Bailey and colleagues, 48 percent of the monozygotic co-twins of lesbians were themselves lesbian or bisexual, compared with only 16 percent of the dizygotic female co-twins.[14] In a relatively small British study that published combined data for male and female twins, 25 percent of the monozygotic pairs were concordant, compared with 12.5 percent of the dizygotic pairs.[15] Thus, although the actual rates vary considerably from study to study, there is agreement that the incidence of homosexuality is approximately twice as high in the monozygotic co-twins of homosexual men and women as in the dizygotic co-twins.

What one wants from these studies is not the concordance rates themselves but an estimate of the *heritability* of sexual orientation, that is, the fraction of the variability in sexual orientation seen in a given population that is attributable to genetic differences among individuals. Heritability can be calculated from the concordance rates if two other numbers are known—the base rate of homosexuality in the population and the *ascertainment bias*. The latter is a measure of the tendency, if any, for homosexual individuals to volunteer for the study more readily if they have a homosexual co-twin than if they have a heterosexual co-twin. It might be, for example, that a gay man whose identical twin was also gay would volunteer more readily because he perceived the concordance as being helpful to the study. On account of uncertainties about these numbers, Bailey and his colleagues had to be satisfied with a broad range of values instead of an single exact value for the heritability of sexual orientation: they estimated that it was somewhere between 30 percent and 75 percent in both men and women.

In 1995 Michael Bailey and N. G. Martin undertook a new study in an attempt to get away from problems with ascertainment bias. Instead of advertising for volunteers, they used a preexisting registry of twins that has been maintained in Australia. Using rather strict criteria for concordance, they found that the concordance rate for male monozygotic twins in their sample was 20 percent, while the rate for the male dizygotic twins was 0 percent. For women, the rates were 24 percent and 11 percent respectively. If they relaxed the criteria, the rates went up to 37.5 percent and 6.3 percent for men and 30 percent and 30 percent—that is, no effect of zygosity at all—for women. On the basis of these results, Bailey and Martin concluded that there very likely had been substantial ascertainment bias in the previous studies. The true heritabilities could not be calculated with any confidence, however, because of the limited sample size.[16]

There is yet another potential problem with the twin studies, which is that they make the assumption that any nongenetic factors influencing sexual orientation are shared to the same degree by monozygotic and dizygotic co-twins. This may not be the case. Let us assume, for the sake of argument, that a hostile father causes his son to become gay. Let us further assume that the fathers of monozygotic twins are generally about equally hostile or loving to both twins, while the fathers of dizygotic male twins tend to be considerably more hostile to one son than the other. In that case a higher concordance rate would be seen in monozygotic than in dizygotic twins, even in the absence of any genes predisposing to homosexuality. In actual fact, this scenario does not seem to be the case: if anything, concordant twins recall being treated *less* alike than discordant twins. Nevertheless, it is difficult to rule out this potential problem without knowing what the non-genetic factors are.

In fact, there is room for complex interactions between genes and environment in the generation of the observed results. Pursuing the example just given, for example, one might hypothesize that, due to their genetic similarity, monozygotic twins seem about equally attractive to their fathers, while dizygotic twins have genetic differences that cause one twin to seem less attractive to his father than the other, thus generating the hostility that eventually causes him to become homosexual. In this case the responsible genes "predispose" to homosexuality only in a very indirect sense. In fact, different genes might predispose to homosexuality in different twin pairs, depending on what traits the particular fathers found attractive or unattractive.

I mention these potential problems only as a cautionary note, not with the intention of dismissing the twin studies out of hand. No one has demonstrated that these potential problems are actually confounding the data. On the whole the twins studies offer substantial if not totally watertight evidence that there is a genetic influence on sexual orientation, at least in men. Furthermore, we shall see that other lines of evidence support the conclusions drawn from the twin studies.

Particularly interesting to behavioral geneticists are twins who are reared apart from birth. If they are monozygotic, they share their genetic endowment but have different postnatal environments. Thus, any characteristic that they tend to share more frequently than expected by chance is likely to be influenced by genetic factors or by factors operating during their shared intrauterine life. A research team at the

University of Minnesota, led by Thomas Bouchard, Jr., has carried out a long-running study of twins reared apart and has concluded that there is substantial heritability for intelligence and a number of personality traits.[17]

The Minnesota group have reported on six pairs of monozygotic twins reared apart (two male, four female) in which at least one twin was homosexual or bisexual.[18] In each of the four female cases, the co-twin was unambiguously heterosexual. Of the two male pairs, one was clearly concordant. In fact the two men, who had not previously known that they were twins, met for the first time after one was mistaken for the other at a gay bar, and they subsequently became lovers. The other male pair was more ambiguous. One twin identified as bisexual until age nineteen, but later became exclusively homosexual, while the other had a homosexual affair between the ages of fifteen and eighteen, but later married and regarded himself as exclusively heterosexual. The pair might be regarded as partially concordant. Although the numbers in this study are obviously too low for a meaningful statistical analysis, they are consistent with the idea that genes do influence men's sexual orientation but may play little or no role in the development of sexual orientation in women.

Molecular Genetic Studies

The most interesting recent development in the field has come from the laboratory of Dean Hamer, a molecular geneticist at the National Cancer Institute.[19] Until 1992, Hamer worked on a fairly obscure set of genes in yeast, genes that have nothing to do with sex. But he was motivated by Pillard's family studies and Bailey's twin data to attempt to find the actual genes that influence sexual orientation. He has recounted the story of the ensuing search in an engaging book, *The Science of Desire*.[20] In the book he describes his reasons for getting into this field of research as a combination of personal and scientific curiosity, as well as boredom with his previous line of research.

Hamer and his colleagues (they include one very "out" lesbian, Angela Pattatucci[21]) began their project by examining the family trees

of gay men. Up to then, the evidence for family clustering of homosexuality had come almost entirely from studies of siblings. Such studies say little about the exact mode of inheritance. Hamer's group
therefore reconstructed pedigrees of families that contained a number of gay men over two or more generations.

A striking pattern emerged from inspection of these family trees
(see figure 9.1). The gay men within a pedigree tended to be connected
by the female line. For example, a gay man in the first generation might
have no gay sons himself, but his sister might have one or more gay
sons. In turn, these second-generation gay men might have no gay sons,
but *their* sister might have a gay son in the third generation. It was as
if gay men could inherit genes predisposing to homosexuality from
their mothers, but not from their fathers.

To verify this apparent pattern of maternal inheritance, Hamer's
group performed a statistical study. They first selected a group of sev-
enty-six gay men and asked them about the existence of other gay men
in their families. It turned out that none of the fathers or sons of these
gay men were themselves gay. Only three kinds of relatives had an
above-chance incidence of homosexuality. These were brothers (13.5
percent of whom were gay), maternal uncles (7.3 percent), and cousins
who were the sons of maternal aunts (7.7 percent). Other relatives who
were not linked through the maternal line (paternal aunts and the other
three kinds of cousins) had chance levels of homosexuality. Nephews
and grandchildren were not examined.

The data became even stronger when Hamer's group looked at the
families, not of randomly selected gay men, but of pairs of gay brothers (with the additional condition that there be no evidence of father-
to-son transmission and no more than one lesbian relative.) Because
of the presence of two gay brothers, such families might be especially
likely to carry genes predisposing to homosexuality. In fact, the rates
of homosexuality in the maternally linked relatives were even higher
in this group than in the randomly selected group: 10 percent of the
maternal uncles and 13 percent of the cousins who were sons of maternal aunts were themselves gay (highly significant findings in both
cases), whereas the incidence in the other kinds of relatives was not
significantly different from chance levels.

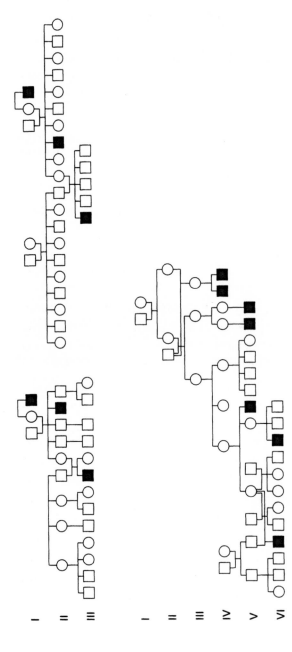

Figure 9.1

Three family trees that suggest maternal inheritance of male homosexuality, from the study by Dean Hamer and colleagues (see text). Filled squares represent gay males, open squares represent nongay males, and open circles represent nongay females. In the top two families, a gay man in the first generation has a gay nephew through *his* sister, and this man in turn has a gay nephew through *his* sister. In the lower family, the seven gay males in generations IV through VI are connected to each other exclusively through females. It seems that the woman in generation I passed a gene for male homosexuality to her two daughters, to her three granddaughters, to at least three of her five great-granddaughters, and to at least two of her great-great-granddaughters. Alternatively, the man who sequentially married the two sisters in generation II may have been a nongay carrier of the gene.

Although there are several possible explanations for this pattern of inheritance, the simplest and most intriguing is that it is caused by a gene that is located on the X chromosome. In the most straightforward model, the gene would come in two versions, one (the more common) that predisposes its owner to become heterosexual and a rarer version that predisposes it owner to become gay. Because men have only a single X chromosome, they could only possess one version of the gene, and they must have inherited this gene from their mother, because fathers do not pass on X chromosomes to their sons. Thus a gene of this kind can be transmitted to two men in the same kinship only if they are related exclusively through women. (The same is true for some well-known X-linked conditions such as hemophilia and anomalous color vision.) Even the relative percentages of gay uncles and cousins in the study spoke for an involvement of the X chromosome, for a slightly complicated reason which I have relegated to a footnote.[22]

Having identified a particular chromosome as a candidate for the location of the gene or genes of interest, Hamer's group applied molecular genetic techniques to localize it even more narrowly. These techniques depend on the existence of *linkage markers* (see figure 9.2). These are sites scattered along the chromosomes where there are known to be slight differences in the exact DNA sequence from one individual to another, differences that can be spotted by rather simple enzymatic tests. Women carry two X chromosomes, and most of the linkage markers are likely to differ between the two, because the two X's derive from unrelated individuals—the woman's two parents. Each of the woman's sons receives from her a single X chromosome, and this is generally a composite made of recombined fragments of her two X's. It is a matter of chance whether any particular region of a son's X chromosome is derived from one or the other X chromosome of the mother. Therefore, if one compares any linkage marker on the X chromosomes of two brothers who have been selected at random, the markers have about a 50 percent chance of being the same (meaning than the markers happened to come from the same maternal chromosome) and a 50 percent chance of being different (meaning that

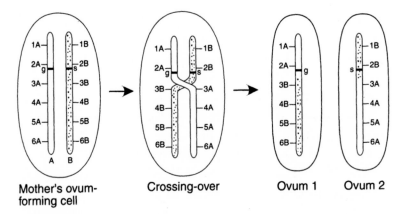

Mother's ovum-   Crossing-over   Ovum 1   Ovum 2
forming cell

Figure 9.2

How the technique of linkage analysis takes advantage of "crossing-over" between homologous chromosomes to pinpoint the location of a gene of interest, in this case a gene influencing male sexual orientation located on the X chromosome. At left, an egg-forming cell in the mother contains two X chromosomes ("A" and "B"). Scattered along the chromosomes are numerous "linkage markers"—locations where the DNA sequence is variable and thus likely to differ between the A and B chromosomes (shown schematically as markers 1 to 6). Let's assume that a gene influencing male sexual orientation is located near marker 2 (shown by horizontal bar); the A chromosome carries the version of the gene that predisposes its owner to become gay ("g"), while the B chromosome carries the version that predisposes its owner to become straight ("s"). During the development of the ova, the X chromosomes "cross over" and recombine (middle panel) at one or more random locations; here the site of crossing-over is shown as about half-way between linkage markers 2 and 3. Of the two resulting "hybrid" chromosomes, one becomes part of the mature ovum ("ovum 1" or "ovum 2") and the other degenerates. A son who develops from ovum 1 carries the "g" gene and also linkage marker 2A, while a son who develops from ovum 2 carries the "s" gene and linkage marker 2B. Because marker 2 is so close to the gene, it is unlikely that crossing-over will take place between the marker and the gene; therefore all sons in this family who carry the "g" version are likely to have the 2A marker, while all sons who carry the "s" version are likely to have the 2B marker. The other markers are far enough away from the gene that one or more crossings-over may occur between the markers and the gene. Therefore, two brothers who are both gay on account of their carrying the "g" gene are likely to share the same linkage marker at location 2, but have only a 50:50 chance of sharing markers at other locations. If this relationship holds up across many families, one can infer that a gene influencing sexual orientation is indeed located near linkage marker 2.

they came each from a different maternal chromosome). If, however, the two brothers are selected on the basis of both being gay and their homosexuality is caused by a gene on the X chromosome, then there is an increased chance that the two brothers will inherit identical X-chromosome linkage markers. The chances are highest for markers very close to the location of the actual gene, because there is relatively little likelihood that a recombination event has occurred between the gene and a nearby marker. The chances decrease to 50 percent for markers far away from the gene.

When Hamer's group compared the linkage markers in a large number of pairs of gay brothers, they obtained a striking result. For most of the length of the X chromosome the brothers coinherited the same markers 50 percent of the time, but there was a small region near one end of the chromosome, a region designated Xq28, where the rate of coinheritance was substantially elevated. With conservative statistical tests, Hamer's results indicate, with a confidence of greater than 99 percent, that there is a gene in the Xq28 region of the X chromosome that influences sexual orientation in men—at least in the case of families with two gay brothers. Even in such families, however, this gene is evidently not all decisive, because there were some pairs of brothers who were discordant for linkage markers in the Xq28 region.

Since publishing their initial report, Hamer's group have extended their studies in various ways.[23] They first replicated their findings. In the replication study, the data were not quite as strong as in the earlier study but were still statistically significant. On the basis of the combined results, the statistical confidence levels rose to an astronomical level: the results could have occurred by chance only about once in 100,000 times.

Hamer and his colleagues also confirmed the validity of their approach in another way, by looking at sibships in which there was at least one heterosexual brother in addition to two gay brothers. They found, as one would hope, that the heterosexual brother generally had different markers in the Xq28 region from the markers shared by the two gay brothers. This result suggested that, not only is there a gene predisposing to homosexuality at Xq28 but that, at least in the kinds of families examined, possessing this gene generally does lead to homosexuality—there do not seem to be large numbers of straight brothers with the "gay" version of the gene. In technical language, the gene seems to be fairly *penetrant.* Finally, Hamer's group showed that the Xq28 region is not linked to homosexuality in women.

It should be emphasized that, so far, Hamer and his colleagues have not actually identified an actual gene or genes in the Xq28 region that influence sexual orientation. The region is large enough to contain hundreds of genes, most of which have not yet been identified. None of the genes that are already known to lie in this region are especially promising candidates: that is, none of them are known to play a specific role in the sexual differentiation of the brain or the regulation of sexual feelings or behavior. To home in on the actual gene, if it is located there, will require study of more families and the use of more linkage markers. Alternatively, it may happen within the next few years that the entire DNA sequence of the Xq28 region is determined in the course of the human genome project. If so, it will be a relatively straightforward matter to search for the gene or genes whose DNA sequence differs between heterosexual and homosexual men, or some fraction of them. After the gene has been identified, it will be possible to address a whole series of important questions: When during development does the gene exert its effect? Where in the brain or body is the gene active? What is the protein coded for by the gene? What does this protein do—is it a gene-regulating factor, an enzyme, a hormone, a receptor, or something else? How do the "gay" and "straight" versions of the gene differ, and how do these differences ultimately influence men to say "I'm gay" or "I'm straight"? And how, if at all, is the possession of this gene linked to the various traits that seem to go along with male homosexuality—gender nonconformity in childhood, artistic ability, and so on? In a word, the molecular approach offers the hope of connecting the genetics, the neurobiology, and the psychology into a more comprehensive picture of the development of male sexual orientation.

Very recently, a group of researchers at the University of Western Ontario, led by molecular geneticist George Ebers, announced that they had failed to replicate Hamer's results.[24] The Canadian researchers performed the same two kinds of study as Hamer did: a pedigree analysis of the families of gay men and a linkage analysis of the X chromosome in pairs of gay brothers. In the pedigree analysis they found a maternal bias, as did Hamer. The bias, however, was smaller and, according to the researchers, was most likely due to a reporting bias (that is, to the fact that women know more about their relatives than men do). In the linkage study, they failed to find any markers linked to sexual orientation at Xq28 or anywhere else on the X chromosome. At this point, the Canadian study is not available for detailed analysis. All one can say is that the Xq28 linkage is likely to remain contentious until it is solidly replicated or refuted by a number of other laboratories.

There is another molecular genetic approach which is an alternative to the linkage analysis method. This second method involves making a guess as to which gene or genes might be involved, based on our knowledge of the molecular biology of sexual development, and then comparing the DNA sequence of these genes in homosexual and heterosexual individuals. If successful, such an "educated-guess" or "candidate-gene" approach could shortcut years of molecular-genetic footslogging.

Around 1991, it occurred simultaneously to several researchers that one particular gene—the gene that codes for the androgen receptor—was an especially good candidate for such an approach. As mentioned in chapter 5, androgens such as testosterone exert their effects by binding to specific receptor molecules that are present in the cells of the developing brain, as well as in many other tissues. The receptors are present in particularly high concentrations in the medial preoptic area of the hypothalamus as well as in other sexually dimorphic regions of the brain. If a chromosomal male suffers from a mutation in the androgen receptor gene that completely knocks out the receptor, this person will develop with the external anatomy of a female, will consider herself a woman, and will generally be sexually attracted to men. This condition—the *androgen insensitivity syndrome*—is of course not the same thing as homosexuality. But what if the androgen receptor, instead of being completely knocked out, were modified in function by a more subtle mutation of the receptor gene? Perhaps there could be a mutation that would cause the gene to be less than usually active in the hypothalamus but fully functional in other tissues. In this case, the hypothalamus might develop in a sex-atypical fashion, while the rest of the body developed in a sex-typical fashion. There are even peculiarities of the androgen receptor gene that make such a scenario especially plausible. The gene contains several regions where the same sequence of three nucleoides (the letters of the DNA alphabet) repeats itself a number of times. Such "triplet repeats" are known to be sites of unusually high genetic variability among individuals—it as if the gene-copying machinery easily loses count when it has to repeat the same thing over and over. In several genes, including the androgen receptor gene, larger-than-usual numbers of triplet repeats are associated with alterations of gene function that can be restricted to certain tissues.[25]

During 1992 the word on the academic grapevine was that several groups of researchers were working furiously to identify differences between the androgen receptor genes of gay and straight men. In the following year, researchers in two labs (Hamer's lab and that of Jeremy Nathans at Johns Hopkins Medical School) published their combined results: they could find no evidence at all that the DNA sequence of the androgen receptor gene in gay men differed from that found in straight men.[26] Other laboratories have not published their results, presumably because they too drew a blank.

More recently Günter Dörner's group in Berlin came up with another "educated guess," although a pretty arcane one.[27] As was recounted in earlier chapters, Dörner has long been wedded to the notion that testosterone levels are lower than normal in male fetuses that are destined to become homosexual. Among other factors controlling testosterone levels is the activity of a complex network of enzymes that manufacture and break down steroid hormones. Dörner has recently claimed that one of these enzymes, named 21-hydroxylase, is defective in both gay men and lesbians, and that this deficiency leads to lower-than-normal androgen levels in male fetuses and higher-than-normal levels in female fetuses—a conclusion that, if true, would dovetail neatly with his endocrinological theories of homosexuality.

Furthermore, he reported that a particular stretch of DNA known as CYP21A is altered in gays and lesbians. CYP21A is generally believed to be a "pseudogene," that is, a piece of DNA that eons ago used to be a functional gene (for 21-hydroxylase in this case), but that in the course of evolution has mutated into an inoperative state, its functions taken over by another 21-hydroxylase gene. It is not at all clear how a further mutation in such an apparently useless stretch of DNA could turn someone into a homosexual. Given that several of Dörner's previous assertions about the causes of homosexuality remain very controversial, it will take exceptionally strong evidence to convince the scientific community that he is right this time.

The trouble with the "educated-guess" approach is that, if any particular guess is wrong, it advances the search very little, given that 100,000 or so genes remain to be tested. It is certainly worthwhile to test candidate genes, but we should not be surprised if this approach fails: we simply do not yet understand development well enough to be able to make confident predictions as to which genes might be responsible for particular outcomes. This is most especially true of the brain, which is the product of the combined efforts of many thousands of genes, most of them still unidentified.

The search for genes that might influence sexual orientation in women does not seem to be making much progress. Aside from Dörner's report of the potential involvement of CYP21A, nothing positive has been reported, even though Pattatucci and Hamer, among others, have been working hard to find something. They have established, for example, that homosexuality in women does not map to the Xq28 region.

It should be understood that the finding that Xq28 may play a role in male sexual orientation depended on a lucky circumstance, namely, that the gene or genes were located on a chromosome that exhibits a special pattern of inheritance. Finding genes on other chromosomes requires lengthy and painstaking linkage studies. It may simply be a matter of time before genes influencing sexual orientation in women are discovered. Alternatively, if the heritability of sexual orientation in women is lower than in men, as some studies suggest, there may not be much to find.

The fact that the "gay" version of the gene at Xq28 does not pre-dispose to homosexuality in women doesn't necessarily mean that it has *no* effect in women. One possibility is that it predisposes to *heterosexuality*. After all, homosexuality in men and heterosexuality in women can be viewed as the same thing—sexual attraction to men. (For this reason the word *androphilia* is sometimes employed to emphasize the similarity of the two phenomena. Conversely, the term *gynephilia*—sexual attraction to women—is sometimes used to stress the equivalence of heterosexuality in men and homosexuality in women.) The "gay" version of the gene at Xq28 could not be the principal cause of female heterosexuality because it is too rare, but it might conceivably enhance a woman's already existing attraction to men, making her as it were "hyperheterosexual."

Homosexuality and Evolution

This train of thought leads naturally into the wider question of why genes predisposing to homosexuality exist at all, considering that they would seem likely to decrease their owner's chances of having children, and thus might be expected to die out over a few generations. When faced with this question, gays and lesbians "in the street" will tend to argue that the genes are kept going because of the important contributions that gays and lesbians have always made to human society. They might quote evidence that, in a wide variety of cultures, gender-variant people have played a special role as shamans, mediators, artists, helpers, and so on. Because of this value to the community their genes have persisted.

Such arguments cut no ice with evolutionary biologists, who are paid to be hardnosed about concepts like "value." Value to whom, they will ask. Genes persist, according to them, when they do as well or better at helping their owners reproduce than do any alternative genes that random mutations might generate, or that might already be in the population. Genes are selfish, and this is the ultimate reason why human beings are selfish.[28] The fact that a gene predisposing to homosexuality might have value to the entire community is of little relevance, because the entire community is not the unit on which natural selection operates.

A number of potential explanations have been put forward to explain the apparent paradox of "gay genes."[29] One simple explanation would be that such genes do indeed rapidly die out because of nonreproduction, but that new mutations are occuring at a rapid enough rate to keep the trait in existence. This would parallel the situation seen with some severe genetic disorders. For example, in a Swedish study of males with the X-linked disorder hemophilia B, it has been reported that the majority of the cases are caused by de novo mutations in the germ-cell line of the patient's maternal grandfather.[30] Male homosexuality is far more common than hemophilia B, and it strains credibility to think that new mutations could account for a sizeable fraction of the total incidence. But genes seem to vary greatly in their susceptibility to mutation, so a definitive judgment on this possible explanation must await the identification of the gene or genes involved.

Another simple explanation would be to say that homosexuality is not in fact associated with decreased reproduction, or was not during a significant part of human evolution.[31] We know that in many contemporary cultures there is social or economic pressure to marry, regardless of the individual's sexual inclinations. Furthermore, some men and women (especially the latter) do not become aware of or accept their homosexual orientation until after they have had one or more children. The statistics in the United States today are interesting in this regard. According to what is probably the most objective national study of the issue, the 1994 survey by Yankelovich Partners, Inc., about the same fraction of women who identified as lesbian said they were mothers as did women who identified as heterosexual (67 percent versus 72 percent; they were not asked about the number of children). For men, on the other hand, identifying as gay was associated with markedly lower reproduction: only 27 percent of the gay men said they were fathers, compared with 60 percent of the heterosexual men.[32] Thus in our culture it would appear that, to whatever extent genes may predispose people to homosexuality, such genes do much more "reproductive harm" in gay men than in lesbians. Yet it is in men that the best evidence for "gay genes" exists.

Outside of our contemporary culture, no reliable data on the reproductive success of gays and lesbians exist. We do know that there is a widespread cross-cultural tradition of transgenderal homosexuality that is associated with nonreproduction, even in societies where marriage is near universal. This is exemplified by the *xanith* of Oman, a traditional Islamic state on the Persian Gulf.[33] The xanith—biological males who adopt an intermediate gender role and who frequently work as prostitutes serving conventional men—are by tradition exempted from many of the activities expected of males, including marriage. Thus, to the extent that the xanith status may have a genetic predisposition, there is clearly a reproductive harm associated with such genes. Much less clear is the reproductive status of more conventionally gendered gays and lesbians—if indeed such labels are appropriate at all—in cultures like Oman's.

Although data are lacking, it seems likely that genes predisposing to male homosexuality have generally being associated with lowered reproduction. Being a male is a far riskier business than being a female: there is much greater variability in the number of offspring parented by males than by females, among humans as among other species. Males need all the help they can get in the struggle to reproduce, and exclusive homosexuality is assuredly no help at all.

Given that the foregoing two explanations, although simple, are not very persuasive, evolutionary biologists have looked for other, more complicated ones. In general, these theories demand that one look not just at the help or hindrance that a particular genetically controlled trait offers to the reproductive success of its owner, but at the wider question of how well it promotes its own survival in an entire kinship. This is known as a trait's *inclusive fitness*.

One way to look beyond the immediate value of a gene-mediated trait to its owner's reproduction is to ask whether the gene confers any reproductive benefit on heterozygous carriers.[34] A particularly well-studied example concerns the gene for sickle-cell anemia, which is quite prevalent in Africa and among African Americans. Sickle-cell anemia is a serious disease that, at least in the past, markedly reduced the reproductive success of the people who suffered from it. It is caused by a mutation of the gene for hemoglobin, and in order to show the disease one must be *homozygous* for the gene, that is, one must have two copies of the gene—one on each of the two homologous chromosomes that carry the hemoglobin gene. Carrying just one copy of the sickle-cell gene (or being *heterozygous*) causes little pathology, but it does alter the hemoglobin sufficiently to make life difficult for malaria parasites, which spend much of their lives inside red blood cells. Thus the gene for sickle-cell anemia is also a gene for resistance to malaria. It is believed that the benefit of malaria resistance to the heterozygous individuals keeps the gene in the population, and the occasional person who is unlucky enough to be homozygous is just that—unlucky. Although the sickle-cell example is the best studied example of this phenomenon, it is believed that other "defective" genes may be kept in the population by a similar mechanism. For example, it has been proposed that the cystic fibrosis gene—cause of the most common inherited disease among white Americans—may confer resistance to cholera on heterozygous carriers of the gene. Of course, malaria and cholera no longer present a significant risk to people in the United States, but it will take many generations before the sickle-cell and cystic fibrosis genes die out.

In the case of a gene on the X chromosome, such as the gene at Xq28, the rules are slightly different. Just a single copy of the gene will be sufficient to exert the gene's full effect in men, because they only have one X chromosome. Therefore there are no heterozygous male carriers. There will however be heterozygous female carriers, including some of the sisters of the men who carry the "gay" version of the gene. Therefore interest focuses on any possible reproductive benefit that the gene might confer on these sisters. Furthermore, as sociobiologist Robert Trivers has pointed out, the reproductive benefit of an X-linked gene to females is more important (to its own evolutionary survival) than its benefit to males.[35] This is because females have two X chromosomes, males only one; as a consequence, over the generations an X chromosome is acted on by natural selection twice as often in a female body as a male body.

One such possible benefit would be the "hyperheterosexuality" postulated earlier, which might cause these women to have more offspring than they would have had otherwise. But there could be some other benefit not obviously connected with sex at all. After all, genes work by affecting basic chemical processes, processes that can end up influencing quite disparate aspects of our lives. In that vein one geneticist, William Turner, suggested at a recent meeting that a gene predisposing to male homosexuality might persist because it gave heterozygous carriers resistance to smallpox. His evidence? He asserted that, according to historical records, the sisters of gay men have been accounted unusually beautiful—a sign, he supposes, that their skin was never touched by smallpox. Obviously there is more imagination than hard science to ideas like this. When the actual genes have been identified, it may be easier to evaluate the likelihood of this and other theories.

The notion of inclusive fitness has been particularly useful in explaining the existence of altruistic behavior and of genes that might predispose to such behavior.[36] The basic idea here is as follows: for a gene to perpetuate itself, it does not necessarily have to help its owner reproduce, because identical copies of the gene exist in some of its owner's relatives. For example, an autosomal gene that exists in a particular man will have a 50 percent chance of also existing in each of that man's brothers and sisters. Suppose that this gene made its owner homosexual, thus preventing him from having, say, two children. The statistical cost to the gene of this homosexuality is one lost copy in the next generation (because any gene has a 50 percent chance of being passed on to any particular child). But let us suppose that this same gene causes its owner to assist the reproduction of his siblings, say by providing them with food or other resources, and that this assistance causes the siblings to have four more offspring between them than they otherwise would have had. This confers a benefit to the gene of one extra copy in the next generation (statistically, these nephews and nieces are 25 percent related to the man, and thus each has a one-in-four chance of carrying a copy of the gene). The costs and benefits in this example cancel out, so the gene is just as likely to persist as an equivalent gene predisposing to heterosexuality.

Of course, humans have not one gene but about 100,000 genes. Human behavior, sociobiologists argue, reflects the statistical equilibrium reached among all these genes as they individually influence their owner's actions, survival, and fertility, sometimes in conflicting ways. The only thing that can be said with confidence about this equilibrium state is that it will tend to make the person selfish, but that he or she will show some altruism toward close relatives. This is of course what is generally observed.

Thus we can see that genes can predispose to homosexuality in ways that go beyond the specific action of a gene like that the one at Xq28. We might all have genes in common that predispose us to become homosexual in certain situations. If, for example, it becomes apparent that our chances of having children ourselves are low, our genes might influence us to adopt an "altruistic" strategy. For example, a boy who is small and weak, perhaps on account of illness early in life, might become homosexual as a result of an unconscious calculation: that he can do better (for the survival of his genes) if he gives up the hopeless quest to have children and becomes homosexual, devoting his resources to helping his siblings have children. In this case, the immediate cause of this boy's homosexuality—the disease that struck him in infancy—is entirely environmental, but genes are the ultimate reason why any boy in his circumstances would make the same "choice." Realistically, the genes responsible for this behavior would probably vary somewhat across the population, so that some individuals would opt for homosexuality after a rather small loss of reproductive potential, while others would continue to put their money on heterosexuality until all chances of reproductive success were lost.[37]

One problem with this general line of thought is that homosexuality is not simply the abandonment of sex in favor of altruistic behavior toward one's relatives; rather it involves the adoption of a different sexuality, one that can be quite costly in terms of time and resources. Although this behavior could bring advantages, such as the assistance of a partner in dealing with life's demands, it also represents a considerable and risky investment. It is not easy to estimate whether such investment could be worthwhile. Perhaps the continued study of homosexuality in non-western cultures, or even among animals, may throw more light on the question.[38]

10

Against Nature?

In the previous chapters I have made frequent reference to scientific studies in which homosexual behavior and same-sex partner preference has been produced experimentally in animals by, for example, treating them with hormones early in life. But to what extent does homosexual behavior or homosexual orientation occur naturally in animals?

The question of whether animals engage in same-sex sexual behavior has been debated for centuries, most often in the context of efforts to stigmatize homosexuality. Three classes of answers have generally been offered: "Animals don't do it, therefore it's unnatural"; "Animals *do* do it, therefore it's bestial"; and "*Some* animals do it, and those are the unclean animals".

Historian John Boswell, in his book *Christianity, Social Tolerance and Homosexuality*,[1] compiled many examples of arguments of this kind. For example, he cited the following passage from Ovid's *Metamorphoses*.

> Cows do not burn with love for cows, nor mares for mares;
> The ram is hot for the ewe, the does follows the stag.
> So also do birds mate, and among all the animals
> No female is seized with desire for the female.

Sometimes this "animal's don't do it" argument is reinforced with the assertion that even animals known for their filthy habits or lack of morals do not engage in gay sex. In 1995, for example, Robert Mugabe, president of Zimbabwe, urged the populace to arrest people who were "behaving like homosexuals," adding that "they are worse than dogs and pigs. If dogs and pigs do not do it, why must human beings?"[2]

In contrast, medieval bestiaries contain many passages that label certain species as "unclean" because of homosexuality or other sexual irregularities, such as the following passage cited by Boswell.

> The law says, "You shall not eat the hyena or anything like it." The Physiologus has written of it that it is male-female; that is, at one time male and at another female. It is therefore an unclean animal, because of this sex change. This is why Jeremiah says, "Never will the den of the hyena be my inheritance." You must not, therefore, become like the hyena, taking first the male and then the female nature; these, he says, the holy Apostle reproached when he spoke of "men with men doing that which is unseemly."

Occasionally, gay people have joined the debate, putting their own spin on the matter. Boswell cites the following passage from *Affairs of the Heart*, a work by an unknown late-Roman author:

> Is it any wonder that, since animals have been condemned by nature not to receive from the bounty of Providence any of the gifts afforded by intellect, they have with all else been deprived of gay desires? Lions do not have such a love, because they are not philosophers either. Bears have no such love, because they are ignorant of the beauty that comes from friendship. But for humans wisdom coupled with knowledge has after frequent experiments chosen what is best, and has formed the opinion that gay love is the most stable of loves.

Only quite recently have scientific studies been made of homosexual behavior among animals. As has been documented by Ronald Nadler, researchers have had diverse motives in undertaking these studies.[3] In some cases, there was an explicit desire to understand and perhaps even justify human homosexuality. Nadler cites G. V. Hamilton, a pioneer in the study of sexual behavior in monkeys, as stating that sexual behavior considered abnormal in humans "may be of normal manifestation and biologically appropriate somewhere in the phyletic scale."[4] On the other hand, some researchers explicitly dissociated themselves from such a point of view, preferring to stress the intrinsic worth of studying animal sexuality. Thus the British anatomist Solly Zuckerman, who also made extensive study of sexual behavior in nonhuman primates, wrote:"I totally fail to see how any analogical comparisons with the ways of monkeys and apes can help in the understanding of what some see as the major problems of human behaviour today." He went on,"I fail to see any reason why...the fact that cows mount cows, dogs dogs, a baby monkey its mother, or a monkey mother its baby will help resolve the social problems or prejudices associated with human homosexuality."[5]

Animal studies have demonstrated that sexual acts between males or between females are common in a wide variety of species. Just among anthropoid primates (monkeys and great apes), homosexual behavior has been described in thirty-three species, according to a recent review by Paul Vasey.[6] In this chapter, rather than review the entire literature on animal homosexuality, I take a few examples that offer potentially interesting parallels to homosexuality in humans.

Rats

In the course of experiments described in the previous chapters, scientists have found that even untreated, off-the-shelf laboratory rats show a certain diversity in their sexual behavior. For example, a variable proportion of male rats display little or no mounting behavior when paired with an estrous female, or are unusually ready to perform lordosis when paired with a stud male.[7] As part of a study of prenatal stress, Richard Anderson and his colleagues at Brigham Young University examined the sex behavior and brain structure of twenty-five "control" rats, that is, rats whose mothers had not been stressed during pregnancy. Six of the twenty-five consistently refused to mount receptive females (their performance with males was not tested). In these six animals, the sexually dimorphic nucleus of the medial preoptic area of the hypothalamus was about half the size of the nucleus in the rats that did perform.[8] Thus it seems that there is some source of variability that affects both brain structure and sexual behavior in male laboratory rats. It is not known whether such variability also exists in wild rat populations.

An even more interesting kind of sexual diversity is seen in female rats. A minority of females will readily mount other females. This behavior becomes even more marked when they are given testosterone, but the hormone treatment is not necessary to see it. Lynwood Clemens and his colleagues at Michigan State University showed that the willingness of a female to mount other females depends on a seemingly inconsequential aspect of its fetal life, namely, its position in the uterus with respect to male fetuses.[9] Those females who, as fetuses, lay adjacent to males are much more likely to mount other females than those whose neighbors in the uterus were females. Later it was shown that only males on one side of the female, namely, the side from which the uterine blood flows, play any role in producing the effect.[10] Thus it is likely that a substance, probably testosterone, is carried in the bloodstream from male to female fetuses and influences the development of their brains, producing a partial masculinization of behavior in adulthood.[11]

Obviously, the uterine contiguity effect could be a rather general mechanism for producing diversity in female sexuality in many species. It might also produce diversity in other sex-linked traits. It has been reported, for example, that female mice that spent their fetal lives next to males are more aggressive than those that had females as neighbors, presumably as a consequence of the same mechanism.[12]

An intriguing question is whether the mechanism might be operative in humans too—for the small number of humans who spent their fetal life with an opposite-sex twin. Because of differences in reproductive anatomy, such effects would not likely be so pronounced in humans as in rodents. Nevertheless, there has been speculation, supported by a certain amount of data, that women who had male co-twins may be partially masculinized in some psychological traits.[13] An obvious problem in interpreting these studies is that women with male co-twins are generally exposed to a masculine influence from the co-twin during childhood: it is difficult to disentangle the social influence from the supposed influence of hormones before birth. There is no evidence, as far as I am aware, that the sexual orientation or sexual behavior of such women is any different from women who were singletons or had female co-twins.

Sheep

In 1988 a sheep farmer came to the United States Department of Agriculture's Sheep Experimental Station in Dubois, Idaho with a problem: every year, about 10 percent of the rams that had been raised to be studs failed to perform: when paired with estrous ewes, they showed no sign of sexual arousal and refused to mount. They had been raised at considerable expense and to no avail. The scientists at Dubois, led by animal psychologist Anne Perkins, studied the problem assiduously for a few months and came back with a startling answer: the sheep were gay.

What Perkins had found was that many of the rams that had expressed no sexual interest in ewes did readily mount and copulate (anally) with other rams.[14] Some of them even formed what seemed to be bonded pairs, in which the two rams would take turns in mounting each other. Further study indicated that homosexual rams show up, in roughly similar proportions, in many varieties of domesticated sheep.

Perkins and her colleagues have compared the brains of their homosexual and heterosexual sheep. So far, they have turned up two interesting findings. First, the activity level of the enzyme aromatase in the medial preoptic area is about twice as high in the heterosexual rams as in the homosexual rams.[15] If this was also true during the rams' early development, it might have caused different degrees of masculinization of the hypothalamus. (It will be remembered from chapter 5 that blocking aromatase in developing male rats demasculinizes their sex behavior in adulthood.)

The second finding had to do with estrogen receptor levels in the *amygdala*, a brain structure near the hypothalamus that is sexually dimorphic and plays some role in the processing of sexually relevant stimuli (see chapter 6). Generally, estrogen receptor levels are about four times higher in the amygdala of rams than in ewes; but in the homosexual rams Perkins's group found that estrogen receptor levels were about the same as in ewes, and one-quarter the level seen in the heterosexual rams.[16] Again, such differences, if present during early development, might cause the amygdala to develop in a sex-atypical fashion. Perkins's group is now looking for structural brain differences between the heterosexual and homosexual rams, and they are also doing breeding studies to see if genetic differences play any role.

What is especially interesting about Perkins's sheep is that their sexual orientation toward their own sex is not accompanied by any obvious reversal of sex behavior. They mount and ejaculate like other males; the only difference is the sex of their preferred partners. In this respect they may be better animal models for human homosexuality than the hormonally manipulated rats, for in the rats there seems to be an almost invariable linkage—at least in the way that the tests have been performed—between an atypical sexual orientation and an atypical sexual *role*: for example, between a male choosing a male as a sex partner and being mounted by that partner. Perhaps with this in mind, Perkins refers unabashedly to her sheep as "homosexual," rather than using more neutral designators like "male-oriented," "sex-atypical," and so forth.

Of course, domesticated sheep are not natural—if by "natural" we mean untouched by human agency. It is very possible that some of these sheep became homosexual because of peculiarities in their rearing conditions, or through genetic changes that arose during the process of domestication. But there may also be a connection to the sex lives of sheep in the wild. Male Bighorn sheep spend most of their lives in all-male troops, and there is extensive sexual activity among members of a troop.[17] Whether some individual males in the wild would consistently mount a male in preference to a female is not known. What is clear, however, is that some males get few or no opportunities to copulate with females in their entire lifetime. In this context, the emergence of homosexually oriented rams makes more intuitive sense than in a situation where every ram has a good prospect of siring young (see also chapter 9).

Seagulls

"Lesbian" seagulls were discovered by George L. Hunt, Jr. and Molly Warner Hunt, ecologists at the University of California, Irvine.[18] During the 1970s the Hunts were engaged in monitoring the breeding colonies of western gulls on Santa Barbara Island and the other Channel Islands off the coast of Southern California. They noticed that a sizeable fraction of the nests—14 percent of all the nests they visited in 1974—contained too many eggs. These "supernumerary clutches" consisted of four, five, or even six eggs, whereas a single female gull does not normally lay more than three eggs. In attempting to discover the cause of these large clutches, the Hunts discovered that the pairs of gulls responsible for them consisted, not of one male and one female, but of two females, both of whom laid eggs in the same nest. This discovery was not as simple to make as one might imagine, because in western gulls the two sexes cannot be reliably distinguished by eye. The Hunts had to look inside the birds' abdomens through a small incision, a procedure that leaves the gulls unharmed.

Over the ensuing seasons, the Hunts and their colleagues made a detailed study of the behavior of the female-female pairs.[19] The two birds in a pair courted each other and, at least in some instances, copulated repeatedly. In pairs that did copulate, one of the birds did all of the mounting; however, this bird was not masculizined in its general behavior. When mounting occurred, the two birds were often arranged head-to-tail rather than head-to-head.

Of the eggs laid by the female-female pairs, only about 13 percent were fertile, compared with about 80 percent of the eggs of male-female pairs. The fact that any eggs were fertile, however, indicated that some of the birds in the female-female pairs had also copulated with males—presumably the males of neighboring heterosexual pairs who were not averse to some extramarital sex. When chicks were hatched, the two females shared the tasks of finding food and guarding the nest, just as male-female pairs do. In the majority of instances, the two females remained paired for more than one season.

Because of the similarities between the female-female pairing observed by the Hunts and lesbian pairing in humans, their discovery attracted a certain amount of attention in the lesbian and gay media. They seemed particularly relevant during the late 1970s, when religion-based homophobia was making an unexpected comeback. Jim Weinrich recalls one editorial cartoon from 1977 in which antigay crusader Anita Bryant "was looking angrily up at a flock of gulls overhead, wiping something out of her eye."[20]

In 1993, twenty years after the original discovery of the lesbian seagulls, the Institute of Gay and Lesbian Education (with which I am affiliated) organized a boat trip to Anacapa Island to revisit the birds. Guided by George Hunt, and with reporters from the *Los Angeles Times* in tow, forty or fifty lesbians and gay men combed the island in search of supernumerary clutches. They could not find any.

Behind the apparent disappearance of the lesbian seagulls is a story that, as well as any, highlights the fragile connection between "queer science" and gay people's quest for acceptance and equal rights. When the Hunts first discovered the birds, they suggested that the formation of female-female pairs was an adaptive response to an imbalance in the sex ratio in the breeding population—specifically, a shortage of males. If there were not enough males to go round, they reasoned, the leftover females would do best to pair with each other. The Hunts and their colleagues established that there was indeed a drastic shortage of males on the islands.[21] This can happen naturally when colonies are first established, because, contrary to human custom, it is mainly the females that set out to colonize new territories. But the Santa Barbara colony was not new.

The puzzle was solved by an avian physiologist at the University of California, Davis, Michael Fry, along with his graduate student Cyndi Toone.[22] They found that the shortage of males had been produced through the efforts of the Montrose Chemical Corporation, that during the 1960s had discharged millions of pounds of the pesticide DDT into Los Angeles sewers, and thus into the ocean. DDT weakened and sterilized the male gull embryos, making it impossible for them to fly to the breeding colonies or, once there, to participate in the rites of spring. After DDT was banned in the early 1970s, the sex ratio on the islands slowly began to even out again, and by the 1990s female-female pairs were a rarity.

Since the Hunts' initial discovery, female-female pairing has been described in several species of gulls, as well as in some nongull species.

Usually the numbers of female-female pairs are much lower than those observed on Santa Barbara Island, and the fraction of their eggs that are fertile are much higher. It seems that, in a colony with healthy males, getting inseminated by a neighbor is a simple matter.

So female-female pairing does seem to be a natural, adaptive response by female gulls to a particular circumstance, namely a shortage of males. To that extent, they may help people see lesbians and gay men as part of the Divine Plan. But the major outbreak of homosexuality among California's gulls in the 1970s was not God's work, but Mammon's.

Primates

According to Vasey's review,[23] homosexual behavior is rare or nonexistent among prosimians (lower primates such as galagos, lemurs, and lorises). It is fairly common among New World monkeys, but it tends to involve relatively brief contacts that are not fully comparable to the sexual contacts between opposite-sex pairs. Among Old World monkeys and apes it is both common and more obviously sexual—for example, sexual contacts are more frequently continued to ejaculation or accompanied by signs of orgasm.

The individual primates who engage in homosexual behavior generally engage in heterosexual behavior too, or would do so if opposite-sex partners were available. There is little evidence in the primatological literature for the existence of individual animals with an enduring preference for same-sex contacts. "Homosexuality," in the sense that I have generally used it in this book, seems to be a rarity among non-human primates, if it exists at all. Rather, some degree of "bisexuality" is the rule in many species.

Attempts to explain homosexual behavior in primates has focused on a number of specific hypotheses, which have been critically reviewed by Vasey. In many species, both same-sex and opposite-sex mounting occurs as a part of juvenile play, suggesting that its function is that of rehearsal for adult sexual contacts.[24] In some species, homosexual behavior increases when fewer opposite-sex partners are available, suggesting that it is to some extent a "second-best" phenomenon—providing a release of sexual energy that cannot find its preferred object.[25] According to some studies, the individual who mounts a same-sex partner generally stands higher in the dominance hierarchy, suggesting that the behavior plays a role in the establishment or maintenance of the hierarchy.[26] It has also been hypothesized that same-sex contacts play a role in the formation of social alliances or serve to reduce social tensions.[27] Same-sex behavior between females may serve to attract nearby males, thus increasing the females' reproductive success.[28] In a particularly devious sociobiological hypothesis, it has been suggest that females mount other females as a part of the competition for males: by providing these other females with sexual gratification, the argument goes, they are decreasing their interest in males and hence increasing their own chances of being inseminated.[29] Finally, higher primates may have discovered the pleasures of gay sex coincidentally, as a byproduct of some other aspect of evolutionary development, without obtaining any particular evolutionary advantages from it.[30] (The evolutionary significance of homosexuality is also discussed in chapter 9.) I pick two primate species, somewhat arbitrarily, to illustrate some of these points.

Hanuman Langurs

The Hanuman langurs (*Presbytis entellus*) are the sacred monkeys of India. As related in the Ramayana, they aided in the rescue of princess Sita from the garden of the giants and, as a bonus, brought the mango fruit back with them. In gratitude, Indians provide food for semiwild populations of langurs. This practice ties the langur troops to particular locations, facilitating their study by ethologists.

The langurs live in "harems"—groups of ten to twenty adult females with their young, along with only one mature male. Other males live on the periphery of the harem or in free-ranging troops: from time to time they organize assaults on the harem with the aim of displacing the harem owner from his position.

Homosexual behavior takes place both among the females in the harem and among the males in the free-ranging troops. A particularly thorough study of this behavior has been carried out by an Indian/ German research group that includes the primatologist Volker Sommer.[31] As his writings make clear, a part of the motivation for Sommer's research has been to establish gay people's place in nature.[32]

Sexual acts between females in the harem resemble heterosexual sex in most respects. One monkey (the "mountee") solicits by means of a head-shaking movement, and presents her rump; the other mounts from the rear and thrusts with her pelvis against her partner's buttocks. The mountee may receive direct clitoral stimulation, but the mounter does not. The mount is usually brief—about five seconds in duration. Neither partner exhibits signs of orgasm; however, females of this species do not show such signs even during male-female sex.

Every female in the harem engages in female-female sex, and every female plays both mounter and mountee roles at one time or another. Nevertheless, there is a clear relationship between mounting role and dominance: in 84 percent of the mounting episodes observed by Sommer and his colleagues, the mounting female was higher in the dominance hierarchy than the mountee. The researchers caution against inferring that the function of the female-female mounts is to maintain dominance relationships: as they point out, even heterosexual sex in langurs involves a dominant (male) mounter and subordinate (female) mountee, but its purpose is sexual, not to establish dominance. Also speaking in favor of a sexual function is the observation that the females most frequently engage in female-female mounting around the time of ovulation, just as they do with male-female sex.

In considering the possible functions of female-female sex among langurs, Sommer and colleagues place most weight on the "devious" hypothesis mentioned above: the notion that a female who mounts another female provides some amount of sexual satisfaction to the mountee, thereby decreasing her likelihood of soliciting the male harem owner. As a consequence, the mounter's behavior helps ensure that there will be sperm available for her to be impregnated and also helps reduce the number of offspring other than her own, thus improving her own offspring's chances of obtaining sufficient resources for growth and reproduction. This hypothesis seems unlikely to have much relevance to sex between women. Even among langurs, the hypothesis runs up against one problem, which is that female-female sex is often solicited by the mountee—the individual who, if the hypothesis is correct, stands most to lose by it.

Bonobos

Bonobos or "pygmy chimpanzees" are closely related to humans—98 to 99 percent of their DNA is the same as ours. They are believed to resemble the common ancestor of chimpanzees and humans (who lived about eight million years ago) more closely than do either humans or common chimpanzees.

Sexual behavior between male and between female bonobos is common. Two males may have genital contact by facing away from each other and rubbing their rumps, especially their scrotums, together; alternatively, they may face each other and rub their erect penises together ("penis fencing"). Females have a very striking behavior in which they embrace front-to-front and rub their clitorises together with a side-to-side motion ("genito-genital rubbing"). The bonobo's clitoris is far more erectile than the human's, and females sometime achieve vaginal intromission, which is accompanied by pelvic thrusting similar to that seen in heterosexual intercourse.[33]

Observations on bonobos both in the wild and in zoos have suggested that same-sex behavior, especially between females, has a specific role in the maintenance of bonobo society. Typically, sex occurs when animals are in a situation of potential conflict over resources such as food. Either animals "trade" sex for access to food, thus preventing conflicts, or sex is used to reconcile them after conflicts occur. In addition, sex is used to integrate "strangers" into the group. When a young bonobo female joins an established group of animals, she forms a liaison with one or two of the senior females, a liaison that is cemented by frequent bouts of genito-genital rubbing.[34] Thus bonding occurs between animals of the same sex that are unrelated. According to Amy Parish, a graduate student at the University of California, Davis, who has made extensive studies of bonobos, sex between females is part of a cooperative strategy that raises the overall status of females in bonobo society, freeing them to a considerable extent from male dominance and aggression. Parish is not shy of drawing a moral for feminism: "This ability found in our closest living relatives," she writes, "lends hope that women's failure to bond ... may not be so inevitable after all." She does not spell out whether this bonding is to be achieved through a broad expansion of sex between women or through some other means.[35]

Of course, men need help in bonding, too, and Parish's moral may be equally applicable to them. If we look, for example, at the homosexual initiatory rites of the Sambia, as described by Gilbert Herdt, we see a theme that seems to echo what Parish describes in bonobos. Fellatio occurs between unrelated, potentially hostile males within the same tribe.[36] Ideally, a youngster will fellate many or most of the available males before he becomes old enough to switch roles. Thus, besides imbuing the fellator with maleness (the acknowledged function of the ritual), it may also serve to tighten the bonds among the population of male adolescents, the tribe's future warriors. Since, before contact with Westerners, the Sambia were engaged in almost incessant inter-tribal warfare, this cementing of male-male loyalty across kinship lines may have been essential for the tribe's survival.

Overview

As the examples cited in this chapter are intended to illustrate, homosexual behavior has been observed in a wide variety of species and takes a wide variety of forms. Some of these forms mimic certain kinds of homosexual behavior and homosexual relationships seen in humans. But what, if anything, does this say about the nature, causes, or moral status of homosexuality in men or women?

Although homosexual *behavior* is very common in the animal world, it seems to be very uncommon that individual animals have a long-lasting predisposition to engage in such behavior to the exclusion of heterosexual activities. Thus, a homosexual *orientation*, if one can speak of such a thing in animals, seems to be a rarity. Even the "lesbian" seagulls do not quite fit the bill: it has not been shown that one of these birds, should she lose her mate, will preferentially pair with another female. Ann Perkins's homosexual male sheep may be the only compelling example, but even there it should be borne in mind that she is studying a domesticated species; truly homosexual sheep have yet to be described in wild sheep populations. Of course, the limited number of studies, the difficulties of observation, as well as the possible prejudices of ethologists may explain why homosexual animals have not been observed more commonly. But on the basis of the current literature, it seems that bisexuality, rather than homosexuality or even heterosexuality, is the predominant mode of animal sexuality.

In the branches of the animal kingdom most closely related to humans, there is a progressive loosening of the connection between sex and reproduction. This is illustrated not just by the frequency of homosexual behavior but also by that of nonprocreative heterosexual sex (especially copulation between males and nonovulating females), as well as play sex between juveniles of either sex and autosexual behavior. Humans seem to cap this evolutionary trend by their "invention" of exclusive homosexuality, as well as by certain aspects of heterosexual culture such as contraception and induced abortion. Undoubtedly, sex has developed social functions of some kind, besides or instead of its purely reproductive function. In bonobos particularly, sex seems to have acquired an abstract value, rather like money, and the value seems to lie in the sex act itself, not in an implicit promise to "have your baby." It is a little puzzling, though, to understand how nonprocreative sex can maintain its value (how it can resist inflation, to stick with the financial analogy). After all, food is a limited resource, but nonprocreative sex would seem to be cheap and essentially limitless. There must be something "bankable" about sex—as if it is a token for altruistic behavior that can be stored in the vaults of memory and brought out later when reciprocation is needed.

Whatever the exact functions of homosexual and other nonprocreative sex in animals, it is obviously a challenge to traditional Christian teachings on the subject. Protestants, to be sure, have long accepted that sex serves a social function—to cement the matrimonial bond. The Roman Catholic Church, however, has only recently begun to accept that sex has any function other than procreation, and certainly does not yet recognize any acceptable function for sex between men or between women (see chapter 14). It seems possible that the study of sexual behavior in animals, especially in non-human primates, will contribute to the liberalization of religious attitudes toward homosexual activity and other forms of nonprocreative sex. Specifically, these studies challenge one particular sense of the dogma that homosexual behavior is "against nature": the notion that it is unique to those creatures who, by tasting the fruit of the tree of knowledge, have alone become morally culpable.

Perhaps the most heartening observation about animals and same-sex behavior is this: there seems to be no homophobia in the animal kingdom. Sommer and his colleagues, for example, recount how langurs simply leave copulating same-sex couples in peace whereas, ironically, they often harass male-female pairs. In biological terms, homophobia is deeply incomprehensible. What could be more helpful in the struggle to reproduce than to have one's competitors waste their seed on each other? Even in anthropology homophobia is by no means ubiqituous. If it is indeed culture-bound, then by identifying and modifying those aspects of culture that are responsible for homophobia, we should be able to eradicate it.

11

Sickness or Health?

Is homosexuality a disease? In the United States, the official answer to this question is "no." It has been "no" since 1973, when the board of trustees of the American Psychiatric Association voted to delete homosexuality from the *Diagnostic and Statistical Manual of Mental Disorders (DSM)*. That vote, together with the Stonewall riots four years earlier, marked a turning point in the history of the American gay-rights movement. It was the end of a long era in which gay people had allowed themselves to be defined in the language of medicine, and the beginning of a new period in which they have demanded, with increasing success, to be treated as a political entity—a "sexual minority." In this chapter we revisit the struggle that preceded the declassification of homosexuality, with a particular focus on the ways in which scientific research was used by the advocates of both sides. We also ask whether the issues that were so hotly debated then have been clarified by research over the ensuing twenty-three years.

What Is a Disease?

In chapter 2 I surveyed the debate over whether the concepts "homosexual" and "heterosexual" are objective, definable categories of people, or whether they are subjective labels that create the very categories they define. In a similar way, there has been a long debate as to whether "disease" and "health" are objectively definable states of being. I will briefly review this general debate before proceeding to the specific instance of homosexuality.

One straightforward definition of "healthy" or "normal" is to say that it corresponds to the average or most common state within the group to which a person belongs, or to a range of states defined by their closeness to the average. For example, a fifty-year old man might be said to "have hypertension" if his blood pressure is higher than that of 95 percent of men his age. There is clearly some validity to this kind of definition, and it is used extensively in clinical practice. If all your physical and mental parameters are close to average, it is unlikely that paramedics will rush you to the nearest hospital. This kind of definition helps explain why, say, the inability to focus the eyes close up (to "accommodate") is considered a disorder in a ten-year-old but not in a seventy-year-old. Similarly, it explains why a man with breasts "has gynecomastia," while a woman with breasts is considered healthy.

The problem with the "healthy = average" definition, taken alone, is that it faces numerous exceptions and contradictions. Some diseases (like colds) are extremely common; some nondiseases (mathematical genius, say) are rare. Some characteristics (eye color, for example) are distributed in such a way as to defy averaging. And what is the group to which any particular individual should be compared? Most ninety-year-olds, for example, are dead. Is that then the healthiest state for people of that age?

Faced with this kind of problem, some people have taken the view that disease and health can be defined objectively with respect to the self-evident functions of body parts and body systems. Often, the proponents of this point of view have used man-made devices as analogies. C. Daly King, a Yale neuroanatomist, wrote an article in 1945 on

"The meaning of normal," in which he took the example of circular man-made objects, such as wheels.[1] The function of circularity, according to King, is the ability to revolve smoothly, therefore a deviation from circularity is an objective defect. Certainly, a bicycle wheel that is to any degree oval has the defect of "out-of-roundness," but what about an oval plate or serving dish? The general circularity of pottery has as much to do with ease of manufacture or with esthetics, as with its function. King in fact demonstrated the weakness of his argument by following it to what seems (to me at least) an absurd conclusion, which was that human beings are the only normal animals, because "no other creature behaviorally manifests the integration of intellectual, affective, and sensorimotor response which characterizes man, or, if any do, then by no means to the same degree of completeness."

In a more recent and sophisticated presentation of the "argument from design," Christopher Boorse[2] gave the example of a 1965 Volkswagen. Such a car, if it still conforms to the designer's specifications, is in "perfect mechanical condition"; if not, it is defective. Although human beings are not the product of conscious design, and have diverse goals, nevertheless there are two "apical goals"—survival and reproduction—that are made possible by the harmonious interaction of numerous subsystems: the heart, the kidneys, the genitalia, the brain, and so on. The contributions of these subsystems to survival and reproduction are just as self-evident as, say, the contribution of an intact gas tank is to the purpose of a motor vehicle. A disease is when one or more of these systems fails to interact properly with the whole person, so as to reduce (even if only to a slight degree) the achievability of the apical goals. Although there are values associated with disease— its undesirability to its bearer, an entitlement to special treatment, and so on, these are not part of the disease itself but constitute the socially constructed apparatus around the disease—what Boorse calls "illness." In a later formulation, however, Boorse even rejected the notion that "illness" is value-bound, preferring instead to simply consider it as disease severe enough to be systemically incapacitating.[3]

A third view—probably the leading one at this time—is that values are intrinsic to the definition of disease. Most especially, it has been claimed that a key feature of a disease is its undesirability, although opinions differ as to *by whom* and *for whom* (the sufferer, doctors, or society) the disease is judged undesirable. This "normative" view of disease does not necessarily rule out objectively definable malfunctions of the body or mind, but holds that such malfunctions do not become diseases until the sufferer, his doctors, and/or society at large find them a matter of concern.[4]

There has generally been more eagerness to take a normative view of mental disease than of bodily disease. A particularly good example of this is the work of the "antipsychiatrist" Thomas Szasz, who published several influential books and articles on mental illness, including homosexuality, in the decade leading up to the APA vote. Szasz raised no objection to considering physical disease as a biologically definable entity. In fact, physical disease was the *only* kind of disease: in a psychiatric context the word "disease" was no more than a metaphor, designed to strengthen the authority of psychiatrists. "Psychiatric diagnoses," he wrote in 1961, "are stigmatizing labels, phrased to resemble medical diagnoses and applied to persons whose behavior annoys or offends others."[5] Szasz's British counterpart, R. D. Laing, went even further, claiming that ". . .sanity or psychosis is tested by the degree of conjunction or disjunction between two persons where the one is sane by common consent."[6] In other words, the madman was the existential Outsider, whose speech, if one would only step outside of the group to listen to him, made as much sense as anyone's.

Szasz's ideas had a certain persuasiveness in a period when psychology was more or less divorced from biology. The brain was known to use synapses and bioelectrical signals, of course, but the interesting aspects of the mind, whether healthy or unhealthy, were generally seen as complex, emergent properties that did not depend in any strong way on the details of the biological hardware. More recently this barrier has been breached: it is commonplace these days for researchers to offer explanations for high-level mental phenomena, including mental diseases, in terms of basic neurobiological or molecular genetic processes, and even to present some evidence in support of such explanations. Just one neurotransmitter, serotonin, has been made to carry half the world's woes on its shoulders, and just one gene (according to Dean Hamer) can significantly influence a man toward homosexuality. In this atmosphere, the distinction between medical and psychiatric disease, as made by Szasz, has come to look decidedly artificial. Either one must liberate bodily diseases too from the tyranny of diagnosis, or one must accept that mental diseases can be as real as bodily ones.

Homosexuality—The Early Skirmishes

The pioneers of the gay-rights movement were quite ambivalent on the question of whether homosexuality was a disease. Hirschfeld devoted his life to the proposition that homosexuality was a normal variation of human sexuality, yet he was disconcertingly willing to use phrases like "curse of Nature" to describe the condition. The American leaders of the "homophile movement"—the gay and lesbian movement from 1950 until the late 1960s—adhered in part to the notion of homosexuality as a disease. American gay-rights pioneer Harry Hay, in his 1948 prospectus for a homophile organization that became the Mattachine Society, referred to homosexuals as having "physiological and psychological handicaps."[7] The pioneering lesbian organization, the Daughters of Bilitis, invited psychiatrists to lecture on possible "cures," acknowledged the right of homosexuals to seek such cures, and generally deferred to medical expertise when the question of the disease status of homosexuality came up.

In spite of all this, the homophile leaders made some attempts to argue that homosexuality was healthy. In the same Mattachine prospectus, Hay described homosexuals as forming 10 percent of the population—a reference to the findings of the 1948 Kinsey Report. This could be seen as an appeal to the "healthy = average" argument, rejecting the disease status because homosexuality, if not the average state, at least was more common than most conditions that were considered to be serious psychiatric disorders. Furthermore, the homophile organizations laid great stress on demonstrating that lesbians and gay men could be happy and productive citizens. Such arguments tended to undermine a disease status that was based either on undesirability or on the argument from design—if homosexuality was undesirable, why were some homosexuals happy, and if it was against design, how did homosexuals remain functional?

In 1956 gays and lesbians got help from an unexpected quarter. A young UCLA psychologist, Evelyn Hooker, gave a lecture at a meeting of the American Psychological Association under the title "The Adjustment of the Male Overt Homosexual." Hooker described the results of a study in which she had subjected gay and straight men to three tests, including the Rorschach inkblot test, that were supposed to give some objective indication of mental health. The test results had been rated "blind" by leading experts in the field: they were unable to figure out who were the gay and who were the straight subjects.

Hooker's findings, which were published the following year,[8] were a challenge to the prevailing notion that male homosexuality was invariably associated with florid psychopathology. Looking back at her work from a present-day viewpoint, one can see that it had distinct limitations. For one thing, the gay subjects were expressly selected on the basis that they seemed to be in good mental health, were functioning well in society, were not too conflicted about their sexual orientation, and so on. Thus, one could not draw any conclusions about statistical differences between the mental health of homosexuals and heterosexuals, only that *some* gay men existed who seemed to be healthy on the basis of the test results.

Another shortcoming (from our perspective) was the lack of a group of "positive controls," that is, individuals who, by common agreement, had serious mental disorders that were interfering with their lives. In the 1950s the mental-health community had enough faith in the Rorschach and the other tests to make such a control group seem unnecessary. Nowadays there is much less consensus on this point. Many psychologists and psychiatrists would say that the results of such tests, to the extent that they have any diagnostic significance, do so only within the context of a broader familiarity with the person being studied. Probably only a minority of mental-health professionals today would claim that a firm statement about mental health or illhealth could be made purely on the basis of the tests Hooker employed.

The power of Hooker's findings, though, were not so much to prove that gay men were as healthy as straight men but to say to the mental health profession, "Your own instruments, used impartially, do not indicate pathology." Her findings challenged the disease label based on the argument from design: some gay men at least were not falling apart, therefore they must not all be defective. They also strongly suggested that bias and homophobia might be affecting the psychiatric profession's attitude toward homosexuality.

Hooker extended her findings in subsequent studies,[9] and other researchers confirmed her findings, at least in part, and extended them to women.[10] Oftentimes the significance of the findings in refuting a pathological image of homosexuality was made especially obvious by the extremist, brook-no-exceptions stance of those who defended the disease model. Charles Socarides, for example, wrote in 1968 that "In all cases of homosexuality the sense of identity is lost, floundering or severely disturbed."[11] This was easily refuted by psychologist Marvin Siegelman, who showed that in nonclinical populations many gay men scored as high as or higher than heterosexuals on tests of ego strength or sense of identity.[12]

Although Evelyn Hooker was (and still is) heterosexual, there was more than a hint of gay activism in her research. As she has been very forthright in acknowledging, she was motivated to undertake her research by her close friendship with a gay male couple who introduced her to gay society and who suggested the project to her. "We have let you see us as we are," she remembers them telling her in 1945, "and now it is your scientific duty to make a study of people like us. . . . We're homosexual, but we don't need psychiatrists. We don't need psychologists. We're not insane. We're not any of those things they say we are."[13] After her research was published, she became something of a patron saint for the gay community: her writings were printed or reprinted in the *Mattachine Review*, she has been given a number of awards by gay organizations, and a documentary about her has made the rounds of the gay film festivals. It seems most unlikely that Hooker's progay "bias" distorted her results or her interpretation of them, given that she took pains to have the data evaluated by independent experts.

But her case illustrates that, in research on homosexuality, the direction of potential bias cannot be deduced solely from the researcher's own sexual orientation.

In the same year that Hooker's pioneering study was published (1957), the Wolfenden Committee, appointed by the British government to review the laws relating to homosexuality and prostitution, published its report. The committee wrote that, to be counted a disease, a condition must satisfy three requirements: it must have a cause, it must have demonstrable pathology, and it must lead to abnormal symptoms. Homosexuality, in the committee's view, fulfilled none of these requirements. Although many causes had been suggested, none seemed well established. Suggestions of mental pathology were mere theoretical constructions, not observed facts. Abnormal symptoms were not always present, and to they extent that they did occur, they were more likely to have resulted from stigmatization than to be intrinsic to the condition. The committee therefore rejected the notion that homosexuality was a disease. For this and other reasons, the committee recommended that homosexual acts between consenting adults be decriminalized, and Parliament enacted this recommendation a few years later.

Obviously, the Wolfenden Committee did not wrestle with deep issues concerning the nature of health and disease. Nor, indeed, was it terribly logical to argue that homosexuality should be decriminalized because (in part) it was not a disease. Showing that homosexuality *was* a disease would surely have made a stronger argument for decriminalization. But the committee clearly believed, as did Hooker, that some homosexuals at least were pretty average citizens, and that to punish the expression of their sexuality was as unfair as to punish the expression of heterosexuality by straight people.

The Wolfenden Report became a bestseller on its publication in the United States in 1963.[14] The U.S. version was accompanied by an introduction written by the psychiatrist Karl Menninger. This essay was a masterpiece of rhetoric: it praised the report as a "most excellent document," while at the same time it contradicted almost everything in it, damning homosexuality as both an "evil" that "ruins the lives of millions," and a disease that medical science and government policy should be given the opportunity to root out. Menninger made the report seem like the product of Senator McCarthy's committee, not Wolfenden's.

Thomas Szasz paid special attention to homosexuality in his book *The Manufacture of Madness*, published in 1970.[15] The psychiatric perspective on homosexuality, he wrote, "is but a thinly disguised replica of the religious perspective which it displaced," and efforts to treat it were "thinly disguised methods for suppressing it." To Szasz, the moralizing nature of the psychiatric discourse was betrayed by the psychiatrists' very choice of words. He quoted a passage by Menninger in which the psychiatrist stated that he did not condone homosexuality but regarded it rather as a symptom, and commented: "If homosexuality is a 'symptom,' what is there to 'condone' or not 'condone'? Menninger would not speak of 'condoning or not condoning' the fever of pneumonia or the jaundice of biliary obstruction—but he does speak of 'not condoning' a psychiatric 'symptom.' His 'therapeutic' recommendations for homosexuality bear out the suspicion that his medical role is but a cloak for that of the moralist and social engineer" (page 171).

Szasz argued that the psychiatric "diagnosis" of homosexuality was used by psychiatrists to assert and legitimize their prejudices. Beyond that, however, he made a strong case that other social institutions used the psychiatrists to justify their own prejudices. For example, he described how psychiatrists, serving as expert witnesses in court cases, facilitated the execution of laws that forbade the entry of homosexuals into the United States. They would testify that the individual in question was "afflicted with a class A condition, namely, psychopathic personality, sexual deviate." In this way the doctor, through his authority to name a disease, became an agent of the powerful state rather than an ally of the supposedly sick individual.

Szasz's arguments were very persuasive. The only problem was that, for Szasz, homosexuality was merely an example. Szasz believed that every single psychiatric diagnosis could be condemned in the same way. Gay people who were "liberated" by Szasz were liberated in the company of schizophrenics, obsessive-compulsives, the suicidally depressed, pedophiles, and so on—not a constituency that the American public was likely to associate with glowing good health. By taking such an extreme antipsychiatric line, rather than focusing on the validity of psychiatric diagnoses on a disease-by-disease basis, Szasz diminished the usefulness of his work, especially to gay people. This, and the advent of biological psychiatry, made Szasz into something of a fringe figure by the end of his career.

In response to Hooker, Szasz, and their like, conservative psychiatrists laid out at great length the many reasons why homosexuality indeed deserved the label of "disease." The argument from design offered all kinds of supportive evidence. Homosexual sex involved an evident misuse of body parts. The penis and the anus did not fit together. Lesbians were missing a part and had to make do with a dildo—the sexual equivalent of a wooden leg. Sex itself had evolved to serve reproduction, so gay sex, which could not produce offspring, was a biological malfunction. Two men or two women could not relate to each other as a man and a woman naturally did. "Heterosexual object choice," wrote Socarides, "is determined by two-and-a-half billion years of human evolution, . . . from one-celled nonsexual fission to the development of two-celled sexual reproduction, to organ differentiation, and finally to the development of two separate individuals reciprocally adapted to each other anatomically, endocrinologically, psychologically, and in many other ways."[16]

Homosexuality was caused, accompanied, and followed by sickness, therefore it must be a sickness itself. It was caused by abnormal parenting, according to Irving Bieber (see chapter 3). It was accompanied by such a grave disruption to the equilibrium of the individual that "all meaningful relationships in life are damaged from the outset and peculiarly susceptible to breakdown and destruction." (Socarides). Challenged by Hooker's suggestion that homosexuals who were not in psychiatric care were healthier than those who were, Socarides' answer was clear: it was the homosexuals in analysis who were the healthier ones, because "they have begun to see their homosexual mode of existence as meaningless."

Finally, homosexuality was a disease because it was curable. In the 1962 study of psychoanalytic treatment orchestrated by Bieber, 27 percent of the homosexual men were said to have become exclusively heterosexual. Socarides went even better: he claimed that over 50 percent of his "strongly motivated" homosexuals developed full heterosexual functioning, including "profound love feelings for their heterosexual partners." More recently, he has lowered that estimate to 25 percent, but he is still adamant that, with sufficient motivation, sexual orientation can be changed.[17]

In the course of the 1960s, the gay movement in the United States was increasingly influenced by other movements—the black civil-rights movement, women's liberation, and the movement against the war in Vietnam. Inspired by these developments, some gays and lesbians attempted to move the gay community away from the accomodationist stance of the homophile era and toward a more confrontational, gay-rights approach. One gay man who took an especially active role in this development was Frank Kameny, who cofounded the Washington, D.C., Mattachine Society in 1961. Kameny was a scientist by training—he had been dismissed from a government position as an astronomer in 1957 on account of his homosexuality—and perhaps because of this training he was less cowed by the pronouncements of mental-health professionals than many others in the movement.

In 1965 Kameny published an article entitled "Does Research into Homosexuality Matter?" in the *Ladder*, the magazine of the Daughters of Bilitis.[18] In the article he asserted that all studies claiming to show that homosexuality was a disease were scientifically worthless. They were based, he said, on circular reasoning, on the healthy = average argument (according to which, he pointed out, even left-handedness would be a disease), or on biased sampling. He berated the homophile organizations for cooperating with researchers and giving weight to their findings.

I have never heard of a single instance of a heterosexual, whatever problems he may have been facing, inquiring about the nature and origins of heterosexuality, or asking why he was a heterosexual, or considering these matters important. I fail to see why we should make similar inquiry in regard to homosexuality or consider the answers to these questions as being of any great moment to us. The Negro is not engrossed in questions about the origins of his skin color, nor the Jew in questions of the possibility of his conversion to Christianity.

Such questions are of academic, intellectual, scientific interest, but they are NOT—or ought not to be—burning ones for the homophile movement. Despite oft-made statements to the contrary, there is NO great need for research into homosexuality, and our movement is in no important way dependent on such research or upon its findings. . . . Those who do allege sickness have created THEIR need for THEIR research; let THEM do it.

Surprisingly, Kameny retreated from this noble statement of principle in the very next paragraph, where he stressed the quality and importance of a recent Dutch study, whose author, a Dr. Tolsma, claimed to show that homosexuality was not caused by seduction. Apparently, Kameny felt free to pick and choose which scientific studies were worth doing on the basis of their results—as if the results of a study could be known before it was carried out! Kameny's stand seems to have been based on a canny mixture of scientific acumen, political pragmatism, and a strong intuitive sense that "Gay is Good"—the revolutionary slogan he coined for the North American Conference of Homophile Organizations in 1968.

The Attack on the APA

Led by Kameny and like-minded gays and lesbians, the gay community focused on the possibility of using direct action to force the psychiatric profession to change its stance on homosexuality. In 1968 gays and lesbians began to picket and leaflet psychiatric meetings, including the American Medical Association convention in San Francisco, where Socarides was lecturing. The demonstrators demanded the opportunity to present an opposing point of view but were not accommodated.

After the 1969 Stonewall riots, the demonstrations became much more aggressive. In May 1970 gay activists from San Francisco's Society for Individual Rights, led by Larry Littlejohn, disrupted two sessions of the APA's annual convention—one of them a session on aversion therapy and the other a lecture by Bieber. In October of the same year, members of the Gay Liberation Front infiltrated the second annual Behavior Modification Conference in Los Angeles and disrupted the showing of a film about aversion therapy. At the 1971 APA convention, which was held in Washington, D.C., demonstrators led by Frank Kameny disrupted the Convocation of Fellows. Over the protests of irate psychiatrists, Kameny delivered a harangue in which he declared "Psychiatry is the enemy incarnate. Psychiatry has waged a relentless war of extermination against us. You may take this as a declaration of war against you."[19] Kameny was also the organizer of an officially sanctioned panel discussion on "Lifestyles of Non-Patient Homosexuals," where, among other speakers, Del Martin (cofounder of the Daughters of Bilitis) delivered an impassioned attack on the psychiatric profession.

Gay involvement in the APA climaxed in the following year, when Kameny and another tireless activist, Barbara Gittings, were invited to participate in a symposium entitled "Psychiatry: Friend or Foe to Homosexuals?" The high point of this symposium, however, was the speech by "Dr. Henry Anonymous," a gay psychiatrist, who was camouflaged for the occasion by mask, wig, and a voice-altering microphone. He said that he was one of two hundred gay psychiatrists attending the meeting, all of whom were forced to lead a double life, concealing their sexual preference and their intimate relationships for the sake of professional acceptance and advancement. Dr. Anonymous was followed by two sympathetic straight psychiatrists, Judd Marmor and Robert Seidenberg, who stressed the suffering that had been inflicted on gay people in the name of medicine.

Although gay involvement in the 1972 APA meeting was more restrained and interactive than in previous years, another disruption occurred at a meeting later that year. This was a gathering of the Association for the Advancement of Behavior Therapy in New York. A group from the New York Gay Activist Alliance, led by Ronald Gold, interrupted a session devoted to aversion therapy, forcing on the participants a discussion of the antigay bias in their work.

It so happened that a member of the APA's Committee on Nomenclature, Robert Spitzer, was present at this session. He promised the demonstrators to convene a meeting of his committee at which their views could be presented. That meeting took place in February 1973. Charles Silverstein of the Institute for Human Identity (a gay counseling center) made a presentation, backed up by a lengthy written statement, that outlined the arguments against classifying homosexuality as a disease. The committee members were favorably impressed by Silverstein's presentation, and the word soon got out that a possible change in nomenclature was in the offing.

During the following months many individuals and organizations put themselves on record as being for or against a change. Several psychoanalytic organizations urged that homosexuality be kept in the *DSM*, while the northern New England district branch of the APA, at the urging of gay psychiatrist Richard Pillard, voted for deletion. The Nomenclature Committee was divided and never actually made a formal recommendation, but Spitzer sent a position paper to the APA's leadership that suggested deleting homosexuality and substituting "sexual orientation disturbance," the condition of homosexuals who were "either bothered by, in conflict with or wished to change their sexual orientation." This was of course a concession to the analysts and behavior therapists, for it made homosexuality into a disease the moment a homosexual walked into a consulting room and asked for treatment. The board of trustees, after hearing an eleventh-hour appeal from Bieber, Socarides, and Robert McDevitt, voted to accept Spitzer's proposal, and it also adopted a statement urging the repeal of sodomy statutes and the end of antigay discrimination. After Socarides engineered a successful move to have the decision referred to the entire membership, a postal ballot was carried out in 1974. Of the ten thousand psychiatrists who returned their ballots, 58 percent supported the trustees' decision and 37 percent opposed it. As a Philadelphia newspaper put it, "20 Million Homosexuals Gain Instant Cure."[20]

Why the Change?

Gay activism was clearly the force that propelled the APA to declassify homosexuality. Without the efforts of Kameny, Gittings, Littlejohn, and the rest, homosexuality might well still be listed as a disease today. But the APA's decision was not a spineless capitulation to the mob, as Bieber and Socarides declared. Rather, the activists were successful in causing psychiatrists, singly and collectively, to question their time-honored assumptions and prejudices concerning human sexuality. The resulting dialogue, although rancorous by academic standards, was an intellectual process, more than a political or emotional one.

A good example of the psychiatrists' efforts to grapple with the issues was a paper entitled "Homosexuality as a Mental Illness," written by Richard Green in 1972.[21] Green began by acknowledging that the activism of the Gay Liberation movement was the spur to his review. He then went on to frame, in the form of about eighty questions, the issues he considered relevant. He questioned the common belief that sexual behavior develops in humans by mechanisms quite different from those operating in animals.

> To what extent can man consider himself dissociated from his two- and four-legged predecessors? Subhuman species are generally considered to manifest a series of automatic biologic responses, their central nervous system turning on to the distinctive smell or perceptual configuration of another animal, with biologic juices and neuronal circuits carrying them relentlessly on to consummate the copulatory act. It is often stated that as animals ascend the evolutionary scale, they become less and less automatically responsive to this biologic program. Yet the degree to which man, by his extraordinary capacity to remember, symbolize, and abstract, is divorced from these mechanisms is not clear. The limbic system, the endocrine glands, and their secretions have not been abandoned along the evolutionary trail. Rather they have been overlaid with additional components.

Green went on to consider biological studies on sexual orientation. He mentioned the animal studies that revealed the organizing influence of hormones on the prenatal hypothalamus. Then he described some of the human research: a study by Sydney Margolese that reported differences between gay and straight men in the ratio of two sex hormone metabolites in the urine,[22] studies claiming to find atypical urinary and plasma testosterone levels in gays and lesbians, and Kallmann's twin study that suggested an overwhelming genetic influence on sexual orientation. On the other side of the case, he mentioned John Money's studies of intersexes, that seemed to show that the sex of rearing was the paramount influence on gender identity and sexual orientation.

It is sobering to realize that, as has been reviewed in previous chapters, most of this human work has since been discredited. Only the Margolese study, as far as I am aware, has not been contradicted or thoroughly modified by subsequent work, and that may be simply because it did not attract much attention in the first place. In 1991 Green told me that he did not place a whole lot of confidence in the Margolese result either, perhaps in part because, as he confided with a grin, his own urine had tested in the "gay" range.

At any event, Green left the biological issues unresolved and went on to review psychodynamic and social-learning theories. These he considered too theoretical and untested to form an appropriate basis for a disease classification. He was particularly skeptical about the data from the psychoanalytic studies. "First," he wrote, "they emanate from patients who are maladaptive to the extent of seeking extended, expensive psychiatric treatment. Second, they are reported by clinicians who ascribe to a psychological philosophy that takes *as givens* certain universal, instinctual, incestuous drives, coupled with fear of genital mutilation, and who then interpret patient behavior in light of that theoretical matrix."

Green reviewed the evidence from Hooker, Siegelman, and others on the psychological adjustment of homosexuals. He pointed out that psychiatrists were likely to find psychopathology in their patients, whether the patients were homosexual or heterosexual, and he raised the question of how much the psychopathology that *was* observed in homosexuals could be attributed directly to their homosexuality and how much to social stigmatization.

Green then asked why conversions of homosexuals to heterosexuality should be undertaken. He examined the writings of psychiatrists and psychoanalysts who undertook conversion therapy, such as Lawrence Hatterer of Cornell Medical School, and pointed out that they relied heavily on the patient's feelings of guilt about his homosexuality as the motive force for change.[23] "One might question guilt *per se* as an inherent virtue to be harnessed for change. Psychiatry frequently helps assuage guilt in sexual matters. The woman incapable of enjoying intercourse because of early parental-religious prohibitions is helped overcome her guilt. Here guilt seems to be working against the good. Should guilt be reinforced or harnessed for behavioral change if it does not derive from behavior that is harmful to others?" He pointed out that general social values were shifting away from the notion that copulation was for conception and that (heterosexual) marriage was the greatest state of happiness. In this context he asked whether psychistrists were justified in believing that a homosexual would be happier or better off as a heterosexual.

In concluding, Green acknowledged the Szaszian standpoint. "To what extent," he asked, "do all heterosexuals, not only psychiatrists, have an emotional investment in maintaining the given that homosexuality is a disease or is at least inferior, in the traditional manner that any majority has an investment in maintaining a conviction of superiority over a threatening minority?"

Green's article was followed by a set of commentaries that represented much of the diversity of attitudes that then existed. Socarides[24] and Hatterer[25] put foward the conservative viewpoint; Judd Marmor[26] and Martin Hoffman[27] put forward more liberal ones. Hoffman, a San Francisco psychiatrist who had written a book about male homosexuality in the Szaszian vein,[28] wrote that "to define a person as 'ill' when he feels 'well,' or 'unnatural' when he deems himself 'natural,' is an ethical—that is, a philosophic—enterprise." Hatterer wrote, "As for homosexuality being a *sickness*, it most certainly is a *sickness* when it makes a person feel *sick*." These two statements are of course much further apart in attitude than they are in substance. Hoffman's statement seems to concede the possibility that homosexuals who are unhappy about their orientation have a disease (the disease that the trustees called "sexual orientation disturbance," and that eventually went into the *DSM-III* as "ego-dystonic homosexuality"). Hatterer's statement reciprocates by tacitly acknowledging that homosexuals who do not feel sick may not have a disease. The real difference between them, then, was over the question of whether the fact that some homosexuals were ill made homosexuality itself into a disease.

Marmor's commentary was perhaps the one most strongly in favor
of declassification. Marmor was a widely respected, analytically trained
psychiatrist who was later elected president of the APA. Like Hooker,
he knew gays and lesbians socially, and this acquaintance led him to
doubt the sweeping generalizations about homosexuals that he heard
at psychoanalytic meetings.[29] His stance in favor of declassifying homosexuality is believed to have strongly influenced the membership
vote. In his essay, he declared his belief that both prenatal biological
processes—analogous to those that predisposed to left-handedness—
as well as disturbed parent-child relationships could lead to homosexuality. But neither one kind of cause nor the other justified the
disease label. Left-handedness was caused by biological processes and
involved some problems of adaptation in a right-handed world, but
was not labeled a disease or corrected by "treatment." Neither were
religious convictions, which were often the result of parental influence
or other postnatal programming. Marmor summed it up by saying "I
submit that the entire assumption that homosexual behavior per se is
'unnatural' or 'unhealthy' is a moral judgment and has no basis in fact."

Similar debates took place in many forums during the two years
prior to the trustees' decision, but the issues discussed were roughly
the same. What it seemed to come down to, as far as most psychiatrists
were concerned, was the fact that large numbers of gays and lesbians
were leading apparently healthy, happy, useful lives—a fact that seemed
at odds with psychiatrists' usual experience of mental illness. That gay
people could be well adjusted was something that, paradoxically, psychiatrists were least likely to realize, dealing as they did with so many
miserable homosexuals. It was something that, even in the early 1970s,
one had to make a conscious effort to perceive, for the public image
of gay people was still, by and large, very negative. The Hollywood film
The Boys in the Band, for example, that opened in 1970, contained the
memorable line: "You show me a happy homosexual, and I'll show you
a gay corpse."

Scientific research into the *cause* of homosexuality played a relatively
small role in bringing about declassification. Although almost all those
who were against declassification were adherents of psychodynamic

or social-learning theories of homosexuality, those who were for declassification were not generally wedded to genetic or other "biological" theories. Probably the majority of them felt that the determinants of sexual orientation had not been firmly established and were likely to be complex. The consensus seemed to be that the cause of homosexuality was not as significant as its *results*. And here research such as Hooker's played a significant role. For what, to most of us, could easily be learned by getting to know a few gays and lesbians was for many psychiatrists only persuasive in the form of inkblots and multiphasic inventories.

Conclusions

Since 1973 the APA's decision has been strengthened in various ways. Other organizations, such as the American Psychological Association, the American Medical Association, and the American Psychoanalytical Association, put themselves on record as supporting the APA decision. "Ego-dystonic homosexuality" was itself removed from the *DSM* in 1987. Curiously, "gender identity disorder of childhood"—now known to be, in most cases, a precursor to normal homosexuality—*is* still listed.[30]

If the 1974 membership ballot was repeated today, it is probable that many more than 58 percent of the members would agree that homosexuality should not be classified as a disease. Whether research carried out since 1973 has promoted this trend is unclear. Recent research has certainly strengthened the notion that prenatal processes, partly under genetic control, significantly influence a person's sexual orientation. The idea that parent-child interactions or social learning are the major determinants of sexual orientation is far less prevalent than it was, although few researchers would rule out *any* role for such environmental processes. But, much more important than any research findings, has been the collective coming-out of gays and lesbians in so many walks of life, including psychiatry. At this point, only willful blindness can prevent one seeing how normally gay people function in society and in their intimate relationships. In fact, the pendulum has swung over to the point that, as described in chapter 7, gay and gay-friendly psychologists now dig deep to find the subtle differences that *do* exist between the minds of gay and straight people.

That the decision to declassify homosexuality was so strongly influenced by nonpsychiatrists meant, to people like Socarides, that it was unscientific. Ultimately, in my view, Socarides was right. Science is one thing, medicine another. Scientists describe, classify, explain, and predict. Doctors intervene, and in doing so they deal of necessity with values—the diverse values that different people put on different facets of the human experience. Every single human being probably wants to become and do something unique with his or her life, and has his or her own ideas about what would be a desirable life course for others. Of all these myriad "life plans," virtually all would be vitiated by, say, a fatal cancer in childhood. That is why we can, to a close approximation, treat such a cancer as an objectively defined "disease." Most life plans would be vitiated by a breakdown in communication with others, and this is one reason why schizophrenia is generally, although not universally considered a disease. Some life plans would be vitiated by a failure to reproduce, but far from all, whether we are talking about gay or straight people, Shakers or Catholics, career women or housewives. The fact that exclusive homosexuality is nonprocreative simply does not ruin enough people's life plans to make it a reason to confer disease status. And similarly with every other aspect of homosexuality.

Nobody is perfectly healthy, in the sense that their bodies and minds allow them to achieve all the goals that they might wish for themselves or that others might wish for on their behalf. Heterosexuals are forever excluded from that branch of human experience, valued by many, that is called homosexuality, and vice versa. But that does not make either straight or gay people sick.

12

Science and the Law

Since time immemorial, nations have framed laws to oppress gay people. Central among these have been the sodomy statutes, the laws that criminalize some of the sexual acts—especially anal and oral intercourse—that gays and lesbians may engage in. For this reason, overturning the sodomy statutes has been a major focus of gay activism ever since the day in 1867 when Karl Heinrich Ulrichs made his historic speech before the Congress of German Jurists (see chapter 1). But laws have also harmed gay people in many nonsexual aspects of their lives: by forbidding same-sex marriage, by negating gays' and lesbians' rights as parents, and by permitting discrimination in employment, housing, and services.

Scientists and doctors have been drawn into the struggle over gay rights since Hirschfeld's time or before—sometimes as neutral experts, sometimes as pro- or antigay partisans whose objectivity might be open to question. It is the uneasy interaction between science and the law that is the topic of this chapter.

It is odd, in a way, that government or the courts have even listened to scientists' views on homosexuality and homosexual behavior, because the sodomy statutes are based on value judgments about the worth or morality of this behavior, judgments about which science can say little. Many sodomy statutes have made this clear by their very wording. The 1671 statute of Plymouth Colony, for example, made the words of the Old Testament into the law of the land.

> If any Man lyeth with Mankind, as he lyeth with a Woman, both of them have committed Abomination; they both shall surely be put to Death, unless the one party were forced, or be under fourteen years of Age: And all other Sodomitical filthiness, shall be surely punished according to the nature of it.[1]

As recently as 1986, the U. S. Supreme Court, in refusing to declare sodomy statutes unconstitutional, wrote that "[t]he law...is constantly based on notions of morality, and if all laws representing essentially moral choices are to be invalidated...the courts will be very busy indeed." In concurring with the majority decision, Chief Justice Warren Burger wrote that "[t]o hold that the act of homosexual sodomy is somehow protected as a fundamental right would be to cast aside millenia of moral teaching."[2]

One way that scientists have injected themselves into the legal debate is by challenging on scientific grounds the very notion that homosexuality or homosexual behavior could be conceptualized in moral terms. In petitioning the German Reichstag to repeal paragraph 175, for example, Hirschfeld included the following two clauses.

> Emphasizing that it is now virtually proven that this phenomenon [homosexuality], which at first sight is so mysterious, actually results from developmental conditions linked to the early bisexual (hermaphroditic) state of the human fetus, and as a consequence no moral blame should be laid on a person for possessing the capacity for such feelings;
> Considering that this capacity for same-sex attraction generally seeks physical expression with the same strength as does the normal sex drive, and often even more strongly; . . .

This attempt to deny a volitional element in homosexuality, and hence to remove it from the moral arena, suffered from two defects. First, the origin of homosexuality in a bisexual state of the early fetus was not, by any stretch, "virtually proven." Hirschfeld compromised his integrity as a scientist by presenting a speculative theory as established fact. Second, paragraph 175, like all sodomy statutes, criminalized homosexual *behavior*, not homosexual *feelings*. Hirschfeld was not very successful in arguing that people lack volitional control over the physical expression of their sexual feelings. Crime in general involves giving way to "basic instincts"—greed, aggression, lust, and so on. The function of moral teaching is to restrain these instincts for the good of society as a whole. Hirschfeld failed to show what was special about homosexual feelings that made their physical expression inevitable. In fact, during the long era when there was near-universal disapproval of homosexual behavior, countless gay people must have chosen not to act on their same-sex desires, and some indeed still do.

In the contemporary United States, progay legal action has focused on two distinct areas. In one, the argument has been put forward that sodomy statutes unconstitutionally violate the right to privacy of persons who engage in same-sex behavior. In the other, it has been argued that sodomy statutes, as well as laws and regulations that permit discrimination against gays and lesbians, violate gay people's right to equal protection of the laws. Both approaches have involved scientists and psychiatrists in one way or another.

Right to Privacy

The U. S. Constitution does not explicitly mention a right to privacy, but the Supreme Court, in a 1965 decision,[3] deduced the existence of such a right from various other rights that have explicit protection. The right to privacy has been held to protect a person's right to use contraceptives, to marry across racial lines, to terminate a pregnancy, and to live together in nontraditional family units.

Some of the Supreme Court's judgments seemed to suggest that the right to privacy might extend to homosexual behavior. For example, in *Eisenstadt v. Baird*, a 1972 case in which the Court asserted that the right to use contraceptives is not restricted to married couples, the Court wrote: "If the right of privacy means anything, it is the right of the *individual*, married or single, to be free from unwarranted government intrusion into matters so fundamentally affecting a person as the decision whether to bear or beget a child."[4]

In 1982 a gay man, Donald Baker, brought suit in a federal district court in Texas to have that state's sodomy statute struck down.[5] Baker argued that the statute violated his right to privacy (as well as the equal protection clause of the Fourteenth Amendment and the establishment of religion clause of the First Amendment). In ruling in favor of Baker, Judge Buchmeyer laid especial weight on the testimony of two experts, psychiatrist Judd Marmor (see chapter 11) and sex researcher William Simon (coauthor of an important sociological study of human sexuality[6]). On the basis of their testimony, Judge Buchmeyer wrote:

> Obligatory homosexuality is not a matter of choice: it is fixed at an early age— before one even begins to participate in sexual activities—and only a small minority can be changed or "cured," if at all. Although there are different theories about the "cause" of homosexuality, the overwhelming majority of experts agree that individuals become homosexuals because of biological or genetic factors, or environmental conditioning, or a combination of these and other causes—and that sexual orientation would be difficult and painful, if not impossible, to reverse by psychiatric treatment. Indeed, homosexuality is not a "disease" and it is not, in and of itself, a mental disorder.[7]

Evidently, Judge Buchmeyer was concerned with distinguishing between "choice" and a variety of "nonchoice" factors as causes of homosexuality. Although his ruling does not make this explicit, it seems that the underlying consideration was a moral one and was not that different from Hirschfeld's position. Like Hirschfeld, Judge Buchmeyer concluded that the connection between homosexual feeling and homosexual behavior was so strong as to make the behavior more or less inevitable. Relying on Marmor's and Simon's testimony, he wrote that "[c]riminal sanctions do not deter homosexual sodomy—because 'sex, next to hunger and thirst, is the most powerful drive that human beings experience,' and it is unrealistic to think that such laws will force total abstinence."

The *Baker* ruling was reversed on appeal, on account of a Supreme Court precedent[8] that was interpreted to mean that sodomy statutes were constitutional. The Texas statute lived on to face (and survive) further legal and legislative challenges in the 1990s. Although it has been subject to so much attack, the Texas statute is, in fact, one of the mildest among the states' sodomy laws: it makes sodomy into a mere

"Class C misdemeanor," punishable by a fine of no more than 200 dollars—a far cry from Plymouth Colony's death penalty or even from the twenty years' imprisonment prescribed by the current Massachusetts statute.[9]

The most important challenge to the sodomy statutes on a right-to-privacy basis was *Bowers v. Hardwick*, the case that ended in 1986 with the US Supreme Court affirming the constitutionality of Georgia's sodomy law.[10] *Hardwick* was not fought over the issues of the nature or causation of homosexuality, but over the question of whether the sphere of constitutionally protected privacy extended beyond matters of family, marriage, and contraception to include anal and oral sex, especially when committed by a same-sex couple. The Court decided that it did not. Thus, until or unless *Hardwick* is overturned, gay people have no fundamental right to engage in these forms of sex. Furthermore, the Court declared that upholding traditional moral values was sufficient rational basis for Georgia's statute.

On its face, *Hardwick* was about conduct (sodomy). Because the case focused on homosexual rather than heterosexual sodomy, however, it has been interpreted by some courts as being about the *status* of gays and lesbians. In effect, it has been seen as denying them a status, and instead reducing them to the behaviors that they are thought likely to engage in. Thus, the *Hardwick* ruling, like many others before and after, can be seen as following Saint Paul in his belief that there is nothing more to homosexuality than straight people acting wrongly (see Introduction).

Equal Protection

The right to equal protection of the laws is guaranteed by the Fifth and Fourteenth Amendments to the Constitution. Equal protection offers disfavored groups in society some shelter from the tyranny of the majority. If a law or other government action sets some group of citizens at a disadvantage, equal-protection doctrine offers two avenues for relief. One avenue focuses on the nature of the disadvantage—specifically, whether it constitutes an encroachment on a *fundamental right.* If a court decide that it does, it must rule the goverment action unconstitutional, unless it can be shown that a compelling state interest is at stake. I will mention later the use of this avenue in one important gay-rights case, *Evans v. Romer,* the case that challenged the constitutionality of an antigay initiative passed by the citizens of Colorado in 1992.

The second avenue focuses on the *kind of group* that has been set at a disadvantage. This approach acknowledges that different groups in society may need or deserve different levels of protection. Left-handers, for example, do not need special protection because they have not, in recent times, been subject to any great discrimination and because many openly left-handed individuals (such as ex-president George Bush) have risen to positions of power, by means of which they can look after the political interests of left-handers in general. Shoplifters, to take another example, do not deserve special protection because, unless they suffer from the disease of kleptomania, they can readily escape from the disfavored group by giving up shoplifting. There is also good reason to punish shoplifters in that this helps protect property.

On the basis of this kind of thinking, the courts have set up a three-tiered hierarchy of groups that have been accorded different levels of protection. At the top of the hierarchy are the "suspect" classifications, so-called because judges are to suspect that laws discriminating on the basis of these characteristics reflect social prejudice. Race and national origin are the prime examples of suspect classifications. The courts are expected to strictly scrutinize laws that discriminate against suspect classes and to strike them down unless they serve a "compelling state interest." Even if they do serve such an interest, they must accomplish their goal by the least discriminatory means possible. An intermediate level of protection is afforded to "quasi-suspect" classifications—the main examples are classifications by sex and by legitimacy. The courts are supposed to strike down laws that discriminate against quasi-suspect classes unless they are substantially related to a legitimate governmental objective. All other, "nonsuspect" classes are protected only to the extent that laws discriminating against them must have a rational basis.

As we have seen in the case of *Hardwick*, such a basis can be as slim as the perpetuation of traditional morality.

What qualifies groups to belong to the suspect or quasi-suspect classes? The main factors that the courts have taken into consideration are as follows. First, a group must in fact have been subject over a considerable period of time to intentional discrimination. Second, the group must have been denied the opportunity to redress this discrimination through the usual political processes, perhaps because it is numerically a small group. Third, the group should be identified by some immutable or obvious characteristic—a kind of fixed identifier, like skin color, that stays with a person from birth, or at least cannot be easily shed.

The reason that classification by sex has a lower level of protection than by race is simply that there are objective differences between men and women that may, in some contexts, justify differential treatment: women are on average shorter, physically weaker, and longer-lived than men, and only women can become pregnant and bear children. Thus not every law that treats men and women differently can be assumed to be based on prejudice—it all depends on the relevance of sex to the topic of the law. With race and national origin, on the other hand, the courts are to assume that these traits are never relevant.

The U.S. Supreme Court has never ruled on whether gays and lesbians constitute a suspect or quasi-suspect class. At present, therefore, most courts go on the assumption that they do not. Thus, laws that discriminate or permit discrimination against gays and lesbians need only have a rational basis. Although courts (such as Judge Buchmeyer in *Baker*) have occasionally ruled antigay laws unconstitutional on these grounds, in general they have held that these laws have enough justification to fulfill this relatively lax criterion.

Considerable efforts have been made to persuade courts to elevate sexual orientation to a higher level of protection. But are the required conditions fulfilled? Certainly, gays have been subject to a long history of discrimination. It can also be strongly argued that gays and lesbians are unable to obtain redress through the normal political channels,[11] although this claim is perhaps less than watertight, given some of the legislative successes that gay people have scored over the last twenty years. Most vexing, and most dependent on scientific and medical evidence, is the question of the immutability of sexual orientation.

The immutability criterion was first spelled out by the Supreme Court in the 1973 decision, *Frontiero v. Richardson*,[12] which named sex as a protected classification. A plurality of the Court wrote that "sex, like race and national origin, is an immutable characteristic determined solely by the accident of birth." For this reason, discrimination on the basis of sex "would seem to violate 'the basic concept that legal burdens should bear some relationship to individual responsibility.'" In other words, one should not generally punish people or set them at a disadvantage for things they cannot help—a bedrock concept of fairness that underlies much of the law. The connection between immutability and responsibility was made especially clear in another case, *Plyer v. Doe*,[13] in which the Supreme Court ruled that the children of illegal aliens are a quasi-suspect class but that their parents are not. In the case of the children, discrimination against them was based on "a legal characteristic over which children can have little control," while for adults, joining the class of illegal aliens is "the product of voluntary action."

Of course, as the Court emphasized in *Frontiero*, the mere fact that a group is characterized by an immutable trait does not by itself make it into a suspect class. People of low intelligence, for example, may legitimately be set at a disadvantage in many ways, because intelligence may be relevant to many decisions, such as in employment. In a more recent decision, *Cleburne v. Cleburne Living Center*,[14] the Supreme Court again emphasized that the relevance of a trait, and not only its immutability, needs to be taken into consideration. In strict logic, then, one could argue that the immutability criterion, and in fact the whole concept of protected classes, is unnecessary: the courts could just decide on a case-by-case basis whether laws that set groups of people at a disadvantage discriminate on the basis of criteria that are relevant to the matter at issue (e.g., job performance).[15] The problem with this approach, however, is that relevance is always contested and uncertain. In gay-rights cases, for example, there will always be expert witnesses to document relevance: that a mother's lesbianism has a bad effect on the child she seeks to raise, that gay service-people undermine morale, and so on. What the suspect classification does is to tell the judges: "You must assume from the start that bigotry is at work here." It flags certain groups as needing the particular attention of the courts and minimizes the effects of whim or prejudice on the part of individual judges.

Military Cases

Military cases are particularly well suited to an equal protection approach, because gays and lesbians have frequently been discharged from the armed forces merely on account of their status as homosexuals, rather than as a result of any homosexual acts that they may have engaged in. In fact, it has traditionally been a valid excuse for a serviceperson caught in a homosexual act to assert that he or she is not "really" homosexual, but participated out of curiosity, immaturity, or the like.[16] Thus the armed forces unquestionably acknowledge the existence of gay people as a class and discriminate against them as a class.

One of the most interesting military cases is *Watkins v. United States Army*.[17] Perry Watkins told the army he was gay when he enlisted in 1967, and he told them again when he reenlisted on two further occasions. In fact, he gave his superiors the names of people he had had sex with, boasted of his activities at the Mine Shaft (New York's most notorious "back room bar"), openly had sex with other servicemen on a daily basis, and was much in demand as a drag entertainer at NCO balls.[18] Only after fifteen years of this did the army attempt to deny him reenlistment, and even then only on the basis of his statement that he was gay, not on account of any homosexual behavior. Watkins sued, and in 1988 a three-judge panel of a federal appeals court found in his favor by a two-to-one majority. The court declared that homosexuals did indeed constitute a suspect class. With regard to immutability, Judge Norris wrote:

> [W]e have no trouble concluding that sexual orientation is immutable for the purposes of equal protection doctrine. Although the causes of homosexuality

are not fully understood, scientific research indicates that we have little control over our sexual orientation and that, once acquired, our sexual orientation is largely impervious to change. [He cited a review of the scientific literature in an 1984 article by H. M. Miller.[19]]. . .It may be that some heterosexuals and homosexuals can change their sexual orientation through extensive therapy, neurosurgery or shock treatment. But the possibility of such a difficult and traumatic change does not make sexual orientation "mutable" for equal protection purposes.

The third member of the panel, Judge Reinhardt, dissented because he felt that *Bowers v. Hardwick* precluded extending suspect classification to gay people. Nevertheless, he took the opportunity of his dissent to deliver a blistering attack on the Supreme Court for its *Hardwick* decision.

When the full appeals court met to reconsider the issue in 1989, it concurred in ordering the army to reenlist Watkins but threw out the broad equal-protection claim. In the same year another federal appeals court, in the case of a lesbian servicewoman, Miriam ben-Shalom, threw out a lower court's ruling that gay people were a suspect class, again on the grounds that the *Hardwick* decision precluded such a ruling.[20]

A more recent case that dealt extensively with the immutability issue was that of Joseph Steffan,[21] a midshipman at the U.S. Naval Academy who was discharged in 1987, six weeks before he was due to graduate, because he stated that he was homosexual. As in the Watkins case, the issue was solely one of Steffan's status as a homosexual, not of any homosexual conduct.

Steffan, represented by the gay community's main legal organization, Lambda Legal Defense and Education Fund, sued in the U.S. District Court for the District of Columbia. The judge in charge of the case, Oliver Gasch, seems to have been somewhat prejudiced against gay people in that he repeatedly used the term "homos" to refer to them. Steffan's lawyers attempted unsuccessfully to have Gasch removed from the case.

The legal action at the district court level took the form of motions and cross-motions for summary judgment. The motion on behalf of Steffan requested that the court declare the military regulations to be unconstitutional; the proposed basis for such a declaration was that gay people are a suspect or quasi-suspect class, and that the regulations do not serve a compelling or substantial governmental interest. The motion was supported by affidavits that laid out the evidence for believing that gay people fulfilled the various requirements to be named a suspect class.

The affidavit that laid out the basis for immutability was written by Richard Green.[22] Green wrote that a homosexual orientation is an immutable characteristic in that it "is not consciously chosen, but, rather, that sexual and affectational feelings are a basic part of an individual's psyche and are established by early childhood." In support of this claim, he mentioned evidence for a genetic and prenatal hormonal influence on sexual orientation. He also described some of the cognitive psychological research, as well as the evidence for prenatal stress as an etiological factor. He laid out some of the history of the efforts to convert gay people to heterosexuality, and their generally poor success. Green also described his own work on the relationship between childhood gender nonconformity and homosexuality.

Green's affidavit was a generally even-handed survey of the field. Nevertheless, in some respects it seems that Green shaded his interpretations to favor Steffan. In arguing for a genetic basis for homosexuality, for example, Green placed considerable emphasis on the old and widely disbelieved Kallmann study, with its 100 percent concordance rate for monozygotic twins (although he did make clear that discordant pairs had been described since Kallmann's time). In describing the Minnesota study of twins reared apart, he mentioned only the pair of twins who were both gay, and not the other male pair who were at least partially discordant, nor the three female pairs, all of whom were discordant (Green's affidavit concerned both male and female homosexuality). Furthermore, when Green added a new affidavit to include a description of my work on the hypothalamus, he did not take the opportunity to mention the newly published twin studies that came up with concordance rates far lower than Kallmann's. In other words, it seems that Green did not afford the court quite so objective a view of the matter as if, for example, he had been lecturing at a scientific meeting.

One can see why researchers may be tempted to shade their testimony by the example of Green's assessment of conversion therapy. This part of his affidavit was very forthright—it mentioned among others the Bieber study that claimed a 27 percent success rate in converting gay or bisexual men to heterosexuality through psychoanalysis. Considering that most of these men were not exclusively homosexual to start with, that they were unusually motivated to change their sexual orientation, that the treatment was extraordinarily arduous and expensive, that the men were not followed up after the termination of their treatment, and that the results were never assessed by anyone except the very analysts who were so committed to this form of "cure"— considering all this, the Bieber study seems more like a testament to the *immutability* of homosexuality than to its mutability. Yet the defense took this 27 percent figure and ran with it, claiming that Green himself had disproved his own case. That was all Judge Gasch needed. "It is not for this Court," he wrote, "to say definitively whether sexual orientation is *always* chosen by the individual, but it is apparent that *sometimes* it is chosen. This realization puts sexual orientation closer to the category of [those] who are not a suspect class. . ."

Gasch ruled in favor of the military, and Steffan appealed. In 1993 a panel of the Court of Appeals for the D.C. Circuit reversed his ruling, stating that the Department of Defense's directives violated the equal-protection rights of gay people on a rational-basis review, thus making it unnecessary to decide whether gays and lesbians were a protected class.[23] In November 1994, however, the full ("en banc") court reversed the decision again, saying that the military regulations banning homosexuals were legitimate. The court placed little value on the distinction—so important for equal-protection argumentation—between homosexual identity and homosexual conduct. "The military may reasonably assume that, when a [service] member states that he is a homosexual, that member means that he either engages or is likely to engage in homosexual acts." Steffan did not appeal to the Supreme Court, probably out of deference to a new test case, *Able v. U.S.A.*, that is currently at the trial court stage and that may end in a Supreme Court ruling.

Colorado's Amendment 2

Another prominent case that has involved a request for a heightened-protection classification is *Evans v. Romer*, the legal challenge to Colorado's Amendment 2. This amendment, passed by Colorado voters in 1992, would have rescinded laws or ordinances that prohibit discrimination against gays and lesbians and would have prevented enactment of such laws in the future. Lambda Legal Defense, along with the three Colorado cities that have such ordinances, brought an action to have the amendment declared unconstitutional. The plaintiffs threw almost the entire Constitution at the state of Colorado, hoping that something would stick: they claimed that Amendment 2 violated the equal protection clause (both because it violated gay people's fundamental right to participate in the political process and because gay people constituted a suspect or quasi-suspect class), as well as the due process clause, the establishment-of-religion clause, the guarantee clause, the supremacy clause, and the rights to free expression, to free association, and to petition for redress.

At the trial in the fall of 1993, the two sides rolled out their biggest guns to contest the immutability issue. Testifying for the plaintiffs were Richard Green, Judd Marmor (now well into his eighties), and Dean Hamer. Lined up against them were Charles Socarides, Harold Voth (another conservative psychoanalyst who had been active in the campaign against the declassification of homosexuality by the A. P.A.), anti-gay psychologist Paul Cameron (see chapter 4), Robert Knight of the Family Research Council, and Edward Eichel (coauthor of a book attacking Alfred Kinsey entitled *Kinsey, Sex and Fraud*[24]). The mudslinging began almost immediately. Green attacked Cameron (a fairly easy target) by listing the various professional organizations that he has been expelled from or censured by. Asked to characterize Eichel's book, Green said that the only person known to have praised it was right-wing politician Patrick Buchanan. The defendants' attorney, Jack Wesoky, accused Hamer of deceiving the National Institutes of Health about the purpose of his research project. He also made frequent reference to the fact that some of the researchers (such as Richard

Pillard and myself) are gay, in an unspoken but still blatant attempt to suggest that our research was biased.

As in the Steffan case, the pressures of the trial drove the expert witnesses to take somewhat more extreme or simplified positions than they might otherwise have done. Hamer, for example, said at one point: "Since people don't choose their genes, they couldn't possibly choose their sexual orientation. The same goes for the question about changing. People can't change their genes. So that part of sexuality that is genetically influenced, of course, cannot be easily changed." This goes beyond the data in two respects. First, it seems to deny any possibility of choice even if the genetic influence is only partial. Yet it is possible to construct a hypothesis whereby both "gay genes" *and* a desire to be homosexual are necessary for a person actually to become homosexual. Second, it equates genetic loading with immutability, a connection that is open to challenge. Joseph Alper and Jonathan Beckwith, perennial critics of "genetic fatalism," have argued that the causes of a trait (e.g., genes versus environment) say nothing about its immutability or malleability.[25]

Nevertheless, Hamer was in general very cautious in interpreting his findings. In particular, he spelled out the difficulty of generalizing from families with two gay brothers (who might be the most genetically loaded toward homosexuality) to the entire population. He said that the Xq28 gene might account for as little as 10 percent of the variance in sexual orientation in the general male population or as much as 80 percent.

One thing everyone involved in the trial seemed to agree on was that biological theories of sexual orientation are "good for" gay rights, whereas environmental theories, and especially anything smacking of choice, are bad for them. Sometimes this seemed to open up the possibility that legal protection should be extended to gay men but not lesbians. The following exchange, for example, occurred during the cross-examination of Judd Marmor.

> Q. Dr. Marmor, I think you testified earlier in the afternoon that homosexuality did not involve a matter of choice. Am I correct in my recollection?
>
> A. That is correct. Homosexual orientation.

Q. Does not involve choice?

A. That is correct.

Q. What about female homosexuals? Is that a matter of choice?

A. Sometimes.

Q. The fact is, you said "it is probable that at least some women choose homosexual relationships because they feel deprived of access to heterosexual intimacy or affection for reasons of shyness, feelings of inadequacy, fear of rejection, or lack of available men." And you said that, didn't you?

A. Yeah. That's a hard choice for a woman to make. That again is talking about heterosexual women who for those reasons have to make that choice for one reason or another.

Q. But they make the choice to engage in homosexual behavior? Yes or no?

A. I have made it clear that women are able to do that while gay men are not able to do that.

Q. So, there's a difference between gay men and lesbians. Is that what you are telling me?

A. Yes.

Q. They aren't the same kind of group then? . . .

A. There is a difference. You cannot draw an absolute parallel between male homosexuality and female homosexuality.

Marmor seemed to become entangled in the effort to distinguish between homosexual orientation as a disposition to experience same-sex attraction and homosexual behavior. In fact, Wesoky was able to find a passage from a 1988 article by Marmor in which he wrote: "Homosexuality can be characterized as behavior involving sexual relations with a member of the same sex." This behavior-based definition of homosexuality (which Marmor repudiated at the trial) is the kiss of death to the case for suspect classification.

Although it had been twenty years since homosexuality was declassified by the APA, the defense saw fit to rehash some of the politics of that decision. By delving into Ronald Bayer's book about the decision,[26] Wesoky portrayed it as the product of gay activism, even gay perfidy. He recounted the story of how a letter soliciting support for declassification had been signed by Marmor and two colleagues and then distributed at the expense of the National Gay Task Force—with no indication in the letter itself of who was financing it. The way

Wesoky presented it, American psychiatrists were hoodwinked by Marmor and the gay lobby and have been burning to reverse the APA's decision ever since.

Two experts—myself and William Byne—were not present at the trial but nevertheless became witnesses *in absentia*. Green and Hamer both discussed my work at length and had to defend it from fairly reasonable criticisms, such as the possibility that I was seeing a disease effect, not something to do with sexual orientation. Byne became a witness for the defense: Wesoky presented some of his arguments challenging the biological point of view. This was perhaps unfair to Byne, for two reasons. First, Byne is a supporter of gay rights and would hardly have testified voluntarily for the defense. Second, although Byne has made some statements that seem to reject the biological approach altogether, the main thrust of his argument has been to question the adequacy of the experimental procedures that have been used, rather than to deny any role for genes, hormones, and so on, in the establishment of sexual orientation. In fact, his most extended treatment of the topic presents sexual orientation as resulting from an interaction between "biological" and environmental or cultural processes.[27]

In his ruling, Judge Jeffrey Bayless did not grant suspect classification. His reasons were not so much to do with any weakness in the "immutability" argument but because, in his view, gay people were not politically powerless in the sense required for heightened scrutiny. Bayless did rule that Amendment 2 violated equal protection on other grounds, however: he held that it interfered with gay people's fundamental right to participate in the political process. In 1994 the Colorado State Supreme Court affirmed Bayless's ruling. The case was appealed to the U.S. Supreme Court, and oral arguments were heard in the fall of 1995. As of this writing, the Supreme Court's ruling is still pending.

Gay Marriage

An equal-protection case that brought the science in through a somewhat unusual channel was *Baehr v. Lewin*, the Hawaii case that deals with the right to same-sex marriage. The trial court dismissed the plaintiffs' claim to this right, but the Supreme Court of Hawaii vacated the trial court's ruling. The justices asserted that prohibiting same-sex marriage, while permitting opposite-sex marriage, discriminated on the basis of sex: a woman who is barred from marrying a woman is suffering discrimination *because she is a woman*, and similarly for a man who is barred from marrying a man. Thus the individual's sexual orientation did not come into the equation. Sex is a suspect classification in the Hawaii constitution; therefore the court told the state of Hawaii that it had to show a compelling governmental interest why same-sex marriage should be prohibited. The Hawaii legislature has since come up with what it considers to be such an interest (the state's interest in procreation), and another round of court review is expected in 1996.

The use of sex rather than sexual orientation as the equal-protection classification is interesting, for it could possibly be used in other contexts, such as the case of sodomy statutes that prohibit same-sex but not opposite-sex sodomy. In addition, however, one of the Hawaii Supreme Court justices, Judge James Burns, wrote a concurring opinion in which he suggested a broadening of the concept of "sex" in its constitutional use. He wrote:

> As used in the Hawaii constitution, to what does the word "sex" refer? In my view, the Hawaii constitution's reference to "sex" includes all aspects of each person's "sex" that are "biologically fated." The decision whether a person when born will be a male or a female is "biologically fated." Thus, the word "sex" includes the male-female difference. Is there any other aspect of a person's "sex" that is "biologically fated"?

Judge Burns mentioned my work on the hypothalamus, taking special note of the fact that the structural differences were in a part of the brain "noted for differences between men and women." He also mentioned the genetic research. He went on:

> If heterosexuality, homosexuality, bisexuality, and asexuality are "biologically fated" then the word "sex" also includes those differences. Therefore, the questions whether heterosexuality, homosexuality, bisexuality, and asexuality are "biologically fated" are relevant questions of fact which must be determined before the issue presented in this case can be answered. If the answers are yes, then each person's "sex" includes both the "biologically fated" male-female

difference and the "biologically fated" sexual orientation difference, and the Hawaii constitution probably bars the State from discriminating against the sexual orientation difference by permitting opposite-sex Hawaii Civil Law Marriages and not permitting same-sex Hawaii Civil Law Marriages.[28]

Judge Burns's opinion comes as close as any in modern jurisprudence to acknowledging that Hirschfeld's "third sex" model of homosexuality might be a basis for the legal protection of gay people. The potential ramifications of his opinion are considerable. For example, if homosexuality were shown to be "biologically fated," then according to Judge Burns's reasoning even gay people as single actors should be protected under the classification of "sex" (in Hawaii at least). Therefore protection would seem to extend to areas such as employment and housing. Furthermore, it would seem that the legal significance of scientific discoveries about sexual orientation would depend on the extent to which such discoveries bolstered the "third sex" model. If Hamer's gene at Xq28, for example, turned out to code for a sex hormone receptor, and thus guided the brain into an alternate pathway of sexual differentiation, his discovery would strengthen Judge Burns's case. If on the other hand the gene turned out to code for a protein not obviously related to sexual differentiation, the discovery might actually weaken the case: it would support the "biological fatedness" of homosexuality, but it would undermine the relevance of this fatedness to the issue of sex discrimination.

All this is idle speculation, given that the majority opinion did not make use of Judge Burns's line of reasoning. It illustrates, though, that the courts might make use of scientific findings in ways that scientists themselves could not be expected to predict.

Politics

This chapter has principally focused on the litigation side of lawmaking, because it is here that the pro- and antigay arguments find their most precise formulations. But gay rights are also affected—perhaps even more strongly—by the legislative process. Constitutional questions like immutability would become irrelevant if legislatures could only be persuaded to make their laws respect the dignity of gay people. Indeed, the passage or repeal of laws, ordinances, and regulations that promote or restrict antigay discrimination currently engages a considerable amount of attention from lawmakers and the electorate. Beliefs about what determines a person's sexual orientation play a major role in this process.

The response of antigay politicians and activists to the recent wave of biological reports on sexual orientation has been a uniform "It ain't so!" When former Vice President Dan Quayle was asked in 1992 about the brain and genetic studies, he said "My viewpoint is that it's more of a choice than a biological situation. . .it is a wrong choice."[29] The Reverend Louis Sheldon, leader of the antigay Traditional Values Coalition, expressed his view of the matter this way:

> Gender identity is something that happens in the environment. Now I think the genes and the hormones can have a bearing on that. But the gender identity, or gender identity conflict that happens to a homosexual, when they have a problem in their opposite-sex attraction, that is something that you develop in your environment. I don't see the alcoholics, I don't see the prostitutes, I don't see other kinds of behavior-based groups all at once demanding special protective rights because of their behavior. Right now, the Los Angeles Unified School District has declared June "Gay and Lesbian Pride Month." Well, this is an abomination. Why? Well, here are impressionable children, with their tax dollars and their parents', being used to force a lifestyle, a value and a belief—not a religion, but like a religion—right down their throats.[30]

Antigay activists like Sheldon, who focus on homosexuality and the school system, may be willing to concede that the sexual orientation of adult men and women is deeply ingrained and hard to change. "I have been a heterosexual all of my adult life," Sheldon said. "Therefore I am in a mold. It's like I could not tomorrow start speaking fluent German or French." Rather than finding the fixity of adult sexual orientation a reason to roll back discrimination, however, people like Sheldon see it as reinforcing the importance of protecting children from progay influences before it is too late. Sheldon was a leading force behind the 1978 "Briggs Initiative" in California, the proposition that would have mandated firing gay teachers and any public education employees who took a positive position on homosexuality. Although that proposition failed, Sheldon has since become a national figure in the antigay movement. In 1995 he was instrumental in persuading House Speaker Newt Gingrich to hold congressional hearings on the topic of progay advocacy in the public-school system. On November 2, 1995, Sheldon was invited to lead the invocation on the floor of the House of Representatives. "His dedication to the Almighty and his strong moral convictions are an inspiration to us all," commented the representative who invited him, Republican Ken Calvert of California.[31]

Because the Christian Right is so invested in the "chosen-lifestyle" theory of homosexuality, which places gay people's sexuality on the very perimeter of their being, the common response of progay activists is to stress what most gay people believe about themselves, namely that their homosexuality is a part of their core identity. Thus the "born-that-way" argument is the leading idea in progay politics, just as it has been since the time of Ulrichs and Hirschfeld. To me, that seems only natural and appropriate, and to the extent that the findings of science lend support to the "born-that-way" argument, this is science well used.

At the same time, it needs to be acknowledged that a significant part of the development of sexual orientation remains unexplained. Furthermore, some people believe that choice *was* an element in their becoming gay or lesbian, or that the categories of gay, lesbian, bisexual, and heterosexual are meaningless or mere vehicles of oppression. To such people, the "born-that-way" argument may smack more of defensiveness or expediency than of self-affirmation. Luckily, there are plenty of other arguments that can be brought into play, including gay people's right to privacy and freedom of expression, the demonstration of the positive benefits of having gay people in society, and the appeal to other marginalized groups for mutual aid. If these arguments do not have quite the potential for a knockout blow that the born-that-way argument seems to carry, they may be more inclusive and more democratic. The benefit of having gay people, for example, is an argument that all lesbians and gay men can make simply by the manner in which they conduct their lives; the "born-that-way" argument, on the other hand, seems to depend on the adjudication of experts.

Overview

The legal battles currently being fought over gay rights seem designed to bring the matter to a head and to force some global resolution of the issue; yet when such resolution will occur, and what form it will take, is very unclear. It may be that, with more scientific data, with more persuasive presentation of the data that exist, or simply with a more sympathetic hearing from the judiciary, gays and lesbians will be recognized as a protected class, and laws permitting discrimination against them will be overthrown. Such an outcome, in my opinion, would be highly desirable and would do justice to gay people's long struggle to establish a social and political identity.

In reality, such an outcome is not especially likely in the near future. The Supreme Court has signaled its reluctance to expand the categories of protected classes, as well as its reluctance to accord gay people any special consideration. Although *Hardwick* was, on its face, about conduct rather than identity, it would be all but absurd for the Supreme Court to grant a globally protected status to gay people while *Hardwick* stands, for gay people are identified by a desire whose physical expression *Hardwick* has permitted to be significantly restricted. Other factors, such as the conservatism of the present Court and the increasing tendency to cede judicial autonomy to the states also make it unlikely that lesbians and gay men will be soon recognized as a class deserving heightened protection. Thus the immutability issue, and the scientific evidence that relates to it, may not play any decisive role in gay-rights litigation in the near future.

Some believe that the quest for suspect classification, or the use of the immutability argument in such a quest, is a fundamentally flawed approach to gay-rights litigation. Legal scholar Janet Halley, for example, has written an extensive critique of the immutability argument from a "weak" social-constructivist perspective. In her conclusion, she writes: "Suspect class analysis (when given its best reading) asks whether the resources of the state are being used to enforce, confirm, and validate social hierarchies. The argument from immutability has never attained the preeminence in suspect class analysis that some pro-gay advocates attribute to it because it carries so little water in that analysis."[32]

To me (a nonlawyer) this seems wrong. Suspect-class analysis does not ask whether the resources of the state are being used to reinforce social hierarchies in general, but specifically whether they are being used to reinforce *unjust* hierarchies. One obvious hierarchy—socioeconomic status—is not touched by suspect class analysis because (the thinking goes) this hierarchy is a just one, in the sense that it rewards people who improve their position by enterprise and hard work. Therefore property laws, which reinforce the socioeconomic hierarchy, are constitutional. Similarly, the carceral hierarchy (free/on probation/in prison) is thought of as a just hierarchy, in the sense that people can avoid incarceration by not committing crimes. Suspect-class analysis is an effort to spell out the moral dimension of equal protection that the framers of the Constitution intended it to possess, and the question of immutability—the impossibility of moving between classes—is a significant factor in that moral dimension, although certainly not the only one.

The social hierarchy based on the Kinsey scale is an unjust one that is strongly reinforced by the state. One aspect of that injustice is the fact that gay people neither choose to be gay nor have the power to escape being gay. In that simple sense, immutability is deeply relevant to what equal protection tries to accomplish.

Halley and others have also argued that, even though a person's sexual orientation, in the sense of whether he or she experiences sexual attraction to the same or the other sex, may indeed be unalterable, the hierarchy reinforced by state action is something different—it is a hierarchy based on sexual behavior, on calling oneself gay or straight, on being in or out of the closet, on joining or not joining gay organizations, and so on. These categories, the ones that the law is concerned with, are mutable; therefore the immutability of a person's sexual feelings is generally irrelevant.

Certainly there is some truth to this. The state does not interrogate adolescents about their emerging feelings and assign them to a favored or disfavored status on the basis of the results. Rather, it lies in ambush, waiting for the young adult to reveal himself through some word or deed. The question is, does the gap between sexual orientation and sexual expression mean that the immutability of orientation is irrelevant to the question of suspect classification?

As we saw in chapter 1, Hirschfeld attempted to bridge this gap by claiming that, in completely homosexual individuals, homosexual behavior was more or less inevitable, thanks to the intensity of their biological sex drive. This argument was useful in making clear to heterosexuals that gay people have a sex drive as strong as their own, but it did not really address the sphere of freely chosen behavior and allegiance that seems to extend from one's sexual orientation without being inevitably tied to it.

As I see it, the umbrella of immutability casts a dense shadow of protection over sexual orientation itself, but beyond this it extends a benign penumbra over the wider sphere of action. Homosexuality did not ineluctably compel Michael Hardwick to commit same-sex sodomy, or Joseph Steffan to tell his commanding officer that he was gay, or Ninia Baehr and her friends to ask for same-sex marriage licenses, but it was centrally relevant to those actions. They could have chosen not to perform those actions, but, on the other hand, hardly anyone would have chosen to perform them who did not experience homosexual feelings. These actions were the natural and appropriate actions of gay people.

The fact that social-constructivist thinking undermines the argument from immutability only reveals, as I see it, the weakness of that school of thought when it comes to matters of practical significance. For social constructivism views human identity as a kind of shell that has precipitated out at the interface of an individual and her environment; within that shell lies a black hole from which nothing can emerge. Yet in truth we have a core identity, of which our sexual orientation is an important element, that radiates outward and richly informs and energizes our lives, helping to making each life unique. The way in which this core identity influences our choice of actions is something that needs to be considered when judging whether action-based categories may lawfully be the target of discrimination. Equally, though, the immutability of core identity can never be a *sufficient* basis for such judgments.

Even if the judiciary declines to recognize that gays and lesbians are a suspect class, equal-protection litigation can still accomplish much. The fundamental-right avenue seems to be bearing fruit in the Colorado Amendment 2 case and may do so more generally. And the simple rational-basis test, to which any group is entitled, may well assist gays and lesbians in escaping some of the worst forms of institutionalized prejudice.[33]

It may also happen that, rather than acceding to a suspect or quasi-suspect classification, the courts will move toward a more "relevance-based" view of equal protection, both for gays and lesbians and for other groups. In such a view, *all* groups will become quasi-suspect, and the permissibility of discrimination will entirely depend on how related the group-defining trait is to the social function with which each law is concerned. This approach offers some benefit to gays and lesbians, for so often, as in the military cases, a good case can be made that sexual orientation is not relevant. Unfortunately, as mentioned earlier, a purely relevance-based approach offers only limited protection against majoritarian prejudice, for relevance can too easily be equated with "perceived relevance." In the military cases, for example, it can too easily be argued that sexual orientation is relevant because, even though gay people may in themselves make good soldiers, the fact that heterosexual soldiers think otherwise is enough to impair military function.

13

Science Fiction—Science Future?

Where is scientific research into homosexuality taking us? Are we heading toward the day when a person's sexual orientation will be discovered by a simple blood test, brain scan, or fingerprint analysis? Will it be possible to predict the future sexual orientation of a child, or even of a fetus? Will the technology become available to change a person's sexual orientation, or future orientation, by some form of brain engineering or genetic manipulation? And if any of these developments do become reality, will they be used for good or ill?

Concern about future abuses of scientific findings is certainly warranted. We have seen how, in the past, assertions about the causes of homosexuality have frequently lead to attempts to "cure" it. Freud's psychoanalytic theories led to the "talking cures," behavioral theories to aversion treatment, endocrinological theories to organotherapy, and brain theories to "treatment" by neurosurgery. If genetic theories have lagged behind in this regard, that is only because, until recently, the technology for genetic manipulation of human beings did not exist.

In *The Twilight of the Golds*, written by gay playwright Jonathan Tolins shortly after my research on the hypothalamus was published, the consequences of this kind of research are painted in especially gloomy colors. Set in what seems to be the near future, the play concerns a gay man, David, and his sister, Suzanne, who is expecting a baby. Suzanne's husband Rob, a biotech executive, persuades Suzanne to have her fetus screened by the most up-to-date tests developed by a company scientist, Dr. Lodge. The results are disconcerting.

> *Rob:* It will probably be like David...We matched the chromosomes from the test with the data compiled in the computer and found the presence of those genes that we've statistically linked to that trait. Then, to double check what we detected, we examined the magnetic image that we made of the brain. And sure enough, the size of the hypothalamus is much smaller than average, even at this early stage of development. Also, the anterior commissure connecting the cortex of the right and left sides of the brain is significantly larger than normal. Those are both in accordance with the latest studies. All of this information taken together has led Dr. Lodge to that conclusion.
>
> *Suzanne:* Oh.
>
> *Rob:* He estimates it's 90% certain. But he has a big ego, so who knows? Still, the evidence suggests that that's what we've got.[1]

Torn between her husband, who pressures her to abort the fetus, and her brother, who pleads with her to save it, Suzanne vacillates until it is almost too late; eventually, she chooses to abort, but complications set in that leave her sterile. Estranged from his family by this event, David later finds out that Dr. Lodge himself is gay—the homosexual equivalent, as David sees it, of an "anti-Semitic Jew."

In the real world, there are certainly some voices that seem to validate Tolins's fears. In 1991, for example, the then Chief Rabbi of the United Kingdom, Lord Jakobovitz, reacted to news reports of my research (and the twin studies) by issuing a statement that said, in part, "If we could by some form of genetic engineering eliminate these trends, we should—so long as it is done for a therapeutic purpose." In 1993 Rabbi Dr. Nisson Shulman, the chief medical ethics advisor to the British rabbinical cabinet, backed up Jakobovitz's remarks, although he made it clear that the proposed program was to be a voluntary one. He told a journalist that "if genetic intervention would help a person voluntarily cure himself of an unnatural tendency which he cannot overcome, or help him reverse a propensity to have homosexual children, then he should be able to do this." He did however rule out abortion as a means to achieve this end.[2]

Techniques to Determine Sexual Orientation

There is already one straightforward and fairly reliable method to find out a person's sexual orientation, and that is simply to ask. Most adults have a clear idea about the relative strength of their sexual attraction to men and to women and are able to verbalize this in response to a question. Yet the question is not often asked. I am not aware of any trade or occupation in the United States today in which potential employees are routinely asked about it—not even in the military (since 1993), the Boy Scouts, or the Roman Catholic Church. Neither are applicants for medical or life insurance, marriage licenses, naturalization or myriad other social benefits.

Of course, it could be argued that people are not asked because they can too easily lie. Countless military recruits *did* lie in the days when they were asked. But then, there is always the plethysmograph. According to Kurt Freund, even men who claim to have been "cured" of homosexuality reveal their true orientation when tested with this device (see chapter 2). But plethysmography is not used either, except in a research setting. On the face of it, then, there is simply no general burning desire to find out people's sexual orientation, or if there is, it has been effectively restrained by law and social convention. Discrimination against gays and lesbians is rampant, but it does not generally take the form of ferreting out the homosexuality of people who are not known to be gay. This fact alone should reduce anxiety about the future use of research findings to identify and disadvantage gay people.

Of the biological markers that seem to be linked to sexual orientation, three merit special attention: fingerprints, brain structure, and genetic markers. In all three cases, we are discussing recent reports that have not yet been replicated, so we cannot yet say that the differences reported in those studies will definitely hold up and offer a basis for future tests of sexual orientation. Also, it should be borne in mind that none of these reports were about lesbians.

The fingerprint differences reported by Hall and Kimura (see chapter 7) are statistical in nature and have very little predictive power when applied to individuals. It is possible that further dermatoglyphic characteristic may be recognized that will allow better discrimination, but that seems doubtful, given that lateralization effects in general tend to be weak.

The difference in hypothalamic structure between gay and straight men, as reported in my study (see chapter 6), was a sizeable one, and overlap between the two groups of subjects was small: one can find a "threshold level" for the size of INAH3 such that only three of the sixteen heterosexual men in the study fell below that level, while only three of the nineteen gay men fell above it (and one of those three in fact identified as bisexual). Yet this does not mean that the size of INAH3 could be the basis for a useful diagnostic test. For one thing, straight men outnumber gay men to such a degree that, even among people with very small INAH3's, there will be plenty of straight men. Therefore, if the point of the test is to identify gay men, there will be a lot of false positive results. In addition, INAH3 is a small nucleus (less than a millimeter across) and it is not demarcated by fiber tracts or aqueous ventricles that would allow it to be imaged in MRI or other scanning technologies. For the near future at least, it will not be possible to measure INAH3 in living subjects.

The other brain structure that has been reported as different between gay and straight men, the anterior commissure, can be visualized and measured in MRI scans. The differences reported by Allen and her colleagues, however, are so small, and the overlap so large, that there is no likely prospect of an informative test based on the size of this structure.

It is possible that useful information could be obtained from techniques that image brain function rather than just the structure. These methods include positron emission tomography, magnetoencephalography, and specialized versions of MRI. There are also techniques, such as single-photon emission computed tomography, that can be used to image the distribution of sex hormone receptors in the brain. So far, these methods have not been applied to study questions of human sexuality, but it is very likely that they will be. What information they might yield about a person's sexual orientation is uncertain.

The most interesting question concerns the development of tests based on genetic markers. We know that such tests will be less than totally accurate, because the heritability of homosexuality is probably no more than about 50 percent even in men, and perhaps even lower in women. But they could still give potentially useful information in some circumstances.

At this point, no actual genes have been identified, but only the approximate location of one gene in the Xq28 region of the X chromosome. Yet in certain limited circumstances, even this knowledge could give some information. Imagine, for example, a family with three sons, ages nineteen, seventeen, and eleven. The two older brothers are homosexual, but the younger boy does not yet know what he is. There are no other known gay or lesbian relatives. Could genetic analysis predict the younger brother's sexual orientation?

On the basis of sibling studies, one can say that this youngster has about a twenty percent to twenty-five percent chance of becoming a gay man, simply by virtue of having gay brothers. Analysis of Xq28 markers, however, might be able to refine this prediction considerably. If (as would be true in the majority of cases, if Dean Hamer's results are correct) both the older brothers share the same Xq28 markers, one could operate on the assumption that these markers are linked to the "gay gene" that they both inherited from their mother. If the younger brother has different Xq28 markers, he would in all probability not have inherited this gene, and his chances of being gay would be reduced below 20–25 percent—probably well below. If his Xq28 markers are the same as his brothers', on the other hand, he probably *would* have inherited the gene, and his chances of being gay would be elevated above 20–25 percent—probably well above. The exact probabilities would depend on information about the penetrance of the Xq28 gene, information that is not yet published. But enough is known to suggest that the discriminatory power of the test for Xq28 markers, in this very particular circumstance, would be considerable. The same would be true if the younger brother were still a fetus, but it is probably unusual for a fetus to have two brothers old enough to know that they are gay.

If the Xq28 results are confirmed and the gene or genes themselves are identified, it should become possible to say whether a person carries the "gay" version of the gene, without having to refer to siblings. Therefore, useful information could be obtained about the sexual orientation of men (or future orientation of boys or male fetuses) who do not have gay brothers. At the present time, it is not clear how much of a role the Xq28 gene plays in the development of gay men who have no gay brothers, but it is very likely to play a role in *some* of these men. Many men, after all, have no brothers at all: if they *did* have brothers, some of these brothers would doubtless have been gay, putting them in the class of men in whom Xq28 is already known to play a role. Furthermore, it is a good possibility that other genes influencing sexual orientation will also be identified, perhaps in both women and men. Therefore the power of genetic tests of sexual orientation will undoubtedly improve. As emphasized earlier, they will never approach 100 percent accuracy. It is possible, however, that the combined application of genetic, brain-imaging, and other tests could yield an accuracy higher than that obtainable by any one test alone.

Techniques to Change Sexual Orientation

In earlier chapters I have described numerous attempts to convert gay people (mostly men) to heterosexuality by a variety of methods derived from research into sexual orientation. All these attempts, as far as I can ascertain, have been unsuccessful. Yet one should not discount the possibility that further research might make such conversions feasible.

Let us make the assumption (a speculative one, to be sure) that sexual orientation is influenced by the size and functional state of a number of brain nuclei including INAH3 and structures connected to it. It is not impossible that these structures in gay men could be altered. Perhaps neurons could be transplanted into the brains of gay men, increasing the size of INAH3 and the other structures to the point that they become capable of mediating heterosexual attraction. If the difference between gay and straight men is a genetic one—say a difference in hormone receptors expressed by the neurons in these brain regions—then the transplanted cells could perhaps be genetically engineered to express the "straight" version of these receptors.

This may sound like the most far-fetched of science-fiction absurdities, and perhaps it is. But in fact, analogous conversions have already been achieved in laboratory animals. There is a group of cells in the hypothalamus known as the *suprachiasmatic nucleus*: it helps regulate the circadian rhythm of daily activity. One particular strain of hamster has an abnormal circadian rhythm—the period is twenty hours rather that the usual twenty-four hours. It has proved possible to restore the twenty-four hour pattern in these animals by destroying their own suprachiasmatic nuclei and transplanting suprachiasmatic nuclei from normal hamsters into their brains; evidently the transplanted neurons integrated themselves into the brains of the host animals and carried out the neural function that was defective.[3] Transplantation has even been successfully accomplished in humans: fetal brain cells, injected into the brains of people with Parkinson's disease, have helped alleviate the symptoms of that disease. It seems conceivable then that changes in a person's sex drive might be achieved by similar means.

Another possibility is that "heterosexual" genes could be inserted into a gay person (an adult, a child, or even a fetus) without transplanting any brain cells. This might be done by an "in situ" procedure, in which the genetic material would be injected directly into the brain regions involved, or by a systemic approach, involving the injection into the bloodstream of genetic material that had been tagged in such a way as to be picked up and incorporated by the relevant brain cells. The in situ method has already been used in attempts to cure cystic fibrosis;[4] the systemic method is still being developed.

There are plenty of reasons why such purely genetic techniques might not work, especially in adults. The gene or genes that influence sexual orientation might normally exert their effects during fetal development, causing the disposition toward heterosexuality or homosexuality to be hard-wired into the brain. In this case, adding new genes in adulthood might well have no effect. The very fact that INAH3, for example, is so much smaller in gay than in straight men makes it likely that it contains fewer neurons in the gay men, and no amount of DNA is going to make new neurons appear in the brains of adults.

These scenarios are alarming whether they work or not. Much suffering has been caused over the last hundred years by unsuccessful and unnecessary attempts to "cure" homosexuality. The idea that this kind of suffering might be continued into the next century is abhorrent.

Getting Homosexuality Out of the Gene Pool

The ultimate technological assault on homosexuality would be the attempt to remove "gay genes" entirely from the population. To the extent that all homosexuality may require *some* degree of genetic predisposition, it is possible that the removal of these genes would eliminate gay people from future generations.

A "low-tech" and inefficient way to do this would be through abortion: embryos or fetuses would be routinely tested for the presence of the offending genes and destroyed if they were found to harbor them. A more sophisticated approach would involve testing early-stage embryos and replacing any "gay" genes with their "straight" counterparts. In this way, all the tissues of the resulting fetus, including its germ-line cells (the potential ova or sperm) would be free of "gay" genes, and the resulting adult would therefore be unable to pass such genes on. In yet another variation, the procedure would be carried out on sperm and/or ova prior to conception. Most probably, these kinds of procedures would be done not simply to eliminate homosexuality, but as part of a general clean-up of the inherited DNA before, at, or soon after conception. The technology to perform this kind of clean-up will surely be in place by the middle of the next century.

Ethical Considerations

The ethical problems associated with these potential developments are of course enormous. Much has been written about them, particularly in the context of the human genome project. The problems apply very generally in human biology, but the specific case of homosexuality focuses them to a burning point, because homosexuality is a trait whose status (sin, crime, sickness, neutral difference, or benefit) is so contentious.

Dean Hamer and his colleagues have put themselves clearly on the record with regard to the ethical issues raised by their work. At the conclusion of their 1993 *Science* paper, they wrote:

> Our work represents an early application of molecular linkage methods to a normal variation in human behavior. As the human genome project proceeds, it is likely that many such correlations will be discovered. We believe that it would be fundamentally unethical to use such information to try to assess or alter a person's current or future sexual orientation, either heterosexual or homosexual, or other normal attributes of human behavior. Rather, scientists, educators, policy-makers, and the public should work together to ensure that such research is used to benefit all members of society.[5]

Hamer also dealt with the issue in his book, *The Science of Desire*. He wrote: "Attempts to interfere genetically with traits that are not life threatening are in my opinion both unwise and potentially dangerous." He laid out three ways in which he himself, as a scientist involved in the research, could help prevent such outcomes: he could publicly oppose genetic tests or "therapies" for homosexuality; he could cooperate with ethics committees and other groups; and he could work to prevent testing technology from becoming available, either through legislation or through patenting of the technology or of the DNA sequences themselves.[6]

Hamer's heart is so obviously in the right place it seems churlish to disagree with him. But I do disagree in some respects. It is too sweeping, in my opinion, to say that the genetic technology should never be used to assess or alter someone's sexual orientation. Surely people should have unrestricted access to genetic information about themselves, so long as the information is reasonably easy to obtain. A prohibition on such access would violate a person's fundamental rights more surely than any sodomy statute. Equally, parents have a right to such information about their children, and pregnant women about their fetuses.

According to Francis Collins, director of the National Center for Human Genome Research at the National Institutes of Health, "[i]t is reasonably likely that by the year 2010, when you reach your 18th birthday you will be able to have your own report card printed out of your individual risks for future diseases based on the genes you have inherited."[7] In fact, there will be no basis in law, ethics, or practicality for restricting the information to those genes that predispose to diseases. Nor will it be possible or desirable to withhold such information *both* from people under eighteen *and* from their parents. After all, many diseases to which genes contribute manifest themselves in childhood, and of those that manifest themselves later, many can be combated by steps taken in childhood. Even more significantly, many people have children before they are eighteen, thus passing on whatever genes they may have. There is clearly a right to this information, if it is available.

It is not just a matter of rights, though. The knowledge that a child or teenager is disposed (or not disposed) to become homosexual has potentially beneficial applications. The thing that is most difficult about becoming gay is that it is so contrary to expectation. A gay teenager has to listen to and trust her or his own feelings without one word of external validation, in fact in the face of myriad contrary signals. In this respect becoming gay (or straight) is quite unlike becoming a man or a woman, where the validating evidence is right there between one's legs. To provide such validation for sexual orientation, whether from genetic tests, brain scans, or other means, could greatly ease gay teenagers' acceptance of their homosexuality. It could also ease their acceptance by their families. Yes, there certainly could be misuse of the information, but to deny the right to that information when there is at least the potential for benefit seems to me autocratic and wrong.

I do not seem to be entirely alone in this belief. Richard Isay, for example, has written as follows:

> If some of these [pre-homosexual] children could be identified early enough, it might be possible to counsel parents and family so that rejection, injury to self-esteem, and negative self-images would be minimized or avoided altogether. Fathers of homosexual sons could, for example, be counseled not to

withdraw but to nourish their son's interests and to share common activities. When necessary and appropriate, mothers would be counseled to encourage these boys to spend more time with their fathers. If the child is made to feel that his same-sex object choice is a normal aspect of his development, he will grow up loving himself and others in spite of being "different" and in spite of the bigotry that surrounds him.[8]

I also do not believe that there should be legal prohibition of the use of genetic or neurosurgical techniques to alter sexual orientation, if such technology becomes available. Certainly there should be regulation to make sure that such procedures are safe and effective: the disasters and disappointments of the past make that abundantly clear. I would also try to persuade anyone who was thinking of undergoing such treatment to abandon the idea. I would tell them (as I firmly believe to be the case) that homosexuality is in every respect as fulfilling a life experience as heterosexuality. But in the end one has to respect an individual's autonomy, at least in the sphere of personal activity that does not harm others. In fact, Hamer himself admits as much when he writes: "My own guiding principle is simple: Everyone has a right to life, liberty, and the pursuit of happiness, so long as they do not infringe upon the rights of others." Hamer wrote that in urging tolerance for gay people, but it should apply equally to those whose idea of happiness is to become straight.

There is a parallel with sex-reassignment surgery. If a woman comes to a doctor and demands to be turned into a man, that doctor surely has an obligation to question her motives, to point out that being a woman is just fine, and to explain the limitations of the operation. The same could be said, perhaps, for plastic surgery that makes "ethnic" features into their Anglo equivalents. But if the desired transformation can be achieved and has no negative consequences, then a person should be free to undergo it, and a surgeon should be free to carry it out. The right to undergo these operations does not derive from proof of disease status—being a woman or a man or having a Jewish or African nose are not diseases or deformations. Rather, the right derives from an individual's fundamental authority over him- or herself.

What then of present-day "conversion therapists" like Socarides and Nicolosi (see chapter 3)? Is what they do ethical? Not in my view, for two reasons. First, far from starting with a reassurance that homosexuality is just fine, both Socarides and Nicolosi attempt to paint homosexuality in the worst possible light, regardless of whether a person wants to be gay or not. By this means they reinforce their clients' internalized homophobia rather than attempting to alleviate it. Second, there is serious question about their ability to perform the transformation that their clients desire. Unless they can show unequivocally that they can turn a substantial fraction of their gay clients into heterosexuals, there will always be the suspicion of deception or self-deception.

What if parents knew that their child was predisposed to become gay? Should they have the right to submit the child to genetic treatment or neurosurgery to change that outcome? Absolutely not, in my view. Parental power has, in large measure, the quality of trusteeship: it should not be exerted arbitrarily in the way that power over one's own person may be. There are innumerable ways in which society limits the autonomy of the parent–child unit without comparably restricting the behavior of parents as single actors.[9] Thus parents should not feel free to subject a child to an invasive medical procedure merely to change that child from one healthy state to another healthy state that is more to the parents' liking.

The legal position on this issue is murky. There is a traditional legal presumption that parents will act in the best interests of their children, and this presumption gives them the power to seek medical treatment for their child, even against the child's will. We saw a dismal example of that with Kyle, the boy who was subjected to operant conditioning in an attempt to get rid of his femininity (see chapter 4). But parental power is restrained, according to the U.S. Supreme Court, by laws that prohibit parents from abusing their children, as well as by the necessity for the physician to independently review the medical appropriateness of the requested treatment.[10] Since homosexuality is no longer classified as a disease, it would seem improper for a physician to carry out a procedure of this type at the parents' request. It is possible, however, that the argument could be made that the procedure was in the interests of the child' mental health because it would spare him or her from ridicule, homophobia, or the like, in the same way as operations to correct normal but "unsightly" physical characteristics such as protruding ears have been justified. This area of law is certain to evolve rapidly in the next few years as parents begin to seek the early fruits of molecular genetic technology, such as recombinant growth hormone, to "improve" their children's height, strength, and so on.

Abortion

Finally we return to Suzanne Gold and her gay fetus. Would such a person in real life choose to abort? If so, is that a problem, and if it is, what should be done about it?

In the specific circumstances of the play, it seems to me fairly implausible that Suzanne would choose to abort. She belongs to a well-educated, affluent, metropolitan sector of society where homophobia is at its weakest. She has an openly gay brother whom she loves and who is successful, healthy, and happy. She has every prospect of having other, heterosexual children after her gay son. By having Suzanne choose abortion, Tolins is telling us that *every* woman in the same circumstances would do so. Tolins's portrayal of Suzanne is, in fact, thoroughly misogynistic: she really has no desire or willpower of her own, but is the passive arena in which the machinations of Dr. Lodge, her husband, and her brother play themselves out. The prospect that Suzanne might simply say: "This is *my* decision, and I want my baby," seems not to lie within Tolins's field of view at all. Contrary to the message of Tolins's play, many women (even among those who have no moral objections to abortion as such) *would* decide to give birth to their gay child and would brook no interference in that decision.

Having said that, I do agree that *some* women would choose to abort a fetus that was predisposed to become gay. In fact, there might also be some lesbians who, desirous of having a lesbian or gay child, would abort a fetus that was predisposed to become heterosexual. As Tolins paints it, this whole situation is to be blamed on the scientists who make it possible. Specifically, he suggests that it is the fault of the closeted gay geneticist who, we are to assume, is giving vent to his internalized homophobia by attempting to eliminate gay people. Tolins's Dr. Lodge is the equivalent, in the scientific domain, of J. Edgar Hoover, the former FBI director who led the legal persecution of gay Americans, while, according to rumor at least, he himself was engaged in a forty-four-year-long homosexual relationship.[11]

In considering this future dilemma—the abortion of gay fetuses—it is useful to consider an equivalent dilemma that is already with us: the abortion of fetuses on account of their sex. Sex-specific abortion first became a possibility in 1955, when it was found that there are structural differences in the nuclei of cells sloughed off by male and female fetuses. These cells can be collected by amniocentesis and examined under the microscope. More recently, it has become commonplace to sex fetuses by directly visualizing the fetal genitalia—something made possible by obstretric ultrasound technology.

Initially, sex-selective abortion was carried out in cases where fetuses of one sex were at high risk of having an inherited sex-linked disease such as hemophilia. Such diseases generally strike males, and thus it was males who were selectively aborted. As amniocentesis and ultrasound became more routine, however, it became more common for women to ask or be told the sex of their fetus, even if it was at no particular risk of disease. Some women, who had had a number of children of one sex and wanted one of the other sex, chose to abort a normal fetus simply because it was of the nonpreferred sex. As the technology for prenatal sex diagnosis spread to developing countries, selective abortion of females has predominated. In India particularly, where bridal payments impose a heavy penalty on the rearing of daughters, abortion of female fetuses has become commonplace: so much so, apparently, as to measurably skew the sex ratio of the youngest generation toward males.

In response to the perceived problem of sex-selective abortion, some bioethicists, such as John Fletcher, have argued that laws should be passed to prevent it.[12] Because the U.S. Constitution, as presently interpreted, protects a woman's right to terminate a pregnancy without test of reasons, the laws would have to be directed against health care professionals; in other words, they would have to criminalize the performance of sex-diagnostic tests or the provision of test results to pregnant women. Such laws, in my view, would be both impractical and offensive to the pregnant woman's autonomy.

Historian Ruth Schwartz Cowan has taken a more liberal approach, framing the problem as an issue in feminist ethics.[13] She argues that a pregnant woman has the autonomous right to bear the child of her choice, because she has taken on the responsibility to nurture that child until it in turn reaches autonomy. The coupling between choice and nurturance makes sense, as Cowan sees it, because it helps ensure a match between the resources of the mother and the demands of the child: optimally, the mother will bring to birth that child whom she is most capable of nurturing. This strategy is not a guarantee against abuse, but simply a more humane and practical solution than anything that could be obtained through regulation. "If nothing else," Cowan concludes, "the history of the twentieth century ought to have taught us that individuals can sometimes behave badly, but they can never behave as badly, or as destructively, as governments can."

In my view, Cowan's arguments apply equally to the future case of "orientation-selective" abortion. I say this knowing well that there will be women who will choose to abort gay fetuses, but believing that any other solution would be worse or impractical.

In the end, the present sex-selective abortion, as well as the future orientation-selective abortion, are the consequences of the lower perceived worth of women and gay people. Yet this perceived worth can be changed—already has been changed, in fact, as far as the worth of women in the United States is concerned. In India one can reasonably hope that feminism will in time engineer a similar change. If not, then the very scarcity of women, induced by the abortion of female fetuses, will force their worth on the attention of the population. Similarly, the perceived worth of gay people can be changed. We know that because this worth has already improved dramatically over the past few decades and because we know of cultures where gay people have been positively esteemed.[14]

There still will remain a problem. Worth to society and worth to the individual are not always the same thing. People may understand that gay people contribute something unique to society or are valuable simply as an instance of human diversity, but they may still see a loss to themselves in rearing a lesbian or a gay man—on account of a diminished prospect for grandchildren, for example. But society faces this kind of problem all the time and deals with it without infringing on people's rights. Typically, society provides incentives of some kind, tailored to the degree of altruism required, whether it be for making charitable donations, developing orphan drugs, or switching to non-polluting fuels. Maybe fifty years from now there will be a tax credit for having a gay child. A far-fetched idea to our twentieth-century ears! But the next century will be different from this one: under the intense pressure of biological discoveries, society will have to find new and inventive ways to balance individual freedom and the good of society.

Eugenics

The eugenics movement of the late nineteenth and early twentieth centuries suffered from deep moral flaws. The movement was lead by the most prominent geneticists of the period—mostly white men—who presumed to judge what constituted a desirable or an undesirable human being. They then attempted to enact a program in which the fundamental rights of people deemed undesirable would be grievously abridged. When their elitist ideas reinforced majoritarian prejudices, the programs were actually carried out, with the most terrible consequences.[15]

As the dimensions of the current revolution in human genetics and neurobiology become apparent, the prospect of a return to the abuses of the past must concern everyone. One common reaction has been to demand that genetic engineering of human beings be totally prohibited or (as Hamer suggested in the passage cited earlier) be restricted to the prevention of "life-threatening" conditions.

In my view, enacting legislation along these lines would be immoral in its own way and would also deprive humanity of most of the benefits that human genome project will have to offer. Are we to say to a child going blind from an inherited retinal degeneration, "Sorry, kid, we could have prevented this, but blindness isn't life-threatening in modern society, and blind people can have a great quality of life, be productive citizens, and so on. We really couldn't tell whether you personally would enjoy being blind or not, so we gave Nature the benefit of the doubt." The child would not merely have a morally justified complaint against us, he or she would also have legal grounds for a "wrongful life" action.[16]

Even if we expand the "life-threatening" criterion, as Hamer does later in his book, to include "quality-of-life" considerations, who is going to decide about the quality of life that merits intervention? Geneticists? An NIH committee? Congress? That would be the worst of eugenics all over again.

It seems to me that no repository of genetic authority can be safer than those very people who will bring the new generation of children into the world and nurture them to adulthood. The issue is not the rights of the infinite multitude of individuals who might have been conceived or born, but never were. The issue is, who is most likely to have an actual future child's interests at heart?

By allowing parents to make these choices, we will introduce a new eugenics—a democratic, "do-it-yourself" eugenics that will circumvent the central evils of the past. The genetically underprivileged, who in the earlier eugenics were deprived of the right to reproduce, will now be free to decide whether they are indeed underprivileged or not, and if so to make the necessary adjustments in their offspring.

Democracy has its own evils. But the keys to successful democracy are education and freedom of speech. So it will be with the new eugenics. No one must understand that more clearly than gay people, who have an urgent and formidable task of persuasion in front of them.

14

Conclusions

So what causes a person to become gay, straight, or bisexual? Has a century of research and controversy produced the answer to this question, or are we still floundering in ignorance and speculation? Is the question itself ill-posed, as social constructivists assert?

At this point, the most widely held opinion is that multiple factors play a role. In 1988 PFLAG member Tineke Haase surveyed a number of well-known figures in the field about their views on homosexuality. She asked: "Many observers believe that a person's sexual orientation is determined by one or more of the following factors: genetic, hormonal, psychological, or social. Based on today's state-of-the-science, what is your opinion?" The answers included the following: "all of the above in concert" (Alan Bell), "all of these variables" (Richard Green), "multiple factors" (Gilbert Herdt), "a combination of all the factors named" (Evelyn Hooker), "all of these factors" (Judd Marmor), "a combination of causes" (Richard Pillard), "possibly genetic and hormonal, but juvenile sexual rehearsal play is particularly important" (John Money), and "genetic and hormonal factors, and perhaps also some early childhood experiences" (James Weinrich). Somewhat discordant with these opinions were those of Lee Ellis ("prenatal factors"), Martin Weinberg ("biological factors for homosexuality and heterosexuality; conditioning for various degrees of bisexuality") and the then director of the Kinsey Institute, June Reinisch ("no one knows").[1] If Haase's survey had been repeated in 1996, there might have been a detectable shift toward "biological" causes, on account of the new scientific findings of the last few years, but most likely there still would be a consensus in favor of "all of the above."

The clearest evidence for multiple factors come from the genetic studies. These offer very strong evidence that genes play a role in influencing sexual orientation, at least in men, but equally they demonstrate that genes are not the whole story. It may be that the genetic influence is very strong or even total in some families, and weak or absent in others. Alternatively, it may be that all gay men have some genetic predisposition toward homosexuality, and this has combined with other predisposing factors to lead to an actual homosexual outcome.

What the nongenetic factors are is uncertain. There might be essentially random processes in prenatal development that influence later sexual orientation. For example, I mentioned in chapter 10 the evidence that, in female rodents, sexual behavior is influenced by position in the uterus: specifically, whether the female fetus has males or females next to her. That is a matter of chance: nature has simply rolled a dice to determine whether she should have male or female neighbors. Most human fetuses are singletons and therefore are not subject to influences from other fetuses, but there are still many ways in which nature could introduce a comparable randomness into the developmental process. It could happen through a complex interaction of many genes, in the same way that a slot machine only pays out when a certain set of symbols come into alignment. It could happen through peculiarities of the site of implantation of the embryo or of the placental blood supply, through chance variations in the development of the fetal brain or endocrine system, or through many other random or near-random events.

Another possibility is that the nongenetic factors are environmental in the usual sense of the word. I have covered many environmental theories earlier in the book: prenatal stress, parenting styles, patterns of childhood reinforcement, early sexual experiences, and so on. Although most authorities, as cited above, are confident that at least some of these factors play a role, I am not sure that there is any compelling reason to believe this, given that genetic differences and random prenatal processes could easily provide all the diversity that exists. But equally, it is impossible at this point to rule out a contribution from postnatal environmental factors.

As I see it, a century of research on sexual orientation has come up with one major clue to the puzzle. This is that homosexuality is not an isolated phenomenon, but is linked with a broader collection of sex-atypical characteristics. These chacteristics include a number of mental traits, brain structures, lateralization of brain functions, and dermatoglyphic patterns. The sex-atypical mental traits are most obvious in childhood, but they are still detectable and quantifiable in adulthood. The sex-atypical brain structures and dermatoglyphic patterns (which have been documented only for gay men, not for lesbians) are presumably life-long characteristics, although that remains to be proved in the case of the brain structures.

It is this "package" of sex-atypical characteristics that Hirschfeld was referring to when he described gay people as a "third sex." He saw gays and lesbians as neither completely male nor completely female, but made up of a mosaic of male and female elements, a mosaic that took them outside of the regular, dichotomous conception of sex. In my view the "third sex" designation was, and still is, a useful way to encapsulate this notion.

In Hirschfeld's time, the word "gender" had not yet been introduced into psychology. (The German language still lacks an equivalent term.) It is very possible that, if Hirschfeld were living today, he would have used the phrase "third gender" rather than "third sex." In fact, he might well have referred to "third and fourth genders," in acknowledgement of the differences between the characteristics of lesbians and gay men. But the basic idea remains unchanged, namely, that homosexuality is one aspect of a broader sex-atypical development.

The term "gender," introduced by John Money, has both advantages and disadvantages. Its main advantage is that it clearly acknowledges the existence of differences between men and women that go beyond anatomical characteristics. Its main disadvantage is that it has fed into a mind-set, initially promoted by Money himself, that these nonanatomical characteristics are exclusively the product of environmental forces. In fact, there are those who believe that environmental causation should be part of the very definition of the word "gender."[2] To me, it would seem a pity to tie a useful word like "gender" to a particular theory of causation, but if that is to happen, then those of us who believe that genetic and other nonenvironmental factors influence "gender" will have to switch to clumsier but more neutral designators such as "the constellation of sex-linked traits."

One main objection that has been raised to the "third sex" concept is that it lumps gay people together and pays no attention to the diversity among them. Yet Ulrichs and Hirschfeld both emphasized that there is a broad spectrum of characteristics within the populations of lesbians and gay men, and this view has been amply borne out by subsequent research. Some gay men have a childhood history of pronounced femininity, some were mildly unmasculine, and some had thoroughly masculine personalities as children. Similarly there is great diversity among girls who become lesbian. Unquestionably there is overlap between the gender characteristics of prehomosexual and preheterosexual children. And the same goes for the adult characteristics that have been described at various places in this book. It is certainly not my aim to collapse gay people into a prototypical lesbian and a prototypical gay man, let alone into a single, prototypical "homosexual."

In this connection, it is useful to bear in mind what we know about the "first two" sexes, men and women. Men and women tend to differ in many characteristics beyond their anatomy (see chapter 7). To ignore this fact, in my view, would be to deny one of the main wellsprings of human diversity, as well as to raise unrealistic expectations about how men and women in a nonsexist world might distribute themselves to different occupations and activities. Yet we must also be aware of the great spread and overlap of the characteristics of men and women. If we ignore this diversity within each sex, then we are not only failing to understand the truth of the matter but we also risk perpetrating injustices on individuals whose characteristics do not correspond to the "average."

So it is with homosexual and heterosexual people. In my view, there is ample scientific evidence that gays and lesbians, on average (and in some characteristics only), are shifted away from the norms for their sex. This shift helps explain why gay people have their own history and culture, why they are overrepresented in certain occupations, and why they are the target of stigmatization. But it is only a shift in the average. Many individual lesbians and gay men have gender characteristics that coincide with the norms for their sex, and this does not make them any less homosexual than those who are gender-nonconformist or less deserving of a place in the gay community. Therefore attempting to understand homosexuality in terms of sex-atypical brain development can only be a first step, though an important one; the diversity within the homosexual (and heterosexual and bisexual) populations will remain to be explained.

A second objection to the "third sex" concept has been a less meritorious one; this is the notion, propounded by some gay men, that acknowledging the gender nonconformity of gay men is buying into a "debased" image of male homosexuality. This notion was explicit in the attitudes of the *Gemeinschaft der Eigenen*, who, as described in chapter 1, attacked Hirschfeld for portraying gay men as effeminate, weak, and so on. Even today this attitude persists to some extent. Many gay men have not fully recovered from a childhood history of teasing or physical abuse on account of their unmasculinity. They may have rejected homophobia, but they have not always rejected "femiphobia," and this may lead to an exaggerated denial of gender nonconformity as an aspect of homosexual identity. Yet the great accomplishments of feminism over the last few decades have not only diminished sexism in a male-female context, they have also, coincidentally, diminished "femiphobia" in the context of male homosexuality. Gender nonconformity is far more recognized and accepted in the gay male community that it was twenty or thirty years ago.

In attempting to account for how a package of sex-linked characteristics might develop in an atypical direction, we surely should look first and foremost at the simplest hypothesis: that they do so through variations in those very mechanisms that cause sex-*typical* development. Specifically, we should consider the hypothesis that both sex-typical and sex-atypical characteristics arise during the prenatal differentiation of the brain under the influence of circulating sex hormones.

Among the pieces of evidence supporting this hypothesis are the results of experimental manipulation of hormone levels in animals, as well as the observations on humans who have inherited defects of steroid metabolism, who were prenatally exposed to synthetic hormones or whose androgen receptors are nonfunctional (see chapter 5). The size difference in INAH3 between heterosexual men and women, and between gay and straight men (see chapter 6), is consistent with this same hypothesis, because prenatal hormone levels are known to be the main factor controlling the size of the sexually dimorphic nuclei in animals.

This hypothesis does not require that the actual levels of circulating sex hormones be different between fetuses that later become homosexual and those that become heterosexual. There may be such differences in some cases: the example of congenital adrenal hyperplasia, where high levels of prenatal androgens lead to a raised incidence of same-sex attraction in adulthood, is the most compelling example. But the sexual differentiation of the brain involves many other elements: the receptors for steroid hormones, converting enzymes like aromatase, control elements in genes that determine whether they are switched on or off by hormone levels, and probably many other molecular factors, any of which might differ between individuals either for genetic or nongenetic reasons.

It is exactly the complexity of these control systems that offer the opportunity for the kind of diversity that we actually encounter. Homosexuality is part of a "package," but it is not tied to a global switch in sex or in sex-associated traits, and the details of the package vary from individual to individual. This could readily be explained by proposing that the molecular factors are themselves variable. In extreme cases, we know this to be true: in the androgen insensitivity syndrome, for example, a genetically nonfunctional androgen receptor causes an individual to have a different external anatomy, different cognitive traits, different gender identity, and different sexual orientation[3] from what that individual would otherwise have had. What I am suggesting (with no claim to originality) is that there is a broad molecular diversity within the pathways of sexual development that permits far more subtle variations in a person's sexuality than simply "all male" or "all female."

Although the sources of this diversity are probably not all genetic, the molecular genetic approach offers by far the best prospect of understanding how sexual diversity arises. The simplest hypothesis is that genes, such as the one at Xq28, are elements in the molecular cascade that controls the sexual differentiation of the brain. If this turns out to be true—and there is absolutely no direct evidence on this as yet—one would have an entry into a realm of inquiry that is presently closed to us. And, although this is a genetic approach, it also offers our best hope of identifying the nongenetic factors that are undoubtedly involved, for the nongenetic factors may very well exert their influence through the same control elements.

Psychodynamic theories, by themselves, are grossly deficient as explanations of why people become gay, straight, or bisexual, but no one can rule out some role for childhood experiences in the establishment of sexual orientation. There are some animal studies indicating that parental treatment and interaction with peers can influence sexual behavior in adulthood.[4] The main difficulty with determining whether childhood experiences play a role in human sexual orientation is the impossibility of performing the necessary experiments. Yet there are some "social experiments" whose results cast doubt on classic psychodynamic theories of causation. An absent or weak father, for example, was one traditional psychoanalytic explanation for male homosexuality. Yet over the last twenty years a whole generation of inner-city African-American youth has been raised by single mothers, so where is the resulting explosion of homosexuality among black male teenagers? It has not happened.

One of the most popular types of psychodynamic theory draws a distinction between a person's homosexuality and other gender-nonconformist aspects of his or her personality, claiming that one of these is inborn, while the other results from an interaction between that inborn trait and some family or social dynamic. In Richard Isay's theory of male homosexuality, mentioned in chapter 3, it is the homosexuality that is inborn; the young boy, who is gay from the start, falls in love with his father and tries to displace his mother in his father's affection by adopting feminine characteristics. The prediction here would be that if a "genetically gay" boy were brought up by a single father, or by a male couple, he would still become gay but he would not show feminine traits.

In another theory, by William Byne and Bruce Parsons,[5] the boy inherits the femininity, or some crucial aspect of femininity such as a low interest in competitive sports. This then leads to rejection by father and peers, and the rejection in turn leads to homosexuality. According to this theory, a feminine boy who is loved and accepted for what he is will not become homosexual.

This theory, like Dörner's stress theory, seems like a "pathological" view of homosexuality. As such, it is at odds with the apparent wellness and normal functioning of homosexual men. More significantly, though, it does not jibe very well with cross-cultural data. In some cultures, there is far greater tolerance of childhood gender nonconformity (in both girls and boys) than there is in the United States. This does not prevent the emergence of homosexuality, however; it merely helps gay and lesbian youth to grow up feeling better about themselves than they often do in this country.[6] The same could be said for the treatment of gender-nonconformist children in Native American cultures, who were often allowed to choose between conventional or amazon/berdache status by means of ritualized trials.[7] There is simply no evidence that parental love, peer-group acceptance, and the like will steer a potentially gay child towards heterosexuality.

Thus, although I acknowledge that interactionist theories of this kind might have some truth to them, they seem to be unduly complex for our present state of knowledge. It is a better strategy, in my view, to see how far more parsimonious explanations of sexual orientation and gender nonconformity can get us, before going on to theories that are more devious and more difficult to test.

Motivation and Bias

The researchers whose work has been discussed in this book have held extremely divergent views about the desirability of homosexuality and the rights of gay people, and how science should influence these rights. Even among the biologically oriented researchers, there have been contradictory views. Hirschfeld, for example, saw a biological theory of homosexuality as being highly advantageous to gay people; he believed it would strengthen their moral status and refute the basis for sodomy statutes and other institutionalized forms of homophobia. Dörner took a very different line: his scientific views about homosexuality are basically very similar to Hirschfeld's, but until recently he has seen the science as a means to get rid of homosexuality altogether, not to foster and protect gays and lesbians.

The same diversity has existed among adherents of psychodynamic theories. Freud, in his public utterances at least, was reasonably positive about gays and lesbians: he disputed that homosexuality was a disease, and he supported the abolition of paragraph 175. Judd Marmor has been very supportive of gays and lesbians for several decades—even during the sixties when his ideas of causation were more or less entirely psychodynamic. Other American analysts like Bieber, Hatterer, and Socarides, whose theories of causation were quite similar to Freud's, nevertheless interpreted their theories as proving the pathological nature of homosexuality. Socarides has consciously used his theories in attempts to deprive gays and lesbians of legal protection (see chapter 12).

Although there is this diversity, it is probably fair to say that, at the present day, researchers who focus on biological hypotheses tend to be better disposed toward gay people than those who emphasize psychodynamic or environmental causes. Many of these biologically oriented researchers are in fact gay themselves—among those whose work is discussed in this book are Angela Pattatucci, Richard Pillard, Richard Isay, Fred Whitam, and myself, as well as several who did not wish their sexual orientation to be mentioned. Of those who are not homosexual, the great majority are thoroughly gay-friendly, supportive of gay rights, and so on. These include Doreen Kimura, Richard Green, Michael Bailey, and many others. Even the exceptions prove the rule: Günter Dörner is a biologist who in the past has been less than friendly to gay people, but the particular theory he espoused—the prenatal stress syndrome—placed the ultimate cause of homosexuality in the environment. Over the past decade, as Dörner has gradually become more positive in his attitude to gay people,[8] he has also talked less about the stress theory and more about possible genetic mechanisms (see chapter 9).

I do not mean to suggest that any researcher who espouses psychodynamic or environmental theories of sexual orientation is homophobic. There are people such as William Byne who believe that parent-child and peer-group interactions are crucial for the development of homosexuality, but who are not in the least antigay. On the whole, though, gay and lesbian academics who reject biological theories of causation reject *all* theories of causation: they are more likely to be social constructivists who see homosexuality, heterosexuality and even bisexuality as nothing more than externally applied labels.

The fact that biologically oriented researchers are more gay-friendly that those who believe in psychodynamic and environmental models echoes a relationship that exists in the wider world. As documented in the Introduction, people who think that gays and lesbians are "born that way" are also the most likely to support gay rights, to be willing to have their children be taught by gay teachers, and so on. This then raises a worrisome question: are the positions taken by researchers merely the expression of their own personal attitudes and prejudices—whether pro- or antigay—that have been dressed up in academic language but that are no more deserving of respect or attention than are the opinions of men and women in the street?

There certainly are people who believe this. Adolf Brand and his groups explicitly accused Hirschfeld of cloaking his gay-rights campaign in a mere show of scientific discourse, and Freud hinted at the same when he called Hirschfeld a "spokesman of the inverts." Conversely, there have been plenty of attempts to impugn the motives of psychodynamically oriented researchers as antigay. I have even done so myself in this book in a few cases, such as when people like Rekers, Socarides, and Nicolosi have written such globally damning statements about homosexuality as to leave no uncertainty about their attitudes towards gay people.

Because my own research on the hypothalamus drew so much public attention, I have myself been the target of many accusations of bias. These accusations have come from several different directions. According to one school of thought, typified by Jack Wesoky, the defending attorney in the Colorado Amendment 2 case, my findings are not to be believed because I am gay. According to another school, my very engagement in biological research on homosexuality proves that I am secretly out to eliminate gay people. This is the point of view of Jonathan Tolins, as expressed in *Twilight of the Golds*. There are even critics who have managed to attack me on both counts. John DeCecco, for example, the editor of the *Journal of Homosexuality*, stated in a television soundbite on the day my research was published that it was "another example of medical homophobia," but a few months later, during the taping of the *Phil Donahue Show*, he said "You're just trying to prove it's not your fault you're gay."

As long as science is conducted by human beings it will be subject to bias of one kind or another. The important question is not whether bias exists but whether science has procedures in place to minimize the effects of such bias. To a considerable degree, it does. These procedures include established methods of conducting research, such as the use of blind procedures (keeping the experimenter ignorant of which subject group each case belongs to while it is being studied), appropriate statistical methods for evaluating the significance of any differences between groups that are found, and peer review of manuscripts submitted for publication. Furthermore, science demands that experiments be described in such a way that they can be repeated by other scientists, some of whom may be biased in a very different direction from the original researchers; it is this replication (or refutation) of scientific findings that in the long term permits some measure of confidence in what science has to tell us. Unfortunately, such replication may take many years, and some of the findings described in this book, such as my own, have not yet been subject to such replication.

The conclusions of these studies must therefore be treated as provisional. Finally, the development of new scientific techniques continually offers new ways to challenge established scientific dogmas: for example, it may ultimately become possible to visualize INAH3 in living, healthy persons, and hence to test directly whether the size differences I reported were or were not a result of the diseases the subjects died of. In my view, biological theories of sexual orientation have held up pretty well over the last century, surviving many false leads, many swings in fashion, and many potentially biased scientists. I predict that they will eventually be firmly established as providing a significant part of the explanation of what makes people gay or straight.

There is one motivation of scientists that all too often gets lost in the acrimony, and that is the simple desire to know what it is that makes us human. Biologists have tended, of course, to study the common modes of our existence: the nuts and bolts of our anatomy, biochemistry, and neurobiology—the hardware we all share. But diversity is the real secret of human success. Humans are said to be genetically the most diverse of all species,[9] and the diversity of human development and culture need no documentation. To understand the basis of this diversity is surely one of the highest goals of science, and it is one on which biologists are increasingly focusing their attention. Differences related to sex and sexual orientation are important aspects of human diversity, well worth studying regardless of the supposed benefit or harm that such research will bring. I am convinced that most contemporary sexologists are driven first and foremost by this intellectual curiosity, not by the potential social consequences of their work.

The Social Consequences

In the previous chapter I discussed some of the potential negative consequences of biological research into homosexuality. I now turn to what I consider to be its main benefit. This is that it helps strengthen the identity of gays and lesbians as a discrete group within the larger society, independent to a considerable extent of the actual sexual behavior they may engage in.

As Michel Foucault and others have emphasized, there was little general recognition before about 150 years ago that there was an objective category of people whose sexual feelings were directed predominantly to persons of the same sex as themselves. Some gays and lesbians themselves may have felt that they belonged to such a category and may have set up their own hidden cultures in the largest cities, but in the general social and legal discourse there was only a behavior—sodomy. Anyone, it was presumed, might be inclined to indulge in this behavior if morality and the law did not stand in the way.

It been mainly the achievement of gay people themselves, not of sexologists, that there is today some recognition of the existence of gays and lesbians, independent of their actual behavior. If a young woman says "I've never had sex with a woman, but I know I'm a lesbian," that statement makes sense to a lot of people, in a way that many analogous statements would not ("I've never written a word of poetry, but I know I'm a poet," or "I've never broken into anyone's house, but I know I'm a burglar"). A substantial fraction of the American population now believes that the predisposition to same-sex attraction, like the predisposition to opposite-sex attraction, is a durable, identifying feature of human personality.

Yet it is still only a fraction of the population that believes this. Another sizable fraction—perhaps as much as half the population—still insist on seeing homosexuality as nothing more than a set of behaviors. It is in this group where most of the homophobia and the organized opposition to civil-rights protection for gay people is lodged. Gays and lesbians, according to Lou Sheldon of the antigay Traditional Values Coalition, are a "behavior-based group," utterly different from identity-based groups such as men and women, ethnic groups, and so on. Indeed, the main thrust of antigay politics is to deny any objective identity to gay people, independent of behavior. This is well illustrated by the text of a state initiative introduced by the Oregon Citizens' Alliance in 1994, which read in part: "Children, students and employees shall not be advised, instructed or taught by any government agency, department or political unit . . . that homosexuality is the legal or social equivalent of race, color, religion, gender, age or national origin."

The reasons for this point of view are clear. If homosexuality is simply a set of behaviors, then anyone is free to judge those behaviors in isolation; to say, in effect, "That behavior is wrong—I want you to stop it." If homosexuality is an aspect of identity, tied in, like heterosexuality, with its owner's most intimate personhood, then homophobia is directed at the individual herself or himself, and it becomes the moral equivalent of racism. Biological research is very much on the side of gay people in their claim to an objective identity and in their efforts to change the focus of public debate from "what we do" to "who we are."

An example of how biological research influence attitudes toward gay people comes from a recent *Jerry Springer Show*, a youth-oriented television talk show. Wrapping up a show devoted to homophobia, Springer delivered the following "final thought."

> You know, hardly a month goes by where we don't read of some new study suggesting or confirming that being gay or at least being disposed to being gay is a genetic circumstance determined at birth, not something someone chooses; the latest such research being that the fingerprint patterns of gays is different than that of heterosexuals. But whatever the evidence presented, from the ridges of one's fingerprints to the analysis of chromosome patterns, the impact of such studies could be profound. Because, you see, arguing that gays are doing something deviant or sinful loses some of its steam if it's determined that some people are simply born that way through no choice of their own. It'd be like hating people because they're short, or tall, or blonde, or blind. Indeed, we may well pass judgment on people based on what they *do*, the choices they make. But to hate based on what they *are* is prejudice. And by that thinking, it's homophobia that may be sinful.[10]

Of course Springer, like the Arizona newspaper editor whose story was recounted in the Introduction, is just a lay person with no special claim to know what constitutes morality or sinfulness. But some religious professionals have put forward very similar arguments. Episcopal Bishop Walter Righter of New Jersey, for example, who is facing a heresy trial in 1996 for having ordained a noncelibate gay man as a deacon, defended his action by saying "I came to the conclusion gay people are gay because of genetics. No moral decision is involved. The moral decision is how you live out your sexuality."[11] Righter's opinion is a restatement of the argument put forward by Ulrichs over a century ago (see chapter 1) that homosexual behavior is not "against nature" for people who are "by nature" homosexual.

Like the Episcopalians, the Presbyterian Church in the United States is also wrestling with the question of whether to ordain sexually active gays and lesbians. In 1994 I was invited to give a lecture at a church conference devoted to this question. Evidently I had been invited by the "progay" faction. After I finished, I fully expected the other side's response to be that the science was irrelevant to the question of the morality of homosexual behavior—particularly since the Presbyterian Church already accepts the existence of homosexuals as a discrete category of people. Instead, the opposing side presented another scientist, who apparently had memorized one of William Byne's articles. He delivered a line-by-line rebuttal of everything I had said. His implicit message was not "Who cares what makes people gay— it's just plain sinful!" but "If you were right, it would really change things—but you're not."

Some professional philosophers, such as Edward Stein of New York University and Richard Mohr of the University of Illinois, have put forward the view that research into the determinants of sexual orientation can say nothing about the way society should treat gays and lesbians. Therefore we need to wade at least ankle-deep into the waters of academic philosophy, to see what their reasons are and whether one can develop any reasoned response to them.

In an extended treatment of the topic,[12] Stein analyzes the arguments used to link the biology to gay rights, presenting them as a sets of conditionals and consequents where, he argues, at least one consequent does not follow from its conditional. Here is one example, where Stein considers whether establishing a biological basis for homosexuality leads to the conclusion that lesbians and gay men deserve protection against discrimination. Stein writes:

> The specific argument is as follows:
>
> (1) Homosexuality has a biological basis.
>
> ([2]) If homosexuality has a biological basis, then sexual orientation should be a protected category. [By "protected category" Stein is referring not to a legal category but to a category morally entitled to protection.]

([3]) If sexual orientation is a protected category, then lesbians and gay men deserve rights, recognition, and protection against discrimination.
(4) Therefore, lesbians and gay men deserve rights, recognition, and protection against discrimination.

But why should we believe premise [2]? There are, in fact, several reasons for doubting its truth. First, just because a category has a biological basis does not thereby entail that members of it deserve protected status; there are many categories with a biological basis that are not thought to be morally relevant categories, much less, to be categories that warrant protected status. For example, hair color has a biological basis but people with a particular hair color do not constitute a protected category. Being a biologically-based category is thus not a *sufficient* condition for being a category that deserves protected status. It is worth noting that being biologically based is not a *necessary* condition either. For example, being of a certain religious affiliation or nationality are not biologically based but they constitute protected categories.

I interrupt this citation just to comment that the last two sentences are irrelevant, because nowhere in the stated argument is it required that *only* biologically based categories be morally entitled to protection. Other categories may be morally entitled to protection for reasons that are conceptually linked to the biological argument (e.g., through a common basis in a perceived lack of choice, as with nationality) or for some quite different reason (as in the case of religion). Stein continues:

A friend of the "protected group" argument for lesbian and gay rights might respond to the hair-color example by pointing out that *if* people were unjustifiably discriminated against on the basis of hair color, then hair color *should* be a protected category and it should be *because* it is genetically based. Behind this response is the notion that being biologically based is not enough to make a category a protected one; there must be some *further* requirement, perhaps that the category is the basis for unjustified discrimination. While there does seem to be something right about it, the further requirement that there be "unjustified discrimination" against members of a category for that category to warrant special protection is not necessarily connected to the "biologically based" requirement. Any category that is the basis for unjustified discrimination—whether biologically based or not—seems a plausible candidate for a protected category. This very fact—that whether or not the category is biologically based seems to have nothing to do with whether the category should be a protected one—suggests that there is no interesting connection between the causes of sexual orientation and whether sexual orientation should be a protected category. Premise ([2]) is thereby undermined.

I agree that there are people-categorizing traits, such as one's natural hair color, that are biologically based and that do not form the basis of explicit morally protected categories. Nevertheless, by virtue of its inborn nature, natural hair color belongs to the set of "no-choice" traits that are implicitly protected and that would gain explicit protection the instant that people were set at a disdvantage on account of such a trait. What seems misleading about Stein's Aunt Sally argument is the notion that people of a certain hair color must face "unjustified" discrimination before their group becomes morally protected. This suggests that the injustice is somehow separable from the fact that the trait discriminated against is inborn or not chosen. In fact, in most people's moral universe, setting a group at a disadvantage is *made* unjust, or made *more* unjust that it would otherwise have been, if the group-defining trait is inborn or not chosen. As an example, suppose I were the owner of a mortuary and my receptionist one day came in with green hair. I would like to fire him, and I would feel morally free to do so if (as would likely be the case) my receptionist had voluntarily dyed his hair green the previous night. If, on the other hand, the green hair resulted from an algal infection of the kind that plagues polar bears, I would feel morally restrained from firing him, even if my business should suffer as a consequence. In other words, the origin of the trait (in a choice or not in a choice) is relevant to the question of whether setting people at a disadvantage is morally justified or not, even if other factors are also relevant. This is true both for individuals and for groups. Stein has disconnected the morality of discrimination from the cause of the trait discriminated against by the simple expedient of assuming in advance that the discrimination is maximally unjust.

Stein also asserts that the biological argument, to the extent that it offers any protection at all, does so only to the trait of experiencing same-sex attraction, not to any behaviors or allegiances that might follow from that trait. I have discussed this point of view in chapter 12.

Richard Mohr's argument[13] resembles Stein's in some respects. For example, Mohr also brings up an example of a no-choice category where discrimination is considered morally acceptable: the class of people who are disadvantaged by "grandfather clauses." That Mohr digs up such a curious class seems to point up the difficulty of identifying such classes.

But the moral thinking behind grandfather clauses, as I see it, lies in the fact that it is often more burdensome to take away a benefit than to prevent someone acquiring that benefit. For example, telling someone to leave their home because it is situated on a floodplain is far more burdensome than telling someone who is considering where to build a home not to build it on a floodplain. Where there is no such difference in burdens, grandfather clauses generally are not enacted: when tax rates go up, for example, they usually go up both for new taxpayers and for people who previously paid the lower rate. Thus grandfather clauses (except where they have some corrupt purpose) are designed to *minimize* discrimination between citizens, not to *establish* such discrimination.

Mohr asserts that the sources of injustice perpetrated against groups lies mainly in the way society treats a group, not how the group is chosen. "Injustice against minorities," he writes, "lies chiefly in the *manner* or *mode* of social operations rather than in the operations being directed at the wrong *objects*. Consider slavery. Slavery is not a social treatment the remedy for which might be found in a shift in its focus, say, from blacks to blonds." Well, no, not from blacks to blonds, because groups defined by innately light skin are as immutable as groups defined by innately dark skin. But what about a shift from blacks to murderers? Life imprisonment, a condition equivalent in most respects to slavery, is considered a just treatment of murderers because people are considered to have a choice as to whether they kill human beings or not. Of course there are other relevant factors, such as the fact that killing people is exceedingly harmful. Still, the importance of choice in making life imprisonment a moral treatment for murderers is made obvious by the fact a person can escape conviction by demonstrating that he did not make a choice to kill (It was an accident, I was mentally deranged at the time, etc.) If we look at the actual treatments that are unjustly perpetrated against gays and lesbians, such as denial of employment opportunities, we see that these treatments are commonly applied to other groups with no sense of injustice. People without college degrees, for example, are regularly denied employment opportunities. This treatment is justified, the thinking goes, because people can choose to study hard and earn degrees, or not to do so.

But Mohr's main argument is actually more interesting and far-reaching than these points would suggest. He believes that establishing gay people as an objective category (or "natural kind") would not help eliminate unjust treatment of them, because gay people are *already recognized* as a natural kind. The problem, according to Mohr, is that that they are recognized as a morally lesser kind, "like animals, children, or dirt, *not* as failed full moral agents."

Mohr claims to see this in the way people refer to gays and lesbians, especially in slang. He asserts that colloquial references to gay people emphasize, not what gay people do sexually, but what gay people are like: in particular, that they have cross-gendered traits. He cites, for example, a slang expression for "gay man" in American Sign Language that takes the form of dry-licking a fingertip and then stroking an eyebrow with it, as if one were painting them. Because painting one's eyebrows has no direct connection with same-sex desire, the use of the sign indicates a belief that gay men constitute a human kind about whom one can make generalizations, such as that they are feminine.

Actually, many colloquial expressions for gay people seem to be quite the opposite: that is, they reduce gay people to the actual sexual behaviors by which they are believed to consummate their same-sex desire. Examples are "cocksucker," "bugger," and "buttmunch." The fact that both "reductive" and "constructive" expressions for gay people are in currency suggests that people's conceptualization of them is complex and uncertain.

Mohr goes on to say that this moral classification of gay people by status rather than by action is evident in the law (such as immigration policy and marital law), religion, and medicine. Thus, at most of the levels at which prejudice against gay people is manifested, that prejudice is directed against a recognized class, not a behavior.

Again, this is only partially true. Let's take marital law, for example. What the law says is that one's marriage partner must be of the other sex. There is no explicit or implicit legal hindrance against gay people marrying, so long as they marry someone of the other sex. Therefore marital law fails to recognize gay people as a group to be either favored or disfavored. The requirement that one marry someone of the other sex, however, is clearly premised on the belief that homosexual behavior is wrong and that the law should not facilitate such behavior by allowing two men or two women to marry. In other words, marital law has the practical effect of setting gay people at a disadvantage, but not through a conscious legal recognition of gay people as a natural kind. Immigration law, on the other hand, did for many years discriminate against gay people by virtue of their status as homosexual. The law seems mixed-up and inconsistent in whether to treat gays by status or by behavior—an inconsistency that is at the heart of the Supreme Court ruling in *Bowers v. Hardwick* (see chapter 12).

Turning to religion, we find that organized churches are also divided in their view of gay people. Many denominations that oppose gay rights reduce gay people to a behavior; this is generally true of fundamentalist Christian churches in America and is exemplified by the phrase "behavior-based group" used by the Reverend Lou Sheldon (see above). The Roman Catholic Church, however, takes a more status-based view. It is worth taking a moment to see how this affects official Catholic policies toward gay people.

The Catholic Church takes the position that homosexuals fall into two groups, "temporary" and "permanent." According to a position paper issued by the second Vatican Council in the 1970s, the latter group may have become homosexual "because of a constitutional defect presumed to be incurable." The document goes on:

> Many argue that the condition of the second type of homosexuals is so natural that it justifies homosexual relations for them[.]...Certainly, pastoral care of such homosexuals should be considerate and kind. The hope should be instilled in them of one day overcoming their difficulties and their alienation from society. Their culpability will be judged prudently. However, it is not permissible to employ any pastoral method or theory to provide moral justification for their actions, on the grounds that they are in keeping with their condition. Sexual relations between persons of the same sex are necessarily and essentially disordered according to the objective moral order. Sacred scripture portrays them as gravely depraved and even portrays them as the tragic consequence of rejecting God.[14]

Thus the official Catholic line is immune to the "argument from biology," unless biologists can show, as Hirschfeld attempted to do, that homosexual *behavior* is as hard-wired as homosexual orientation. Furthermore, because the Catholic view is grounded in an "objective moral order," it is applicable to every human being, whether Catholic or not. Thus the Catholic Church feels itself entitled, even obliged, to intervene in spheres far removed from its own constituency. It has lobbied successfully against the enactment of antidiscrimination regulations by several states, including New York, as well as by influential private organizations such as college accreditation boards.[15] It leads (along with the Mormon Church) the campaign against same-sex *civil* marriage in Hawaii. As a nation-state in its own right (the Vatican City), it has used its seat in the United Nations to campaign against antidiscrimination measures of potentially worldwide significance.[16] And it has consistently opposed gay-positive sex education, condom distribution as an AIDS-prevention strategy, and the like.

Yet, by engaging in this campaign against the civil rights of gays and lesbians around the world, the Catholic Church has undercut the very basis of its own moral position. To escape the "biological argument" the Church has emphasized the culpability of homosexual behavior, not of homosexual identity. But its political campaign is directed against the civil liberties of a set of individuals who are identified by what the Church recognizes to be an immutable characteristic— same-sex desire. If, as a consequence of the Church's campaign, gays and lesbians are to be denied protection against discrimination in employment, housing, services, college admission, civil marriage, and the like, regardless of what they may or may not do in bed, is this not the exact opposite of the Church's moral position, which is to attack the sin, not the sinner?

Sensing this contradiction, the Vatican has more recently attempted to justify discrimination against gay people themselves, regardless of behavior. According to a 1992 Vatican statement, "'sexual orientation' does not constitute a quality comparable to race, ethnic background, etc., in respect to nondiscrimination. Unlike these, homosexual orientation is an objective disorder. . .and evokes moral concern. There are areas in which it is not unjust discrimination to take sexual orientation into account, for example, in the placement of children for adoption or foster care, in employment of teachers or athletic coaches, and in military recruitment." Even discrimination against gays and lesbians in housing may be permissible, the statement suggests, because

preventing such discrimination may negatively influence "the housing needs of genuine families." Furthermore, gay people bring discrimination on themselves by being open about their sexual
orientation. "As a rule, the majority of homosexually oriented persons who seek to lead chaste lives do not publicize their sexual orientation. Hence the problem of discrimination in terms of
employment, housing, etc., does not usually arise."[17]

These harsh pronouncements illustrate very clearly the limits of the
"argument from biology." It is evident that Richard Mohr's point of
view is applicable to the case of the Catholic Church. But it is far from
universally true.

In particular, I believe it is not true at the level of heterosexual people's "instinctive" response to homosexuality—the deepest source of
homophobia. As I see it, when straight people are faced with the fact
that some people are sexually active with members of their own sex,
they go through the following mental process. They first place themselves conceptually in the shoes of such people: they imagine themselves engaging in homosexual behavior, and they experience the
same aversion that they would feel if they themselves (as heterosexuals) were engaged in such behavior. They then apply this aversion to
the people who actually do engage in this behavior. Thus, "instinctive" homophobia results from an *insufficient* distancing of gay people:
a failure to place them in a distinct category where the test-by-empathy would be inappropriate. In comparison, people see animals do
all kinds of potentially disgusting or immoral things, but because they
view animals as natural kinds distinct from their own kind, they do
not generally apply the test-by-empathy and consequently do not hate
animals for their behavior, even if they use animals allegorically for
moralizing purposes (see chapter 10).

Gay people, I believe, go through a similar process in their attitude
toward heterosexual behavior. But, because of culture, the "otherness"
of heterosexual people is immediately obvious. They may perceive
themselves as the misfits, but they rarely fail to perceive the lack of fit
itself. They conceptualize straight people as a distinct category of people who in their sexual lives operate by different mental rules from
those governing gay people, and generally they leave it at that.

Thus, I believe that science helps improve relationships between straight and gay people when it strengthens gay people's status as an objective category of human beings. But I agree fully with Mohr and others when they assert that the question of how gay people should be treated is at base a moral question, not a scientific one. Science can only provide grist for the mill of moral discourse. It can only be an "underlaborer," as Mohr puts it. Science can describe and measure gay people, and maybe figure out how they got that way; science can study the effects that the existence of gay people has on society, its institutions, its economy, and so on. But ultimately, it is not a scientific judgment as to how society should treat gay people, or whether gay people are "worth having," because the assessment of worth is a moral judgment, a judgment that every individual makes according to his or her own conscience.

In this sphere of worth, it is the words and deeds of gays and lesbians themselves that ultimately provide the evidence on which judgments are made. As gay people are becoming more open about their sexual orientation and more active on behalf of their community, it seems inevitable that the special contributions made to society by gay people will become more apparent and that damaging myths about them—that they are "antifamily," for example—will be exposed as false. It will also become clearer that gay people live in a fashion that is appropriate to their kind. Thus it is likely that their perceived worth, both in a practical and a moral sense, will increase, science or no science.

What the biology does say is this: If you believe you have grounds in reason, morality, or mere emotion to think poorly of homosexuality, or to rate it below heterosexuality on your scale of worth, so be it. But don't try to fool yourself that a person's homosexuality can be segregated off from the remainder of his or her being; that it can be gathered into some corner of the psyche, to be locked up and forgotten, or to be neatly cut away by some exercise of medicine, law, or religion. The biology reinforces what gay people know about themselves: that their homosexuality is an integral, defining aspect of their being and that an assault on their homosexuality is an assault, not just on their behavior, their rights, or their pride, but on their very selves.

Notes

Introduction

1. There has been controversy about the interpretation of Aristophanes' speech. The interpretation I present corresponds roughly to the traditional view (see, for example, J. Boswell, "Revolutions, universals, and sexual categories," reprinted in M. Duberman, M. Vicinus, and G. Chauncey, Jr., *Hidden from History: Reclaiming the Gay and Lesbian Past* [New York: Meridian Books, 1990], pp. 17-360). David Halperin, a literature professor who believes that homosexuality is a social construction, has argued that Aristophanes did not recognize a category of homosexual people, but only the separate categories of men-loving men and women-loving women. Furthermore, he asserts that Aristophanes divided men-loving men into two independent "sexualities"—the love of youths for adult men and the love of adult men for youths. This argument is somewhat strained, given that the two kinds of love are represented by Aristophanes as being different stages of a single life course. (D. M. Halperin, *One Hundred Years of Homosexuality and Other Essays on Greek Love* [New York: Routledge, 1990], pp. 18–21.)

2. The late historian John Boswell (*Christianity, Social Tolerance, and Homosexuality: Gay People in Western Europe from the Beginning of the Christian Era to the Fourteenth Century* [Chicago: University of Chicago Press, 1980], pp. 112–113) argued that "[i]t cannot be inferred from this that Paul considered mere homoerotic

attraction or practice morally reprehensible, since the passage strongly implies that he was not discussing persons who were by inclination gay. . ." A similar argument has been made by journalist Andrew Sullivan (*Virtually Normal* [New York, Alfred A. Knopf, 1995], pp. 28–30). There is no indication, however, that Paul acknowledged the existence of such persons. Boswell's line of reasoning exemplifies the attempt to read homophobia out of the Bible—a hopeless undertaking, in my estimation.

3. J. Schmalz, *New York Times*, March 5, 1993.

4. J. E. Aguero, L. Bloch, and D. Byrne, "The relationship among beliefs, attitudes, experience, and homophobia," *Journal of Homosexuality* 10: 95–107 (1984); B. E. Whitley, Jr., "The relationship of heterosexuals' attributions for the causes of homosexuality to attitudes towards lesbians and gay men," *Personality and Social Psychology Bulletin* 16: 369–377 (1990).

5. K. E. Ernulf, S. M. Innala, and F. L. Whitam, "Biological explanation, psychological explanation, and tolerance of homosexuals: A cross-national analysis of beliefs and attitudes," *Psychological Reports* 65: 1003–1010 (1989).

6. J. Piskur and D. Degelman, "Effect of reading a summary of research about biological bases of homosexual orientation on attitudes towards homosexuals," *Psychological Reports* 71: 1219–1225 (1992).

7. J. Taylor, producer, *Born That Way?* (London: Windfall Films, 1992).

8. This is of course a simplification, in that I do not distinguish between necessary and sufficient causes, nor between signal-dependent and default pathways of development. I do not assert that there must be a detailed complementarity of homosexual and heterosexual development, but only that there must be at least one point of development (and quite likely more than one) where the roads to homosexuality and heterosexuality diverge. Identifying that branch point or those branch points should shed light equally on why one person becomes gay and another straight.

9. J. Lever, "Sexual revelations: The 1994 Advocate survey of sexuality and relationships: The men," *The Advocate* (August 23, 1994), pp. 17–24.

10. J. Lever, "Lesbian sex survey: The 1995 Advocate survey of sexuality and relationships: The women," *The Advocate* (August 22, 1995), pp. 22–30. It should be borne in mind that the gay and lesbian readers sampled by *The Advocate* were probably more "out" and more politically conscious than most gays and lesbians in the population.

11. D. Y. Rist, "Are homosexuals born that way?" *The Nation* 255 (October 19, 1992), pp. 424-429 .

12. In a recent study of mostly well-educated gay male and heterosexual youths, no significant difference in self-esteem was found between the two groups (R.

C. Savin-Williams, "An exploratory study of pubertal maturation timing and self-esteem among gay and bisexual male youths," *Developmental Psychology* 31: 56–64 [1995]). While economically disadvantaged and strongly gender-nonconformist gay and lesbian youth may have lowered self-esteem, these populations are also responding to altered social attitudes and to youth-oriented outreach programs (see, for example, G. Herdt and A. Boxer, *Children of Horizons: How Gay and Lesbian Teens Are Leading a New Way Out of the Closet* [Boston: Beacon Press, 1993]).

Chapter 1

1. This account is principally based on H. Kennedy, *Ulrichs: The Life and Works of Karl Heinrich Ulrichs, Pioneer of the Modern Gay Movement* (Boston: Alyson Publications, 1988). A collection of Ulrichs's pamphlets is available in English translation as K. H. Ulrichs, *The Riddle of "Man-Manly" Love: The Pioneering Work on Male Homosexuality* , M. A. Lombardi-Nash, trans. (Buffalo: Prometheus Books, 1994).

2. K. H. Ulrichs, (Numa Numantius, pseudonym), *Inclusa: Anthropologische Studien über mannmänliche Geschlechtsliebe* (Leipzig: Mathes, 1864), reprinted in K. H. Ulrichs, *Forschungen über das Rätsel der mannmännlichen Liebe* (New York: Arno Press, 1975).

3. K. H. Ulrichs, (Numa Numantius, pseudonym), *Formatrix: Anthropologische Studien über urnische Geschlechtsliebe* (Leipzig: Mathes, 1865), reprinted in K. H. Ulrichs, *Forschungen über das Rätsel der mannmännlichen Liebe* (New York: Arno Press, 1975).

4. K. H. Ulrichs, *Critische Pfeile: Denkschrift über die Bestrafung der Urningsliebe* (Leipzig: Otto and Kadler, 1979). The relevant portion is reprinted in translation in Kennedy, *Ulrichs* , pp. 196–198.

5. M. Hirschfeld, *Berlins Drittes Geschlecht* (Berlin: H. Seemann, 1904). The cited excerpts are my translation.

6. H. Ostwald, *Männliche Prostitution: Erste umfassende, Aufsehen erregende Schilderung dieser verderblichen Erscheinung* (Leipzig: Ernst Müller-Verlag, 1906), reprinted as *Männliche Prostitution im kaiserlichen Berlin* (Berlin: Janssen-Verlag, 1991).

7. M. Hirschfeld, (Th. Ramien, pseudonym), *Sappho und Socrates: Wie erklärt sich die Liebe der Männer und Frauen zu Personen des eigenen Geschlechts?* (Leipzig: Max Spohr, 1896).

8. In her biography of Hirschfeld (*Magnus Hirschfeld: A Portrait of a Pioneer in Sexology* [London: Quartet Books, 1986], p. 35), Charlotte Wolff gives a seriously erroneous account of this part of *Sappho and Socrates*: She has Hirschfeld asserting that the development of a lesbian identity is accompanied by atrophy of the clitoris. This is based on a misinterpretation of the phrase "Rückgang der

männlichen Außenteile," which, as the comparable passage on the development of heterosexual women makes clear, simply refers to the normal process of female bodily development.

9. I have made a new, rather literal translation of the petition (based on the German version reprinted in the *Jahrbuch für sexuelle Zwischenstufen* [1899], pp. 239–241), because the English version most readily available, by Charlotte Wolff (*Magnus Hirschfeld*, pp. 445–448), fails to capture the official tone of the document and also contains several errors, most notably the statement that the petition was addressed to the judiciary rather than to the legislature.

10. R. Dyer, *Now You See It: Studies on Lesbian and Gay Film* (London: Routledge, 1990), pp. 10–27.

11. Wolff, *Magnus Hirschfeld*, p. 73.

12. J. D. Steakley, "Iconography of a scandal: Political cartoons and the Eulenburg affair in Wilhelmin Germany," in M. Duberman, M. Vicinus, and G. Chauncey, Jr., eds., *Hidden from History: Reclaiming the Gay and Lesbian Past* (New York: Meridian, 1990), pp. 233–263.

13. Hirschfeld's writings on homosexuality culminated in the encyclopedic 1914 book, *Die Homosexualität des Mannes und des Weibes* (Berlin: Louis Marcus). An English translation of the second, 1920 edition is in preparation (*The Homosexuality of Men and Women*, M. A. Lombardi-Nash, trans. [Buffalo: Prometheus Books]). A perhaps more original work was *Die Transvestiten: Eine Untersuchung über den erotischen Verkleidungstrieb* (Berlin: A. Pulvermacher, 1910; available in English translation as *Transvestites: The Erotic Drive to Cross-Dress*, M. A. Lombardi-Nash, trans. (Buffalo: Prometheus Books, 1991). This pioneering work showed that transvestism and homosexuality are different entities; however, it failed to make a clear distinction between heterosexual transvestic fetishism, homosexual cross-dressing ("drag queens and kings"), and transsexuality of the homosexual type. For a recent review of the topic, see K. J. Zucker and R. Blanchard, "Transvestic fetishism: Psychopathology and theory," in D. R. Laws and W. O'Donohue, eds., *Handbook of Sexual Deviance: Theory and Application* (New York: Guilford Press, in press).

14. *Die Homosexualität* , chapter 5.

15. E. Steinach, "Willkürliche Umwandlung von Säugetier-Männchen in Tiere mit ausgeprägt weiblichen Geschlechtscharakteren und weiblicher Psyche. Eine Untersuchung über die Funktion und Bedeutung der Pubertätsdrüsen," *Pflüger's Archiv der gesamten Physiologie des Menschen und der Tiere* 144: 71–108 (1912).

16. E. Steinach, "Operative Behandlung der Homosexualität," *Jahrbuch für sexuelle Zwischenstufen* 17: 189 (1917). Testicular transplantations were sometimes performed for the purpose of "rejuvenation" in men. Already in the 1880s the

pioneering endocrinologist Charles Brown-Séquard had purportedly reversed his own aging process by repeated injections of testicular extracts.

17. *Die Homosexualität*, preface to second edition.

18. M. Hirschfeld, *Geschlechtskunde* (Stuttgart: Julius Puttmann, 1930) vol. 3, p. 537. (Cited in M. Herzer, *Magnus Hirschfeld: Leben und Werk eines jüdischen, schwulen und sozialistischen Sexologen* [Frankfurt: Campus Verlag, 1992], p. 81). My translation.

19. S. Freud, "Leonardo da Vinci and a memory of his childhood," in J. Strachey, ed. and trans., *Standard Edition of the Complete Psychological Works of Sigmund Freud, Vol. 11* (London: Hogarth Press, 1957), p. 100.

20. W. McGuire, ed., *The Freud/Jung Letters: The Correspondence between Sigmund Freud and C. G. Jung*, R. Manheim and R. F. C. Hull, trans. (London: Hogarth Press, 1974), p. 453.

21. H. Oosterhuis and H. Kennedy, eds., *Homosexuality and Male Bonding in Pre-Nazi Germany* (New York: Harrington Park Press, 1991).

22. Benedict Friedländer, *Denkschrift für die Freunde und Fondszeichner des Wissenschaftlich-Humanitären Komitees* (Berlin: privately printed, 1907) (reprinted in Osterhuis and Kennedy, *Homosexuality and Male Bonding*, pp. 71–84).

23. Herzer, *Magnus Hirschfeld*, pp. 87–88.

24. For a description of Hirschfeld and the institute, see C. Isherwood, *Christopher and His Kind* (New York: Avon Books, 1976), chapter 2. The following paragraph is of particular interest: "Then, one afternoon, André Gide paid them a visit. He was taken on a tour of the premises personally conducted by Hirschfeld. Live exhibits were introduced, with such comments as: 'Intergrade. Third Division.' One of these was a young man who opened his shirt with a modest smile to display two perfectly formed female breasts. Gide looked on, making a minimum of polite comment, judiciously fingering his chin. He was in full costume as the Great French Novelist, complete with cape. No doubt he thought Hirschfeld's performance hopelessly crude and un-French. Christopher's Gallophobia flared up. Sneering, culture-conceited frog! Suddenly he loved Hirschfeld—at whom he himself had been sneering, a moment before—the silly solemn old professor with his doggy mustache, thick peering spectacles, and clumsy German-Jewish boots . . . Nevertheless, they were all three of them on the same side, whether Christopher liked it or not. And later he would learn to honor them both, as heroic leaders of his tribe" (pp. 16–17).

25. Herzer, *Magnus Hirschfeld*, p. 22.

26. Research of Rüdiger Lautmann, cited in R. Plant, *The Pink Triangle: The Nazi War against Homosexuals* (Henry Holt, 1986), p. 154; G. Grau, *Hidden Holocaust? Gay and Lesbian Persecution in Germany 1933–45*, P. Camiller, trans. (London: Cassell, 1995), p. 6.

27. M. Dannecker and R. Reiche, *Der gewöhnliche Homosexuelle in der Bundesrepublik* (Frankfurt/Main: Fischer, 1974), p. 27. (Cited by Herzer, *Hirschfeld*, p. 12.) My translation.

28. Grau, *Hidden Holocaust*, p. 165; see also H. Oosterhuis, "Male Bonding and Homosexuality in German Nationalism," in Oosterhuis and Kennedy, *Male Bonding*, pp. 241–263.

29. P. Russell, *The Gay 100: A Ranking of the Most Influential Gay Men and Lesbians, Past and Present* (New York: Citadel Press, 1995), pp. 15–18.

30. J. N. Katz, *Gay American History: Lesbians and Gay Men in the U.S.A.* (New York: Meridian Books, 1992), p. 393.

31. S. Timmons, *The Trouble with Harry Hay, Founder of the Modern Gay Movement* (Boston: Alyson Publications, 1990), p. 141.

32. G. Schiller, director, *Before Stonewall: The Making of a Gay and Lesbian Community* (1986). (Documentary film.)

33. Timmons (p. 43) has also recounted how one of Hay's lovers told him about the Chicago Society of Human Rights in 1930. According to Timmons, ". . . the notion of an organized group of 'temperamental' men fascinated Harry, and the idea took a deep hold."

34. P. Gay, *Freud: A Life for Our Time* (New York: W. W. Norton, 1988), pp. 144, 181, 460.

Chapter 2

1. *Ortiz v. Bank of America*, 547 F. Supp. 550 (E.D. Cal. 1982), p. 565.

2. A. C. Kinsey, W. B. Pomeroy, and C. E. Martin, *Sexual Behavior in the Human Male* (Philadelphia: Saunders, 1948); A. C. Kinsey, W. B. Pomeroy, C. E. Martin, and P. H. Gebhard, *Sexual Behavior in the Human Female* (Philadelphia: Saunders, 1953).

3. Kinsey, *Human Male*, p. 647.

4. For example, he wrote "The heterosexual male finds a regular outlet if he locates a single female who is acceptable as a wife in marriage. The homosexual male is more often concerned with finding a succession of partners, no one of whom will provide more than a few contacts, or perhaps not more than a single contact" (*Human Male*, p. 632).

5. Kinsey, *Human Male*, p. 664.

6. K. Wellings, J. Field, A. M. Johnson, and J. Wadsworth, *Sexual Behavior in Britain: The National Survey of Sexual Attitudes and Lifestyles* (London: Penguin Books, 1994).

7. E. O. Laumann, J. H. Gagnon, R. T. Michael, and S. Michaels, *The Social Organization of Sexuality: Sexual Practices in the United States* (Chicago: University of Chicago Press, 1994).

8. D. Hamer and P. Copeland, *The Science of Desire: The Search for the Gay Gene and the Biology of Behavior* (New York: Simon and Schuster, 1994).

9. J. M. Bailey and R. C. Pillard, "A genetic study of male sexual orientation," *Archives of General Psychiatry* 48: 1089–1096 (1991).

10. M. T. Saghir and E. Robins *Male and Female Homosexuality: A Comprehensive Investigation* (Baltimore: Williams and Wilkins, 1973); A. P. Bell and M. S. Weinberg,, *Homosexualities: A Study of Diversity among Men and Women* (New York: Simon and Schuster, 1978); S. Hite, *The Hite Report: A Nationwide Study of Female Sexuality* (New York: Dell, 1981); S. Hite, *The Hite Report on Male Sexuality* (New York: Dell, 1982); J. Lever, "Lesbian sex survey: The 1995 Advocate survey of sexuality and relationships: The women," *The Advocate* (August 2, 1995), pp. 22–30.

11. K. W. Freund, F. Sedlácek, F., and K. Knob, "A simple transducer for mechanical plethysmography of the male genital," *Journal of the Experimental Analysis of Behavior* 8: 169–170 (1965).

12. G. Sintchak and J. A. Geer, "A vaginal plethysmograph system," *Psychophysiology* 12: 113–115 (1975).

13. K. W. Freund, "Male homosexuality: An analysis of the pattern," in J. A. Loraine, ed., *Understanding Homosexuality: Its Biological and Psychological Bases* (New York: Elsevier, 1974), pp. 25–81.

14. E. Laan, J. Sonderman, and E. Janssen, "Straight and lesbian women's sexual responses to straight and lesbian erotica: No sexual orientation effects," poster presented at the International Academy of Sex Research, 21st Annual Meeting, Provincetown, Massachusetts (1995).

15. A. M. L. Pattatucci and D. H. Hamer, "Development and familiality of sexual orientation in females," *Behavior Genetics* 25: 407–420 (1995).

16. P. C. Rust, "'Coming out' in the age of social constructionism: Sexual identity formation among lesbian and bisexual women," *Gender and Society* 7: 50–77 (1993).

17. J. Lever, "Sexual revelations: The 1994 Advocate survey of sexuality and relationships: The men," *The Advocate* (August 23, 1994), pp. 17–24.

18. M. Foucault, *The History of Sexuality, Volume I* (New York: Pantheon, 1978).

19. D. M. Halperin, *One Hundred Years of Homosexuality and Other Essays on Greek Love* (New York: Routledge, 1990).

20. R. D. Mohr, *Gay Ideas: Outing and Other Controversies* (Boston: Beacon Press, 1992), pp. 221–242.

21. Halperin's position is already a step away from the extreme social constructivism of Foucault, in that he concedes that sex itself defines objective categories given in nature. For a survey of the finer gradations of social constructivism, see

C. S. Vance, "Social construction theory: Problems in the history of sexuality," in D. Altman, C. Vance, M. Vicinus, and J. Weeks, eds., *Homosexuality, Which Homosexuality?* (London: GMP Publishers, 1989).

22. J. E. Halley, "The construction of heterosexuality," in M. Warner, ed., *Fear of a Queer Planet: Queer Politics and Social Theory* (Minneapolis: University of Minnesota Press, 1993), pp. 82–102.

23. The diversity in homosexual relationships across different cultures is discussed at greater length (along with references to the literature) in S. LeVay and E. Nonas, *City of Friends: A Portrait of the Gay and Lesbian Community in America* (Cambridge, MA: MIT Press, 1995), chapter 2.

24. W. L. Williams, *The Spirit and the Flesh: Sexual Diversity in Native American Culture* (Boston: Beacon Press, 1986).

25. G. H. Herdt, *Guardians of the Flutes: Idioms of Masculinity* (New York: Columbia University Press, 1981).

26. For a discussion of the difference between homosexuality as a trait and culturally imposed or age-limited homosexual behavior, see W. Gapaille, "Cross-species and cross-cultural contributions to understanding homosexual activity," *Archives of General Psychiatry* 37: 349-356 (1980).

27. F. L. Whitam, "Culturally invariant properties of male homosexuality: Tentative conclusions from cross-cultural research," *Archives of Sexual Behavior* 12: 207–226 (1983); F. L. Whitam and R. M. Mathy, *Male Homosexuality in Four Societies: Brazil, Guatemala, the Philippines and the United States* (New York: Praeger, 1986); F. L. Whitam and R. M. Mathy, "Childhood cross-gender behavior of homosexual females in Brazil, Peru, the Philippines and the United States," *Archives of Sexual Behavior* 20: 151–170 (1991).

28. S. Timmons, *The Trouble with Harry Hay: Founder of the Modern Gay Movement* (Boston: Alyson Publications, 1990), pp. 136–137.

29. Richard Mohr, for example, writes of ". . .that but 5 or so percent of the population that is gay and male" (i.e., 10 or so percent of the male population) (*Gay Ideas: Outing and Other Controversies* [Boston: Beacon Press, 1992], p. 247).

30. ACSF Investigators, "AIDS and sexual behavior in France," *Nature* 360: 407–409 (1992).

31. J. M. Sundet, I. L. Kvalem, P. Magnus, and L. S. Bakketeig, "Prevalence of risk-prone behavior in the central population of Norway," in A. F. Fleming, M. Carballo, and D. F. Fitzsimons, eds., *The Global Impact of AIDS* (London: Alan R. Liss, 1988).

32. S. M. Rogers and C. F. Turner, "Male-male sexual contact in the U. S. A.: Findings from five sample surveys, 1970–1990," *Journal of Sex Research* 28: 491–519 (1991); J. O. G. Billy, K. Tanfer, W. R. Grady, and D. H. Klepinger, "The

sexual behavior of men in the United States," *Family Planning Perspectives* 25: 52–60 (1993); E. O. Laumann, J. H. Gagnon, R. T. Michael, and S. Michaels, *The Social Organization of Sexuality: Sexual Practices in the United States* (Chicago: University of Chicago Press, 1994).

33. *A Yankelovich MONITOR Perspective on Gays/Lesbians* (Norwalk, CT: Yankelovich Partners, Inc., 1994).

34. R. L. Sell, J. A. Wells, and D. Wypij, "The prevalence of homosexual behavior and attraction in the United States, the United Kingdom and France: Results of national population-based samples," *Archives of Sexual Behavior* 24: 235–248 (1995). The most serious problem with the study was that respondents were asked to report their behavior *as a way of* describing their feelings toward their own sex. In reality, same-sex behavior can and does take place without same-sex attraction (e.g., experimentation, prostitution, molestation, rape, lack of opposite-sex opportunity such as in boarding school or prison, or simply to please one's partner). In addition, sexual behavior was assayed with a question about "numbers of sex partners," a vague phrase that might include noncontact or nongenital-contact relationships. Finally, the results are not published in a form that allows the balance of same-sex and opposite-sex attraction or behavior to be estimated. The authors also wrongly claim that prior national studies did not examine attraction.

35. See, for example, H. Taylor, "Number of gay men more than 4 times higher than the 1 percent reported in a recent survey," *The Harris Poll* 20: 1–4 (1993). This article criticizes the study of Billy et al. However, the Louis Harris agency itself carried out the methodologically flawed survey authored by Sell et al.

36. K. Ellingwood, "The 'gay Camelot' grows up," *Los Angeles Times* (June 27, 1994), pp. A1+.

37. Laumann et al., *Social Organization of Sexuality*.

38. Fred Whitam has described how Tobias Schneebaum's fictitious visit to the all-gay "Akaramas" of Peru, recounted in his book *Keep the River on Your Right* (New York: Grove Press, 1969), was taken seriously by some sexologists (F. L. Whitam, "Culturally invariant properties of male homosexuality: Tentative conclusions from cross-cultural research," *Archives of Sexual Behavior* 12: 207–226 [1983]).

39. Two examples: "One thing is certain and that is that the centre from which homosexuality has spread so widely is to be sought in Asia. From there it found its way among the Greeks and Romans and finally the Teutons as well. It can already be seen from this path of radiation that homosexuality is alien in kind to the Nordic race." (From a lecture by Josef Meisinger, chief of the Reich Office for the Combating of Homosexuality and Abortion, April 1937, cited in G.

Grau, *Hidden Holocaust? Gay and Lesbian Persecution in Germany 1933–45*, P. Camiller, trans. [London: Cassell, 1995], p. 110); "When Kabul was conquered by the Muslims and the Ispahbad of Kabul adopted Islam, he stipulated that he not be bound to eat cow's meat nor to commit sodomy (which proves that he abhorred one as much as the other)" (eleventh-century scholar cited in A. Sharma, "Homosexuality and Hinduism," in A. Swidler, *Homosexuality and World Religions* [Valley Forge, PA: Trinity Press International, 1993], pp. 47–80).

40. F. L. Whitam, "Culturally invariant properties of male homosexuality: Tentative conclusions from cross-cultural research," *Archives of Sexual Behavior* 12: 207–226 (1983).

Chapter 3

1. S. Freud, *Three Essays on the Theory of Sexuality*, James Strachey, trans. (Basic Books, 1962), p. 11 (footnote).

2. Ibid., p. 48.

3. Ibid., p. 49.

4. S. Freud, "Psychoanalytic notes on an autobiographical account of a case of paranoia (dementia paranoides)," in J. Strachey, ed., *The Standard Edition of the Complete Works of Sigmund Freud* (London: Hogarth Press, 1958), vol. 12, p. 466.

5. J. M. Bailey, S. Gaulin, Y. Agyei, and B. A. Gladue, "Effects of gender and sexual orientation on evolutionarily relevant aspects of human mating psychology," *Journal of Personality and Social Psychology* 66: 1081–1093 (1994).

6. S. Freud, *Some Neurotic Mechanisms in Jealousy, Paranoia and Homosexuality*, in Freud, *Standard Edition* (1955), vol. 18, pp. 223–232.

7. S. Freud, "The Psychogenesis of a Case of Homosexuality in a Woman," in Freud, *Standard Edition* (1955), vol. 18, pp. 147–172.

8. "Affecting her intimately" is my revision of the translator's obsolete "touching her nearly."

9. S. Freud, letter of April 9, 1935, cited in E. Jones, *The Life and Work of Sigmund Freud* (New York: Basic Books, 1955), pp. 208–209.

10. Actually, the sibling-rivalry theory does involve a neurotic mechanism and therefore should be treatable.

11. L. Ovesey, *Homosexuality and Pseudohomosexuality* (New York: Science House, 1969).

12. M. Duberman, *Cures: A Gay Man's Odyssey* (New York: Dutton, 1991).

13. C. W. Socarides, "Homosexuality: Findings derived from 15 years of clinical research," *American Journal of Psychiatry* 130:1212–1213 (1973).

14. C. W. Socarides, *Homosexuality* (New York: Jason Aronson, 1978), pp. 83–85. This is a summary except for the verbatim passage placed within quotation marks.

15. Richard Socarides is a prominent gay activist who has served on the Board of Lambda Legal Defense and is now White House liaison to the Department of Labor.

16. The interview was shown as part of the British documentary film *Born That Way?* (London: Windfall Films, Jeremy Taylor, producer), but the portion described was excised at Socarides' request.

17. J. Nicolosi, *Reparative Therapy of Male Homosexuality*, (Northvale, NJ: Jason Aronson, 1991), pp. 109–110.

18. I. Bieber, T. B. Bieber, H. J. Dain, P. R. Dince, M. G. Drellich, H. G., Grand, R. H. Gundlach, M. W. Kremer, A. H. Rifkin, and C. B. Wilbur, *Homosexuality: A Psychoanalytic Study* (Northvale, NJ: Jason Aronson, 1988).

19. H. E. Kaye, S. Berl, J. Clare, M. Eleston, B. S. Gerschwin, P. Gerschwin, L. S. Kogan, C. Torda, and C. B. Wilbur, "Homosexuality in women," in *Archives of General Psychiatry* 17: 626-634 (1967).

20. H. MacIntosh, "Attitudes and experiences of psychoanalysts in analyzing homosexual patients," *Journal of the American Psychoanalytic Association* 42: 1183–1207 (1994). Among the 285 analysts surveyed by MacIntosh, 62 percent agreed with the statement that homosexual patients can "sometimes" change to heterosexuality. Of the lesbian patients treated by these analysts, 20 percent were reported to have changed to heterosexuality, while 24 percent of the gay male patients did so. There is some reason for skepticism concerning these results; in particular, MacIntosh phrased his survey as a referendum on a statement by the outspoken gay analyst, Richard Isay, a strategy that seemed calculated to evoke a response antagonistic to Isay's position. In addition, there was no reported follow up or third-party investigation of the "converted" gays and lesbians.

21. P. Wyden and B. Wyden, *Growing Up Straight: What Every Thoughtful Parent Should Know About Homosexuality* (New York: Stein and Day, 1968).

22. See especially J. Marmor, ed., *Sexual Inversion* (New York: Basic Books, 1965); J. Marmor, ed., *Homosexual Behavior: A Modern Reappraisal* (New York: Basic Books, 1980).

23. E. Marcus, *Making History: The Struggle for Gay and Lesbian Equal Rights, 1945–1990* (New York: HarperCollins, 1992), p. 251.

24. He cites S. Coates and E. S. Person, "Extreme boyhood femininity: Isolated behavior or pervasive disorder?" *Journal of the American Academy of Child Psychiatry* 24: 702–709 (1985).

25. R. C. Friedman, *Male Homosexuality: A Contemporary Psychoanalytic Perspective* (New Haven: Yale University Press, 1988), p. 193.

26. W. L. Williams, *The Spirit and the Flesh: Sexual Diversity in American Indian Culture* (Boston: Beacon Press: 1986).

27. E. K. Sedgwick, "How to bring your kids up gay," in M. Warner, ed., *Fear of a Queer Planet: Queer Politics and Social Theory* (Minneapolis: University of Minnesota Press, 1993), pp. 69–81.

28. K. Lewes, *The Psychoanalytic Theory of Male Homosexuality* (New York: Simon and Schuster, 1988), pp. 236–238.

29. R. A. Isay, *Being Homosexual: Gay Men and Their Development* (New York: Farrar, Straus and Giroux, 1989).

30. R. A. Isay, *Becoming Gay: The Journey to Self-Acceptance* (New York: Pantheon Books, 1996).

31. B. Burch, *On Intimate Terms: The Psychology of Difference in Lesbian Relationships* (Urbana: University of Illinois Press, 1992); N. O'Connor and J. Ryan, *Wild Desires and Mistaken Identities: Lesbianism and Psychoanalysis* (New York: Columbia University Press, 1993); J. M. Glassgold and S. Iasenza, eds., *Lesbians and Psychoanalysis: Revolutions in Theory and Practice* (New York: Free Press, 1995).

32. L. Deutsch, "Out of the closet and on to the couch: A psychoanalytic exploration of lesbian development," in Glassgold and Iasenza, eds., *Lesbians and Psychoanalysis:*, pp. 19–37.

33. B. Burch, "Heterosexuality, bisexuality, and lesbianism: Rethinking psychoanalytic views of women's sexual object choice," *Psychoanalytic Review* 80: 83–99 (1993).

34. M. Suchet, "Having it both ways: Rethinking female sexuality," in Glassgold and Iasenza, eds., *Lesbians and Psychoanalysis*, pp. 39–61.

35. Dianne Fuss, for example, has criticized Freud's search for the "etiology" of female homosexuality as "a question that can only assume in advance what is purports to demonstrate." (D. Fuss, "Freud's fallen women: Identification, desire, and 'A case of homosexuality in a woman'," in M. Warner, ed., *Fear of a Queer Planet*, pp. 42–68.)

Chapter 4

1. W. Churchill, *Homosexual Behavior among Males: A Cross-Cultural and Cross-Species Investigation* (New York: Hawthorn Books, 1967).

2. P. Cameron and K. Cameron "Does incest cause homosexuality?" *Psychological Reports* 76: 611–621 (1995).

3. According to a large British survey (K. Wellings, J. Field, A. M. Johnson, and J. Wadsworth, *Sexual Behavior in Britain: The National Survey of Sexual Attitudes and Lifestyles* [London: Penguin, 1994], pp. 204–209), men and women who attended such schools are about three times more likely to have experienced same-sex genital contact than those who did not, but the type of school attended has no significant impact on the likelihood that they have engaged in homosexual behavior in the five years prior to the survey (i.e., in adulthood).

4. R. J. McGuire, J. M. Carlisle, and B. G. Young, "Sexual deviations as conditioned behaviour: A hypothesis," in *Behavior Research and Therapy* 2: 185–190 (1965).

5. K. Freund, "Some problems in the treatment of homosexuality," in H. Eysenck, *Behavior Therapy and the Neuroses* (London: Pergamon Press, 1960), pp. 312–326. See also K. W. Freund, "Should homosexuality arouse therapeutic concern?" *Journal of Homosexuality* 2: 235–240 (1977).

6. B. James, "Case of homosexuality treated by aversion therapy," *British Medical Journal* 1: 768–770 (1962).

7. N. McConaghy, "Subjective and penile plethysmograph responses following aversion-relief and apomorphine therapy for homosexual impulses," *British Journal of Psychiatry* 115: 723–730 (1969); N. McConaghy, "Subjective and penile plethysmograph responses to aversion therapy for homosexuality: A follow-up study," *British Journal of Psychiatry* 117: 555–560 (1970); N. McConaghy, "Penile response conditioning and its relationship to aversion therapy in homosexuals," *Behavior Therapy* 1: 213–221 (1970); N. McConaghy, "Aversive relief of homosexuality: Measures of efficacy," *American Journal of Psychiatry* 127: 141–144 (1971); N. McConaghy, D. Proctor, and R. Barr, "Subjective and penile plethysmography responses to aversion therapy for homosexuality: A partial replication," *Archives of Sexual Behavior* 2: 65–78 (1972).

8. J. Money, "Strategy, ethics, behavior modification and homosexuality," *Archives of Sexual Behavior* 2: 79–81 (1972).

9. R. Bayer, *Homosexuality and American Psychiatry: The Politics of Diagnosis* (New York: Basic Books, 1981), p. 103.

10. N. McConaghy, "Is a homosexual orientation irreversible?" *British Journal of Psychiatry* 129: 556–563 (1976).

11. N. McConaghy, "Should biological theories of sexual orientation ignore feelings?" *International Behavioral Development Symposium: Biological Basis of Sexual Orientation and Sex-Typical Behavior* (Minot State University, May 1995), p. 58.

12. M. P. Feldman and M. J. MacCulloch, *Homosexual Behavior: Therapy and Assessment* (Oxford: Pergamon, 1971).

13. For example, L. Birk, "Group psychotherapy for men who are homosexual," *Journal of Sex and Marital Therapy* 1: 29–52 (1974).

14. J. Bancroft, "Aversion therapy of homosexuality: A pilot study of 10 cases," *British Journal of Psychiatry* 115: 1417–1431 (1969).

15. B. A. Tanner, "Shock intensity and fear of shock in the modification of homosexual behavior in males by avoidance learning," *Behaviour Research and Therapy* 11: 213–218 (1973).

16. M. F. McBride, "Effect of visual stimuli in electric shock therapy," Ph.D. dissertation, Brigham Young University, 1976.

17. D. D. Harryman, "With all thy getting, get understanding," in R. Schow, W. Schow, and M. Raynes, eds., *Peculiar People: Mormons and Same-Sex Orientation* (Salt Lake City: Signature Books, 1991), pp. 23–35.

18. J. R. Cautela, "Treatment of compulsive behavior by covert sensitization," *Psychological Record* 16: 33–42 (1966); J. R. Cautela, "Covert sensitization," *Psychological Reports* 20: 459–468 (1967).

19. E. J. Callahan and H. Leitenberg, "Aversion therapy for sexual deviation: Contingent shock and covert sensitization," *Journal of Abnormal Psychology* 81: 60–73 (1973).

20. N. M. Owensby, "Homosexuality and lesbianism treated with metrazol," *Journal of Nervous and Mental Disease* 92: 65–66 (1940).

21. G. N. Thompson, "Electroshock and other therapeutic considerations in sexual psychopathology," *Journal of Nervous and Mental Disease* 109: 531–539 (1949).

22. J. N. Katz, *Gay American History: Lesbians and Gay Men in the U.S.A.* (New York: Meridian, 1992), pp. 201–207.

23. J. M. Bailey and K. J. Zucker, "Childhood sex-typed behavior and sexual orientation: A conceptual analysis and quantitative review," *Developmental Psychology* 31: 43–55 (1995).

24. H. Bakwin, "Deviant gender-role behavior in children: Relation to homosexuality," *Pediatrics* 41: 620–629 (1968); P. S. Lebovitz, "Feminine behavior in boys: Aspects of its outcome," *American Journal of Psychiatry* 128: 1283–1289 (1972); J. Money and A. J. Russo, "Homosexual outcome of discordant gender identity/role: Longitudinal follow-up," *Journal of Pediatric Psychology* 4: 29–41 (1979); B. Zuger, "Early effeminate behavior in boys: Outcome and significance for homosexuality," *Journal of Nervous and Mental Disease* 172: 90–97 (1984); R. Green, *The "Sissy Boy Syndrome" and the Development of Homosexuality* (New Haven: Yale University Press, 1987).

25. J. Money, J. G. Hampson, and J. L. Hampson, "Imprinting and the establishment of gender role," *Archives of Neurology and Psychiatry* 77: 333–336 (1957).

26. R. Green, *Sexual Identity Conflict in Children and Adults* (New York: Basic Books, 1974).

27. G. A. Rekers and O. I. Lovaas, "Behavioral treatment of deviant sex-role behaviors in a male child," *Journal of Applied Behavior Analysis* 7: 173–190 (1974); see also G. A. Rekers, O. I. Lovaas, and B. Low, "The behavioral treatment of a 'transsexual' boy," *Journal of Abnormal Child Psychiatry* 2: 99–116 (1977).

28. G. A. Rekers, *Shaping Your Child's Sexual Identity* (Grand Rapids, MI: Baker Book House, 1982), p. 139.

29. Green, *The "Sissy-Boy Syndrome,"* pp. 292–319.

30. S. F. Morin and S. F. Schultz, "The gay movement and the rights of children," *Journal of Social Issues* 34(2): 137–148 (1978).

31. A. C. Rosen, G. A. Rekers, and P. M. Bentler, "Ethical issues in the treatment of children," *Journal of Social Issues* 34(2): 122–136 (1978).

32. Rekers, *Shaping Your Child's Sexual Identity* , pp. 87–88.

33. K. J. Zucker and S. J. Bradley, *Gender Identity Disorder and Psychosexual Problems in Children and Adolescents* (New York: Guilford Publications, 1995).

34. J. Money and A. A. Ehrhardt, *Man & Woman, Boy & Girl: The Differentiation and Dimorphism of Gender Identity from Conception to Maturity* (Baltimore: Johns Hopkins University Press, 1972), pp. 118–123.

35. D. D. Kelly, "Sexual differentiation of the nervous system," in E. R. Kandel and J. H. Schwartz, *Principles of Neural Science*, 2d edition (New York: Elsevier, 1985), pp. 771–783. The cited passage was dropped from the third (1991) edition.

36. M. Diamond, "Sexual indentity, monozygotic twins reared in discordant sex roles and a BBC follow-up," *Archives of Sexual Behavior* 11: 181–186 (1982).

37. M. Diamond, "Some genetic considerations in the development of sexual orientation," in M. Haug et al., eds., *The Development of Sex Differences and Similarities in Behavior* (Amsterdam: Kluwer Academic Publishers, 1993), pp. 291–309; M. Diamond and H. K. Sigmundson, "Sex reassignment at birth: A long-term review and clinical implications" (manuscript in preparation).

38. P. Mussen and L. Distler, "Masculinity, identification, and father-son relationships," *Journal of Abnormal and Social Psychology* 59: 350–356 (1959); E. M. Hetherington and G. Frankie, "Effects of parental dominance, warmth, and comfort on imitation in children," *Journal of Personality and Social Psychology* 6: 119–125 (1967); E. M. Hetherington and J. Duer, "Effects of father absence on child development," *Young Children* 26: 233–248 (1971).

39. L. Kohlberg, "A cognitive-developmental analysis of children's sex-role concepts and attitudes," in E. E. Maccoby, ed., *The Development of Sex Differences* (Stanford: Stanford University Press, 1966), pp. 82–173.

40. M. Lewis, "Early sex differences in the human: Studies of socioemotional development," *Archives of Sexual Behavior* 4: 329–335 (1975).

41. S. Cahill, "Reexamining the acquisition of sex roles: A social interactionist approach," *Sex Roles* 9: 1–15 (1983).

42. S. Freud, "The psychogenesis of a case of homosexuality in a woman," in J. Strachey, ed., *The Standard Edition of the Complete Works of Sigmund Freud* (London: Hogarth Press, 1955), pp. 147–172. Citation on p. 168.

Chapter 5

1. E. Pfeiffer, "Ein geheilter Fall von Homosexualität durch Hodentransplantation," *Deustche medizinische Wochenschrift* 48: 660–662 (1922).

2. For brief biographies of Marker and many other sex-research pioneers, see V. L. Bullough, *Science in the Bedroom: A History of Sex Research* (New York: Basic Books, 1994).

3. C. A. Wright, "Endocrine aspects of homosexuality: A preliminary report," *Medical Record* 142: 407–410 (1935).

4. S. J. Glass, H. J. Deuel, and C. A. Wright, "Sex hormone studies in male homosexuality," *Endocrinology* 26: 590–594 (1940); R. Neustadt and A. Myerson, "Quantitative sex hormone studies in homosexuality, childhood, and various neuropsychiatric disturbances," *American Journal of Psychiatry* 97: 524–551 (1940).

5. C. A. Wright, "Results of endocrine treatment in a controlled group of homosexual men," *Medical Record* 154: 60–61 (1941).

6. S. J. Glass and R. H. Johnson, "Limitations and complications of organotherapy in male homosexuality," *Journal of Clinical Endocrinology* 4: 540–544 (1944).

7. H. S. Barahal, "Testosterone in psychotic male homosexuals," *Psychiatric Quarterly* 14: 319–330 (1940).

8. A. C. Kinsey, testimony cited in R. M. Brown (chairman), *Preliminary Report of the Subcommittee on Sex Crimes of the Assembly Interim Committee on Judicial System and Judicial Process* (Sacramento: California Legislature, 1950), pp. 103–122. I do not know of other references to these experiments and I am somewhat skeptical that they took place as described.

9. This account is based on Nazi documents published in G. Grau, ed., *Hidden Holocaust? Gay and Lesbian Persecution in Germany 1933–45*, P. Cammiller, trans. (London: Cassell, 1995).

10. S. Rosenzweig and R. G. Hoskins, "A note on the ineffectualness of sex-hormone medication in a case of pronounced homosexuality," *Psychosomatic Medicine* 3: 87–89 (1941). (Reprinted in J. N. Katz, *Gay American History: Lesbians and Gay Men in the U.S.A.* [New York: Meridian, 1992], pp. 167–169.)

11. C. W. Dunn, "Stilbestrol-induced gynecomastia in the male," *Journal of the American Medical Association* 115: 2263–2264 (1940).

12. F. L. Golla and R. S. Hodge, "Hormone treatment of the sexual offender," *Lancet* 256(1): 1006–1007 (1949).

13. A. Hodges, *Alan Turing: The Enigma* (New York: Simon and Schuster, 1983).

14. Katz, *Gay American History*, pp. 23–24. The penalty of castration replaced the earlier death penalty.

15. A. Karlen, *Sexuality and Homosexuality: A New View* (New York: W. W. Norton, 1971), p. 334.

16. Grau, *Hidden Holocaust*, pp. 246–262.

17. For a review of these studies, see H. F. L. Meyer-Bahlburg, "Psychoendocrine research on sexual orientation. Current status and future options," *Progress in Brain Research* 61: 375–398 (1984).

18. Data reviewed by Meyer-Bahlburg.

19. C. H. Phoenix, R. W. Goy, A. A. Gerall, and W. C. Young, "Organizing action of prenatally administered testosterone propionate on the tissues mediating mating behavior in the female guinea pig," *Endocrinology* 65: 369–382 (1959).

20. K. L. Grady, C. H. Phoenix, and W. C. Young, "Role of the developing rat testis in differentiation of the neural tissues mediating mating behavior," *Journal of Comparative and Physiological Psychology* 59: 176–182 (1965).

21. F. Neumann, R. von Berswordt-Wallrape, W. Elger, H. Steinbeck, J. D. Hahn, and M. Kramer, "Aspects of androgen-dependent events as studied by antiandrogens," *Recent Progress in Hormone Research* 26: 37–410 (1970).

22. Reviewed in W. W. Beatty, "Gonadal hormones and sex differences in nonreproductive behaviors," in A. A. Gerall, H. Moltz, and I. L. Ward, eds., *Handbook of Behavioral Neurobiology: Vol. 11. Sexual Differentiation* (New York: Plenum Press, 1992), pp. 85–128.

23. R. W. Goy, "Differentiation of male social traits in female rhesus macaques by prenatal treatment with androgens: Variation in type of androgen, duration and timing of treatment," in M. J. Novy and J. A. Resko, eds., *Fetal Endocrinology* (New York: Academic Press, 1981), pp. 319–339. By the "male role" in play-sex I mean the double-footclasp mount, in which the animal raises itself on the hind legs of the other in order to mount it.

24. S. M. Pomerantz, M. M. Roy, J. E. Thornton, and R. W. Goy, "Expression of adult female patterns of sexual behavior by male, female and pseudohermaphroditic female rhesus monkeys," *Biology of Reproduction* 33: 878–889 (1985); S. M. Pomerantz, R. W. Goy, and M. M. Roy, "Expression of male-typical sexual behavior in adult pseudohermaphroditic rhesus: Comparisons with normal males and neonatally gonadectomized males and females," *Hormones and Behavior* 20: 483–500 (1986).

25. R. W. Goy, F. B. Bercovitch, and M. C. McBrair, "Behavioral masculinization is independent of genital masculinization in prenatally androgenized female rhesus macaques," *Hormones and Behavior* 22: 552–571 (1988).

26. G. Dörner, "Tierexperimentelle Untersuchungen zur Frage einer hormonellen Pathogenese der Homosexualität," *Acta Biologica et Medica Germanica* 19: 569-584 (1967); G. Dörner, "Zur Frage einer neuroendokrinen Pathogenese, Prophylaxe und Therapie angeborener Sexualdeviationen," *Deutsche Medizinische Wochenshrift* 94: 390–396 (1969).

27. G. Dörner, I. Poppe, F. Stahl, J. Kölzsch, and R. Uebelhack, "Gene- and environment-dependent neuroendocrine etiogenesis of homosexuality and transsexualism," *Experimental and Clinical Endocrinology* 98: 141–150 (1991). Dörner states in the article that his teacher Walter Hohlweg studied with Steinach from 1925 to 1928.

28. G. Dörner, *Hormones and Brain Differentiation* (Amsterdam: Elsevier, 1976), p. 229.

29. V. Sigusch, E. Schorsch, M. Dannecker, and G. Schmidt, "Official statement by the German Society for Sex Research (Deutsche Gesellschaft für Sexualforschung e.V.) on the research of Prof. Dr. Günter Dörner on the subject of homosexuality," *Archives of Sexual Behavior* 11: 445–449 (1982). Note that Dannecker also attacked Hirschfeld's biological views for supposedly paving the way for the Nazi persecution of gay people (see chapter 1).

30. H. H. Feder, "Hormones and sexual behavior," *Annual Reviews of Psychology* 35: 165–200 (1984). See also H. F. L. Meyer-Bahlburg, "Psychoendocrine research on sexual orientation: Current status and future options," in G. J. DeVries, J. P. C. DeBruin, H. B. M. Uylings, and M. A. Corner, eds., *Progress in Brain Research, Vol. 61: Sex Differences in the Brain* (Amsterdam: Elsevier, 1984), pp. 375–398.

31. For a clear statement of the issues involved, see E. Adkins-Regan, "Sex hormones and sexual orientation in animals," *Psychobiology* 16: 335–347 (1988).

32. B. J. Meyerson, M. Eliasson, and J. Hetta, "Sex-specific orientation in female and male rats: Development and effects of early endocrine manipulation," in A. M. Kaye and M. Kaye, eds., *Advances in the Biosciences, Vol. 25: Development of Responsiveness to Steroid Hormones* (Oxford: Pergamon Press, 1980), pp. 451–460; F. H. de Jonge, J.-W. Muntjewerff, A. L. Louwerse, and N. E. van de Poll, "Sexual behavior and sexual orientation of the female rat after hormonal treatment during various stages of development," *Hormones and Behavior* 22: 100–115 (1988); J.Vega Matuszczyk, A. Fernandez-Guasti, and K. Larssen, "Sexual orientation, proceptivity, and receptivity in the male rat as function of neonatal hormonal manipulation," *Hormones and Behavior* 22: 362–378 (1988); T. Brand and A. K. Slob, "Neonatal organization of adult partner preference behavior in male rats," *Physiology and Behavior* 49: 107–111 (1991); T. Brand, J. Kroonen, J. Mos, J., and A. K. Slob, "Adult partner preference and sexual behavior of male rats affected by perinatal endocrine manipulations," *Hormones and Behavior* 25: 323–341 (1991); J. Bakker, T. Brand, J. van Ophemert, and A. K. Slob, "Hormonal regulation of adult partner preference behavior in neonatally ATD-treated male rats," *Behavioral Neuroscience* 107: 480–487 (1993).

33. W. A. Johnson and L. Tiefer, "Sexual preferences in neonatally castrated male golden hamsters," *Physiology and Behavior* 9: 213–218 (1972).

34. E. R. Stockman, R. S. Callaghan, and M. J. Baum, "Effects of neonatal castration and testosterone propionate treatment on sexual partner preference in the ferret," *Physiology and Behavior* 34: 409–414 (1985); M. J. Baum, M. S. Erskine, E. Kornberg, and C. E. Weaver, "Prenatal and neonatal testosterone exposure interact to affect the differentiation of sexual behavior and partner preference in female ferrets," *Behavioral Neuroscience* 104: 183–198 (1990).

35. E. Adkins-Regan, P. Orguer, and J. P. Signoret, "Sexual differentiation of reproductive behavior in pigs: Defeminizing effects of prepubertal estradiol," *Hormones and Behavior* 23: 290–303 (1989). The authors found that in pigs the period of sensitivity to the organizing effects of gonadal steroids extends almost until puberty.

36. E. Adkins-Regan and M. Ascenzi, "Social and sexual behavior of male and female zebra finches treated with oestradiol during the nestling period," *Animal Behaviour* 35: 1100–1112 (1987).

37. A. A. Ehrhardt and S. W. Baker, "Fetal androgens, human central nervous system differentiation and behavior sex differences," in R. C. Friedman, R. M. Richart, and R. L. Vande Wiele, eds., *Sex Differences in Behavior* (New York: Wiley, 1974), pp. 33–51; M. Matheis and C. Förster, "Zur psychosexuellen Entwicklung von Mädchen mit dem adrenogenitalen Syndrom," *Zeitschrift für Kinder- und Jugendpsychiatrie* 8: 5–17 (1980); R. W. Dittmann, M. H. Kappes, M. E. Kappes, D. Börger, H. Stegner, R. H. Willig, and H. Wallis, "Congenital adrenal hyperplasia I: Gender-related behavior and attitudes in female patients and sisters," *Psychoneuroendocrinology* 15: 401–420 (1990); S. A. Berenbaum and M. Hines, "Early androgens are related to childhood sex-typed toy preferences," *Psychological Science* 3: 203–206 (1992); S. A. Berenbaum and E. Snyder, "Early hormonal influences on childhood sex-typed activity and playmate preferences: Implications for the development of sexual orientation," *Developmental Psychology* 31: 31–42 (1995); S. M. Resnick, S. A. Berenbaum, I. I. Gottesman, and T. J. Bouchard, "Early hormonal influences on cognitive functioning in congenital adrenal hyperplasia," *Developmental Psychology* 22: 191–198 (1986).

38. J. Money, M. Schwartz, and V. G. Lewis, "Adult erotosexual status and fetal hormonal masculinization and demasculinization: 46,XX congenital virilizing adrenal hyperplasia and 46,XY androgen-insensitivity syndrome compared," *Psychoneuroendocrinology* 9: 405–414 (1984); R. M. Mulaikal, C. J. Migeon, and J. A. Rock, "Fertility rates in female patients with congenital adrenal hyperplasia due to 21-hydroxylase deficiency," *New England Journal of Medicine* 316: 178–182 (1987); R. W. Dittmann, M. E. Kappes, and M. H. Kappes, "Sexual behavior in adolescent and adult females with congenital adrenal hyperplasia," *Psychoneuroendocrinology* 17: 153–170 (1992); K. J. Zucker, S. J. Bradley, G. Oliver, J. E. Hood, J. Blake, and S. Fleming, "Psychosexual assessment of women with congenital adrenal hyperplasia: Preliminary analyses." Paper presented at International Academy of Sex Research, 18th Annual Meeting, Prague, Czechoslovakia, July 1992.

39. D. A. Edelman, *DES/Diethylstilbestrol—New Perspectives* (Boston: MTP Press, 1986).

40. H. F. L. Meyer-Bahlburg, A. A. Ehrhardt, L. R. Rosen, R. S. Gruen, N. P. Veridiano, F. H. Vann, and H. F. Neuwalder, "Prenatal estrogens and the development of homosexual orientation," *Developmental Psychology* 31: 12–21 (1995).

41. An alternative explanation for the lesser influence of DES might be that the doses used in many of the women were not high enough or prolonged enough to activate all the estrogen receptors throughout the critical period. Unfortunately, information about the amounts of DES that were administered is generally no longer available.

Chapter 6

1. A. E. Fisher, "Maternal and sexual behavior induced by intracranial chemical stimulation," *Science* 124: 228–229 (1956); J. M. Davidson, "Activation of the male rat's sexual behavior by intracerebral implantation of androgen," *Endocrinology* 79: 783–794 (1966); R. D. Lisk, "Reproductive capacity and behavioral oestrus in the rat bearing hypothalamic implants of sex steroids," *Acta Endocrinologica* 48: 209–219 (1965); G. Dörner, F. Döcke, and S. Moustafa, "Differential localization of a male and a female hypothalamic mating centre," *Journal of Reproduction and Fertility* 17: 583–586 (1968).

2. A. Soulairac and M. L. Soulairac, "Effets de lésions hypothalamiques sur le comportement sexuel et le tractus génital du rat male," *Annales d'Endocrinologie (Paris)* 17: 731–745 (1956); L. Heimer and K. Larsson, "Impairment of mating behavior in male rats following lesions in the preoptic-anterior hypothalamic continuum," *Brain Research* 3: 248–263 (1966/67); D. W. Pfaff and Y. Sakuma, "Deficit in the lordosis reflex of female rats caused by lesions in the ventromedial nucleus of the hypothalamus," *Journal of Physiology (London)* 288: 203–210 (1979); S. Hansen, C. H. Kohler, M. Goldstein, and H. V. M. Steinbusch, "Effects of ibotenic acid-induced neuronal degeneration in the medial preoptic area and the lateral hypothalamic area on sexual behavior in the male rat," *Brain Research* 239: 213–232 (1982).

3. N.-A. Hillarp, H. Olivecrona, and W. Silferskiold, "Evidence for the participation of the preoptic area in male mating behavior," *Experientia* 10: 224 (1954); C. W. Malsbury, "Facilitation of male rat copulatory behavior by electrical stimulation of the medial preoptic area, *Physiology and Behavior* 7: 797–805 (1971); D. W. Pfaff and Y. Sakuma, "Facilitation of the lordosis reflex of female rats from the ventromedial nucleus of the hypothalamus," *Journal of Physiology (London)* 288: 189–202 (1979).

4. Y. Oomura, S. Aou, Y. Koyama, and H. Yoshimatsu, "Central control of sexual behavior," *Brain Research Bulletin* 20: 863–870 (1988).

5. J. J. Singer, "Hypothalamic control of male and female sexual behavior in female rats," *Journal of Comparative and Physiological Psychology* 66: 738–742 (1968).

6. J. C. Slimp, B. L. Hart, and R. W. Goy, " Heterosexual, autosexual and social behavior of adult male rhesus monkeys with medial preoptic-anterior hypothalamic lesions," *Brain Research* 142: 105–122 (1978).

7. G. Dörner, F. Döcke, and G. Hinz, "Homo- and hypersexuality in rats with hypothalamic lesions," *Neuroendocrinology* 4: 20–24 (1969);

8. The passage from Dörner's film that contains this quotation is included in the British documentary film *Born That Way?* (J. Taylor, producer), Windfall Films, London, 1992.

9. G. Dörner, *Hormones and Brain Differentiation* (Amsterdam: Elsevier, 1976), pp. 227–228.

10. F. D. Roeder, "Stereotaxic lesion of the tuber cinereum in sexual deviation," *Confinia Neurologica* 27: 162–163 (1966).

11. F. Roeder and D. Müller, "Zur stereotaktischen Heilung der pädophilen Homosexualität," *Deutsche Medizinische Wochenschrift* 9: 409–415 (1969); D. Müller, H. Orthner, F. Roeder, A. König, and K. Bosse, "Einfluss von Hypothalamusläsionen auf Sexualverhalten und gonadotrope Funktion beim Menschen: Bericht über 23 Fälle," in G. Dörner, G., ed., *Endocrinology of Sex* (Leipzig: Barth, 1974), pp. 80–105; G. Dieckmann and R. Hassler, "Unilateral hypothalamotomy in sexual delinquents," *Confinia Neurologica* 37: 177–186 (1975); G. Dieckmann, H.-J. Horn, and H. Schneider, "Long-term results of anterior hypothalamotomy in sexual offences," in E. R. Hitchcock., H. T. Ballantine, Jr., and B. A. Meyerson, eds., *Modern Concepts in Psychiatric Surgery* (Amsterdam: Elsevier, 1979), pp. 187–195; G. Dieckmann, B. Schneider-Jonietz, and H. Schneider, "Psychiatric and neuropsychological findings after stereotactic hypothalamotomy in cases of extreme sexual agressivity," *Acta Neurochirurgica,* Supplement 44: 163–166 (1988).

12. According to current American usage as spelled out in *DSM-IV*, pedophilia refers to sexual activity with a prepubescent child.

13. F. Garner, "Homosexuality 'burned out': German surgeon claims hypothalamotomy normalizes sex drive," *Medical World News* 11(39) (September 25, 1970), pp. 20–21.

14. G. Dörner, W. Rohde, F. Stahl, L. Krell, and W.-G. Masius, "A neuroendocrine predisposition for homosexuality in men," *Archives of Sexual Behavior* 4: 1–8 (1975).

15. In some writings, as in my own earlier book *The Sexual Brain*, GnRH is referred to by another name, "luteinizing hormone releasing hormone" or LHRH.

16. The control of the menstrual cycle is more complex, and involves more hormones, than indicated here. For a fuller account, see M. Johnson and B. Everitt, *Essential Reproduction,* 3rd edition (Oxford: Blackwell, 1988), chapters 4 and 5.

17. T. Swelheim, "The influence of a single high dose of oestradiol benzoate on the ICSH-content in the serum of gonadectomized male and female rats," *Acta Endocrinologica (Copenhagen)* 49: 231–238 (1965).

18. G. Dörner and F. Döcke, "Sex-specific reaction of the hypothalamo-hypophysial system of rats," *Journal of Endocrinology* 30: 265–266 (1964); F. Döcke and G. Dörner, "Tierexperimentelle Untersuchungen zur Ovulationsauslösung mit Gonadotropinen und Östrogenen. 4. Mitteilung: Zur neurohormonalen Regulation der Ovulation," *Zentralblatt für Gynäkologie* 88: 273–282 (1966).

19. L. Gooren, "The neuroendocrine response of luteinizing hormone to estrogen administration in heterosexual, homosexual and transsexual subjects," *Journal of Clinical Endocrinology and Metabolism* 63: 583–588 (1986).

20. L. Gooren, "The neuroendocrine response to estrogen administration in the human is not sex specific but dependent on the hormonal environment," *Journal of Clinical Endocrinology and Metabolism* 63: 589–593 (1986).

21. B. A. Gladue, R. Green, and R. E. Hellman, "Neuroendocrine response to estrogen and sexual orientation," *Science* 225: 1496–1499 (1984).

22. S. E. Hendricks, B. Graber, and J. F. Rodriguez-Sierra, "Neuroendocrine responses to exogenous estrogen: No differences between heterosexual and homosexual men," *Psychoneuroendocrinology* 14: 177–185 (1989).

23. F. J. Karsh, D. J. Dierschke, and E. Knobil, "Sexual differentiation of pituitary function: apparent difference between primates and rodents," *Science* 179: 484–486 (1972); J. K. Hodges, "Regulation of oestrogen-induced LH release in male and female marmoset monkeys, (*Callithrix jacchus*)," *Journal of Reproduction and Fertility* 60: 389–398 (1980).

24. R. L. Norman and H. G. Spies, "Cyclic ovarian function in a male macaque: additional evidence for a lack of sexual differentiation in the physioligical mechanisms that regulate the cyclic release of gonadotropins in primates," *Endocrinology* 118: 2608–2610 (1986).

25. D. F. Swaab and M. A. Hofman, "Sexual differentiation of the human brain: A historical perspective," *Progress in Brain Research* 61: 361–373 (1984); C. D. Ankney, "Sex differences in relative brain size: The mismeasure of woman, too?" *Intelligence* 16: 329–336 (1992); J. P. Rushton, "Cranial capacity related to sex, rank, and race in a stratified random sample of 6,325 U.S. military personnel," *Intelligence* 16: 401–413 (1992). In an earlier book, *The Sexual Brain* (Cambridge, MA: MIT Press, 1993), p. 101, I implied wrongly that sex differences in brain size are fully accounted for by differences in body size.

26. R. Lynn, "Sex differences in intelligence and brain size: A paradox revisited," *Personality and Individual Differences* 17: 257–271 (1994).

27. C. D. Ankney, "Sex differences in brain size and mental abilities: comments

on R. Lynn and D. Kimura," *Personality and Individual Differences* 18: 423–424 (1995).

28. D. F. Swaab and M. A. Hofman, "An enlarged suprachiasmatic nucleus in homosexual men," *Brain Research* 537: 141–148 (1990); S. LeVay, "A difference in hypothalamic structure between homosexual and heterosexual men," *Science* 253: 1034–1037 (1991); L. S. Allen and R. A. Gorski, "Sexual orientation and the size of the anterior commissure in the human brain," *Proceedings of the National Academy of the U.S.A.* 89: 7199-7202 (1992). Given that these studies examined relatively few brains, and were focused on other issues than overall brain size, the possibility that they missed a small difference in average brain size cannot be excluded.

29. R. A. Gorski, J. H. Gordon, J. E. Shryne, and A. M. Southam, "Evidence for a morphological sex difference within the medial preoptic area of the rat brain," *Brain Research* 148: 333–346 (1978).

30. G. Greer, *The Female Eunuch* (New York: McGraw-Hill, 1971).

31. For example, C. Gilligan, *In a Different Voice: Psychological Theory and Women's Development* (Cambridge, MA: Harvard University Press, 1982).

32. K.-D. Döhler, M. Hines, A. Coquelin, F. Davis, J. E. Shryne, and R. A. Gorski, "Pre- and postnatal influence of testosterone propionate and diethylstilbestrol on differentiation of the sexually dimorphic nucleus of the preoptic area in male and female rats," *Brain Research* 302: 291–295 (1984); K.-D. Döhler, S. S. Srivastava, J. E. Shryne, B. Jarzab, A. Sipos, and R. A. Gorski, "Differentiation of the sexually dimorphic nucleus in the preoptic area of the rat brain is inhibited by postnatal treatment with an estrogen antagonist," *Neuroendocrinology* 38: 297–301 (1984); R. W. Rhees, J. E. Shryne, and R. A. Gorski, "Termination of the hormone-sensitive period for differentiation of the sexually dimorphic nucleus of the preoptic area in male and female rats," *Developmental Brain Research* 52: 17–23 (1990).

33. M. Hines, F. C. Davies, A. Coquelin, R. W. Goy, and R. A. Gorski, "Sexually dimorphic regions in the medial preoptic area and the bed nucleus of the stria terminalis of the guinea pig brain: a description and an investigation of their relationship to gonadal steroids in adulthood," *Journal of Comparative Neurology* 144: 193–204 (1985); D. Commins and P. Yahr, "Adult testosterone levels influence the morphology of a sexually dimorphic area in the Mongolian gerbil brain," *Journal of Comparative Neurology* 224: 132–140 (1984); S. A. Tobet, D. J. Zahniser, and M. J. Baum, "Sexual dimorphism in the preoptic/anterior hypothalamic area of ferrets: Effects of adult exposure to sex steroids," *Brain Research* 364: 249–257 (1986); J. A. Cherry, M. E. Basham, C. E. Weaver, R. W. Krohmer, and M. J. Baum, "Ontogeny of the sexually dimorphic male nucleus in the preoptic/anterior

hypothalamus of ferrets and its manipulation by gonadal steroids," *Journal of Neurobiology* 21: 844–857 (1990); W. Byne (personal communication).

34. Reviewed in L. W. Swanson, "The hypothalamus," in A. Björklund, T. Hökfelt, and L. W. Swanson, eds., *Handbook of Chemical Neuroanatomy, Vol. 5, Integrated Systems of the CNS, Part I* (Amsterdam: Elsevier, 1987), pp. 1–124; see also R. B. Simerly and L. W. Swanson, "Projections of the medial preoptic nucleus: A *Phaseolus vulgaris* leucoagglutinin anterograde tract-tracing study in the rat," *Journal of Comparative Neurology* 270: 209–242 (1988).

35. M. Hines, L. S. Allen, and R. A. Gorski, "Sex differences in subregions of the medial nucleus of the amygdala and the bed nucleus of the stria terminalis of the rat," *Brain Research* 579: 321–326 (1992).

36. J. A. Cherry and C. Baum, "Effects of lesions of a sexually dimorphic nucleus in the preoptic/anterior hypothalamic area on the expression of androgen- and estrogen-dependent sexual behaviors in male ferrets," *Brain Research* 522: 191–203 (1990).

37. E. Terasawa, S. J. Wiegand, and W. E. Bridson, "A role for the medial preoptic nucleus on afternoon of proestrus in female rats," *American Journal of Physiology* 238: 533–539 (1980); R. Bleier, W. Byne, and I. Siggelkow, "Cytoarchitectonic sexual dimorphism of the medial preoptic area and anterior hypothalamic areas in guinea pig, rat, hamster and mouse," *Journal of Comparative Neurology* 212: 118–183 (1982); Y. Arai, M. Nishizuku, S. Murakami, M. Miyakawa, M. Machida, H. Takeuchi, and H. Sumida, "Morphological correlates of neuronal plasticity to gonadal steroids: Sexual differentiation of the preoptic area," in M. Haug et al., eds., *The Development of Sex Differences and Similarities in Behavior* (Amsterdam: Kluwer Academic Publishers, 1993), pp. 311–323.

38. L. S. Allen, M. Hines, J. E. Shryne, and R. A. Gorski, "Two sexually dimorphic cell groups in the human brain," *Journal of Neuroscience* 9: 497-506 (1989). A Dutch group had previously reported that a different cell group in the preoptic area (now identified as INAH1) was sexually dimorphic (D. F. Swaab and E. Fliers, "A sexually dimorphic nucleus in the human brain," *Science* 228: 1112–1115 [1985]), but neither Allen's group, nor myself, nor William Byne (personal communication) have been able to replicate that finding. The Dutch group compared INAH1 in gay and straight men and found no difference, and argued from that that the theory of sex-atypical brain development in gay men was incorrect (D. F. Swaab and M. A. Hofman, "Sexual differentiation of the human hypothalamus: Ontogeny of the sexually dimorphic nucleus of the preoptic area," *Developmental Brain Research* 44: 314–318 [1988]). If INAH3 is not sexually dimorphic, however, the lack of a difference between gay and straight men is not informative.

39. L. S. Allen and R. A. Gorski, "Sex differences in the bed nucleus of the stria terminalis of the human brain," *Journal of Comparative Neurology* 302: 697–706 (1990); L. S. Allen (personal communication).

40. L. S. Allen and R. A. Gorski, "Sexual dimorphism of the anterior commissure and massa intermedia of the human brain," *Journal of Comparative Neurology* 312: 97–104 (1991).

41. See LeVay, *The Sexual Brain*, pp. 101–102.

42. S. LeVay, "A difference in hypothalamic structure between heterosexual and homosexual men," *Science* 253: 1034–1037 (1991). For further description of the study, and a consideration of possible confounding factors, see LeVay, *The Sexual Brain*, pp. 120–123.

43. My reasons include: the lack of frank pathology in the hypothalamus, the large size of INAH3 in a control group of heterosexual AIDS patients, the lack of correlation between INAH3 size and a number of clinical variables such as length of survival, the lack of any size differences in nearby cell groups (INAH 1, 2, and 4), and the small size of INAH3 in one gay man who died of non-AIDS causes. See *The Sexual Brain*, p. 121.

44. L. S. Allen and R. A. Gorski, "Sexual orientation and the size of the anterior commissure in the human brain," *Proceedings of the National Academy of Sciences of the U.S.A.* 89: 7911–7202 (1992).

45. W. Byne and R. Bleier, "Medial preoptic sex dimorphisms in the guinea pig, II: An investigation of their hormonal dependence," *Journal of Neuroscience* 7: 2688–2696 (1987); W. Byne, J. Warren, and I. Siggelkow, "Medial preoptic sexual dimorphisms in the guinea pig, II: An investigation of medial preoptic neurogenesis," *Journal of Neuroscience* 7: 2697–2702 (1987).

46. W. Byne and B. Parsons, "Human sexual orientation: The biologic theories reappraised," *Archives of General Psychiatry* 50: 228–239 (1993); W. Byne, "Is homosexuality biologically influenced? The biological evidence challenged," *Scientific American* 270(5): 50–55 (1994); W. Byne, "Science and belief: Psychobiological research on sexual orientation," *Journal of Homosexuality* (in press).

47. W. Byne, "Apparent homologues of the rat's sexually dimorphic nucleus of the preoptic area in the human and rhesus monkey," American Psychiatric Association Annual Meeting, Miami, Florida (May 1995), Abstracts; W. Byne (personal communication).

Chapter 7

1. D. Kimura, "Sex differences in the brain," *Scientific American* (September): 119–125 (1992).

2. M. C. Linn and A. C. Petersen, "A meta-analysis of gender differences in spatial ability: Implications for mathematics and science achievement," in J. S. Hyde and M. C. Linn, *The Psychology of Gender* (Baltimore: Johns Hopkins University Press, 1986), pp. 67–101; D. F. Halpern, *Sex Differences in Cognitive Abilities* (Hillsdale, NJ: Erlbaum, 1986).

3. E. E. Maccoby and C. N. Jacklin, *The Psychology of Sex Differences* (Palo Alto: Stanford University Press, 1974); B. Sanders, M. P. Soares, and J. D'Aquila, "The sex difference on one test of spatial visualization: A non-trivial difference," *Child Development* 53: 1106–1110 (1982); D. Kimura and E. Hampson, "Neural and hormonal mechanisms mediating sex differences in cognition," in P. A. Vernon, ed., *Biological Approaches to the Study of Human Intelligence* (Norwood, New Jersey: Ablex Publishing, 1993), pp. 375–397.

4. R. Jardine and N. G. Martin, "Spatial ability and throwing accuracy," *Behavior Genetics* 13: 331–340 (1983); N. V. Watson and D. Kimura, "Nontrivial sex differences in throwing and intercepting: Relation to psychometrically defined spatial functions," *Personality and Individual Differences* 12: 375–385 (1991).

5. L. Galea and D. Kimura, *Sex Differences in Route Learning* (London, Ontario: University of Western Ontario, 1991); T. Bever, "The logical and extrinsic sources of modularity," in M. Gunnar and N. Maratsos, eds., *Modularity and Constraints in Language, Minnesota Symposia on Child Psychology,* volume 25 (Hillsdale, NJ: Lawrence Erlbaum, 1992), pp. 179–211.

6. T. Tiffin, *Purdue Pegboard Examiner Manual* (Chicago: Science Research Associates, 1968).

7. C. P. Benbow and J. C. Stanley, "Sex differences in mathematical ability: Fact or artifact?" *Science* 210: 1262–1264; C. P. Benbow and J. C. Stanley, "Sex differences in mathematical ability: More facts," *Science* 222: 1029–1031 (1983).

8. E. E. Maccoby, *The Development of Sex Differences* (Stanford: Stanford University Press, 1966); R. H. Harshman, E. Hampson, and S. A. Berenbaum, "Individual differences in cognitive abilities and brain organization, Part 1: Sex and handedness differences in ability," *Canadian Journal of Psychology* 37: 144–192 (1983); J. S. Hyde and M. C. Linn, "Gender differences in verbal ability: A meta-analysis," *Psychological Bulletin* 104: 53–69 (1988). Reported sex differences in verbal abilities are relatively small and inconsistent.

9. D. Lunn and D. Kimura, "Spatial abilities in preschool-aged children," *University of Western Ontario, Department of Psychology Research Bulletin, No. 681* (1989). See also E. S. Johnson and A. C. Meade, "Developmental patterns of spatial ability: An early sex difference," *Child Development* 58: 725–740 (1987); K. A. Kerns and S. A. Berenbaum, "Sex differences in spatial ability in children," *Behavior Genetics* 21: 383–396 (1991).

10. N.V.Watson and D. Kimura, "Nontrivial sex differences in throwing and intercepting: Relation to psychometrically-defined spatial functions," *Personality and Individual Differences* 12: 375–385 (1991).

11. S. M. Resnick, S. A. Berenbaum, I. I. Gottesman, and T. J. Bouchard, Jr., "Early hormonal influences on cognitive functioning in congenital adrenal hyperplasia," *Developmental Psychology* 22: 191–198 (1986).

12. J. Imerato-McGinley, M. Pichardo, T. Gautier, D. Voyer, and M. P. Bryden, "Cognitive abilities in androgen-insensitive subjects: Comparison with control males and females from the same kindred," *Clinical Endocrinology* 34: 341–347 (1991).

13. J. L. M. Dawson, Y. M. Cheung, and R. T. S. Lau, "Developmental effects of neonatal sex hormones on spatial and activity skills in the white rat," *Biological Psychology* 3: 213–229 (1975); C. L. Williams and W. H. Meck, "The organizational effects of gonadal steroids on sexually dimorphic spatial ability," *Psychoneuroimmunology* 16: 155–176 (1991).

14. E. Hampson and D. Kimura, "Reciprocal effects of hormonal fluctuations on human motor and perceptual-spatial skills," *Behavioral Neuroscience* 102: 456–459 (1988); D. Kimura, "Sex differences in the brain," *Scientific American* (September):119–125 (1992); G. Sanders and D. Wenmoth, "A decrease in left ear performance across the menstrual cycle, from menses when oestrogen is low to the mid-luteal phase when oestrogen is high, underlies reciprocal changes in functional asymmetry for dichotic verbal and music tasks." Oral presentation at International Behavioral Development Symposium: Biological Basis of Sexual Orientation and Sex-Typical Behavior (Minot State University, May 1995).

15. See, for example, P. Kitcher, *Vaulting Ambition: Sociobiology and the Quest for Human Nature* (Cambridge, MA: MIT Press, 1985).

16. B. Milner, "Psychological studies of focal epilepsy and its neurological management," *Advances in Neurology* 8: 299–321 (1975); E. De Renzi, *Disorders of Space Exploration and Cognition* (New York: Wiley, 1982); G. Deutsch, W. T. Bourbon, A. C. Papanicolaou, and H. M. Eisenberg, "Visuospatial tasks compared via activation of regional cerebral blood flow," *Neuropsychologia* 26: 445–452 (1988); B. A. Shaywitz, S. E. Shaywitz, K. R. Pugh, R. T. Constable, P. Skudlarski, R. K. Fulbright, R. A. Bronen, J. M. Fletcher, D. P. Shankweiler, L. Katz., and J. C. Gore, "Sex differences in the functional organization of the brain for language," *Nature* 373: 607–609 (1995).

17. A. Beaton, *Left Side, Right Side: A Review of Laterality Research* (London: Batsford, 1985); B. A. Shaywitz, S. E. Shaywitz, K. R. Pugh, R. T. Constable, P. Skudlarski, R. K. Fulbright, R. A. Bronen, J. M. Fletcher, D. P. Shankweiler, L. Katz, and J. C. Gore, "Sex differences in the functional organization of the brain for language," *Nature* 373: 607–609 (1995).

18. Kimura and Hampson, "Neural and hormonal mechanisms mediating sex differences in cognition," pp. 375–397.

19. P. G. Hepper, S. Shahidullah, and R. White, "Handedness in the human fetus," *Neuropsychologia* 11: 1107–1111 (1991).

20. For reviews see D. Halpern, *Sex Differences in Cognitive Abilities*, 2d edition (Hillsdale, NJ: Lawrence Erlbaum, 1992); S. Coren, *The Left-Hander Syndrome* (New York: Free Press, 1993). See also I. B. Perelle and L. Ehrman, "An international study of handedness: The data," *Behavior Genetics* 24: 217–227 (1994).

21. S. F. Witelson, "Hand and sex differences in the isthmus and genu of the human corpus callosum," *Brain* 112: 799–835 (1987); V. H. Denenberg, A. Kertesz, and P. E. Cowell, "A factor analysis of the human's corpus callosum," *Brain Research* 548: 126–132 (1991) (these reports find structural differences related to handedness in men only); S. F. Witelson and D. L. Kigar, "Sylvian fissure morphology and asymmetry in men and women: Bilateral differences in relation to handedness in men," *Journal of Comparative Neurology* 323: 326–340 (1992).

22. J. S. Hyde, "How large are gender differences in aggression? A developmental meta-analysis," *Developmental Psychology* 20: 722–736 (1984); A. H. Eagly and V. J. Steffen, "Gender and aggressive behavior: A meta-analytic review of the social psychological literature," *Psychological Bulletin* 100: 309–330 (1986); M. Daly and M. Wilson, *Homicide* (Hawthorne, NY: Aldine De Gruyter, 1988); L. Ellis, "The victimful-victimless crime distinction, and seven universal demographic correlates of victimful criminal behavior," *Personality and Individual Differences* 9: 525–548 (1988); L. Ellis, "Sex differences in criminality: An explanation based on the concept of r/K selection," *Mankind Quarterly* 30: 17–37 (1989), 399–417 (1990).

23. A. A. Ehrhardt, R. Epstein, and J. Money, "Fetal androgens and female gender identity in the early-treated adrenogenital syndrome," *Johns Hopkins Medical Journal* 122: 160–167 (1968); S. W. Baker and A. A. Ehrhardt, "Prenatal androgen, intelligence, and cognitive sex differences," in R. C. Friedman, R. Richart, and R. Vande Wiele, eds., *Sex Differences in Behavior* (New York: Wiley, 1974), pp. 53–76; E. Hampson, J. F. Rovet, and D. Altmann, "Sports participation and physical aggressiveness in children and young adults with congenital adrenal hyperplasia," *International Behavioral Development Symposium: Biological Basis of Sexual Orientation and Sex-Typical Behavior, Abstracts* (Minot State University, May 1995), p. 39. The observations on aggression in CAH females relate primarily to childhood characteristics.

24. W. W. Beatty, "Hormonal organization of sex differences in play fighting and spatial behavior," *Progress in Brain Research* 61: 315–330 (1984); R. W. Goy and B. S. McEwen, *Sexual Differentiation of the Brain* (Cambridge, MA: MIT Press, 1980), see especially pp. 44–54.

25. M. B. Oliver and J. S. Hyde, "Gender differences in sexuality: A meta-analysis," *Psychological Bulletin* 114: 29–51 (1993).

26. D. M. Buss and D. P. Schmitt, "Sexual strategies theory: An evolutionary perspective on human mating," *Psychological Review* 100: 204–232 (1993).

27. M. S. Clark and E. Hatfield, "Gender differences in receptivity to sexual offers," *Journal of Psychology and Human Sexuality* 2: 39–55 (1989).

28. J. M. Bailey, S. Gauling, Y. Agyei, and B. A. Gladue, "Effects of gender and sexual orientation on evolutionary relevant aspects of human mating psychology," *Journal of Personality and Social Psychology* 66: 1081–1093 (1994).

29. D. T. Kenrick and R. C. Keefe, "Age preferences in mates reflect sex differences in human reproductive strategies," *Behavioral and Brain Sciences* 15: 75–133 (1992).

30. J. M. Townsend and G. Levy, "Effects of potential partners' physical attractiveness and socioeconomic status on sexuality and partner selection," *Archives of Sexual Behavior* 19: 149–164 (1990); J. M. Towsend and G. D. Levy, "Effect of potential partners' costume and physical attractiveness on sexuality and partner selection," *Journal of Psychology* 124: 371–389 (1990).

31. Townsend and Levy, "Effects of potential partners' physical attractiveness and socioeconomic status on sexuality and partner selection"; D. M. Buss, "Sex differences in human mate preferences: Evolutionary hypotheses tested in 37 cultures," *Behavioral and Brain Sciences* 12: 1–49 (1989).

32. D. M. Buss, R. J. Larsen, D. Westen, and J. Semmelroth, "Sex differences in jealousy: Evolution, physiology and psychology," *Psychological Science* 3: 251–255 (1992).

33. Bailey, Gauling, Agyei, and Gladue, "Effects of gender and sexual orientation on evolutionary relevant aspects of human mating psychology"; D. M. Buss and D. P. Schmitt, "Sexual strategies theory: A contextual evolutionary analysis of human mating," *Psychological Review* (in press).

34. J. M. Connor and L. A. Serbin, "Behaviorally based masculine- and feminine-activity-preference scales for preschoolers: Correlates with other classroom behaviors and cognitive tests," *Child Development* 48: 1411–1416 (1977); M. B. Liss, "Patterns of toy play: An analysis of sex differences," *Sex Roles* 7: 1143–1150 (1981).

35. A. A. Ehrhardt, R. Epstein, and J. Money, "Fetal androgens and female gender identity in the early-treated adrenogenital syndrome," *Johns Hopkins Medical Journal* 122: 160–167 (1968); A. A. Ehrhardt and H. F. L. Meyer-Bahlburg, "Prenatal sex hormones and the developing brain: Effects on psychosexual differentiation and cognitive function," *Annual Review of Medicine* 30: 417–430 (1979); S. A. Berenbaum and M. Hines, "Early androgens are related to childhood sex-

typed toy preferences," *Psychological Science* 3: 203–206 (1992); S. Berenbaum and E. Snyder, "Early hormonal influences on childhood sex-typed activity and play-mate preferences: implications for the development of sexual orientation," *Developmental Psychology* 31: 31–42 (1995).

36. N. A. Krasnegor and R. S. Bridges, eds., *Mammalian Parenting: Biochemical, Neurobiological and Behavioral Determinants* (New York: Oxford University Press, 1990).

37. For example, A. Fausto-Sterling, *Myths of Gender: Biological Theories About Women and Men* (New York: Basic Books, 1985).

38. J. Hall and D. Kimura, "Sexual orientation and performance on sexually dimorphic motor tasks," *Archives of Sexual Behavior* 24: 395–407 (1995).

39. It has been suggested that the female superiority in fine motor tasks such as the pegboard task may be a consequence of women having smaller fingers (M. Peters, P. Servos, and R. Day, "Marked sex differences on a fine motor skill task disappear when finger size is used as a covariate," *Journal of Applied Psychology* 75: 87–90 [1990]).

40. G. Sanders and L. Ross-Field, "Sexual orientation and visuo-spatial ability," *Brain and Cognition* 5: 280–290 (1986); B. A. Gladue, W. W. Beatty, J. Larson, and R. D. Staton, "Sexual orientation and spatial ability in men and women," *Psychobiology* 18: 101–108 (1990); C. M. McCormick and S. F. Witelson, "A cognitive profile of homosexual men compared to heterosexual men and women," *Psychoneuroendocrinology* 16: 459–473 (1991). For negative results see G. E. Tuttle and R. C. Pillard, "Sexual orientation and cognitive abilities," *Archives of Sexual Behavior* 20: 307–318 (1991); B. Glaude and J. M. Bailey, "Spatial ability, handedness, and human sexual orientation," *Psychoneuroendocrinology* 20: 487–497 (1995).

41. C. M. McCormick and S. F. Witelson, "Cognitive abilities in lesbians," *Society for Neuroscience Abstracts* 16: 2 (1990); B. A. Gladue, W. W. Beatty, J. Larson, and R. D. Staton, "Sexual orientation and spatial ability in men and women," *Psychobiology* 18: 101–108 (1990); G. E. Tuttle and R. C. Pillard, "Sexual orientation and cognitive abilities," *Archives of Sexual Behavior* 20: 307–318 (1991).

42. M. Willmott and H. Brierley, "Cognitive characteristics and homosexuality," *Archives of Sexual Behavior* 13: 311–319 (1984).

43. B. A. Gladue, W. W. Beatty, J. Larson, and R. D. Staton, "Sexual orientation and spatial ability in men and women," *Psychobiology* 18: 101–108 (1990).

44. C. M. McCormick and S. F. Witelson, "A cognitive profile of homosexual men compared to heterosexual men and women," *Psychoneuroendocrinology* 16: 459–473 (1991); G. E. Tuttle and R. C. Pillard, "Sexual orientation and cognitive abilities," *Archives of Sexual Behavior* 20: 307–318 (1991).

45. G. Sanders and L. Ross-Field, "Sexual orientation, cognitive abilities and cerebral asymmetry: A review and a hypothesis tested," *Italian Journal of Zoology* 20: 459–465 (1986).

46. C. M. McCormick and S. F. Witelson, "Functional cerebral asymmetry and sexual orientation in men and women," *Behavioral Neuroscience* 108: 525–531 (1994). The study did report a complex interaction between sexual orientation, handedness, and cerebral lateralization as measured in a dichotic listening task.

47. In Hirschfeld's data, left-handers formed 7 percent of the gay male population, compared with 4 percent of unselected Army recruits (M. Hirschfeld, *Die Homosexualität des Mannes und des Weibes*, 2nd edition (Berlin: Louis Marcus, 1920), chapter 6.

48. C. M. McCormick, S. F. Witelson, and E. Kingstone, "Left-handedness in homosexual men and women: Neuroendocrine implications," *Psychoneuroendocrinology* 15: 69–76 (1990); D. W. Holtzen, "Handedness and sexual orientation," *Journal of Clinical and Experimental Neuropsychology* 16: 702–712 (1994).

49. J. Lindesay, "Laterality shift in homosexual men," *Neuropsychologia* 25: 965–969 (1987); J. T. Becker, S. M. Bass, M. A. Dew, L. Kingsley, O. Selnes, and K. Sheridan, "Hand preference, immune system disorder, and cognitive function among gay/bisexual men: The Multicenter AIDS Cohort Study (MACS)," *Neuropsychologia* 30: 229–235 (1992); K. O. Götestam, T. J. Coates, and M. Ekstrand, "Handedness, dyslexia, and twinning in homosexual men," *International Journal of Neuroscience* 63: 179–186 (1992).

50. L. D. Rosenstein and E. D. Bigler, "No relationship between handedness and sexual preference," *Psychological Reports* 60: 704–706 (1987); S. E. Marchant-Haycox, I. C. McManus, and G. D. Wilson, "Left-handedness, homosexuality, HIV infection and AIDS," *Cortex* 27: 49–56 (1991); P. Satz, E. N. Miller, O. Selnes, W. Van Gorp, L. F. D'elia, and B. Visscher, "Hand preference in homosexual men," *Cortex* 27: 295–306 (1991); B. A. Gladue and J. M. Bailey, "Spatial ability, handedness, and human sexual orientation," *Psychoneuroendocrinology* 20: 487–497 (1995); A. F. Bogaert and R. Blanchard, "Handedness in homosexual and heterosexual men in the Kinsey interview data," *Archives of Sexual Behavior* (in press).

51. D. Hamer, "The role of genes in sexual orientation and sex-typical behavior." Oral presentation at International Behavioral Development Symposium, Biological Basis of Sexual Orientation and Sex-Typical Behavior (Minot State University, May 1995).

52. D. Kimura, *Neuromotor Mechanisms in Human Communication* (New York: Oxford University Press, 1993).

53. D. Kimura, "Body asymmetry and intellectual pattern," *Personality and Individual Differences* 17: 53–60 (1994).

54. J. Hall and D. Kimura, "Dermatoglyphic asymmetry and sexual orientation in men," *Behavioral Neuroscience* 108: 1203–1206 (1994).
55. Pairs of different words are presented simultaneously to the left and right ears through headphones. A subject will more readily comprehend the words presented to the right ear if language is represented in the left hemisphere of the brain, because the connections between ear and brain are crossed. If language is represented in the right hemisphere, the subject will hear the words presented to the left ear better, and if language is represented bilaterally, neither ear will have an advantage.
56. J. A. Hall and D. Kimura, *Neuroscience Abstracts* 19: 561 (1993).
57. S. B. Holt, *The Genetics of Dermal Ridges* (Springfeld, IL: Charles C. Thomas, 1968).
58. There have been recent studies suggesting that homosexual men may be slightly shorter and lighter than heterosexual men: R. Blanchard, R. Dickey, and C. L. Jones, "Comparison of height and weight in homosexual versus nonhomosexual male gender dysphorics," *Archives of Sexual Behavior* 24: 543–554 (1995); R. Blanchard and A. F. Bogaert, "Biodemographic comparisons of homosexual and heterosexual men in the Kinsey interview data," *Archives of Sexual Behavior* (in press); A. F. Bogaert and R. Blanchard, "Physical development and sexual orientation in men: Height, weight, and age of puberty differences," (submitted for publication). The authors suggest that the differences may be related to a slightly earlier onset of puberty in homosexual men. There have also been claims that lesbians, or some subset of lesbians, are taller and/or heavier than heterosexual women, or have narrower hips: F. E. Kenyon, "Physique and physical health of female homosexuals," *Journal of Neurology, Neurosurgery and Psychiatry* 31: 487–489 (1968); M. W. Perkins, "Female homosexuality and body build," *Archives of Sexual Behavior* 10: 337–345 (1981). These two studies leave a lot to be desired in terms of sampling techniques and comparison groups. It has been reported that the faces of highly gender-nonconformist boys are physically *more* attractive (when rated blindly by adult men and women) than those of a comparison group of boys, whereas the faces of highly gender-nonconformist girls are *less* attractive that those of controls girls: K. J. Zucker, J. Wild, S. J. Bradley, and C. B. Lowry, "Physical attractiveness of boys with gender identity disorder," *Archives of Sexual Behavior* 22: 23–36 (1993); S. R. Fridell, K. J. Zucker, S. J. Bradley, and D. M. Maing, "Physical attractiveness of girls with gender identity disorder," *Archives of Sexual Behavior* 25: 17–30 (1996). Whether these results are correct or not, the results are capable of many different explanations, ranging from the purely biological to the purely psychosocial.

59. R. Blanchard, J. G. McConkey, V. Roper, and B. Steiner, "Measuring physical aggressiveness in heterosexual, homosexual and transsexual males," *Archives of Sexual Behavior* 12: 511–524 (1985).

60. R. Green, *The "Sissy Boy Syndrome" and the Development of Homosexuality* (New Haven: Yale University Press, 1987), p. 60. (Because Green's boys were selected on the basis of "femininity," it is uncertain to what extent the findings apply all prehomosexual boys.)

61. J. Harry, "Defeminization and adult psychological well-being among male homosexuals," *Archives of Sexual Behavior* 12: 1–19 (1983).

62. L. Ellis, H. Hoffman and D. M. Burke, "Sex, sexual orientation and criminal and violent behavior," *Personality and Individual Differences* 11: 1207–1212 (1990). As Ellis and colleagues made clear, lumping lesbian and bisexual women together for analysis introduces a potential problem. Women who admit to some degree of bisexuality may also be more ready to admit to having performed criminal acts. This could have generated an artefactual relationship between homosexuality and criminality in women. For men, the comparison was between exclusively homosexual and exclusively heterosexual individuals.

63. B. A. Gladue and J. M. Bailey, "Aggressiveness, competitiveness and human sexual orientation," *Psychoneuroendocrinology* 20: 475–485 (1995).

64. A. P. Bell and M. S. Weinberg, *Homosexualities: A Study of Diversity Among Men and Women* (New York: Simon and Schuster, 1978), pp. 85–101.

65. In many surveys of heterosexual behavior, conducted in diverse cultures, men report having had more different sex partners than do women (e.g., D. Serwadda, M. J. Wawer, S. D. Musgrave, N. K. Sewankambo, J. E. Kaplan, and R. H. Gray, "HIV risk factors in three geographic strata of rural Rakai District, Uganda," *AIDS* 6: 983–989 [1992]; Centers for Disease Control, "Number of sex partners and potential risk of exposure to human immunodeficiency virus," *Morbidity and Mortality Weekly Report* 37: 565–568 [1988]; ACSF Investigators, "AIDS and sexual behaviour in France," *Nature* 360: 407–409 [1992]; K. Wellings, J. Field, A. M. Johnson, and J. Wadsworth, *Sexual Behavior in Britain: The National Survey of Sexual Attitudes and Lifestyles* [London: Penguin Books, 1994]). In the British study, for example, a quarter of the men, but only 7 percent of the women, had had ten or more partners. It is possible that the sex difference results in part from reporting biases (overreporting by men and/or underreporting by women). Alternatively, the "excess" partners reported by men may be a small number of highly promiscuous women (such as prostitutes) who are typically missed or undersampled in the surveys.

66. D. Symons, *The Evolution of Human Sexuality* (New York: Oxford University Press, 1979).

67. J. M. Bailey, S. Gauling, Y. Agyei, and B. A. Gladue, "Effects of gender and sexual orientation on evolutionarily relevant aspects of human mating psychology" (in press).
68. W. R. Jankowiak, E. M. Hill, and J. M. Donovan, "The effects of sex and sexual orientation on attractiveness judgments: An evolutionary interpretation," *Ethology and Sociobiology* 13: 73–85 (1992).

Chapter 8

1. G. Dörner, T. Geier, L. Ahrens, L. Krell, G. Münx, H. Sieler, E. Kittner, and H. Müller, "Prenatal stress as possible aetiological factor of homosexuality in human males," *Endokrinologie (Leipzig)* 75: 365–368 (1980).
2. For a review of stress mechanisms and their interaction with the reproductive system, see R. M. Sapolsky, "The neuroendocrinology of the stress-response," in S. M. Becker, S. M. Breedlove, and D. Crews, eds., *Behavioral Endocrinology* (Cambridge, MA: MIT Press, 1992), pp. 287–324.
3. I. L. Ward, "Prenatal stress feminizes and demasculinizes the behavior of males," *Science* 143: 212–218 (1972); I. L. Ward, "Exogenous androgen activates female behavior in noncopulating prenatally stressed rats," *Journal of Comparative and Physiological Psychology* 91: 465–471 (1977); I. L. Ward and J. Reed, "Prenatal stress and prepuberal social rearing conditions interact to determine sexual behavior in male rats," *Behavioral Neuroscience* 99: 301–309 (1985).
4. W. Rohde, T. Ohkawa, K. Dobashi, K. Arai, S. Okinaga, and G. Dörner, "Acute effects of maternal stress on fetal blood catecholamines and hypothalamic LH-RH content," *Experimental and Clinical Endocrinology* 82: 268–274 (1983); T. Ohkawa, W. Rohde, S. Takeshita, G. Dörner, K. Arai, and S. Okinaga, "Effect of an acute maternal stress on the fetal hypothalamo-pituitary-adrenal system in late gestational life of the rat," *Experimental and Clinical Endocrinology* 98: 123–129 (1991).
5. I. L. Ward and J. Weisz, "Differential effects of maternal stress on circulating levels of corticosterone, progesterone and testosterone in male and female fetuses and their mothers," *Endocrinology* 114: 1635–1644 (1984).
6. J. Weisz, B. L. Brown, and I. L. Ward., "Maternal stress decreases steroid aromatase activity in brains of male and female rat fetuses," *Neuroendocrinology* 35: 374–379 (1982).
7. R. H. Anderson, R. W. Rhees, and D. E. Fleming, "Effects of prenatal stress on differentiation of the sexually dimorphic nucleus of the preoptic area (SDN-POA) of the rat brain," *Brain Research* 332: 113–118 (1985); R. H. Anderson, D. E. Fleming, R. W. Rhees, and E. Kinghorn, "Relationship between sexual activity, plasma testosterone, and the volume of the sexually dimorphic nucleus of the

preoptic area in prenatally stressed and non-stressed rats," *Brain Research* 370: 1–10 (1986); M. Kerchner and I. L. Ward, "SDN-MPOA volume in male rats is decreased by prenatal stress, but is not related to ejaculatory behavior," *Brain Research* 581: 244–251 (1992).

8. J. L. Humm, K. G. Lambert, and C. H. Kinsley, "Paucity of c-*fos* expression in the medial preoptic area of prenatally stressed male rats following exposure to sexually receptive females," *Brain Research Bulletin* 37: 363–368 (1995).

9. D. E. Fleming, R. H. Anderson, R. W. Rhees, E. Kinghorn, and J. Bakaitis, "Effects of prenatal stress on sexually dimorphic asymmetries in the cerebral cortex of the male rat," *Brain Research Bulletin* 16: 395–398 (1986); J. Stewart and B. Kolb, "The effects of neonatal gonadectomy and prenatal stress on cortical thickness and asymmetry in rats," *Behavioral and Neural Biology* 49: 344–360 (1988).

10. C. H. Kinsley, "Prenatal stress-induced variability in the expression of sex-typical physiology and behavior," *International Behavioral Development Symposium: Biological Basis of Sexual Orientation and Sex-Typical Behavior, Abstracts* (Minot State University, May 1995), p. 48.

11. W. Grisham, M. Kerchner, and I. L. Ward, "Prenatal stress alters sexually dimorphic nuclei in the spinal cord of male rats," *Brain Research* 551: 126–131 (1991).

12. P. W. Harvey and P. F. D. Chevins, "Crowding or ACTH treatment of pregnant mice affects adult copulatory behavior of male offspring," *Hormones and Behavior* 18: 101–110 (1984).

13. L. G. Dahlöf, E. Hård, and K. Larssen, "Influence of maternal stress on offspring sexual behavior," *Animal Behavior* 25: 958–963 (1977).

14. R. W. Rhees and D. E. Fleming, "Effects of malnutrition, maternal stress, or ACTH injection during pregnancy on sexual behavior of male offspring," *Physiology and Behavior* 27: 879–882 (1981).

15. F. S. vom Saal, "Variation in infanticide and parental behavior in male mice due to prior intrauterine proximity to female fetuses: Elimination by prenatal stress," *Physiology and Behavior* 30: 675–681 (1983); W. M. Miley, "Prenatal stress suppresses hunger-induced rat-pup killing in Long-Evans rats," *Bulletin of the Psychonomic Society* 21: 495–497 (1983); P. W. Harvey and P. F. D. Chevins, "Crowding pregant mice affects attack and threat behavior of male offspring," *Hormones and Behavior* 19: 86–97 (1985).

16. C. H. Kinsley and R. S. Bridges, "Prenatal stress and maternal behavior in intact virgin rats: Response latencies are decreased in males and increased in females," *Hormones and Behavior* 22: 76–89 (1988); P. J. McLeod and R. E. Brown, "The effects of prenatal stress and postweaning housing conditions on parental and sexual behavior of male Long-Evans rats," *Psychobiology* 16: 372–380 (1988).

17. I. L. Ward., O. B. Ward., R. J. Winn, and D. Bielawski, "Male and female sexual behavior potential of male rats prenatally exposed to the influence of alcohol, stress, or both factors," *Behavioral Neuroscience* 108: 1188–1195 (1994); I. L. Ward and O. B. Ward., "Environmental and pharmacological factors that alter sexual differentiation of males during fetal life," *International Behavioral Development Symposium, Biological Basis of Sexual Orientation and Sex-Typical Behavior, Abstracts* (Minot State University, May 1995), p. 79.

18. G. Dörner, B. Schenk, B. Schmiedel, and L. Ahrens, "Stressful events in prenatal life of bi- and homosexual men," *Experimental and Clinical Endocrinology* 81: 83–87 (1983).

19. G. Schmidt and U. Clement, "Does peace prevent homosexuality?" *Archives of Sexual Behavior* 19: 183–187 (1990).

20. R. Wille, D. Borchers, and W. Schultz, "Prenatal distress: a disposition for homosexuality?" Meeting, International Academy of Sex Research, Tutzing, Germany, 1987 (Abstract).

21. L. Ellis, M. A. Ames, W. Peckham, and D. Burke, "Sexual orientation of human offspring may be altered by severe maternal stress during pregnancy," *Journal of Sex Research* 25: 152–157 (1988).

22. J. M. Bailey, L. Willerman, and C. Parks, "A test of the maternal stress theory of human male homosexuality," *Archives of Sexual Behavior* 20: 277–293 (1991).

23. E. J. Sachar, "Hormonal changes in stress and mental illness," in D. T. Krieger and J. C. Hughes, eds., *Neuroendocrinology* (New York: H. P. Publishing, 1980), pp. 173–183.

24. R. M. Sapolsky, "The neuroendocrinology of the stress-response," in Becker, Breedlove, and Crews, eds., *Behavioral Endocrinology*, pp. 287–324.

Chapter 9

1. Castration (see chapter 5) was performed on some gay men in the United States and Europe, but it was done with the aim of extinguishing homosexual behavior or simply as a punitive act, rather than to prevent the passing on of homosexual genes.

2. The studies are summarized in T. Lang, "Studies on the genetic determination of homosexuality," *Journal of Nervous and Mental Disease* 92: 55–64 (1940).

3. M. Pritchard, "Homosexuality and genetic sex," *Journal of Mental Science* 108: 616–623 (1962).

4. K. Jensch, "Weiterer Beitrag zur Genealogie der Homosexualität," *Archiv für Psychiatrie und Nervenkrankheit* 112: 679–696 (1941); L. Ellis, "Sibling sex ratios and birth orders among male and female homosexuals," poster presentation at

International Behavioral Development Symposium, Minot State University, May 1995. Some studies have indicated that the excess of brothers is seen only or predominantly in gender-dysphoric or very feminine homosexual men, and not in conventional gay men or gender-dysphoric heterosexual men (R. Blanchard and P. M. Sheridan, "Sibship size, sibling sex ratio, birth order, and parental age in homosexual and heterosexual gender dysphorics," *Journal of Nervous and Mental Disease* 180: 40–47 [1992]; R. Blanchard, K. J. Zucker, S. J. Bradley, and C. S. Hume, "Birth order and sibling sex ratio in homosexual male adolescents and probably prehomosexual feminine boys," *Developmental Psychology* 31: 22–30 [1995]). A number of studies, including several of the foregoing, have reported that gay men tend to be relatively late-born (in the order of siblings), but the possibility that this effect is due to ascertainment bias cannot be excluded. Both the sibling-ratio and birth-order effects are susceptible to a variety of biological or psychosocial explanations.

5. F. J. Kallmann, "Comparative twin studies on the genetic aspects of male homosexuality," *Journal of Nervous and Mental Disease* 115: 283–298 (1952).

6. A certain reorganization of the genome occurs in some tissues, for example, the immune system, after conception. It is not generally believed that such changes contribute to normal variations in personality between monozygotic twins, but there are biologists, such as Cassandra Smith of Boston University, who consider this hypothesis worth exploring.

7. W. W. Schlegel, "Die Konstitutionsbiologischen Grundlagen der Homosexualität," *Zeitschrift der menschlichen Vererbung und Konstitutionslehre* 36: 341–364 (1962).

8. J. D. Rainer, A. Mesnikoff, L. C. Kolb, and A. Carr, "Homosexuality and heterosexuality in identical twins," *Psychological Medicine* 22: 251–259 (1960); G. K. Klintworth, "A pair of male monozygotic twins discordant for homosexuality," *Journal of Nervous and Mental Disease* 135: 113–125 (1962); A. I. Meskinoff, J. D. Rainer, L. C. Kolb, and A. C. Carr, "Intrafamilial determinants of divergent sexual behavior in twins," *American Journal of Psychiatry* 119: 732–738 (1963); N. Parker, "Homosexuality in twins: A report on three discordant pairs," *British Journal of Psychiatry* 119: 732–738 (1964); L. L. Heston and J. Shields, "Homosexuality in twins: A family study and a registry study," *Archives of General Psychiatry* 18: 149–160 (1968); K. Davison, H. Brierley, and C. Smith, "A male monozygotic twinship discordant for homosexuality," *British Journal of Psychiatry* 118: 675–682 (1971); R. Green and R. J. Stoller, "Two monozygotic (identical) twin pairs discordant for gender identity," *Archives of Sexual Behavior* 1: 321–327 (1971); R. C. Friedman, F. Wollesen, and R. Tendler, "Psychological development and blood levels of sex steroids in male identical twins of divergent sexual orientation,"

Journal of Nervous and Mental Disease 163: 282–288 (1976); B. Zuger, "Monozygotic twins discordant for homosexuality: Report on a pair and significance of the phenomenon," *Comprehensive Psychiatry* 17: 661–669 (1976); N. McConaghy and A. Blaszczynski, "A pair of monzygotic twins discordant for homosexuality, sex-dimorphic behaviour and penile volume responses," *Archives of Sexual Behavior* 9: 123–131 (1980).

9. D. Rosenthal, *Genetic Theory and Abnormal Behavior* (New York: McGraw-Hill, 1970), pp. 250–255.

10. R. C. Pillard and J. D. Weinrich, "Evidence of familial nature of male homosexuality," *Archives of General Psychiatry* 43: 808–812 (1986).

11. R. C. Pillard, "The Kinsey scale: Is it familial?" in D. P. McWhirter, S. A. Sanders, and J. M. Reinisch, *Homosexuality/Heterosexuality: Concepts of Sexual Orientation* (New York: Oxford University Press, 1990) pp. 88–100; J. M. Bailey and D. S. Benishay, "Familial aggregation of female sexual orientation," *American Journal of Psychiatry* 150: 272–277 (1993); J. M. Bailey and A. P. Bell, "Familiality of female and male homosexuality," *Behavior Genetics* 23: 313–322 (1993); M. L. Pattatucci and D. H. Hamer, "Development and familiality of sexual orientation in females," *Behavior Genetics* 25: 407–420 (1995).

12. J. M. Bailey and R. C. Pillard, "A genetic study of male sexual orientation," *Archives of General Psychiatry* 48: 1089–1096 (1991).

13. F. L. Whitam, M. Diamond, and J. Martin, "Homosexual orientation in twins: A report on 61 pairs and three triplet sets," *Archives of Sexual Behavior* 22: 187–206 (1993).

14. J. M. Bailey, R. C. Pillard, M. C. Neale, and Y. Agyei, "Heritable factors influence sexual orientation in women," *Archives of General Psychiatry* 50: 217–223 (1993).

15. M. King and E. McDonald, "Homosexuals who are twins: A study of 46 probands," *British Journal of Psychiatry* 160: 407–409 (1992).

16. J. M. Bailey and N. G. Martin, "A twin registry study of sexual orientation," poster presentation at the International Academy of Sex Research, 21st Annual Meeting, Provincetown, Massachusetts, 1995.

17. T. J. Bouchard, Jr., "Twins reared together and apart: What they tell us about diversity," in S. W. Fox, ed., *Individuality and Determinism* (New York: Plenum Press, 1984).

18. E. D. Eckert, T. J. Bouchard, J. Bohlen, and L. H. Heston, "Homosexuality in monozygotic twins reared apart," *British Journal of Psychiatry* 148: 421–425 (1986).

19. D. H. Hamer, S. Hu, V. L. Magnuson, N. Hu, and A. M. L. Pattatucci, "A linkage between DNA markers on the X chromosome and male sexual orientation," *Science* 261: 321–327 (1993).

20. D. Hamer and P. Copeland, *The Science of Desire* (New York: Simon and Schuster, 1994).

21. K. Brandt, "Doctor Angela Pattatucci: Not your typical government scientist," *Deneuve* (December1993), pp. 44–46; see also S. LeVay and E. Nonas, *City of Friends: A Portrait of the Gay and Lesbian Community in America* (Cambridge, MA: MIT Press, 1995), pp. 194–195.

22. For most genes, the likelihood that two relatives will share the same version of the gene (the same *allele*) decreases by half with every step in relatedness: a man has 50 percent genetic similarity with his mother, 25 percent with his uncle, 12.5 percent with his cousin, and so on. This rule does not apply to genes on the X chromosome, however, because a man has only one X chromosome and must therefore pass on the identical X-linked genes to all his daughters. Simple calculation shows that, with respect to X-linked genes, a man is more closely related to the son of his maternal aunt than he is to his maternal uncle. The rates of homosexuality found by Hamer in these two kinds of relatives fits this pattern: there were more gay cousins who were sons of maternal aunts than there were gay maternal uncles.

23. S. Hu, A. M. L. Pattatucci, C. Patterson, L. Li, D. W. Fulker, S. S. Cherny, L. Kruglyak, and D. H. Hamer, "Linkage between sexual orientation and chromosome Xq28 in males but not in females," *Nature Genetics* 11: 248–256 (1995).

24. G. Rice, C. Anderson, N. Risch, and G. Ebers, "Male homosexuality: Absence of linkage to micro satellite markers on the X-chromosome in a Canadian study," poster presentation at the International Academy of Sex Research, Provincetown, MA, 1995.

25. G. J. Riggins, L. K. Lokey, J. L. Chastain, H. A. Leiner, S. L. Sherman, K. D. Wilkinson, and S. L. Warren, "Human genes containing polymorphic trinucleotide repeats," *Nature Genetics* 2: 186–191 (1992).

26. J. P. Macke, N. Hu, S. Hu, J. M. Bailey, V. L. King, T. Brown, D. Hamer, and J. Nathans, "Sequence variation in the androgen receptor gene is not a common determinant of male sexual orientation," *American Journal of Human Genetics* 53: 844–852 (1993).

27. G. Dörner, I. Poppe, F. Stahl, J. Kölzsch, and R. Uebelhack, "Gene- and environment-dependent neuroendocrine etiogenesis of homosexuality and transsexualism," *Experimental and Clinical Endocrinology* 98: 141–150 (1991); G. Dörner, R. Lindner, I. Poppe, R. Weltrich, L. Pfeiffer, H. Peters, and J. Kölzsch, "Gene and environment dependent brain organization, sexual orientation, and sex-typical behavior," *International Behavioral Development Symposium: Biological Basis of Sexual Orientation and Sex-Typical Behavior, Abstracts* (Minot State University, May 1995) p. 31.

28. R. Dawkins, *The Selfish Gene*, 2d edition. (Oxford: Oxford University Press, 1989).

29. For reviews of these ideas, see J. D. Weinrich, *Sexual Landscapes: Why We Are What We Are, Why We Love Whom We Love* (New York: Scribners, 1987), chapter 13; M. Ruse, *Homosexuality: A Philosophical Inquiry* (Oxford: Basil Blackwell, 1988), chapter 6; Hamer and Copeland, *The Science of Desire*, chapter 11.

30. A. J. Montandon et al., "Direct estimate of the Haemophilia B. mutation rate and variation of the sex-specific mutation rates in Sweden," *Human Genetics* 89: 319–322 (1992). (The reason that the mutation occurs more often in the grand-fathers than in the mothers is simply that sperm are the product of many more cycles of cell division than are ova. For this reason, the majority of all new mutations arise in men.)

31. J. D. Weinrich, "A new sociobiological theory of homosexuality applicable to societies with universal marriage," *Behavioral Ecology and Sociobiology* 8: 37–47 (1987).

32. *A Yankelovich MONITOR Perspective on Gays/Lesbians*, Yankelovich Partners, Norwalk, CT, 1994. (The survey question did not clearly distinguish between being a biological parent and nonbiological co-parenting, adoption, etc. No doubt a somewhat greater fraction of the lesbian than the heterosexual "mothers" were nonbiological.)

33. S. Nanda, *Neither Man nor Woman—The Hijras of India* (Belmont, CA: Wadsworth, 1990).

34. G. E. Hutchinson, "A speculative consideration of certain possible forms of sexual selection in man," *American Naturalist* 93: 81–91 (1959); M. R. Ruse, "Are there gay genes? Sociobiology and homosexuality," *Journal of Homosexuality* 6: 5–34 (1981).

35. R. L. Trivers, "Parent-offspring conflict," *American Zoologist* 14: 249–264 (1974); R. L. Trivers, *Social Evolution* (Menlo Park, CA: Bejamin/Cummings, 1985). See also a more detailed discussion in Hamer and Copeland, *The Science of Desire*.

36. E. O. Wilson, *Sociobiology: The New Synthesis* (Cambridge, MA: Harvard University Press, 1975) (see especially page 555 for discussion of homosexuality); E. O. Wilson, *On Human Nature* (Cambridge, MA: Harvard University Press, 1978).

37. For further review of these and similar ideas see M. Ruse, *Homosexuality: A Philosophical Inquiry* (Oxford: Blackwell, 1988), chapter 6.

38. For examples of anthropological and cross-cultural studies, see C. S. Ford and F. A. Beach, *Patterns of Sexual Behavior* (New York: Harper and Brothers, 1951); G. H. Herdt, *Guardians of the Flutes: Idioms of Masculinity* (New York: Columbia University Press, 1981); F. L. Whitam and R. M. Mathy, *Male Homosexuality in Four Societies: Brazil, Guatemala, the Philippines and the United States* (New York:

Praeger, 1986); W. L. Williams, *The Spirit and the Flesh: Sexual Diversity in American Indian Culture* (Boston: Beacon Press, 1986); Nanda, *Neither Man nor Woman.*

Chapter 10

1. J. Boswell, *Christianity, Social Tolerance and Homosexuality: Gay People in Western Europe from the Beginning of the Christian Era to the Fourteenth Century* (Chicago: University of Chicago Press, 1980). The quotation from Ovid is on page 152; the quotation from a bestiary is on page 142; the passage from *Affairs of the Heart* is on page 153. Translations by Boswell.

2. *The Advocate* (September 19, 1995), p. 12.

3. R. D. Nadler, "Homosexual behavior in non-human primates," in D. P. McWhirter, S. A. Sanders, and J. M. Reinisch, eds., *Homosexuality/Heterosexuality: Concepts of Sexual Orientation* (New York: Oxford University Press, 1990), pp. 138–170.

4. G. V. Hamilton, "A study of sexual tendencies in monkeys and baboons," *Journal of Animal Behavior* 4: 295–318 (1914), p. 295, cited in R. D. Nadler, "Homosexual behavior in non-human primates," in McWhirter, Sanders, and Reinisch, eds., *Homosexuality/Heterosexuality: Concepts of Sexual Orientation*, pp. 138–170.

5. S. Zuckerman, *The Social Life of Monkeys and Apes* (London: Routledge and Kegan Paul, 1981), p. 394, cited in Nadler, "Homosexual behavior in non-human primates," pp. 138–170.

6. P. L. Vasey, "Homosexual behavior in primates: a review of evidence and theory," *International Journal of Primatology* 16: 173–204 (1995).

7. P. Sodersten, S. Hansen, P. Eneroth, C. A. Wilson, and J. A. Gustafsson, "Testosterone in the control of rat sexual behavior," *Journal of Steroid Biochemistry* 12: 337–346 (1980).

8. R. H. Anderson, D. E. Fleming, R. W. Rhees, and E. Kinghorn, "Relationships between sexual activity, plasma testosterone, and the volume of the sexually dimorphic nucleus of the preoptic area in prenatally stressed and non-stressed rats," *Brain Research* 370: 1–10 (1986). The Villanova group failed to replicate this result (M. Kerchner and I. L. Ward, "SDN-MPOA volume in male rats is decreased by prenatal stress, but is not related to ejaculatory behavior," *Brain Research* 581: 244–251 [1992]).

9. L. G. Clemens, B. A. Gladue, and L. P. Coniglio, "Prenatal endogenous androgenic influences on masculine sexual behavior and genital morphology in male and female rats," *Hormones and Behavior* 10: 40–53 (1978).

10. R. L. Meisel and I. L. Ward, "Fetal female rats are masculinized by male littermates located caudally in the uterus," *Science* 213: 239–242 (1981).

11. That the masculinizing agent is an androgen is suggested by the observation that androgen-blocking drugs administered during fetal or perinatal life prevent mounting behavior by females (I. L. Ward and F. J. Renz, "Consequences of perinatal hormone manipulation on the adult sexual behavior of female rats," *Journal of Comparative and Physiological Psychology* 78: 349–355 [1972]).

12. F. S. vom Saal and F. H. Bronson, "*In utero* proximity of female mouse fetuses to males: Effect on reproductive performance during later life," *Biology of Reproduction* 19: 842–853 (1978).

13. S. M. Resnick, I. I. Gottesman, and M. McGue, "Sensation seeking in opposite-sex twins: An effect of prenatal hormones?" *Behavior Genetics* 23: 323–329 (1993); E. M. Miller, "Prenatal sex hormone transfer: A reason to study opposite-sex twins," *Personality and Individual Differences* 17: 511–529 (1994); E. M. Miller and N. G. Martin, "Analysis of Australian opposite sex twin attitudes: Do hormones affect attitudes?" *Acta Geneticae Medicae et Gemellologiae: Twin Research* 44: 41–52 (1995).

14. A. Perkins and J. A. Fitzgerald, "Luteinizing hormone, testosterone, and behavioral resonse of male-oriented rams to estrous ewes and rams," *Journal of Animal Science* 70: 1787–1794 (1992).

15. J. A. Resko, A. Perkins, C. E. Roselli, J. A. Fitzgerald, J. V. A. Choate, and F. Stormshak, "Aromatase activity and androgen receptor content of brains from heterosexual and homosexual rams," *Proceedings of the Endocrine Society, 77th Annual Meeting,* June 1995, p. 135.

16. A. Perkins, J. A. Fitzgerald, and G. E. Moss, "A comparison of LH secretion and brain estradiol receptors in heterosexual and homosexual rams and female sheep," *Hormones and Behavior* 29: 31–41 (1995).

17. V. Geist, *Mountain Sheep: A Study in Behavior and Evolution* (Chicago: University of Chicago Press, 1971); V. Geist, *Mountain Sheep and Man in the Northern Wilds* (Ithaca, NY: Cornell University Press, 1975).

18. G. L. Hunt, Jr. and M. Warner Hunt, "Female-female pairing in western gulls (*Larus occidentalis*) in Southern California," *Science* 196: 1466–1467 (1977).

19. G. L. Hunt, Jr., A. L. Newman, M. H. Warner, J. C. Wingfield, and J. Kaiwi, "Comparative behavior of male-female and female-female pairs among western gulls prior to egg-laying," *The Condor* 86: 157–162 (1984).

20. J. D. Weinrich, *Sexual Landscapes: Why We Are What We Are, Why We Love Whom We Love* (New York: Charles Scribner's Sons, 1987), p. 298.

21. G. L. Hunt, Jr., J. C. Wingfield, A. Newman, and D. S. Farner, "Sex ratios of western gulls on Santa Barbara Island," *The Auk* 97: 473–479 (1980).

22. M. Fry, "The rest of the story," *The Living Bird* (Winter 1993), p. 19. See also M. Cone, "The DDT legacy," *Los Angeles Times,* August 9 and 10, 1995, pp. 1+.

The Montrose Chemical Corporation has suggested that the DDT reached the ocean via farm runoff.

23. P.V.Vasey, "Homosexual behavior in primates: A review of evidence and theory," *International Journal of Primatology* 16: 173–204 (1995).

24. S. Chevalier-Skolnikoff, "Homosexual behavior in a laboratory group of stumptail monkeys (*Macaca arctoides*): Forms, contexts, and possible social functions," *Archives of Sexual Behavior* 5: 511–527 (1976).

25. L. D. Wolfe, "Sexual strategies of female Japanese macaques (*Macaca fuscata*). *Human Evolution* 1: 267–275 (1986); J. Yamagiwa, "Intra- and inter-group interactions of an all-male group of Virunga mountain gorillas (*Gorilla gorilla beringeni*)." *Primates* 28: 1–30 (1987).

26. W. Wickler, "Socio-sexual signals and their intraspecific limitations among primates," in D. Morris, ed., *Primate Ethology* (London: Weidenfield and Nicholson, 1967), pp. 69–147. For a critical review of this hypothesis, see P.V.Vasey, "Homosexual behavior in primates: A review of evidence and theory," *International Journal of Primatology* 16: 173–204 (1995).

27. L. A. Fairbanks, M. T. McGuire, and W. Kerber, "Sex and aggression during rhesus monkey group formation," *Aggressive Behavior* 3: 241–249 (1977).

28. G. A. Parker and R. G. Pearson, "A possible origin and adaptive significance of the mounting behavior shown by some female mammals in oestrus" *Journal of Natural History* 10: 241–245 (1976).

29. P. A. Tyler, "Homosexual behavior in animals," in K. Howells, ed., *The Psychology of Sexual Diversity* (Oxford: Blackwell, 1984), pp. 42–62; A. Srivastava, C. Borries, and V. Sommer, "Homosexual mounting in free-ranging female Hanuman langurs (*Presbytis entellus*)," *Archives of Sexual Behavior* 20: 487–512 (1991).

30. D. J. Futuyama and S. J. Risch, "Sexual orientation, sociobiology, and evolution," *Journal of Homosexuality* 9: 157–168 (1984).

31. Srivastava, Borries, and Sommer, "Homosexual mounting in free-ranging female Hanuman langurs (*Presbytis entellus*)."

32. V. Sommer, *Wider die Natur? Homosexualität und Evolution* (Munich: C. H. Beck, 1990); V. Sommer, "Homosexualität und Evolution," in E. P. Fischer, ed., *Mannheimer Forum 93/94: Ein Panorama der Naturwissenschaften* (Mannheim: Boehringer Mannheim GmbH, 1994), pp. 11–69.

33. E. S. Savage-Rumbaugh and B. J. Wilkerson, "Socio-sexual behavior in *Pan paniscus* and *Pan troglodytes*: A comparative study," *Journal of Human Evolution* 7: 327–344 (1978).

34. F. B. de Waal, "Bonobo sex and society," *Scientific American* 272 (March 1995): pp. 82–88.

35. A. R. Parish, "Sex and food control in the "uncommon chimpanzee": How bonobo females overcome a phylogenetic legacy of male dominance," *Ethology and Sociobiology* 15: 157–179 (1994).

36. G. H. Herdt, *Guardians of the Flutes: Idioms of Masculinity* (New York: Columbia University Press, 1987), p. 238.

Chapter 11

1. C. D. King, "The meaning of normal," *Yale Journal of Biology and Medicine* 17: 493–501 (1945).

2. C. Boorse, "On the distinction between disease and illness," *Philosophy and Public Affairs* 5: 49–68 (1975). See also C. Boorse, "What a theory of mental health should be," *Journal for the Theory of Social Behavior* 6: 61–84 (1976).

3. C. Boorse, "On the distinction between disease and illness," in A. L. Caplan, H. T. Engelhardt, and J. J. McCartney, eds., *Concepts of Health and Disease: Interdisciplinary Perspectives* (Reading, MA: Addison-Wesley, 1981).

4. H. Merskey, "Variable meanings for the definitions of disease," *Journal of Medicine and Philosophy* 11: 215–232 (1986).

5. T. S. Szasz, *The Myth of Mental Illness: Foundations of a Theory of Personal Conduct* (New York: Delta, 1961; 2d edition, New York: Harper and Row, 1974).

6. R. D. Laing, *The Divided Self* (London: Tavistock Publications, 1960; Revised edition, New York: Pantheon Books, 1969), p. 37 of revised edition.

7. S. Timmons, *The Trouble with Harry Hay: Founder of the Modern Gay Movement* (Boston: Alyson Publications, 1990), p. 137

8. E. Hooker, "The adjustment of the male overt homosexual," *Journal of Projective Techniques* 21: 18–31 (1957).

9. E. Hooker, "Male homosexuality in the Rorschach," *Journal of Projective Techniques* 22: 33–54 (1958); E. Hooker, "An empirical study of some relations between sexual patterns and gender identity in male homosexuals," in J. Money, ed., *Sex Research: New Developments* (New York: Holt, 1965), pp. 24–52.

10. J. Chang and J. Block, "A study of identification in male homosexuals," *Journal of Consulting and Clinical Psychology* 24: 307–310 (1960); R. B. Dean and H. Richardson, "Analysis of MMPI profiles of forty college-educated overt male homosexuals," *Journal of Consulting and Clinical Psychology* 28: 483–486 (1964); J. N. DeLuca, "Performance of overt male homosexuals and controls on the Blacky Test," *Journal of Clinical Psychology* 23: 497 (1967); M. Siegelman, "Adjustment of homosexual and heterosexual women," *British Journal of Psychiatry* 120: 477–481 (1972).

11. C. W. Socarides, "A provisional theory of aetiology in male homosexuality:

A case of pre-oedipal origin," *International Journal of Psycho-Analysis* 49: 27–37 (1968).

12. M. Siegelman, "Adjustment of male homosexuals and heterosexuals," *Archives of Sexual Behavior* 2: 9–25 (1972).

13. E. Marcus, *Making History: The Struggle for Gay and Lesbian Equal Rights 1945–1990* (New York: HarperCollins, 1992), p. 18.

14. *The Wolfenden Report: Report of the Committee on Homosexual Offenses and Prostitution* (New York: Stein and Day, 1963).

15. T. S. Szasz, *The Manufacture of Madness: A Comparative Study of the Inquisition and the Mental Health Movement* (New York: Harper and Row, 1970).

16. C. W. Socarides, "Homosexuality—Basic concepts and psychodynamics," *International Journal of Psychiatry* 10 (1): 18–125 (1972).

17. Interview in J. Taylor, producer, *Born That Way?* (London: Windfall Films, 1992).

18. F. E. Kameny, "Does research into homosexuality matter?" *The Ladder* (May 1965), pp. 14–20.

19. *The Advocate* (May 26, 1971), p. 3, cited in Bayer, R., *Homosexuality and American Psychiatry: The Politics of Diagnosis* (Princeton: Princeton University Press, 1981), p. 105.

20. Marcus, *Making History:*, p. 225.

21. R. Green, "Homosexuality as a mental illness," *International Journal of Psychiatry* 10 (1): 77–98 (1972).

22. M. Margolese, "Homosexuality: A new endocrine correlate," *Hormones and Behavior* 1: 151–155 (1970). See also M. S. Margolese and O. Janiger, "Androsterone/etiocholanolone ratios in male homosexual," *British Medical Journal* 3: 207–210 (1973).

23. L. J. Hatterer, *Changing Homosexuality in the Male* (New York: McGraw-Hill, 1970).

24. C. W. Socarides, "Homosexuality—Basic concepts and psychodynamics," *International Journal of Psychiatry* 10(1): 118–125 (1972).

25. L. J. Hatterer, "A critique," *International Journal of Psychiatry* 10(1): 103–104 (1972).

26. J. Marmor, "Homosexuality—Mental illness or moral dilemma?" *International Journal of Psychiatry* 10(1) 114–117 (1972).

27. M. Hoffman, "Philosophic, empirical and ecologic remarks," *International Journal of Psychiatry* 10(1): 105–107 (1972).

28. M. Hoffman, *The Gay World: Male Homosexuality and the Social Creation of Evil* (New York: Basic Books, 1968).

29. Marcus, *Making History:*, p. 252.

30. American Psychiatric Association, *Diagnostic and Statistical Manual of Mental Disorders, Fourth Edition (DSM IV)* (Washington, DC: American Psychiatric Association, 1994).

Chapter 12

1. J. N. Katz, "Plymouth Colony sodomy statutes and cases," in W. B. Rubenstein, ed., *Lesbians, Gay Men and the Law* (New York: The New Press, 1993), pp. 47–53. The words "If . . . Death" are from Leviticus 20:13.
2. *Bowers v. Hardwick*, 478 U.S. 186 (1986).
3. *Griswold v. Connecticut*, 381 U.S. 479 (1965).
4. *Eisenstadt v. Baird*, 405 U.S. 430 (1972).
5. *Baker v. Wade*, 553 F. Supp. 1121 (N.D. Tex. 1982), reversed 769 F.2d 289 (5th Cir. 1985) (en banc).
6. J. H. Gagnon and W. Simon, *Sexual Conduct: The Social Sources of Human Sexuality* (Chicago: Aldine, 1973).
7. Cited in Rubenstein, *Lesbians, Gay Men and the Law*, p. 105.
8. *Doe v. Commonwealth's Attorney*, 425 U.S. 901 (1976).
9. Although still on the books, the Massachusetts law has been without legal force since 1974, when a sister statute relating to "unnatural acts" was held not to apply to sex between consenting adults in private (*Commonwealth v. Balthazar*, 366 Mass. 298, 318 N.E.2d 478 [1974]).
10. *Bowers v. Hardwick*, 478 U.S. 186 (1986).
11. K. Sherrill, "On gay people as a politically powerless group," in M. Wolinsky and K. Sherrill, eds., *Gays and the Military: Joseph Steffan versus the United States* (Princeton: Princeton University Press, 1993).
12. *Frontiero v. Richardson*, 411 U.S. 677 (1973).
13. *Plyer v. Doe*, 457 U.S. 202 (1982).
14. *Cleburne v. Cleburne Living Center*, 473 U.S. 432 (1985).
15. J. E. Halley, "Sexual orientation and the politics of biology: A critique of the argument from immutability," *Stanford Law Review* 46: 503–568 (1994).
16. A. Bérubé, *Coming Out Under Fire: The History of Gay Men and Women in World War Two* (New York: Plume Books, 1990).
17. *Watkins v. U.S. Army*, 837 F.2d 1428 (9th Cir. 1988) amended, 847 F.2nd 1329, different results reached on rehearing, 875 F.2d 699 (9th Cir. 1989) (en banc), certiorari denied, 111 S. Ct. 384 (1990).
18. M. A. Humphrey, "Interview with Perry Watkins," in Rubenstein, *Lesbians, Gay Men, and the Law*, pp. 368–374.

19. H. M. Miller, II, "An argument for the application of equal protection heightened scrutiny to classifications based on homosexuality," *Southern California Law Review* 57: 797 (1984).

20. *ben-Shalom v. Marsh*, 881 F.2d 454 (7th Cir. 1989), certiorari denied *sub nomine ben-Shalom v. Stone*, 494 U.S. 1004 (1990).

21. *Steffan v. Cheney*, 920 F.2d 74 (1990). Documents relating to the District Court proceedings are published in M. Wolinsky and K. S. Sherrill, eds., *Gays and the Military: Joseph Steffan versus the United States* (Princeton: Princeton University Press, 1993).

22. R. Green, "On homosexual orientation as an immutable characteristic," in Wolinsky and Sherrill, eds., *Gays and the Military: Joseph Steffan versus the United States* , pp. 56–83.

23. *Steffan v. Aspin*, 8 F.3d 57 (D.C. Cir. 1993).

24. J. A. Reisman and E. W. Eichel, *Kinsey, Sex and Fraud: The Indoctrination of a People* (Lafayette, LA: Lochinvar-Huntington House, 1990).

25. J. S. Alper and J. Beckwith, "Genetic fatalism and social policy: The implications of behavior genetics research," *Yale Journal of Biology and Medicine* 66: 511–524 (1993).

26. R. Bayer, *Homosexuality and American Pychiatry: The Politics of Diagnosis* (Princeton: Princeton University Press, 1981).

27. W. Byne and B. Parsons, "Human sexual orientation: The biologic theories reappraised," *Archives of General Psychiatry* 50: 228–239 (1993).

28. *Baehr v. Lewin*, 852 P.2d 44 (Hawaii 1993), p. 69.

29. K. De Witt, "Quayle contends homosexuality is a matter of choice, not biology," *New York Times* (September 14, 1992), p. A18.

30. Interviewed by the author, in J. Taylor, producer, *Born That Way?* (London: Windfall Films, 1992).

31. A. Brooke, "The rise of reverend Lou," *Frontiers* (December 1, 1995), pp. 25–30.

32. Halley, "Sexual orientation and the politics of biology."

33. L. J. Rankin, "Ballot initiatives and gay rights: Equal protection challenges to the right's campaign against lesbians and gay men," *University of Cincinnati Law Review* 62: 1055–1103 (1994).

Chapter 13

1. J. Tolins, *The Twilight of the Golds* (New York: Samuel French, 1992), pp. 55–56.

2. J. Ezard, "Top Jews back genetic means to deal with homosexuality," *The Guardian* (London), July 26, 1993.

3. M.A.Vogelbaum, J. Galef, and M. Menaker, "Factors determining the restoration of circadian behavior by hypothalamic transplants," *Journal of Neural Transplantation and Plasticity* 4: 239–256 (1993).

4. W. F.Anderson, "Gene therapy," *Scientific American* 273 (September 1995), pp. 124–128.

5. D. H. Hamer, S. Hu,V. L. Magnuson, N. Hu, and A. M. L. Pattatucci, "A linkage between DNA markers on the X chromosome and male sexual orientation," *Science* 261: 321–327 (1993).

6. D. Hamer and P. Copeland, *The Science of Desire: The Search for the Gay Gene and the Biology of Behavior* (New York: Simon and Schuster, 1994).

7. F. S. Collins, in "Further predictions on medical progress," *Scientific American* 273 (September 1995), p. 140.

8. R.A. Isay, *Being Homosexual: Gay Men and Their Development* (New York: Farrar, Straus and Giroux, 1989), p. 131–132.

9. A simple example: In California, adults are free to choose whether or not to wear helmets while bicycling, but they must place helmets on their children's heads even when neither parents not children wish it.

10. *Parham v. J. R.*, 442 U. S. 584 (1978).

11. M. Greif, *The Gay Book of Days* (New York: Carol Publishing Group, 1989), p. 16. Hoover's biographer, Curt Gentry (*J. Edgar Hoover: The Man and the Secrets* [New York: Norton, 1991]) cites the rumors without reaching any conclusions as to their veracity.

12. J. C. Fletcher, "Is sex selection ethical?" in K. Berg and K. E.Tranoy, *Research Ethics* (New York: Alan R. Liss, 1983), p. 333.

13. R. S. Cowan, "Genetic technology and reproductive choice: an ethics for autonomy," in D. J. Kevles and L. Hood, *The Code of Codes: Scientific and Social Issues in the Human Genome Project* (Cambridge, MA: Harvard University Press, 1992), pp. 244–263.

14. See, for example, W. L. Williams, *The Spirit and the Flesh: Sexual Diversity in American Indian Culture* (Boston: Beacon Press, 1986).

15. D. J. Kevles, *In the Name of Eugenics: Genetics and the Uses of Human Heredity* (Berkeley: University of California Press, 1986).

16. L. B.Andrews, "Legal aspects of genetic information," *Yale Journal of Biology and Medicine* 64: 29–40 (1991).

Chapter 14

1. T. B. Haase, "Why is my child gay?" Pamphlet, Parents and Friends of Lesbians and Gays, Inc., 1988.The relevant portion has been reprinted as "A survey

of scientific views on homosexual orientation," in R. Schow, W. Schow, and M. Raynes, *Peculiar People: Mormons and Same-Sex Orientation* (Salt Lake City: Signature Books, 1991), pp. 230–239. The quotations are brief excerpts from or summaries of more discursive answers.

2. D. A. Gentile, "Just what are sex and gender, anyway?" *Psychological Science* 4: 120–122 (1993).

3. When I say "different sexual orientation," I of course mean that this person, who otherwise would have been sexually attracted to women, is now sexually attracted to men. There has been a change in the sex to which the person is attracted, but this is not a switch from heterosexuality to homosexuality because the anatomical sex has changed also. Taken by itself, the androgen insensitivity syndrome does not help to distinguish prenatal from environmental factors in the determination of sexual orientation.

4. R. W. Goy and K. Wallen, "Experiential variables influencing play, foot-clasp mounting and adult sexual competence in male rhesus monkeys," *Psychoneuroendocrinology* 4: 1–12 (1979); C. L. Moore, "Maternal contribution to the development of masculine sexual behavior in laboratory rats," *Developmental Psychobiology* 17: 347–356 (1984); I. L. Ward, "Sexual behavior: The product of perinatal hormones and prepubertal social factors," in A. A. Gerall, H. Moltz, and I. L. Ward, eds., *Handbook of Behavioral Neurobiology, Vol. 11. Sexual Differentiation* (New York: Plenum: 1992), pp. 157–180.

5. W. Byne and B. Parsons, "Human sexual orientation: The biologic theories reappraised," *Archives of General Psychiatry* 50: 228–239 (1993). For a similar theory, which emphasizes the alienation of gender-variant children from their peers as the key step to homosexuality, see D. J. Bem, "Exotic becomes erotic: A developmental theory of sexual orientation," *Psychological Review* (in press).

6. F. L. Whitam and R. M. Mathy, *Male Homosexuality in Four Societies: Brazil, Guatemala, Philippines, and the United States* (New York: Praeger, 1986); F. L. Whitam and R. M. Mathy, "Childhood cross-gender behavior of homosexual females in Brazil, Peru, the Philippines, and the United States," *Archives of Sexual Behavior* 20: 151–170 (1991).

7. W. L. Williams, *The Spirit and the Flesh: Sexual Diversity in American Indian Culture* (Boston: Beacon Press, 1992).

8. In 1991 Dörner called for the World Health Organization to remove homosexuality from its offical list of mental diseases (G. Dörner, I. Poppe, F. Stahl, J. Kölzsch, and R. Uebelhack, "Gene- and environment-dependent neuroendocrine etiogenesis of homosexuality and transsexualism," *Experimental and Clinical Endocrinology* 98: 141–150 [1991]). This actually came to pass in 1993.

9. D. J. Kevles and L. Hood, *The Code of Codes: Scientific and Social Issues in the Human Genome Project* (Cambridge, MA: Harvard University Press, 1992). The genetic difference between two randomly selected humans corresponds to about ten percent of the genetic difference between a human and the most closely related non-human species (D. Hamer and P. Copeland, *The Science of Desire: The Search for the Gay Gene and the Biology of Behavior* [New York: Simon and Schuster, 1994]).

10. "I'm furious that you're gay," *Jerry Springer Show* (January 19, 1995), Multimedia Entertainment.

11. *Frontiers* (September 22, 1995), pp. 16–17.

12. E. Stein, "The relevance of scientific research about sexual orientation to lesbian and gay rights," in T. F. Murphy, ed., *Gay Ethics: Controversies in Outing, Civil Rights, and Sexual Science* (New York: Harrington Park Press, 1994), pp. 269–308.

13. R. D. Mohr, *Gay Ideas: Outing and Other Controversies* (Boston: Beacon Press, 1992), chapter 8.

14. Sacred Congregation for the Doctrine of the Faith, "Personae humanae (Declaration on certain problems of sexual ethics)," in A. Flannery, ed., *Vatican Council II: More Postconciliar Documents* (Grand Rapids: Wm. B. Eerdmans Publishing, 1982), pp. 486–499. The scriptural authority referred to is Romans 1: 24–27. A more recent statement, written by Cardinal Ratzinger (Sacred Congregation for the Doctrine of the Faith, "The pastoral care of homosexual persons," *Origins: NC Documentary Service* 16, No. 22 [November 13, 1986], pp. 377–382), reemphasizes the distinction between homosexual behavior and homosexual identity, but equivocates on the moral status of the latter. Ratzinger writes "Although the particular inclination of the homosexual person is not a sin, it is a more or less strong tendency ordered toward an intrinsic moral evil and thus the inclination itself must be seen as an objective disorder."

15. As an example, Catholic and other conservative religious schools lobbied the Western Association of Schools and Colleges not to include "sexual orientation" as a nondiscrimination category in the most recent (1994) revision of their diversity statement. WASC did include the category, but also nullified its effect by permitting schools and colleges to exclude openly gay students and to ban same-sex behavior.

16. The most recent example was in September 1995, when the Vatican City persuaded the United Nations Fourth World Conference on Women to drop "sexual orientation" from the antidiscrimination clause in the final platform (R. Tempest, "Sex-orientation references cut in deference to Vatican, Muslims," *Los Angeles Times* [September 15, 1995], p. A10).

17. Sacred Congregation for the Doctine of the the Faith, "Responding to legislative proposals on discrimination against homosexuals," *Origins: CNS Documentary Service* 22, No. 10 (August 6, 1992), pp. 173–177. Archbishop Quinn of San Francisco responded to the Vatican statement by saying: "[M]y policy and the policy of the archdiocese will continue to be what it has always been: to affirm and defend the human and civil rights of gay and lesbian persons; . . . [and] to affirm and defend the church's teaching on the distinction between sexual orientation and behavior." (J. Quinn, "Civil rights of gay and lesbian persons," *Origins: CNS Documentary Service* 22, No. 10 [August 6, 1992], p. 204.)

Index

for Reform of the Law against
Sexual Offenses; Daughters of
Bilitis; Gay Liberation Front;
Gemeinschaft der Eigenen; Lambda
Legal Defense and Education
Fund; Mattachine Society; National Gay Task Force; New York
Gay Activist Alliance; Society for
Human Rights; *Wissenschaftlich-humanitäres Komitee*
Gemeinschaft der Eigenen, 34–36, 37,
38, 276
Gender identity disorder of childhood, 229
Gender nonconformity
in adulthood, 17, 21, 29, 37, 190,
249, 275, 277, 291
in childhood 6, 12, 14, 30, 53, 60,
73–74, 81–82, 84, 97–105, 184,
241, 275, 276, 280
Gene therapy, 172
Genes
for androgen receptor, 126
for aromatase, 126
autosomal, 192
in CAH, 121
for estrogen receptor, 126
evolution of 188–193
predisposing to homosexuality, 5,
55, 113, 125, 171–193, 234, 241,
244, 259–260, 274, 286
Genetic engineering, 256, 270–271
Genetic fatalism, 244
Genito-genital rubbing, 206
Genome project. *See* Human genome
project
Georgia, sodomy statute of, 235
Gerber, Henry, 39
Gerbils, 140, 141
German Society for Sex Research, 119

Germany, brain surgery on gay men
in, 134–137
Germany, gay-rights movement in,
11–40
Germany, gay life in, 16–18, 36–37
Gernreich, Rudi, 39
Giese, Karl, 27, 37
Gingrich, Newt, 250
Gittings, Barbara, 223, 224
Gladue, Brian, 159
Glass, S. J., 110
Glucocorticoids, 164
Gold, Ronald, 223
Gonadotropin releasing hormone
(GnRH), 137–138, 165, 166
Gooren, Louis, 138
Gorski, Roger, 139–140, 142
Goy, Robert, 117
Grandfather clauses, 289–290
Greece, sex in, 58. *See also* Plato,
Aristophanes
Green, Richard, 98–103, 225–227,
241, 243, 246, 273, 282
Greer, Germaine, 140
Growing Up Straight (Wyden), 79–80
Guinea pigs, 115, 140, 146
Gulls, 200–203
Gynephilia, 188

Haase, Tineke, 273–274
Hall, Jeff, 154–155, 157–158, 258
Halley, Janet, 57, 251–252
Halperin, David, 56
Hamer, Dean, 51–52, 54, 156,
178–186, 243–244, 248, 259, 263,
265, 270
Hamilton, G.V., 196
Hampson, Elizabeth, 152
Hamsters, 120
Handedness, 7, 153, 156, 221, 228

Isay, Richard, 82–84, 264, 280, 281
Isherwood, Christopher, 36

Jahrbuch für sexuelle Zwischenstufen, 27, 31
Jakobovitz, Lord, 256
Japan, sex in, 58
Jerry Springer Show, 286
Jews, 11, 25, 37, 222, 256
Johnson, R. H., 110
Judges. *See* Buchmeyer; Burger; Burns; Gasch; Norris; Reinhardt

Kallmann, Franz, 173, 174, 241, 221–223
Kameny, Frank, 221–223, 224
Katz, Jonathan Ned, 97
Kennedy's disease, 126
Kertbeny, Karl Maria, 12
Kimura, Doreen, 152, 154–155, 157–158, 258, 282
King, C. Daly, 212–213
Kinsey, Alfred, 47–50, 61, 62, 215, 243
Kinsey, Sex and Fraud (Eichel), 243
Kinsey scale, 22, 47–48, 50–52, 54, 64, 252
Kleptomania, 97, 236
Knight, Robert, 243
Krafft-Ebing, Richard, 7, 25, 172
Krupp, Friedrich Alfred, 34
"Kyle," 100–101, 266

Laan, Ellen, 53
Ladder, 221
Laing, R. D., 214
Lambda Legal Defense and Education Fund, 240, 243
Lang, Theo, 172–173
Language, brain representation of, 152, 157

Langurs, 204
Lateralization, 145, 153, 258
  differences with sexual orientation, 156, 157
  sex differences in, 152
Law, immigration, 219
Left-handedness, 236
  as disease, 221, 228
Lesions of brain
  in animals, 132
  in humans, 134–137
LeVay, Simon, 143–145, 241, 244, 246, 247, 256, 281
Lewes, Kenneth, 82
Libel, 28
Libido, 68–69, 75, 76. *See also* Sex drive
Linkage analysis, 181–185
Lions, 196
Littlejohn, Larry, 222, 224
Lordosis, 115, 119, 132–133, 134, 165
Lorenz, Konrad, 99
Los Angeles, 202, 249
Luteinizing hormone
  releasing hormone. *See* Gonadotropin releasing hormone
  regulation by CRF, 165
  response to estrogens, 137–139

Macaque monkeys, 141
  influence of hormones in, 117
Magnetic resonance imaging (MRI), 258
Magnetoencephalography, 258
Malaria, 191
Male Homosexuality (Friedman), 81
Malnutrition, 166
Mannling, 14
Manufacture of Madness (Szasz), 219
Marcus, Eric, 81

Lightning Source UK Ltd.
Milton Keynes UK
UKOW02f0603170816

280838UK00001B/96/P